THE
Conquistadors

THE
Conquistadors

BY JEAN DESCOLA

Translated by Malcolm Barnes

NEW YORK: THE VIKING PRESS

1957

CONTENTS

v

Appendixes

MAPS

The Conquistadors

Terra Incognita

"Terra Incognita." These words in Gothic letters on medieval globes, at the place where the Americas are now shown, serve to remind us that until the end of the fifteenth century the world came to an end out in the Atlantic Ocean. Like the Sphinx, "Oceanus Occidentalis" devoured those who were mad enough to try to grasp its secrets. It was in fact *Mare Tenebrosum,* the "Dark Sea," the great devourer of lost paradises and sunken empires. Monstrous sea creatures with fins heavier than bronze disported there ponderously; the waters of the equator seethed like volcanic lava and sometimes spouted upward in black jets. The enemy was everywhere: in the air, on the surface of the waves, under the sea, and especially in the firmament, which was filled with the anger of the gods. Indeed, only the wrath of heaven could explain the waterspouts that had pounded caravels to pieces in a few minutes. This was the way that Spanish and Portuguese sailors, returning from the islands of the Atlantic, reasoned.

It is true that as early as the eleventh century some hardy Vikings had reconnoitered Iceland and Greenland and had probably reached the North American coast, without suspecting that it continued southward. Two hundred years later, Genoese sailors had reached the Azores, the Canaries, and Madeira. Another two centuries, and the Portuguese discovered the Cape Verde Islands. But the extreme limit of human daring seemed to have been reached. Beyond an imaginary line drawn from Iceland to Cape Verde lay darkness— a darkness peopled with fantastic imaginings. But the farther the sailors advanced into the Dark Sea as they prolonged their voyages from African shores, the higher their spirits rose. At each new point traced on the charts by cosmographers whose hands trembled with excitement, at each new island discovered, they imagined others. For had not Ptolemy suggested as many as twenty-seven thousand? Here lay the Archipelago of the Satyrs, the Island of Antilia (known also as the Island of the Seven Cities), the Island of Merops, and the island where Briareus, son of Heaven and Earth, watched beside the sleeping Saturn. And here, most wonderful of them all, lay Atlantis.

Atlantis

Legend precedes history. Dreams give rise to action. By pursuing chimeras, we reach reality. Would the flame of the conquest have burned so fiercely had it not been fanned by the myths that lured men on? So it was with Christopher Columbus, who, setting out to make an alliance with the Great Khan, ended by discovering America.

The idea of Atlantis was at the threshold of the discovery; it was a necessary mirage, without which the discovery would not have taken place. If we wish to enter into the outlook of the Conquistadors, we must first of all share their nostalgias and rediscover their dreams. The enigma of the Atlantic did more for the conquest than did the politics of princes. The lure of gold would not have provoked such a rush for the New World but for an attraction that was greater—a mystery.

Atlantis is discussed in two of Plato's writings, *Timaeus* and *Critias*. In the first of these dialogues, in which Socrates, Hermocrates, Timaeus, and Critias take part, Critias recounts the revelations made to Solon by the priests of Sais during his journey in Egypt: "[The Atlantic] sea indeed was then navigable, and had an island fronting that mouth which you in your tongue call the Pillars of Hercules; and this island was larger than Libya and Asia put together; and there was a passage hence for travelers of that day to the rest of the islands, as well as from those islands to the whole opposite continent that surrounds the real sea. For as respects what is within the mouth here mentioned, it appears to be a bay with a kind of narrow entrance; and that sea is indeed a true sea, and the land that entirely surrounds it may truly and most correctly be called a continent. In this Atlantic island, then, was formed a powerful league of kings

who subdued the entire island, together with many others, and parts
also of the continent; besides which they subjected to their rule the
inland parts of Libya, as far as Egypt, and Europe also, as far as
Tyrrhenia. Subsequently, however, through violent earthquakes and
deluges which brought desolation in a single day and night, the
Atlantic island itself was plunged beneath the sea and entirely disappeared; whence even now that sea is neither navigable nor to be
traced out, being blocked up by the great depth of mud which the
subsiding island produced."

In *Critias*, Plato completes this story:

"Poseidon, in particular, took as his lot the Atlantic island. . . .
Toward the sea, but in the center of the whole island, was a plain,
which is said to have been the fairest of all plains, and distinguished
for its excellence. On this plain, and at its center, about fifty stadia
distant, was a mountain with short acclivities on every side. On this
dwelt one of those men who in primitive times sprang from the earth,
by name Evenor, who lived with a wife, Leucippe; and they had an
only daughter, Clito. Now when this girl arrived at marriageable
age, and her mother and father were dead, Poseidon, becoming
enamored, made her his mistress. . . . To the eldest of his sons who
was the king, he gave the name of Atlas, from whom, as the first
sovereign, both the island and sea were termed Atlantic; and to the
twin born after him, who had received for his share the extreme
parts of the island toward the Pillars of Hercules, as far as the region
which now in that country is called Gadeirica, he gave the titular
name, which we Greeks call Eumelus, but which the people of that
country term Gadeirus."

So Atlantis was situated beyond the Strait of Gibraltar, which was
known to the ancient world as the Pillars of Hercules: at its eastern
extremity it approached Cádiz, while its western shores were washed
by the Caribbean Sea.

Plato records the gigantic works achieved by the Atlanteans:
temples, palaces, ports, and dry docks for triremes. The outer wall
of the island was covered with brass, melted tin covered the inner
wall, and orichalcum shone on the walls of the citadel itself. "The
temple of Poseidon himself was a stadium in length, three plethra in
breadth, and of a height to correspond, having something of a barbaric appearance. All the outside of the temple, except the pinnacles,

they lined with silver, but the pinnacles with gold; and as to the interior, the roof was formed wholly of ivory variegated with gold and orichalcum; and as to all the parts—the walls, pillars, and pavements—they lined them with orichalcum. They also placed in it golden statues, the god himself standing on a chariot holding the reins of six winged horses, of such size as to touch the roof with his head, and round him a hundred nereids on dolphins. . . . Round the outside of the temple likewise golden images were placed of all the men and women that were descended from the ten kings."

Each of the ten kings of Atlantis had the power of life and death over his subjects, within the limits of his province. He legislated by taking orders from Neptune, which were transmitted to him by sovereign law and figured upon a column raised in the temple, being engraved on the orichalcum.

So long as the godhead from which they sprang lived on in the souls of the people of Atlantis, their conduct remained wise and their government just. But the more they mixed with earthly creatures, so that the human tended to prevail over the divine, the more the sons of the sea god degenerated. Their virtues were weakened by contact with the children of men; they were corrupted and lent an ear to thoughts of violence and ambition. . . .

Homer, Strabo, Plutarch, Pliny, and many others continued the marvelous story of Atlantis. Some denied that it had existed, and a twentieth-century scholar has forcefully stated that "the Atlantic civilization did not exist at any epoch; it has its place only outside time, just as it is outside space. It did not exist anywhere. It has never existed." But nobody in the Middle Ages doubted the Platonic story. No sailor steering west but saw in his mind's eye the drowning of Atlantis or thought he could hear the voice of the gods across the ocean crying: "People of Atlantis! You must perish." The divine island had existed for centuries in the memories of the poets, and it haunted the minds of the navigators. It gave rise to the discovery and urged on the discoverers. In fact, the story of the Conquistadors begins at the Pillars of Hercules.

Although absorbed by his great political plans, could Christopher Columbus forget Atlantis when he took his bearings from the forecastle of the *Santa María*? Scarcely had he left the port of Palos than he came to Cádiz—the rock of Gadir, the remains of a continent ruled by the brother of Atlas. Then, having called at the Canaries, he steered due west. Running past the peak of Tenerife, the Genoese knew that he was close to one of the summits of the submerged chains of Atlantis, prolonged by the Azores, Cape Verde, and the Bermuda plateau. And he doubtless recognized in the Sargasso Sea that trapped his caravels the sea described by Plato as impracticable to navigation because of the mud and the shallows, the remains of the submerged island. In this state of mind, which paradoxically allied an acute sense of reality to something prophetic, dreams quite naturally merged with action. Christopher Columbus sailed in search of the Great Khan but did not despair of encountering on his way the island of the Saturnian gods, the empire of bronze and of sun.

Similarly, when Pizarro's companions penetrated the outlying parts of Cuzco, the royal city of the Incas, they still thought of the cities of Atlantis and doubtless considered the Temple of the Sun and the "metallic garden," with terraces that ran down in tiers to the Río Huatanay and were plated with pure gold, an astounding replica of the Temple of Neptune. And when Cortés set eyes on Tenochtitlán, the capital of the Aztec Empire, surrounded by lakes and canals, did he not think that this perhaps was Plato's Poseidonis?

But we must leave Atlantis. To sum up: It was said that more than ten centuries before the Christian era, an enormous continent stretching from the shores of Portugal and Morocco to the Caribbean Sea had been swallowed up in a cataclysm singularly recalling the Biblical tradition of the Flood; but this is something which today is no longer of interest except to geologists. Here we have only to imagine what it must have meant to the sailors of Isabella or Charles V while fitting out in Andalusian ports to sail for unknown lands.

Europe Looks East

Europe's vital preoccupation at the end of the fifteenth century was the East.

Antiquity had left the Middle Ages with an obsession for Asia, and the Middle Ages had passed it on to the Renaissance. The Holy Land and the Holy Sepulcher were there: the focal point of the Crusades and the Apostolate. Farther on lay India, Japan ("Cipango"), and China ("Cathay"), and the paradisial islands of

Oceania. To take the Holy Sepulcher from the Mussulmans, to conquer the Asiatic markets, and to convert the yellow races to the True Faith was the triple contest that was fought between Europe and the East for several centuries. The capture of Constantinople by Mohammed II, barring to Western Christians the road to the Christian East, had stimulated the enthusiasm for conquest among the navigators. While Vasco da Gama prepared to round the Cape of Good Hope, bold adventurers prospected the Indian and Chinese coasts. Long before Marco Polo, the route to the Indies was known and diplomatic contacts had been established between the European powers and the Asiatic princes. But to Europe the West remained a closed book; Europe took no interest in it and did not believe in it.

Meanwhile, in the last quarter of the fifteenth century, Europe entered upon an era of knowledge and curiosity. In Italy, Portugal, and Spain, eyes were turned toward Africa and Asia. These young kingdoms, scarcely freed from Islamic occupation, needed an outlet for their overflowing energies. Further, the light of the Renaissance had just succeeded the noble gloom of the Middle Ages. Gutenberg had perfected his processes, and the printing presses restored honor to the writings of antiquity and at the same time made known the most recent discoveries. No one doubted any longer that the earth was round. A certain Pole, named Copernicus, had even revealed the movement of the planets both with respect to one another and around the sun, like a gigantic clock. All Europe took a large bite at the still-green fruit of the Tree of Knowledge, and its strong flavor turned the coolest heads.

While the printing presses creaked, the furnaces of the alchemists had never known greater activity. Crouched over their retorts and white-hot alembics, the experts still hoped to find the philosopher's stone that would turn base metal into gold. But would it not be easier to go and find the gold where it lay? It was believed at this time that gold extracted from mines was sunlight petrified by the action of time. So the sunny lands had to disgorge their gold.

Gold for High Policy

Europe in the fifteenth century was divided among four kings: Louis XI of France, Maximilian of Germany, Henry VII of England,

and Ferdinand of Spain. Each of these monarchs—all by Divine Right
—secretly dreamed of remaking the Western Empire to his own
profit, and from this arose the need to create a grand policy that
would be the first step toward the conquest of Europe. The two
instruments of these politics of prestige were arms and finance.

At the end of the fifteenth century, military art had reached its
zenith. It was the age when charging armored cavalry, men and
horses in steel armor, began to be seen on the battlefields, while along
the roads of Italy heavy pieces of artillery rolled on four wheels.
Battles were skillfully fought with carefully chosen mercenaries.
Louis XI had his Swiss, Maximilian his *Landsknechte*, and Gonzalo
de Córdoba created the terrible "Spanish Infantry," the Queen of
Battles. In truth, never did war have a better-instructed or more attentive personnel at its disposal than in the last years of the fifteenth
century.

But an army is the most expensive of luxuries for an ambitious
prince. The cannon foundry, the gunsmith's factory, remounting,
and especially the soldiers' pay required that the treasury be refilled
constantly. "No money, no Swiss!" No army any more. So gold was
needed to maintain the grand policy.

This metal was rare in Europe. When Christopher Columbus
embarked for the West Indies, Europe's store of gold and silver did
not exceed a thousand million gold francs (at the 1914 valuation)*
—a heap of silver weighing 3200 metric tons and equal to two fifths
of the annual world production of silver in 1937, and a heap of inferior gold weighing 90 metric tons and representing one twelfth
of the annual world production for the same year. Cast in a single
ingot, all Europe's gold would have formed a cube only two meters
in each dimension.

So the main aim of the rulers of Europe was to acquire this precious
metal and build up as large a stock of it as possible. To have at one's
disposal sufficient liquid money to be able to pay ready cash was the
great preoccupation of the candidates to the empire, a preoccupation the more serious as they saw themselves halted in their under-
takings by lack of "liquidities." No grand policy without a rich
treasury: that was the dilemma in which the four princes were
caught.

* Equivalent value in 1914: about £40,000,000 or $200,000,000.

Europe lacked gold. What was looted from Turkish coffers, the few nuggets brought back from Africa by Portuguese explorers, and the melting down of gold plate had increased the reserves of metal very little. How could the sacks of the recruiting officers be filled, as well as the money wagons that followed the armies? How could the suppliers be paid? The coin in circulation was not enough for the growing appetites of the continental kingdoms, so on the margins of open conflict another battle was carried on: a battle for gold. Localized for a long time to the land routes of Oriental caravans and the sea routes along the African coasts, the battle for gold was soon to spread to the Dark Sea. Where could gold be found, indeed, if not in the Indies?

Caravels against Islam

But science and gold were only the means. Christian Europe, so long humiliated by Arab power, felt a renewed taste and vocation for the Crusades. Two hundred years had passed since Saint Jean d'Acre had fallen into the hands of the Saracens and Saint Louis had died before Carthage. The defeat of Islam had to be completed. To drive the Moor from Granada and to take him from the rear in Africa: to succeed in this double operation would revenge El Mansûra and Guadalete.

The end of the fifteenth century in Europe was marked by signs of confusion. Though one might think that the new learning was being substituted for the old, nothing of the kind took place. Never did the real and the marvelous get on so well together. Travelers' tales and the observations of the scholars, far from destroying the legends, helped to accredit them. Chimeras are not so easily forsaken!

A confusion of knowledge and a confusion of plans. Europe was like a great famished body long shackled to the earth. Its bonds had just been broken. It stretched its numbed limbs slowly. It rose up and looked around. A fearful and obscure covetousness grew within it. This was the Renaissance—the rebirth.

One Portuguese united in his person the contradictory passions of the age. This was Dom Henrique, better known as Prince Henry the Navigator, the son of King John I of Portugal, himself the natural son of Peter the Cruel and founder of the Aviz dynasty.

In his youth he had been among those who had conquered Ceuta. Though by his bravery he had won his spurs, he turned a fascinated eye upon the ocean and the violet line of the Atlas Mountains. On his return to Portugal, his father appointed him Grand Master of the Order of Christ, founded to fight the Mussulmans. From then on he devoted his life to this double objective: the conquest of Africa and the ruin of Islam—a confusion of ends and means. By conquering Africa he would enrich himself. He would use the fabulous gold that was said to abound in Africa to finance an expedition against the Mussulmans of Barbary, whom he thought to pursue as far as Jerusalem. Who could prevent him, then, from retaking the Holy Places?

Prince Henry the Navigator was never to navigate. He did better: he became the educator of Portugal. Appointed by his father as governor of Algarve, the southern province, he stayed there all his life. Close to Cape St. Vincent, on the Sagres promontory that thrusts far out into the ocean, he set up an astronomical observatory and founded a cosmographic school. Men who were learned in marine matters came to him from all parts. Portuguese, Catalans, Majorcans—even Jews and Moroccan Moors—installed themselves at Sagres and set to work.

So here indeed was the great brotherhood of learning! Speaking different tongues and following different religions, the students of Sagres for a time forgot their lands and their gods. They deliberately turned their backs on Europe. They wanted to forget what was happening there. Meanwhile, in Spain the favorite, Alvaro de Luna, confiscated royal power to his own benefit and led the nobility a hard life. Portugal alternately flattered and bullied her Spanish neighbor. Italy was a jigsaw, and foreign princes fought over the pieces; while Florence, the Medici capital, was about to give birth to the Renaissance. In France, Charles VII, "le Bien Servi," galvanized by Joan of Arc, drove out the English. The Hundred Years' War had ended, and Europe entered a new era. But the scholars of Sagres paid no attention. The future of Europe, they reckoned, would be settled on the sea. Africa had to be reconnoitered and its farthest point had to be turned so that the way to the Indies could be found.

Sagres was not merely a scientific seminary; it was also a naval dockyard. Under the direction of Italian experts, caravels were armed and took to sea. They went as far as they could, then returned laden with strange merchandise, but more than that, with astonishing information. During the half century that Prince Henry devoted to his folly, the Portuguese navigators had covered more than half the route that separated Lisbon from the future Cape of Good Hope. A half century to effect this African circuit: Madeira, the Canaries, the Cape Verde Islands, Senegal, the Gambia, Guinea and its gulf. Thus they had reached the equatorial region that Aristotle and Plato had declared uninhabitable.

Prince Henry's death did not extinguish the eager curiosity of the explorers. The drive went on. While the merchants landed on the coasts, penetrated inland, and boldly ascended the rivers, the Portuguese sailors continued their southward way. Diogo Cão, accompanied by the astronomer Martin Behaim, discovered the Congo in 1484, two years before Christopher Columbus presented himself to the Catholic monarchs. Two years afterward, Bartholomeu Diaz reached the southern point of Africa. This was the Cabo Tormentoso (a fearful storm there had nearly smashed his vessels), which King John II of Portugal later named the Cape of Good Hope.

Diaz returned to Lisbon. He reported his expedition to the king. He was complimented. But was he quite sure that this cape marked the end of Africa? Had he really rounded it? For everything was before them, including the eternal objective, the way to the Indies.

Bartholomeu Diaz never returned to the Cape of Good Hope. He died in a storm. Had not Adamastor, the Spirit of the Cape, declared: "I will wreak vengeance upon him who is the first to come and disturb my peace?" Diaz was certainly the first. The second was Vasco da Gama, who rounded the Cape of Good Hope ten years later.

Two Fashionable Authors: Marco Polo and Jehan à la Barbe

Two hundred years before the death of Prince Henry the Navigator, two Venetian merchants had traveled the road to the Indies, but by the overland route. A young man of seventeen years went with them on their second journey: Marco, son of the elder brother, and the future historian of the journey. They went from Acre through Baghdad and Ormuz, then north and east across the Pamirs and the Gobi Desert to China (Peking), and finally returned by way of the

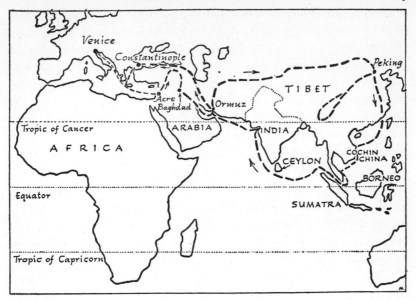

Marco Polo's Itinerary

China coast, Sumatra, India, Persia, and Constantinople. This fantastic journey—in the thirteenth century, moreover—was interrupted by long sojourns in the countries they visited, and lasted twenty-four years. When the three Polos returned to Venice, no one recognized them. Indeed, they spoke Venetian with difficulty, and their costume, like their manners, was Asiatic. Then they gave a great banquet at which members of their family and the city worthies were present. During dessert, the Polos ripped open the seams of their coarse cloth garments. A flood of precious stones—sapphires, emeralds, rubies—tumbled out, and the flood opened the eyes of the guests. Men so rich could not lie! All Venice then recognized the Polos. Marco became "Messer Millione," and he undertook to write the tale of their journeys.

When the fifteenth century ended, the book had not lost its fascination. It made the simple people dream and the scholars ponder. It was the bedside book of the lovers of marvels, and it was the Bible of future explorers. It was in the baggage of the Conquistadors and in the captains' chests. What does this book, which is at once a novel, a piece of reporting, and a treatise, relate?

It concerns the time when Kublai, grandson of Genghis Khan, reigned over the immense Mongol Empire that stretched from Poland to the China Sea. A formidable warrior, like his grandfather, Kublai had invaded Chinese territory at the head of a powerful Mongol army. It took him only a few years to subdue the whole country and to create a state three times larger than Europe. Founder of the Mongol dynasty of the Yüans, he and his successors governed China for a century, until the advent of the Mings. His residence was at Peking not far from the Great Wall, in the very heart of China. He was called the Great Khan. His palace, which was decorated with gold and silver, was as large as a town. The banquet hall could hold six thousand guests. As he suffered from gout, the Khan went to the hunt lying on a litter hung with lion skins and cloth of gold, and drawn by four elephants. Ten thousand falconers were his escort. Roads, canals, and causeways of astonishing dimensions cut through the Mongol Empire. Laden with spices and commodities unknown to Europe, thousands of boats passed up and down rivers that were as wide as the sea. Marco Polo knew how to please Kublai. He remained seventeen years in his service.

Vested by the Great Khan with diplomatic and commercial missions, Marco Polo traveled throughout China. He witnessed battles fought between lancers on elephants and archers on foot. He visited Quinsay (Hankow) on the river Yangtze Kiang and felt he was back in his native city, for Quinsay was built on a group of islands. Twelve thousand marble bridges spanned the canals. There were six hundred thousand houses and four thousand bathhouses, and— an extraordinary fact—Christian churches that were ministered over by Nestorian priests, followers of Nestorius, the originator of the doctrine attributing to Christ two persons and two natures, divine and human. Three times a week the market attracted more than fifty thousand persons.

After China came the wondrous island of Cipango—Japan. Marco Polo had not been there. But he had been told about it and about its gold and its rose-colored pearls. Java, homeland of nutmeg and clove; Sumatra, peopled with monkeys called by Marco Polo "men with tails"; Ceylon, where the pebbles were rubies and topazes.

No one before Marco Polo had told Europe that beyond the nameless deserts were towns as imperial as Toledo, ports as flourishing as Seville, and dynasties as noble as the Medici.

There was another book that also stirred the men of the fifteenth century. It was a novel attributed to a certain English gentleman, Sir John Mandeville, though the real author was an astronomer of Liége known to some as Jehan à la Barbe and to others as Jehan de Bourgogne. Written fifty years after Marco Polo's story, Jehan à la Barbe's book was a condensation in novel form of the geographical knowledge of the period. It concerned India, China, and the Malayan islands. The fabulous ruler was no longer the Great Khan but Prester John, a mysterious person who seems to have reigned over central Asia before Genghis Khan. He was confused in tradition with the priest-king, the Negus of Abyssinia.

Sir John Mandeville was present at ceremonies the splendor of which was allied to the Eastern liturgy. He saw mountains studded with diamonds, men with dogs' heads, and fights between pygmies and cranes. Near the sources of the Ganges the natives fed exclusively on perfumes and the odor of apples. Others had enormous ears that they wrapped around themselves like cloaks. He also saw one-eyed tribes. Finally—it was here that the book excited the geographers— he stated that a European, having set out in the direction of the Indies and visited more than five thousand islands, found himself in a country where his own language was spoken, where the farm workers, dressed like himself, drove their cattle using familiar words. He had come back to his starting point. So the earth was round. Europe, Asia, and Africa formed a single continent washed by a single ocean.

The world, as conceived by this supposedly English gentleman, was a single continent surrounded by a little water. A few archipelagoes were scattered about the water.

The fifteenth century ended in a stirring atmosphere. Intoxicated by books with ink that had scarcely time to dry, following step by step the progress of the navigators, the minds of men could not distinguish between truth and legend. For the geographer, the second half of the fifteenth century was like the first half of the twentieth for the technician: a period of sudden progress. The world opened in a rush. Everyone was in a hurry to turn the pages of the great book. To the caravels they whispered: "Faster and farther." They were eager to replace the broken line of the cosmographers by the firm line of certainty. An island reconnoitered, an anchor dropped at a new shore, and for a time the thirst for the fabulous was quenched. Then the dream took on the solid consistency of reality. Everyone marveled at how the discovered lands surpassed in splendor the lands that had been imagined.

The icy glow of Samarkand silks; the scent of burning sandalwood in Java; the pepper and nutmeg of Malabar; the glittering gems of Cipango; were these not the means to intoxicate the contemporaries of Leonardo da Vinci and Pico della Mirandola, the one symbolical of prescience and the other of science? This time, what was known surpassed what had been foretold.

But gold and spices were not everything. The cupidity of the merchants, the ambition of the navigators, and the imagination of the poets concealed political ulterior motives of the widest extent. It was certain, first of all, that the conquest of the "Ultramar" would assure the mastery of Europe. Would it be Spain or Portugal? Both were well placed. But Italy was watchful. As for the Papacy— the arbiter of princes, and spiritual ruler of the lands that had been discovered and were still to be discovered—was it not the guarantor of the part that God would play?

The domination of Europe was fine; but why not that of the world? It was only a matter of renewing the alliance with the Great Khan that had been outlined two centuries earlier by the three Polos. It was thought that he favored Christian ideas. Once in association, would these two forces permit a third force to continue? Certainly not. The armies of His Catholic Majesty and those of the Tartar emperor would set out to meet one another and make contact at Constantinople. Thus the jaws of these formidable pincers would close upon Islam. They would crush the old enemy of Europe like a nutshell.

The first essential of this grandiose plan was to find a way to the Great Khan.

For the moment there was only one route to the Indies: the eastern route, Marco Polo's, involving thousands of miles across hostile lands. Many started out, but few got beyond the Caucasian plateaus.

It was said that Vasco da Gama, the Portuguese, was about to try the route to the Indies by circling the Cape of Good Hope. But what a voyage!

It was said also that in a western direction . . .

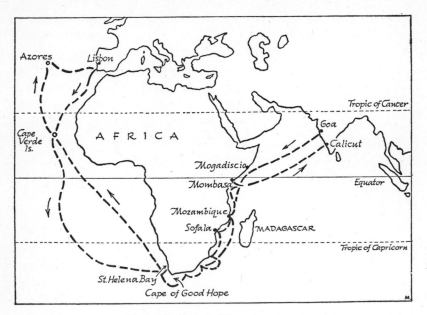

Vasco da Gama's Voyage, 1497-99

PART ONE

Master Christopher the Unlucky;
OR
A World Discovered by Mistake

*I sent His Majesty a map drawn by my own hand.
In it was defined the whole western part of the
known world from Ireland to Guinea, as well as all
the islands one encountered on this route. Immediately facing them, due westwards, were reproduced
the beginnings of India, with its islands and cities....*
—Letter from Toscanelli to the Confessor of King John II of Portugal.
Florence, June 25, 1474.

Islands Discovered by Columbus

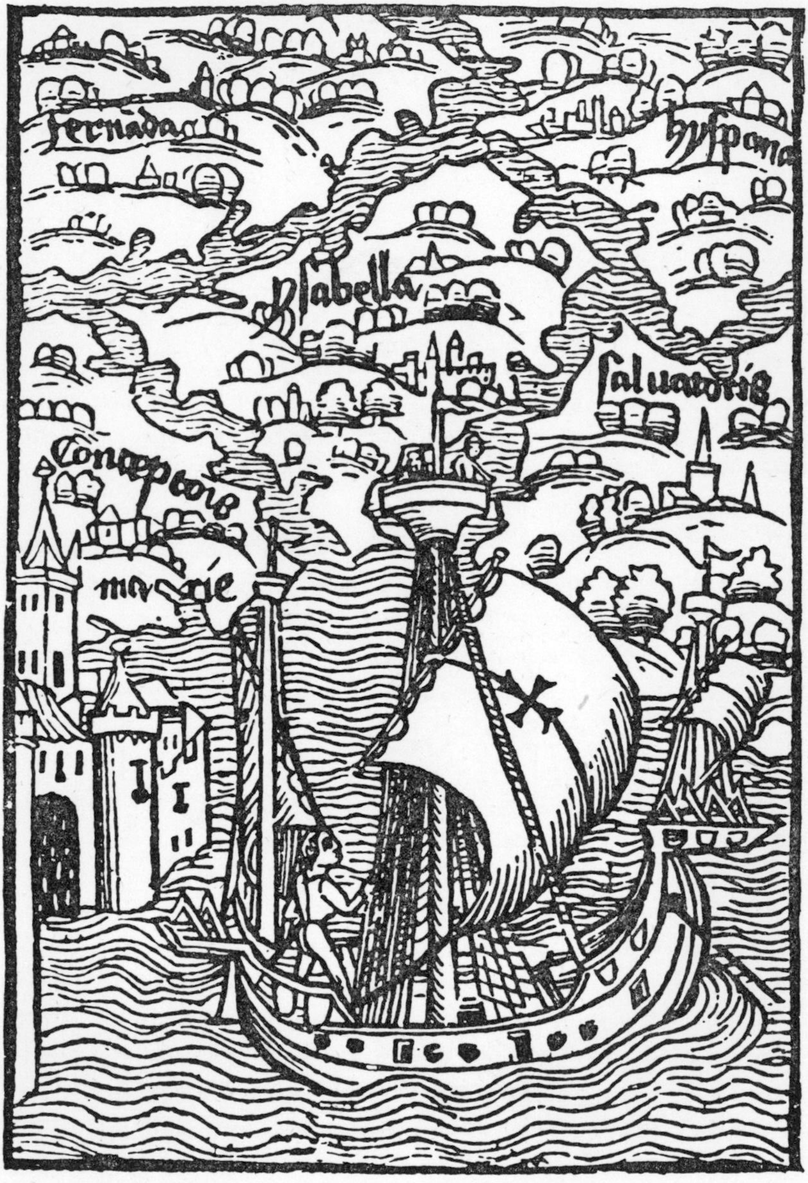

CHAPTER I

In Search of the Great Khan

A Castilla y a León   Nuevo mundo dió Colón.

Though it was Christopher Columbus who gave a new world to Spain, the first Conquistador was not himself a Spaniard. A propagator of the Christian faith, he was probably of Jewish descent. A geographer, he was not sure that the world was round, for no one had ever given proof that could be shown on the map. A mathematician, he could barely count, and his astronomical knowledge was no better than Ptolemy's. *Almirante Mayor de la Mar Oceana*, an admiral in fact, he made errors in charting his course and reckoned his sea routes by guesswork. Discoverer of America, he actually thought he was in Asia.

These fundamental contradictions throw an obscure light on the peculiar character of Columbus. This man at first sight shows signs of inconsistency, even perhaps of imposture. But does this mean that Christopher Columbus was an imposter?

Actually, he was at one and the same time more simple and more complex. There is no way of describing him in one word. It is by following him step by step throughout a career that was by turns extremely lucky and extremely unlucky that we succeed gradually in isolating the essential elements of his personality, which are so varied that their synthesis seems impossible. He is a man with a hundred faces: visionary and practical, candid and crafty, a sage and a man of business, an ascetic and a voluptuary, Columbus can be grasped only in his details. His characteristics are superimposed one on another; they are not complementary. His defects set him off rather than debase him. The mere adding of one characteristic to another does not form the whole. Yet something in the moral aspect of Christopher Columbus imposes itself on one forcefully. Inversely, as the curve of his fortune fell, the spiritual curve rose. This continuous progress began with his third voyage, a progress toward asceticism, toward a sort of heroic wisdom, a superhuman serenity that serves to make almost a saint of this boastful and adventure-hungry Genoese.

This unlucky man's reward was not of this world—this world that he merely glimpsed and that others would steal from him. But after so many failures on the way—for there was not one of his victories but was followed by a bitter morrow—his was a great moral triumph, for his greatest discovery was himself.

His Mysterious Origin

One day, accompanied by a child, a vagabond presented himself to the prior of the monastery of La Rábida. Exhausted by hunger, he had fallen upon the steps of the cross that stood before the portal. The doorkeeper lifted these two unfortunate creatures and took them to the Superior. The vagabond and his child were Christopher Columbus and his son, Diego.

At this time Christopher Columbus was well past his thirtieth year. What had he done until then? Whence had he come? He was at an age when men of his calling already have a past, are already in mid-career, while some have even ended it. Columbus seemed only at the beginning of his life.

Eleven Italian towns claim that he first saw light within their walls: Genoa, Savona, Cuccaro, Nervi, Pradello, Oneglia, Finale, Quinto, Palestrella, Albissola, and Cosseria. Melodious names, of which we need remember only one: Genoa. But that is not all, for at Calvi they will show you the house where he was born, while some Spaniards claim, with supporting evidence, that he was born in Estremadura, that his ancestor was Pablo de Santa María, Rabbi of Cartagena, who was converted to Catholicism and became archbishop of Burgos. Possibly, also, he was born in Galicia of a Jewish mother, in the province of Pontevedra. Fourteen birthplaces, but the most likely is Genoa. *"Essendo io nato en Genova . . ."* Columbus said in his testament. His Jewish origin, on which much evidence agrees, is probable, and it is to be found in many aspects of his behavior. A Ligurian with a touch of the Semite? Very probably, although it cannot be said for certain.

His father's name was Domingo. He was a wool carder and kept a wineshop. His mother bore the lovely name of Susanna Fontana-rossa, and he had two brothers: Bartholomew and Diego. His early childhood was spent with his parents, but it seems that he went to sea at a very early age: "at the age of fourteen years," he was to say later. Between two short voyages along the Italian coasts he came ashore, helped his father in his modest business with wool and wine, and then set off again. Aboard ship his job was unpretentious: while he scrubbed the deck or assisted the carpenter, he educated himself, though not in practical matters alone. For this ship's apprentice was a dreamer. Lying on the scorching quayside at Genoa, or leaning on his elbows at a gangway's rail, he read such books as Cardinal d'Ailly's *Imago Mundi,* which had just been printed; Pomponius Mela's *Chronographia,* Ptolemy's *Astronomy,* Marco Polo's *Travels,* Enea Sylvio Piccolomini's *Historia Rerum,* and Plutarch's *Lives.* Such was his insatiable appetite for knowledge that he read everything that came into his hands. He was self-taught, and he lacked a teacher to direct and coordinate his ill-assorted reading. This amalgam of confused knowledge was the first leaven to ferment his dreams. But what gaps there were in this too voraciously swallowed knowledge!

"De muy pequeña edad, entré en la mar, navegando. . . ." So he sailed, still very young. After his lessons in sail, he traveled on business. At Chios, the little island in the Greek archipelago where Homer first saw light, he went in search of a kind of resin called mastic, much esteemed by Andalusians: they rubbed the insides of their jars with it, and as a result their wine was sweeter than honey. For several years Christopher Columbus sailed in the Mediterranean, selling merchandise or carrying cargoes; obscure years they were, filled with one knows not what, and about which Columbus was later discreet or reticent.

Is there any truth in the statement that he may have visited the British Isles? Later he was to tell of an expedition to Thule, the end of the world in a northerly direction, and in reality one of the Shetland Islands; and of the adventure that befell him in the

neighborhood of Cape St. Vincent. As he was on his way to England, the vessel on which he had sailed was attacked by pirates and
set afire. He threw himself into the sea and, bestriding a piece of
timber, was able to reach the Portuguese coast. But was he perhaps
one of the pirates?

Another adventure is recorded, and this time a warlike affair.
He was in command of one of the Duke of Anjou's ships, the *Bon
Roi René*, and was struck down under his flag in Tunisia. He also
served Portugal against the Venetians, and Spain against the Moors.
But there is no proof of these often contradictory feats of arms.

Was he a *condottiere* or a commercial traveler? Undoubtedly he
was both. A complete mystery envelops the youth of Columbus,
and he did nothing to disperse it; on the contrary, it might be said
that he took care to confuse his tracks. Loquacious as he was, he
knew how to be silent when necessary.

A Balcony above the Dark Sea

Having been lost to sight for several years, Christopher Columbus
turns up again at Lisbon. What was he doing there? Probably he
was on business. He was very nearly thirty years old. Each morning
(for his piety was very great) he went to hear Mass in the chapel
of the monastery at Lisbon where the penniless orphans of men
who had served Portugal were brought up. There he met the young
Dona Felipa Perestrello e Moniz, whose father had been a sailor
in the service of the Infante Prince Henry and had helped in the
discovery of the island of Porto Santo, close to Madeira.

What did these two young people talk about at the beginning?
Doubtless, the famous island of Porto Santo. The Infante had given
it to Perestrello, thinking to favor him, for it seemed easier to
cultivate than nearby Madeira, which was covered with the immense
woodlands from which its name derived. Perestrello's companions,
not knowing how to clear Madeira, decided to set it afire. The
fire lasted for seven years, and when the island was no more than
flat open country and ashes, the settlers planted sugar canes and vine
stocks brought from Portugal. The fine Madeira wine made the
fortunes of those whom the Infante thought to injure. As to Perestrello, lord and master of Porto Santo, he obtained excellent results

at once, but an imprudent act destroyed his labors. It occurred to him to take a couple of rabbits to Porto Santo, and these and their progeny multiplied at such a rate that in a few years all the crops were destroyed.

Felipa tearfully told Christopher of these events; her father had died a hopeless and ruined man. Her brother governed the desolate island, which was henceforth the poor relation of its powerful neighbor.

Christopher Columbus married Felipa and went to settle with her at Porto Santo, beside his brother-in-law, the governor.

Why did Christopher Columbus marry Felipa? She was young and pretty, no doubt, but not at all rich. Though he had an eye for beauty, the Genoese had a greater regard for wealth. What rhyme or reason was there, then, for this apparently purely sentimental marriage? Columbus saw farther, far beyond love and immediate profit; he reached out for his wife's dowry: the marine maps, observations, and documents of Perestrello, who was a poor administrator but an excellent navigator. This heap of manuscripts and yellowed parchments contained the sum total of the navigational and geographical knowledge of the time. There were also personal notes and observations, the fruit of a long career, and these were solid nourishment for a man hungry for knowledge, which the hasty and muddled reading of his youth had been unable to satisfy. Felipa brought her husband something more precious than gold: she brought him the road to gold itself.

Columbus ransacked this mass of papers, hugging it to his bosom as a miser his treasure, and took it with him to Porto Santo. He stayed there for three years, a strange honeymoon on an island swept by the Atlantic winds. But it was an important period in the life of Columbus, for it was at Porto Santo that his confused dreams took shape. Thanks to his father-in-law's documentation, he was to complete and enrich his stock of knowledge, which until then was rudimentary. Moreover, this scrap of storm-tossed earth was a fine, advanced post in the ocean, a balcony above the New World of the future. The Portuguese had already taken possession of the Azores, the Canaries, and the Cape Verde Islands. The westerly invasion was on the march. It spread fanwise from the Portuguese coasts to the African littoral. The volcanic archipelagoes were conquered. Where would the next stage in this race toward the unknown lead? From this moment Columbus's gaze upon the Dark Sea was that of a master: for three years it was to be as from a promontory, embracing the sky and the sea and the bronze-colored massing of the waves and clouds, seeking how to tear the mystery apart. This avid, aching contemplation of the Atlantic was for Columbus a sort of novitiate. He needed the rough bite of the Atlantic breeze and, above all, the constant view of that fluid desert to complete and vitalize the lessons he had drawn from his books. Doubtless, too, the docile presence of Felipa played its catalytic role.

Failure in Portugal

Three years had passed. The dream took shape. The idea had become a plan, then a project. It had to be realized. And the project was this: to reach the Indies by the westward route.

The idea was not a new one. It had been discussed for a long time and was already inscribed upon the maps of the time. The "Catalonian World Map," Paolo Toscanelli's map, Martin Behaim's globe, and Cardinal d'Ailly's *Imago Mundi* were in agreement on one point: that Portugal was very near the eastern extremity of Asia, that is to say, Cipango—Japan. The world was not nearly so big as had been thought, and Asia formed its largest part. As to the sea, it occupied only a seventh of the globe. Moreover, Toscanelli had calculated precisely the comparative dimensions of the European and Asiatic lands and of the ocean: no more than 700 leagues, about 2500 miles, separated Lisbon from the empire of the Great Khan. It had all been proved by mathematics; it was only a matter of taking to sea and steering westward. Provided a straight line was strictly followed along the 28th parallel, not deviating by a single degree, one could be sure of reaching the first Indian port after a crossing of several weeks.

This, then, was the true route to the Indies, swift and direct, and economical, too, free from natural and human obstacles. It would supplant Marco Polo's out-of-date route. It would also supplant the route that Vasco da Gama dreamed of tracing on the sea by rounding the Cape of Storms—assuming that he would ever succeed in achieving that crazy circuit.

To reach India by the west: what, in short, could be simpler?
Toscanelli, a Florentine doctor, was the inventor of the idea
and had put it on a map for the first time. Columbus knew of the
existence of this map; its author had sent it to John II, King of
Portugal. Columbus needed it most urgently, so he wrote to Toscanelli, who without hesitation sent him this famous map; one
admires his disinterest. Trembling with joy, the hermit of Porto
Santo spread it out, and it was just as he had imagined. With his
finger he followed the 28th parallel from east to west: from Lisbon
to Cipango was no distance at all! The figures were there: Europe
and Asia together occupied 270 degrees, while the ocean that separated the western point of Europe from the eastern extremity of
Asia filled only 90 degrees.

Toscanelli had sent with his map a copy of his request to John II
through the latter's confessor. "Do not be astonished," he wrote,
"to see that I name as the Occident the places where the spices
grow, for it is generally said that they flourish in the East. But he
who continues to sail westward will encounter these places in the
west. And he who travels by the land route in an easterly direction,
without stopping, will reach these regions by the east."

Columbus did not fail to thank the Florentine and took the
opportunity of revealing his plan. Toscanelli replied: "I am very
pleased that you regard the voyage as not only possible, but certain,
and that there is no doubt about its realization. . . . This route
leads to powerful kingdoms, and famous cities and provinces, where
will be found in masses all those things of which we have read,
for example all sorts of spices in plenty and precious stones in
superabundance. . . . These princes and kings to whom we shall
have access should rejoice, even more than ourselves, to enter into
relations with the Christians of our lands, since many of them are
Christians. . . ."

Nothing could be better, in the opinion of Christopher Columbus:
gold and souls. For in the seething mind of the Genoese the desire
for lucre was already inseparable from apostleship. It was not enough
that some subjects of the Great Khan were already Christians: all
must be so. The route to the Indies led to the possession of the world,
but it came back to Christ.

It is good to conceive an idea, but better still to know that it is realizable. Christopher Columbus now needed someone of rank to be the confidant of his dreams. Above all, he needed a partner, but not an active one. Where could one be found except at court?

In the year 1483 Columbus succeeded in obtaining an audience with John of Portugal. The new monarch—he had just ascended the throne—continued the work begun by Henry the Navigator. Having doubted it for a long time, he had been convinced that Portugal's future was on the sea. In his palace at Lisbon he busied himself less with diplomacy than with astronomy and navigation. Like the Infante of Sagres, he had gathered a group of scholars about him. He was in correspondence with foreign experts, especially with Abraham Zacuto, a Jewish professor of mathematics at Salamanca. It therefore seemed that Columbus should find a favorable reception at court.

Walking across the palace flagstones with rapid steps, his head held high, and tightly grasping a roll of papers, Christopher Columbus advanced to meet the King. His appearance was good: of medium height but well proportioned, with eyes that were light blue, and a skin that was very pale, with a few scattered freckles. He was bearded, and his hair was long and fair, tending toward red. One curious feature—especially as he does not appear to have been much more than thirty—was that he was already white at the temples. His nose was aquiline, while in the middle of his broad and clear brow was a vertical furrow, the sign of an uncommon will. His worn but tidy costume was that of a man of rank. In his hand he carried a plush cap slashed with silk, and he was wrapped in a green cloth tabard—a short mantle with a turned-down hood, worn over armor and made fashionable among Christians by the Moors of Granada. Blue breeches could be seen beneath its skirts. On his feet were red boots of Córdoba leather, and at his belt hung the wide short sword customary with sea captains.

The exalted and learned assembly before which he appeared did not intimidate Columbus. Like an advocate at the bar, he opened his brief, spread out his maps, and displayed his plans. Above all, he talked, and his fluency was staggering. He piled up his figures and his references; he cited texts; he invoked Aristotle, Seneca, Ptolemy, and the masters of yesterday and today; and he poked fun at the Reverend Cosmos Indicopleustes, the ecclesiastical traveler of the early Middle Ages who represented the earth as a disk around which the sun turned. Cautiously, because the Church was suitably represented at the gathering, he deplored the mistakes of Saint Augustine and certain doctors. How was it that these absurd theories had for so long received the approval of official circles, and were even treated as dogma, when for several centuries the Mussulmans in their academies, the Jews in their synagogues, and simple monks in their monasteries had shown that they were false? Was it not an Arab, al-Farghani, who in the ninth century had proved that the earth was round? Christopher Columbus recited by heart whole passages from authors formerly rejected by the Church.

This discourse was not to the taste of the royal assembly. The bishops scowled, the scholars tightened their lips. John II repressed a smile and dryly interrupted Columbus. "What are you getting at?" he asked.

Columbus's tone then became pompous. He had not come as a beggar but as a donor. His clothes told against him. Nevertheless, he had a secret that was worth gold. This secret he did not wish to keep to himself; he intended to offer it to Portugal, his adopted country. Triumphantly he flourished his plan of a route to the Indies.

The Portuguese sovereign, the scholars and ecclesiastics leaned over Columbus's parchment stretched out on the marble table. Martínez, the King's confessor, exclaimed: "But this is Toscanelli's map!" In fact, the measurements were the same, and on Columbus's sketch could be found the contours outlined by the Florentine doctor. The project was not a new one! Nevertheless, it was discussed, but without much conviction. Actually, the King had never taken Toscanelli's plan seriously. What faith could he place in this Italian who was versed in the natural sciences but had never studied geography and had navigated even less? The Toscanelli affair was well known: his family—one of the richest in Florence—had made a fortune in the spice trade. By capturing Constantinople and thus cutting the land route to the Indies, the Turks had ruined the Toscanellis. Paolo was now an old man, but his thirst for gold was greater than ever and he did not want to die without renewing contact with his warehouses. So, in retirement, he had invented a new route for reaching the lands where, he said, "there was much to gain"—the dreams of a miser, delirious and senile, which a serious mind could not take into consideration. The royal mathematicians leaned scornfully over Columbus's map: his measurements were wrong, he had confused Euclid's degrees with Ptolemy's, and the Arab miles of al-Farghani with those of Behaim. But Christopher Columbus did not admit defeat. He stood up to the assembly. Even if the measurements were inexact, would not gold be found? Not only gold, but also an alliance with the most powerful ruler on earth, which would mean the end of Islam.

The Royal Chancellor cut Columbus short. His plan had been in the archives for a long time. It had been dealt with fully in the bull sent thirty years earlier by Pope Nicholas V to King John II's predecessor, regarding the conquests of Henry the Navigator. The royal official delivered a lecture about it: "The Infante, recalling that no one had ever, in the memory of man, been known to navigate this ocean . . . believed that it would give God the greatest evidence of submission if, through his care, this ocean could be made navigable as far as the Indies that were said to be obedient to Christ. If he should enter into relations with these peoples, he would move them to come to the aid of the Christians of the West against the Saracens and the enemies of the Faith. At the same time he would, with royal permission, subdue the heathens of these countries, not yet infected by the Mohammedan plague, making them recognize the name of Christ. . . ."

This time it was Christopher Columbus's turn to smile. Now they were drawing upon Prince Henry for evidence! During Henry's lifetime he had been regarded as mad and had nearly been shut up. What was madness yesterday was wisdom today! Columbus bit his lips and kept the reflection to himself.

The Portuguese court knew what it had to do; it needed no foreigner to remind it of its duties. The material and political interest of the route to the Indies had never escaped it. This contact with the Great Khan, which was highly desirable both for Europe and for Christianity, would be achieved on the day when the ships rounded the Cape of Good Hope and reached the eastern tip of Asia. The studies were already far advanced. Portugal was rich enough in men of courage and talent to expect that soon some navigator would extend and complete Bartholomeu Diaz' exploit. But the western route was madness. Columbus said nothing, but thought of Henry and of other madmen who had been proved right.

The audience was drawing to an end. Half serious and half amused, John II asked Columbus what would be his conditions if he were given command of a westward expedition. Imperturbably the Genoese named them: the title of Admiral of the Ocean Sea, the viceroyalty and the government of all the lands discovered and to be discovered, transmissible to his heirs, the tenth part of the prize, and the exclusive right to legislate in the territories conquered.

Columbus's demands were received with a burst of laughter. Someone remarked that Portuguese were not in the habit of making money out of services to their country. His tales, moreover, were grotesque. Already he had abused the royal patience enough. The audience was ended.

Christopher Columbus picked up his papers, bowed to the King, and without a glance at the assembly, left the room. As he crossed the threshold he lightly shrugged his shoulders. If Portugal did not want his plan, he would suggest it to some other nation. Should it be France or Spain?

Victory at Granada

He decided upon Spain.

His repulse at the hands of the King of Portugal had cruelly wounded his self-esteem, for he was very impressionable despite his outward hardness. For some months he wandered about the streets of Lisbon like a lost soul. Would it be true to say that he was a vagabond? What did he live on? Very little, certainly, and even that was borrowed. His position in Portugal became untenable. He could expect no more of that ungrateful kingdom but further affronts and perhaps imprisonment for debt. So he fled.

For it was in reality a fugitive who one winter evening fell at the foot of the cross that stood before the monastery of Santa María de la Rábida. He was exhausted, half dead with hunger. He held a child of four years by the hand: his own son, Diego. What had he done with his wife, the gentle Felipa? Why had he left her in Portugal? Was this premeditated desertion? Was she perhaps dead? So far as we are concerned, she was, for the touching bride of Porto Santo was effaced forever from the tale of Columbus.

The Franciscan monastery of La Rábida, which is the Arabic for "watchtower," lay some sixty miles from Seville, and two hours on foot from Huelva. With its whitewashed walls and its trees bent by the ocean breeze, it was more a *granja*—a family house—than a monastery. It comprised only two inner cloisters, a small church, and scarcely more than a dozen cells. But its dome could be seen far out at sea and served as a guide to pilots. Around the monastery grew aloes and palms, though the terraces, supported by walls of dried earth, had collapsed beneath the weight of the orchards: vines, lemon trees, fig trees, and caper bushes. It was an African landscape. Built on a shaded hill, the monastery overlooked the mouths of the Odiel and the Tinto, and from its high windows could be seen the Gulf of Cádiz. Four miles farther on lay Palos de la Frontera, whence Columbus eventually set sail.

At that moment he was thinking of setting out for France, where Charles VIII had just succeeded Louis XI. It was said that he was a man of great imagination. Columbus would bring him something that would satisfy it. While he mused sadly as he leaned against the stone stylobate, the gatekeeper came toward him. Columbus pointed to Diego and murmured simply: "Bread and water for my child!" Moved by such misfortune and struck by the nobility and bearing of the stranger, the monk went off to inform the prior, Juan Pérez. The prior left his cell, came out of the monastery door, looked at Columbus for a moment, and laid a hand on his shoulder. He drew him toward the monastery. The door closed behind them.

Antonio de Marchena, a monk well versed in geographical knowledge, was present at the first interview between Juan Pérez and Christopher Columbus, and the two men lent an attentive ear to the vagabond's words. The old books were opened, the maps were unrolled, and the Franciscan subjected Columbus to something like an examination. It seems to have been decisive. The plan merited study. The adventure was perhaps worth an attempt, but support and enormous subsidies would be needed. Juan Pérez was Queen Isabella's former confessor, but he had continued to maintain contact with the court. In short, he was so affected by the man and his words that he was inclined to use these contacts in Columbus's favor.

What developed from this three-sided conversation? Nothing

precise and nothing immediate except for an agreement on principle and a formal promise of support. For the moment Christopher Columbus needed nothing more. He was one of those who, always poised between dream and action, knew how to be content with the one, provided that it prepared the way for the other. He entrusted his child to the Franciscans and vanished.

Once again there is an obscure gap in his life. For two years only glimpses of him can be had. He made frequent trips between La Rábida and Seville, sojourned at Huelva (with a sister-in-law?), and then is lost to sight once more. Anyway, it seems that his affairs were in a better state. The intervention of the prior Juan Pérez must have borne fruit. In fact, he often visited with the great lords of Seville, the Andalusian business magnates, always in search of a grant that would make it possible for him to pass at last into the realm of reality. First he was received by the Duke of Medina Sidonia, a rich shipowner of Seville who had the tunny-fishing monopoly in the Gibraltar region. Then, having been unsuccessful with this gentleman fisherman, he approached another, the Duke of Medina Celi; in his domain at Puerto de Santa María this duke had a flotilla of caravels and three-masters with a dual purpose: they were used for commerce and also for pursuing the war against the Moors of Granada. Medina Celi allowed himself to be convinced by Columbus. At the end of the western route to the Indies, the Duke could catch the odor of spices. The adventure was worth the risk of two vessels.

At the last moment Medina Celi changed his mind. On reflection, the business was beyond him. It was within the province of the court. Furthermore, the most urgent matters demanded his attention, for he was called to Córdoba with his men-at-arms, where King Ferdinand had need of all the available forces in Christian Spain. The final assault on Granada had begun. God knew how long it would last!

In Spain the question of the day that excited public opinion and preoccupied the princes was to complete the reconquest. Ferdinand III, the Saint, King of Castile and León, had carried his frontiers to Córdoba and Seville. James I of Aragon, the Conqueror, had taken possession of the Balearics and Murcia. But two centuries had passed since that time. Incredible as such a halt may seem, more than two hundred years passed between the capture of Córdoba and the capture of Granada. Civil wars, dynastic rivalries, and local particularisms explain the interval. Almost all Spain had become Christian again except the kingdom of Granada, which stretched along the Mediterranean coast from Gibraltar to Almería and in the north reached to the sources of the Guadalquivir. Two centuries to cross a mountain, the Sierra Nevada!

Isabella and Ferdinand, who simultaneously united their loves and their kingdoms, had put the expulsion of the Moors at the top of their political program, and they forced the Cortes to vote the credits necessary to the success of the campaign. It was to cost the treasury a million silver ducats. Pope Sixtus IV had granted them a Bull of Crusade and had thereby given a religious character to the undertaking. A hundred thousand soldiers were drawn up. The final liberation of Spain had its price.

Málaga, Almería, and Cádiz had just fallen into the crusaders' hands. But Granada held out, a thorn in the heel of Christian Spain. It had to be torn out.

The southward movement of the center of gravity in the battle against the Moors had forced the court to move. It was Córdoba, for a long time a frontier city, constantly menaced by Arab incursions, that now became the capital of warring Spain. Deserting Valladolid for a time, the Catholic monarchs were established in Córdoba, a hundred miles from Granada. It was a battle position rather than a royal residence.

Abandoned by the Duke of Medina Celi, his protector, Christopher Columbus left Seville for Córdoba. There he made the acquaintance of a strange man, Gabriel de Acosta, a doctor, astrologer, and geographer. Acosta was interested in the enigmatic character of Columbus, and through Acosta Columbus made contact with the one who was to open a way for him to the throne of the Spanish sovereigns. For it was now Columbus's fixed idea to reach the Catholic monarchs, so as to submit his plan to them.

Tenaciously and by stages, Columbus began his task of approach by way of the clerks of the Royal Chancellery. This stubborn man's reserves of patience were inexhaustible. In a few months he had secured the aid of the Master of the Accounts, Alfonso de Quintanilla, the Grand Chamberlain, Cabrero, and King Ferdinand's secretary-accountant, Luis de Santangel. Passed on from one to another, he ended by being received by the Cardinal of Spain, González de Mendoza, "the third monarch." This prelate, a skillful politician, a valorous warrior and *grand seigneur*, did not understand much of practical science, so he lent a willing ear to the discourses of Christopher Columbus. He was enchanted by the prospects opened up to him by the Genoese. An alliance with the Great Khan seemed to him desirable; it would complete the decisive action which the armies of Their Catholic Majesties were preparing at that moment around Granada. As to the purely scientific arguments advanced by Columbus, the soldier-cardinal was in no position to discuss them, but he understood enough to be persuaded that they merited examination by the experts. Anyway, the matter was one of importance: it could and should be submitted to royal authority.

The year 1486 was a significant one in the life of Christopher Columbus, for it was then that he appeared before the Catholic monarchs. In the same year he met Beatriz Enríquez de Harana, the woman he was to love above all others. Isabella of Castile and Beatriz were respectively the mistress of his destiny and the mistress of his heart.

It was in the former alcazar of the Arab kings, which had now become the palace of the Spanish sovereigns, that the interview took place between Christopher Columbus and Isabella and Ferdinand. Never was the Genoese more eloquent. He well knew that he was playing his last card. He laid stress on the political and religious aspects of the enterprise. He recalled that the Great Khan had for two centuries been touched by grace and that Marco Polo had occupied himself with establishing diplomatic relations between the "King of Kings" and the Papacy. But it had not been possible completely to effect the liaison, for the road from Rome to Peking was long and difficult. The pontifical envoys and those of the Great Khan came to a stop en route. Only two ambassadorships had succeeded: Marco Polo's, in the name of Gregory X, to Kublai, and, in the opposite direction—almost two centuries later—that of Kublai's successor, to Pope Eugenius IV. Since then no one had known what was happening at the court of China. Columbus stated forcefully that it behooved Their Catholic Majesties to resume contact with the Asiatic emperor, to ally themselves to him and thus form the most formidable confederation of peoples that had ever been seen. The Mussulmans would no longer have the balance of power between Europe on one side and Asia on the other. And what a harvest of souls for the Church of Christ! Christopher Columbus was not afraid of taking up the Crusaders' cry: "*Dieu le veult.*"

Isabella and Ferdinand listened attentively to the musical voice that flowed endlessly like the waters of a stream. After having rung like a trumpet while evoking the service of God, it became insinuating regarding the riches of Cathay. Then Christopher added gesture to his words, and with his prophet's hands described the marble quays, the gold-plated palaces, the ships with multicolored sails and prows ornamented with dragons, the endless lines of men carrying on their shoulders cases filled with diamonds and pearls—a theme that had now become familiar to Columbus and which he developed with the ease of an actor at his hundredth performance.

Isabella dreamed, for she was a woman and her love of finery and taste for dress were touched by the stranger's evocations. Precious stones and silk! She had not forgotten her almost poor childhood at Madrigal de las Altas Torres, in the "black lands" of Old Castile. Christopher Columbus was softened at seeing the reflection of gold in her eyes. Would he end by completely believing the story himself?

Ferdinand of Aragon was dreaming, too. He thought of the Portuguese, of their forward march along the African coasts, of their slow and painful penetration of unknown lands. For a long time the Spaniards had laughed at this point-to-point race; what a lot of money had been swallowed up for nothing by Henry the Mad, the paper navigator! But in recent times the business had become a paying one. The gold of Sierra Leone and the maleguetta pepper of Guinea were in a fair way to repaying the expenditures of thirty years, and the cosmographers of Lisbon were forecasting the early opening of the route to the Indies via the Cape of Good Hope. The lead that the Portuguese had achieved over the Spaniards was incontestible, but Columbus's project, if it succeeded, would permit Spain not only to bridge this gap, but even to surpass her rivals. The way to the Indies, immediate and direct, was an exciting prospect.

Alliance with the Great Khan, the ruin of Islam, the eclipse of Portugal, the spiritual and material annexation of hundreds of millions of men, the conquest of the sources of gold and riches—these amounted in all to the possession of the world. The proposition was tempting, too tempting, in fact. For though Ferdinand was ambitious, his prudence was greater. This vagabond who stood before him as wise man and preacher was perhaps right, but he might also be a hoaxer. Moreover, the moment was not propitious for effecting such a new drain on the treasury, already sorely tried by the war against Granada. Inch by inch the Catholic monarchs were in process of reconquering the last refuge of the Arab occupiers, and each inch cost the royal purse dearly. So Ferdinand decided to submit Columbus's plan to a commission of scholars. The monk Talavera, prior of Santa María del Prado at Valladolid, the Queen's confessor and later archbishop of Granada, presided over this commission.

Columbus's cause was once again referred to the experts, which amounts to saying that it was postponed *sine die*. The Genoese expected nothing good from the scholars. They were dogmatists in whom the one master quality, imagination, was lacking. The first meeting of the commission at Córdoba confirmed his fears, for it ended by rejecting his plan, "which did not rest on a firm enough base for the good name of Spain to be exposed in such an enterprise, nor the lives of those who would accompany it."

For this new failure Christopher Columbus consoled himself in the arms of Beatriz Enríquez de Harana, whom he had just met. She was blue-eyed and fair, like Isabella of Castile. He was soon to have a child by her, whom he named Fernando.

The months passed. The war against the Moors of Granada dragged on and on. Christopher Columbus lost heart. He could be seen at the monastery of San Esteban at Salamanca among the Dominicans whom he strove to convince; he could be glimpsed at Málaga, which had become Christian again, in search of available vessels; and despite the unpleasant memories he retained of Portugal, he wrote to John II to offer him his plan a second time. He sent Bartholomew, his brother, to England. But neither the Portuguese sovereign nor Henry VII took Columbus's project seriously. He fell back again on the Spanish sovereigns. Thanks to the friendships he maintained at the court of the Catholic monarchs—particularly that of Father Diego de Deza, tutor to the heir to the throne—he succeeded in getting himself summoned to the camp at Santa Fe, under the walls of besieged Granada.

It was granted to Christopher Columbus to be present at the death throes of Arab rule. What a battle and what a scene! On the three hills where the buttresses of the Sierra Nevada come to an end, the city of Granada rises in tiers: the Vermilion Towers, the Alhambra, the Alcazaba. The perpetual enchantment of the Andalusian landscape, the profusion of arbutus trees, and the sweet scent of orange trees were in striking contrast to the uproar of a people in arms. Isabella and Ferdinand were of course too busy to give audience to Columbus, but they informed him that his business would be examined after the fall of Granada.

After the fall of Granada? Columbus noted those words. Meanwhile he decided to stay in the Santa Fe camp. Lost in the crowd and wandering for several months among the fifty thousand Spanish infantry, the Genoese became bored. He ascended the Zubia, which overlooks Granada. The three hills reddened in the sunlight. On the highest of them the Alhambra rose like a torch. In the shadows he saw in his mind's eye the Court of the Myrtles and the Hall of the Ambassadors. What colors there were, at once violent and voluptuous!—but less violent and less voluptuous than those he saw beyond the Dark Sea.

In the end Boabdil, the last of the Moorish kings, capitulated. The dawn of January 2, 1492, rose over Granada, and the Catholic monarchs, preceded by the banners of Santiago and the Virgin, moved out of the camp of Santa Fe. Beside them rode the Grand Cardinal of Spain. Boabdil, accompanied by fifty knights, came out to meet his conquerors. When he reached the banks of the Genil, the Moor stepped down and handed Ferdinand the keys of the alcazar. Then, while the Christian advance guards entered Granada, Cardinal Mendoza raised the silver pontifical cross and the standard of Castile to the summit of the Comares tower. "Granada to the Catholic monarchs!" a herald proclaimed from the top of the Vela tower. Arab domination, which had lasted for almost eight centuries, was broken, and Mussulman Spain was no more.

Christopher Columbus watched this historic scene from afar. He shrugged his shoulders. What a din over such a small affair! It had taken the Catholic monarchs more than ten years and a million silver ducats to put an end to a usurping kinglet, and though it was fine to see the blackamoor weeping at his mother's skirts, he, Christopher

Columbus, was asking but a few weeks and one caravel in order to seek an empire and the alliance of the Great Khan!

The hour had come for Columbus to confront the Spanish sovereigns once again and for them to keep their word. Granada had fallen. So one morning, when all were still agog over the Christian victory, Columbus made his way to the camp at Santa Fe and to the tent that Their Majesties still inhabited, for they found it preferable to the Alhambra.

He who had been named derisively "the man in the threadbare cloak" presented himself to the Catholic monarchs for the second time like a master. Was he not, after all, a purveyor of kingdoms? And the conversation that had begun at Córdoba six years before was resumed in the same style, for his plan had not changed, nor had his demands. They were those that he had always formulated and of which he was determined to relinquish nothing. He recited them to a stupefied Ferdinand: the title of Admiral of the Ocean Sea, the viceroyalty of the territories discovered, ten percent of the riches he acquired. . . . The King did not let him proceed. Such demands were insane! Isabella, despite her sympathy for Columbus, shared her husband's irritation at such presumption. The Genoese was dismissed coldly, as he had been by John II of Portugal.

This time Christopher Columbus lost patience. Since neither Spain nor Portugal nor England wanted his plan, he would offer it to France. He had held this last card in reserve. He was about to play it.

Where could he find the money to go to France? At the monastery of La Rábida. He left Granada, went to Seville and Huesca, and then, one evening, knocked at the monastery door. Eight years had passed since his first visit, and he had made scarcely any progress since. There he found Pérez, Father de Marchena, and his friends the monks. He told them of his rebuffs and of his resolve. Juan Pérez was moved: Columbus was perhaps mad, but it was a greater madness to let him go. The prior had maintained considerable influence over the Queen, so he did not hesitate to write to her at Santa Fe to beg her to give consideration to Columbus's plan. He did not hesitate to invoke the interest of the Crown and of Christianity, of which Spain, and not France, was the guarantor. Was it desirable that Charles VIII of Valois should accept what Isabella of Castile had refused?

The Queen's reply was not long delayed. She agreed to resume the discussions with Columbus. Would Juan Pérez come to Granada with his protégé? The young sovereign's heart and mind were easily persuaded by her former confessor's arguments, for she had been won over to Columbus's cause ever since the first encounter; but Ferdinand had still to be convinced, hence the necessity for the Franciscan's presence.

Juan Pérez was not the only one to lay siege to the King of Aragon, for he had found allies in the immediate entourage of the Spanish sovereigns. Besides Santangel, the "Grand Treasurer," who had long been favorably disposed toward Columbus's ideas, there were all those who from far and near managed the royal chest and hoped that the discovery of the route to the Indies would enrich the treasury. The gold and spices of Cathay would re-establish the state's finances, and those honest stewards doubtless thought that there would be a pinch left over for themselves.

In short, it was the men of the Church—except for a few cautious theologians—and the Jews who supported Columbus's cause. The former—Juan Pérez, Marchena, Cardinal de Mendoza, Diego de Deza, Talavera—saw that the success of Columbus would mean also the success of a vast political and religious project: the domination of the world under the symbol of the Spanish Christ. The Jews— Cabrero, Santangel, and a certain influential official named Sánchez, all of them "converted" but Jews nevertheless—by upholding Columbus gave evidence of their Christian feelings, since an evangelizing enterprise was involved. It was, in fact, a fine opportunity to display their zeal!—not forgetting that there was gold at the end of the road.

Fervent though these monks and Jews were in their support of Columbus, neither party succeeded in securing Ferdinand's consent, nor did Isabella. As for the great political plan of which Columbus spoke, it was the Queen who bore it within her like a child: she adorned it with all the strange colors of the unknown, for this capable woman had imagination. She coldly computed the risks and chances of the business; she estimated the assets and liabilities; but at the same time she could not prevent herself from dreaming. The cold glow of the real and the glitter of the unreal shone together on the noble forehead of Isabella of Castile.

Gradually, under pressure from his entourage, Ferdinand was convinced by Columbus's arguments. He agreed that the voyage might succeed. He agreed to the idea of an alliance with the Great Khan. He believed in the virtues of gold, which, said Columbus emphatically in a letter written to the sovereign later, was the finest thing in the world. "Gold," he declared somewhat heretically, "rules everything. Its power is such that it is able to deliver souls from Purgatory or open to them the gates of Paradise."

But Ferdinand was not going to decide yet. He certainly agreed to give Columbus his patronage, to facilitate things for him, and to provide all or part of the funds necessary for equipping the fleet. He was ready to sign the contract. But he could not bring himself to give Columbus the honors he demanded. Admiral of the Ocean Sea, viceroy for life, transmissible to his heirs! It would amount to making this adventurer the second personage of the realm—and he was not even Spanish! Perhaps the first, if his discoveries were to imperil the Spanish crown. Ferdinand's pride bled at the thought of this overseas empire which might absorb his own. He was not going to make a potential rival with his own hands.

Ferdinand asked for time to think, but Columbus was firmly determined to abandon none of his claims, and it seemed that the matter was postponed yet again. Columbus then staked everything. This consummate actor staged a showdown. He pretended to abandon his plans. He told those nearest him that the discussions had been broken off and that he was preparing to leave the country. He went even further: he mounted his mule and rode out of Santa Fe, but not without first informing Santangel.

This false departure was certainly Columbus's finest gamble. It was a risky business, for his whole destiny was involved in the subterfuge. What if they did not fetch him back?

Two leagues out of Granada, at the place known as Puente de los Pinos, Columbus heard a horse galloping behind him. It was Isabella's courier! The clatter of hoofs on the dry earth was to Columbus like the sound of a fanfare, and before the royal messenger had even caught up with him, he knew that he had triumphed.

On a fine April morning three months after the capture of Granada, Christopher Columbus and the Catholic monarchs signed the Santa Fe convention. To the Genoese they gave complete satisfaction—and more!

"Columbus, for the duration of his life, his heirs and successors forever, will enjoy, on all the lands and continents he may discover or acquire in the Ocean, the office of admiral, with the honors and prerogatives similar to those enjoyed by the Grand Admiral of Castile.

"He shall be Viceroy and Governor of all the aforesaid lands and continents, with the privilege of nominating three candidates to the government of each island or province, one of whom shall be chosen by the Sovereign.

"He shall have the right to retain for himself, during his Admiralty, the tenth part, after deduction of expenses, of the precious stones, gold, silver, spices, and all other articles of trade by whatever means he obtain them: by purchase, barter, or conquest.

"He and his lieutenant shall be the sole judges of all the suits and causes which might be occasioned by trade between Spain and these lands.

"Finally, he may at all times contribute an eighth part of the costs of arming vessels destined to the discovery and to receive an eighth part of the profits."

Such was the exorbitant contract that Christopher Columbus signed with the Catholic monarchs. Nothing like it had ever been seen or would ever be seen again. Surely this was trafficking with the unknown. Doubtless, too, the Spanish monarchs secretly speculated on the hazards of the undertaking. If Columbus found nothing or perished at sea, the Crown would have made a bad investment, but the cost would be very small. If he won, the Catholic monarchs would know how, in practice, to limit the scope of the agreement. And besides, was it conceivable that Columbus would be able, with a few hundred men and two or three caravels, to defeat the innumerable army of the Great Khan if there should be a battle?

Thus neither Columbus nor Isabella and Ferdinand were entirely sincere. Both sides had mental reservations. Columbus was not sure of success; while the Catholic monarchs reckoned on keeping only part of their promises. Nevertheless, in this mad contest against nature, rulers, and men, begun eight years before, Columbus had won the first round.

CHAPTER 2

Bermejo Sights Land

BETWEEN the mouths of the Guadiana and Guadalquivir the Andalusian coast forms a continuous curve, wide open to the Gulf of Cádiz. Huelva, the property of the dukes of Medina Sidonia, stands on a peninsula formed by the Tinto and the Odiel. Following the palm-fringed left bank of the Odiel, La Rábida is reached in an hour, and in another hour Palos de la Frontera, while in yet another, Moguer. The Río Tinto, which means the "red river" because it is saturated with copper, waters and colors the land. But the province of Huelva was rich not only in minerals; the ship-builders had made it the center of their activity. The regular lie of the coast and its admirable aspect lent themselves excellently to the construction and launching of ships. Farther south lay Sanlúcar de Barrameda and then Cádiz.

Palos, Moguer, La Rábida: blinding white houses, old Arab palaces in Mudejar style, the remains of Roman fortresses, and, on the sandy pine-fringed beaches, immense nets drying in the scorching heat of the Andalusian sun. This was the brilliant scene that witnessed Columbus's final anxieties before departure.

To give an order is one thing, but to carry it out is another, and Columbus was to test this bitter formula to his cost.

Money had been found to finance the expedition. Isabella had not needed to pledge her jewels with the Jews, for by one means or another, scraping the bottoms of drawers, it had been possible to get together the million maravedis in gold that were required to cover the initial cost. It had been foreseen that more would be needed. A month after the agreement of Santa Fe—Columbus had meanwhile secured from the Catholic monarchs the transmission to his descendants of the dignities and prerogatives of the viceroyalty, as well as the title of Don—the new admiral arrived at Palos. He was in possession of royal ordinances commanding the municipality to equip and arm two caravels. A period of ten days was given the inhabitants of Palos to carry them out, and Columbus immediately placed an embargo on the two caravels that seemed to him the best rigged among the vessels anchored in the port. He had now to recruit the crews.

The ten-day period slipped by. The weeks passed. The summer arrived. No one had come to present himself at the enrollment table. What was the reason for this mistrust of Columbus? First, he had no standing in the eyes of the sailors of Palos, for everyone knew that he had done more navigation through the royal antechambers than upon the ocean. Further, he had been seen earlier at La Rábida dressed in rags and sponging on the monks, but now he was wearing an embroidered cloak, with a sword at his side and on his chest a double necklet of amber beads. None could forget the vagabond of yesterday. What right, moreover, had this foreigner to invoke the name of the Catholic monarchs? Further, these old sea dogs—there were some who had even been as far as Guinea—did not believe in Columbus's speeches. They remembered with terror that Sea of Weeds, that liquid prairie that seized the caravels in its grip. Cipango? The Great Khan? Why not the Earthly Paradise? The experienced captains shook their heads.

Columbus was in despair. He had the ships, the money, and the royal guarantee, but now he had encountered an unforeseen obstacle. In fact, not for a second had he thought that crews would be hard to come by. Angrily he had the enrollment table, which had stood before the church of Palos, taken away. Although it had been covered with golden coins, no one had approached it except at a distance and in order to laugh.

Once again Columbus found help and consolation in Juan Pérez. All hope was not lost. Martín Alonso, the most influential and most fortunate of the Pinzón family (by its wealth it ruled Palos and Moguer) had left for the port of Ostia with a cargo of Andalusian wines. He would soon be back. He was a man worth consulting. He was of the country; he was interested in geography; and, above all, he was richer than all the Andalusian dukes put together.

It was at the monastery of La Rábida that Columbus met Martín Alonso Pínzón. It happened that this traveler had been to Rome, where he had been the guest of a friend of Pope Innocent VIII. Turning over the maps in the Vatican library, Pinzón's attention had been attracted by one in which Cipango figured to the west of the Spanish coast. The Andalusian had not imagined that Europe was so close to the Indies—perhaps only a thousand leagues from the Canaries by the sea road. He compared the facts he brought back from Rome with those given by Columbus. The similarity was striking. Pinzón was enthusiastic; Columbus was too, but he concealed his pleasure. He needed Martín Alonso, so much was clear; but it was unnecessary to make it too obvious. Shareholders, collaborators, certainly; but associates, no.

Meanwhile, Columbus drew in his claws. He showed himself conciliatory, even humble, for he wished to win Pinzón over. Through flattery, he easily succeeded. The Andalusian agreed finally to take over the technical direction of the preparations in matters of personnel and material. It might be said that at the right moment Columbus always found the one man to save the situation; he expressed his plans, needs, and even his despair with an eloquence that seems to have derived its unction from the monks, its brilliance from the Italians, its nervous strength from the Spaniards, and its subtlety from the Jews. To know how to talk, that is everything.

Preparations

Martín Alonso was the head of the Pinzón family, of which there were two branches. His own comprised three brothers: Francisco Martín, Vicente Yáñez, and himself, with their numerous children. The other branch, headed by his cousin Diego Martín, known as "the Elder," had a vast progeniture. All of them, father and sons, were sailors. Furthermore, the Pinzóns were allied through various marriages to the most notable families in the land. In brief, it was a dynasty of captains and merchants that reigned over the ports of the Río Tinto and the Río Odiel. Their trade prospered. They trafficked with Guinea and the Canaries and even pushed as far as Sicily.

Martín Alonso's first concern was to examine the two caravels selected by Columbus. One look assured him that they were unsuitable for the expedition. He procured two other caravels, doubtless the best among all those that danced gently on the waters of the port of Palos. They bore the names *Pinta* and *Niña*, since their proprietors were named Pinto and Niño.

A glance at these caravels is indispensable to anyone who wishes to follow Columbus on his mad expedition. They were the same ships as those which, from the beginning of the fifteenth century, had carried the first discoverers safely to port. What could the artisans of the conquest have done without this splendid instrument?

The caravels were a Portuguese invention. Simple merchant vessels by origin, they had been designed for coastal sailing and carrying merchandise. But during increasingly distant cruises they won their title to nobility and became the vessels of the discovery.

All the nations, including the Turks, had adopted this type of vessel—fast, light, and easy to handle. The bottom of the hull was flat for a third of the length of the keel, with very full extremities. Projecting bulkheads and vertical bulwarks (*bularcanas*) strengthened the external structure. At the rear of the deck was a castle (*tolda*), surmounted by the poop (*toldilla*). The forecastle (*castillo*) overhung the stem. The two castles, fore and aft, were very high in relation to the deck. The captain's cabin (*chopa* or *chupeta*) was situated below the toldilla. As for the crew, officers and men, they lodged as best they could under the tolda, protected from the spray by awnings. The rigging comprised three masts and a bowsprit. The mainmast, firmly planted in the keelson and held by guys, carried a large square sail or *treho*. The foremast, fixed to the deck, bore a smaller sail, but also square, called the *trinquete*. The mizzenmast, near the poop, bore a lateen triangular sail. Finally, forward and leaning toward the horizon was the bowsprit, which carried the *cebadera*.

The shallow draft of the caravels facilitated maneuver. Fearing neither reefs nor mud bottom, they could navigate along reputedly dangerous coasts, negotiate channels, and enter rivers.

The caravels took a crew of about forty. Their speed—fast for the period—scarcely exceeded five or six knots. They are sometimes shown covered with gold and carving, but this is false, for caravels were cargo vessels and did not carry passengers normally. Moreover, they were devoid of all comforts and lacked even an inner surfacing. Life on them was hard and the risks were constant. It is a miracle that such ships—nutshells that danced at the will of the waves or that a wind could carry away—were able to conquer the ocean.

The Conquistadors had maps as well as instruments to steer by. To orient themselves they used the compass, astrolabe, portolano, and astronomical tables. The compass, unknown to the ancients but used by the Chinese for more than a thousand years before the Christian era, had been passed on to the Spaniards by the Arabs. It consisted of a needle floating on water in a wooden case. The astrolabe, invented by Hipparchus two centuries before Christ and perfected by the German astronomer John of Königsberg, served to plot the position of the stars and their height above the horizon.

Besides the astrolabe and compass, the sailors consulted the documents drawn up by geographers and astronomers. On the portolano elaborated by scholars or monks they could locate the seaports, the currents, and the tides; in brief, it was a colored calligraph of the known world, kept scrupulously up to date and modified with every discovery. Finally, the astronomical tables gave an approximate picture of the sky. It needed much learning and patience to extract any practical information from these scribblings, unintelligible as they were to the common people.

Such were the technical means available to the navigators when Columbus was preparing to cross the Dark Sea. Yet it should be recorded that the pilots who could use these means properly were few. Audacity did not always go hand in hand with learning. Columbus was incapable of explaining to his crew the variations of the compass, yet the men of his day knew the phenomenon of local declination—the angle made by the magnetic needle with geographical north under the influence of terrestrial magnetism.

The *Pinta* and the *Niña* swung gently in the port of Palos. Columbus could only confirm Pinzón's choice, Pinzón's competence being indisputable. But for his own part he found these caravels very modest for an ambassador of the Catholic monarchs. They would make a poor showing beside the vessels of the Great Khan, with dragons and unicorns carved on their timbers. So, in order not to offend the Andalusian captain, he accepted the *Pinta* and the *Niña*, but suggested at the same time that they add a third caravel for the commander of the fleet, the commander in chief of the expedition— himself. On his arrival at Palos, Columbus had observed a vessel that was distinguished from the rest by its great dimensions: a cock among the chickens. It was certainly more than 120 tons, while the *Pinta* and the *Niña* did not exceed 100 tons. Moreover, its speed was nine knots. It was exactly what suited this commoner, for whom nothing was too noble. For this vagabond and son of a wineshop keeper was constantly obsessed by the matter of appearances. As at Lisbon, Córdoba, and Santa Fe, he was to give evidence in the little city of Palos of the same lofty demands. Caravels? Certainly; but for himself one that was bigger than the rest.

The ship coveted by Columbus bore the gay name of *Mariagalante*. As it had been built in a Galician port, it was also called "the Galician."

The captain of the *Mariagalante* (he was also its owner) was Juan de la Cosa, a native of Santona, a little city halfway between Bilbao and Santander. From the very first he pleased Columbus. This Basque seemed to have all the virtues of his race: seriousness, sobriety, and a quiet earnestness at work. He spoke little, smiled often, and noticed a great deal; in appearance he was gentle, but his strong jaw and deep-sunken eyes revealed that this quiet little man could show himself merciless in grave circumstances. Moreover, the whole crew of the *Mariagalante* was patterned after its skipper. All of them were Basques and accustomed to rough voyages in the Bay of Biscay; they were thick-skinned and did not know how to take a joke. They distrusted everything that was not Galician or Basque. Excellent sailors, but hot-tempered, they obeyed Juan de la Cosa without question. Would they accept another captain?

Columbus knew how to find the words to win Juan de la Cosa to his side. Quite simply, glory and fortune were what he put before him. The Basque agreed to surrender his ship to Columbus, and to it he added himself. Although proprietor and captain of the *Mariagalante*, he wished while on board to remain simply master of the crew and pilot. This would give confidence to his men, who would never consent to enlist under a stranger. Columbus had done an excellent job; a reliable ship—and one that was bigger than the rest!— an experienced pilot, and a trustworthy crew, all without spending a maravedi. Indeed, Juan de la Cosa refused to discuss money. There would be plenty of time when they got back from Cipango to claim repayment of the costs of the expedition from the Catholic monarchs. Columbus was troubled by one last scruple. The name *Mariagalante* was a tiresome reminder of those ladies of light morals who sold their

charms to the soldiers. Was it a fitting name for the flagship of a
Christian fleet? It should not be forgotten that Columbus's embassy
was also apostolic. So a few strokes with a brush put an end to the
profane inscription, and the *Mariagalante* became the *Santa María.*

The problem of armament was settled. There remained, so far as
the *Pinta* and the *Niña* were concerned, the problem of crews. That
was Martín Alonso's business. Like Columbus, the elder Pinzón was
also persuasive, though his method differed from that of the Genoese.
There was no contempt, no conceit, in his attitude toward his men.
He treated them with a mixture of familiarity and respect. "*Señor
Marino* . . ." he addressed the swarthy, hairy fellows that stank of
grease and tar while they mended their nets on the beach at Palos,
and he doffed his hat to them as if at court. "Come to Cipango, the
city of golden roofs!" he added, leading them gently toward the enrollment table. Gradually the heap of gold shrank, and at this point
Columbus began to grow anxious. The Queen's million, to which
Santangel had spontaneously added 140,000 maravedis, had been seriously broached, for the payment of advances to the crews, the re-
fitting of the vessels, and the purchase of munitions and supplies had
consumed a large part of the royal subsidy. To be exact, a further
half million maravedis in gold was still needed, but there was no question of asking for Isabella's help a second time. When Columbus
spoke to him of his anxieties, Martín Alonso smiled. If 500,000 maravedis were still needed, he would find them! In a few days the
Pinzón family had got them together. To those of his family who
were alarmed at being involved without security of any kind, Martín
Alonso replied: "The word of a sailor is worth more than the
scribbles of a notary!"

Martín Alonso's infectious enthusiasm, the contribution of a further half million, and the example of the *Santa María's* crew had their
effect. In the space of three weeks the personnel of the flotilla was
complete: one hundred and twenty men in all, for the most part
natives of the localities along the Río Tinto and Río Odiel. The rest,
other than Juan de la Cosa's Basques, came from every direction.
There was one from Valencia, Juan Martínez de Azogue, four who
had been under sentence of death and taken from the prison at
Huelva, an Englishman, an Irishman, and a few Castilians who happened to be at Palos.

Columbus, "the man in the threadbare cloak," having become admiral, took over the *Santa María*. Juan de la Cosa, assisted by Sancho Ruiz, was her pilot. Juan de Lequeitio, known as Cachu, was mate, and Gil Pérez, an old campaigner of the seas, steward. Columbus's friends took their places aboard the flagship: those who flattered him because he required it, and those who flattered him because by doing so they hoped for everything. Among the former were Rodrigo de Escobedo, notary attached to the fleet, and Rodrigo Sánchez de Segovia, royal comptroller. Among the latter was Diego de Harana, a cousin of Beatriz, who had been promised the office of chief alguazil, or chief justice. Pedro de Terrenos was appointed private steward to the great man.

Martín Alonso Pinzón kept for himself the command of the *Pinta*, reputed to be the best sailer of the three vessels. Both pilot and boatswain were his kinsmen, and the sailors and apprentices were all from Palos and Moguer.

Vicente Yáñez, younger brother of Martín Alonso, commanded the *Niña*, and the crew was made up of cousins, nephews, and childhood friends of the Pinzóns. All, moreover, were excellent sailors, among them Bartolomé Roldán and Juan Bermúdez, who, a few years later, discovered the islands that bear his name.

The two caravels and the flagship were anchored in the port of Palos at the spot called Estero de Domingo Rubio. This was the deepest part of the Río Tinto. La Rábida could be reached by following the bank.

Never had the little port of Palos known such activity as during the month of July 1492. The three ships had to be provisioned for a whole year. The quays were alive with the continuous movement of people. The sailors rolled the barrels to the *fontanilla* to fill them with fresh water. Trains of mules and men laden with boxes came from inland carrying dried vegetables, dried meat, and all the articles needed on a long crossing. But the animation was not only in the port; it was in the hearts and minds of everyone. In the evenings, when the crushing heat of the day began to decline, the inhabitants of Palos and Moguer got together in the wineshops or at the house of that old pilot Pedro Vásquez, who had been as far as the Sea of Weeds thirty years before, quite close to the reputed Island of Seven Cities (as the Portuguese knew it), or Antilia (to use its Spanish name). All night—for it was too hot to sleep—they talked about the West. Seven bishops, Spanish and Portuguese, fleeing from the Moors in the eighth century, had set out upon the ocean with a great number of Christians, and after months of navigation discovered Antilia. Each bishop had founded an island kingdom, of which nothing was now known except that the soil of these islands was gold dust. Later, some Portuguese, having determined to explore the Dark Sea to its limit, had landed on some strange islands: the island of "sheep with bitter flesh," of the "red men," and of "Saint Brendan," which was the realm of a giant converted to Christianity. And they finished by recalling Cipango and its palaces with gold plating as thick as a two-real piece, and the innumerable pearls that the fishermen carried away by the basketful.*

Lulled by the deep voice of old Vásquez, the children dozed. For Columbus's sailors it was like a vigil of arms. The old man's tales, the heavy Andalusian wine, the nervousness of impending departure, and the burning sun of the day fired their already hot heads. But when they thought of the perils to which their husbands, brothers, and sons would be exposed, the women paled—or rather, they called upon the Virgin of Miracles. How could the companions of Columbus ever come back except by a miracle? And although the night was far advanced, none had any desire for sleep. Each, as he watched the bright strip of the rising sun glimmer upon the Andalusian sky, thought of the golden fringe of the Dark Sea away in the far west.

Cast Off! In the Name of God!

It was August 2, 1492, and just seven months since Granada had fallen. On the morrow Columbus's caravels would steer for Cipango. Thanks to Martín Alonso, no time had been lost. A review of men and materials had been completed. It happened that this day was also the traditional feast of the Virgin of Miracles, and the entire people were on their knees to pray. During High Mass at the monastery of La Rábida, the commander had taken the Sacrament.

The next morning, shortly before sunrise, all were aboard. The

* The tale of the seven bishops who founded the Seven Cities is purely traditional and has no basis in fact. Antilia was a ghost island, no more real than Atlantis.

boats had been hauled onto the decks. The sailors were at their posts. No thing or person was missing. Columbus had even thought to bring with him two interpreters who knew Chaldean, Arabic, and Hebrew. He had thought of everything except a priest—a strange oversight on the part of an ambassador of the Catholic monarchs.

On the riverbank at the front of the crowd was Juan Pérez, prior of La Rábida, surrounded by his monks; his eyes never left the flagship. Was it not he who had instigated this unique moment? Beside him stood old Pedro Vásquez and young Diego Columbus and the families of all those who were leaving. Would they ever return? In the Andalusian fashion, the women raised piercing cries. Words of farewell were exchanged. Martín Alonso promised a golden tile to each of his friends. In the sonorous air of early morning—the *madrugada*—the voices blended into a soft murmur. The creak of the cables around the capstans, the slapping of the sails as they were freed from the yards, covered the sobbing murmur of the town of Palos. Motionless at their sterns, their faces lit by the gleam of the lanterns, the three captains surveyed the maneuver. Columbus wore the admiral's uniform with ease: the breeches, coat, and short fur-trimmed cloak were garnet-red, the color of the admirals of Castile. He had just been conducted around his fleet to the sound of trumpets, in accordance with tradition. He wanted all the honors.

Something glistened in the waters of the Río Tinto. A reflection quivered on the tarred sterns of the vessels. The sun! Then Christopher Columbus doffed his cap, bowed, looked toward the mastheads, and in a voice of thunder cried: "Cast off! In the name of God!" And the two Pinzón brothers repeated: "Cast off! In the name of God!" Then all the sails, now unfurled, gave out a thunderous report, and so strongly blew the wind that, as they were launched upon the Río Tinto, the three caravels looked like three white sea birds. They were awkward and rolled heavily. But they drew away. The admiral's flag, bearing the image of Christ nailed to the Cross, flew over the *Santa María*, and from the mainmasts of the *Pinta* and *Niña* flew the banner of the expedition: a green cross and the royal initials surmounted by a crown. This fleet, although it had no chaplain, was nevertheless truly under the sign of God. Its parting hymn was the *Salve Regina*.

The prior of La Rábida had returned to the monastery and from its terrace he blessed the caravels. Carried along by a strong breeze, they were beyond the confluence of the rivers Tinto and Odiel. Then they crossed the bar of the Saltés and in a great shower of foam entered the ocean. For a long time the crews could see the wide brown sleeves of Juan Pérez forming a living cross against the sky. They could hear the moans of the women back in their homes. And, borne along by the swell, the *Salve Regina* would envelop Palos almost to the moment when the high sails of the caravels sank into the sea.

While the sailors were still trying to distinguish the coast, there arose a great sound of lamentation. Was this from Palos, brought to them on the wind, or was it the song of the sirens that legend had promised them? The clamor drew nearer. It took shape. Soon they could see open mouths, for these were men and not phantoms. The three caravels had almost to swing to port to avoid running down about twenty-five vessels of a sinister flotilla which, steering for Africa, cut the ocean with a long foaming wake. The passengers looked wretched: there were old men with rounded backs and hoary chins, enormous women like witches, and fine young women with aquiline noses and complexions like alabaster. They were all singing—if it can be so described—a desperate hymn to the accompaniment of tambourines. For these were the Jews expelled from Spain. The edict of the Catholic monarchs had given them four months— prolonged by nine days through the benevolence of Torquemada —to leave the land of their adoption forever. Preceded by violinists and accompanied by their rabbis, after having wound up their affairs as best they could, on foot or crowded together into carts, they had passed along the Andalusian roads for the last time toward the south- ern ports. A squadron commanded by the corsair Pedro Cabrón awaited them at Cádiz or at Puerto de Santa María. Now they were sailing toward the Moroccan coast.

Columbus's sailors leaned upon the rails as they watched the wretched fleet slip by. The women, like the mourners of antiquity, had wailed for three days and nights without end over the tombs of their ancestors whose bones would remain in Spanish earth. All along the roads leading to the ports they had wept, wringing their hands, and at sea they continued their shrill plaint. Wailing is a Jewish prayer, prolonging through the centuries the cry of the

tribes of Israel as they marched toward Canaan, or of the slaves in
Babylon. But one hopeful note punctuated this propitiatory *lamento*.
A chosen and a persecuted people by turns, the Jews have always
glimpsed at the end of an exodus the lights of the blessed city.
Perhaps these exiles were going to find, buried in the Barbary sands,
the ruins of another Zion. There they would restore the ruins and
build a new Jerusalem.

Leaning with his elbows on the gangway of the castillo, Christopher Columbus mused. He shed no tears for this Hebrew flock,
deported by those same princes who had just made his own fortune,
while expecting him to make theirs. It would be well to keep the
limpia sangre unsullied. But was his own blood so pure? But for
his Jewish friends at court and the Jewish gold of the *marranes*
(the cursed and the damned), would he that day have been in
command of these three caravels?

The *Salve Regina* and the chant of the Psalmist, momentarily
mingled in one entreaty, broke up and then died away. Columbus's
fleet continued southward, while Cabrón's turned eastward. There
was no sound now but that of the sea. A warm night fell, wrapping
the day of August 3 in its heavy folds.

The Crossing

Christopher Columbus headed for the Canaries, the first stage.
From there he planned to turn due west and to sail straight on,
following the 28th parallel. This was the route on which he had
always been determined.

Three days passed without event. The caravels sailed on at a
good pace. The weather was fine and the men seemed contented.
On the morning of the fourth day news reached the admiral that
the *Pinta*'s helm had broken loose. This was bad news indeed. Without a helm the *Pinta* was like a carcass at the mercy of the waves.
Moreover, she was the flotilla's best sailer and, as such, led the *Niña*
and *Santa María*. Martín Alonso tried as best he could to put the
helm back in its pintles. He succeeded. It would hold out as far as
the Canaries. There Columbus wanted to get rid of the *Pinta* and to
change it for another vessel, but Martín Alonso opposed him.
The ship was excellent; it had only to be repaired. For the four

weeks that these labors occupied, from August 9 to September 6, the *Santa María* and the *Niña* sailed from one island to the other: Fuerte Ventura, Lanzarote, and Ferro. Columbus spoke with the natives and derived new assurances from what they told him. It seemed that on certain evenings mysterious summits were outlined above the sea toward the west. And what was the terror of the Spanish sailors at seeing the peak of Tenerife spitting out its flames! The admiral reassured them. There was nothing about this volcanic phenomenon that was not perfectly natural. For Columbus's skill lay in distinguishing the marvelous from the real, according to circumstances. Things were terrifying or normal according to what he had decided they should be.

The *Pinta* was made good. The rudder steered again. The bow was repaired. The sails, too, had been changed: on the foremast and mainmast the lateen or triangular sails had been replaced by square sails. Putting this enforced halt to profit, they had reprovisioned with water and salt meat. Now everything was ready, and Columbus gave the order to depart. It was September 6.

Now renovated and all spick and span, with her new sails flapping in the wind, the *Pinta* once again took the lead. The real voyage now began, and it was time. Three Portuguese caravels cruised in the vicinity with the task of delaying—even of preventing—the Spanish expedition; but Columbus outstripped his adversaries, gave himself plenty of room, then, forcing the pace, steered due west. Soon the Canaries were lost to sight. Farewell to the Fortunate Isles!

From very vague indications Columbus reckoned the distance from the Canaries to the shores of Cipango at 700 leagues. But he was not certain. Furthermore, from the start he compiled two records of the course, one for his own use, made up of the real figures, and the other for the crew, showing lower figures. This childish trick, which did not escape the notice of the Pinzón brothers nor Juan de la Cosa, deceived the sailors throughout the voyage; or so Columbus thought. Tricks and falsehoods were his chief weapons in difficult moments: when he did not know, he invented, and his assurance was such that he convinced the most sceptical. Thus, when on September 13 his men came to him stricken with terror at observing that the compass needle varied from north toward east, the admiral was not disturbed: it was not the needle that had been displaced, he said, but the polestar. The needle was infallible but the stars were wayward. This explanation satisfied the crew, but it was an improvisation, for in fact the phenomenon had astonished him, as his logbook shows: "At nightfall the needle inclined toward the southwest, the point being turned toward the left of north. The next morning it was directed northeastward, the point being to the right of north." He observed and was surprised; but he did not argue. This compass needle, torn between the opposing attractions of the two poles, seemed to him to be mad. He had no idea why it behaved in this way. What did it matter, anyway? The main thing was to follow the 28th parallel vigorously.

On September 14 the sailors on the *Niña* saw a heron, a bird that was believed never to go farther than twenty leagues from the land and was evidence of its proximity. It was warm, like "the month of April in Andalusia," Columbus wrote; and he added: "Only the song of the nightingale was missing." The sky was deep blue and almost unbearable. With the evening, a wonderful meteor, like a streak of fire, sank to the horizon. The crews took fright, but once again the admiral found an explanation: it was a piece of a star that had broken away. Nothing could be more natural.

From September 17 signs multiplied that land was very close. Enormous masses of seaweed slowed the progress of the vessels. This was weed from the Sargasso Sea. The flotilla seemed to be moving over a flooded grassland. The sailors threw out ropes and drew in these conglomerated plants. There was no doubt about it: these were "river weeds" and not marine flora. A living crab hid among them, and this was another good sign, for crustaceans do not venture into the high seas. A flight of birds, whose homeland must certainly be near, once again cleaved the sky. The very sea water—it was surely mixed with river water—bore witness by its singularly fresh flavor to the fact that land was not far off.

The night of the seventeenth to eighteenth passed in a sort of confused excitement. The least phenomenon was interpreted by the crews as a sign of land. Columbus did nothing to dispel the illusion; imprudently, he allowed this atmosphere of enthusiasm to mature and grow. On the morning of the eighteenth the weed-encumbered sea was as smooth and featureless as a board. The next day it rained.

The helmsmen calculated the distance covered since the Canaries, but they could not agree. The *Niña* showed 540 leagues, the *Pinta* 420, and the *Santa María* 400.

September 19, 20, 21, 22, 23, 24, 25. . . . It was nineteen days since the caravels had left Gomera. The crews began to lose patience. They were weary of sky and sea, and Columbus strove to keep them in hand. A bird that got caught in the sails (the admiral asserted that it was a sea gull), the flight of a pelican, the fins of a whale emerging between two waves—no more was needed for Columbus to assure his men that land would soon be in sight. At twilight on September 25 the *Pinta* and the *Niña* drew near to the *Santa María*, as they did each evening and morning. They came "for orders." Columbus and Martín Alonso exchanged their day's observations. According to their calculations and the indications of the maps, they ought that day to encounter Antilia, the island of the Seven Cities. Nevertheless, the sea was featureless and the horizon unbroken. While Columbus and Juan de la Cosa exchanged notes, Martín Alonso, high up on his caravel, scanned the horizon. The sun descended into the sea. It was that fantastic hour at which mirages hold sway. Suddenly there came a cannon shot and a cry "Land!" Columbus fell to his knees. The whole crew did the same. The men of the *Pinta*, who were the first to perceive the land, sang the "Gloria in Excelsis Deo," and the two other caravels took up the canticle. Martín Alonso reckoned the distance still to be covered to the point he had seen as 25 leagues. None could sleep during that night of expectation. Turning slightly southward, the vessels steered carefully. Dawn came, but on the horizon there was nothing: the land glimpsed by the elder Pinzón had been a bank of clouds. They had dispersed. The splendid monotony of sea and sky continued.

The disappointment of the sailors was terrible. Was the fleet condemned to rove miserably until the end of the century? Actually, it had covered half the voyage without knowing it.

On October 1 Columbus verified that the caravels had covered 700 leagues. To his men he gave out about 100 leagues less. The trick was a crude one, for experienced sailors reckoned the distance by guesswork. Seven hundred leagues! Normally, and if his calculations were right, he should be at Cipango. On October 6 Martín Alonso suggested to Columbus that they should steer southwest, the direction clearly indicated by the flight of the birds. But the admiral stuck to his fixed idea: west it must be. The next day the crew of the *Niña* fired a cannon in their turn, but again it was an optical illusion. Martín Alonso then begged the admiral to change course. The situation was grave. The men were discouraged. Land was certainly close. One had only to watch the flight of the birds and to guide oneself by them; that was what the Portuguese did. Columbus let himself be convinced, and he gave the order to steer west-southwest.

Land!

October 10. Thirty-four days since leaving the Canaries! The weather was fine. The sea was as calm as a lake. "One breathes the scented air with delight," Columbus noted in his log. If nature was peaceful, the men were less so. Columbus had been able until then to impose authority by his impassioned speaking, noble bearing, and rank. But gradually his prestige fell. Ignorant as they were, the sailors understood that their commander knew no more than they themselves. His errors of navigation were flagrant. Moreover, the Genoese was harsh with his crew, and his anger was terrible and often unjustified. At the highest level he lacked that social sense, that team spirit, which is traditional at sea. The Basques of the *Santa María* did not hesitate to grumble openly, and in the evening gathered about the galley stove and argued resolutely. An end must be made to this ridiculous expedition. Why not toss this gimcrack admiral into the sea? they asked—then they could turn for home. There was one objection to this plan: the proximity of the other two caravels. The Pinzón brothers had their crews well under control; they were good to their men, who had full confidence in them. But these happy comrades, always ready for a laugh with the sailors, would stand no nonsense in the matter of discipline; they put down the least attempt at rebellion on the *Santa María* with extreme rigor.

The protests from the galley reached the castillo. Columbus fired a cannon shot. The *Pinta*, leading, stopped. The *Santa María* joined her. The *Niña* came into line. From the top of the stern castle Columbus cried: "Captains, my crew are complaining. What, in your opinion, should I do?" Vicente Yáñez Pinzón answered: "Go on for another 2000 leagues and then, if you find nothing, return." A burst of laughter greeted Vicente's sally. But Martín Alonso was not in a mood for trifling. At the top of his voice he cried: "Hang half a dozen of these malcontents and throw them into the sea!" Then he added: "I have sworn, by the royal Crown, that neither I nor any of my kin will return before discovering land. Let those who wish to return, return! For my part, I will go on; I must discover land or die seeking it!" This resounding voice drowned the murmur of the waves. It stifled the murmur of the rebels. Everything returned to normal.

Columbus was the spirit of the expedition, but Martín Alonso was its strength. Without a doubt, Columbus would not have been able to bring it to success without him. His own incontestible gifts as a fine talker and brilliant captain lost their power as the crossing stretched out, for they had not stood up to the trial of daily contact with the men, to a hand-to-hand struggle with elusive nature, to the slow penetration of a horizon that constantly eluded them. To Juan de la Cosa's Basques and the Pinzóns' Andalusians, Columbus was a foreigner, but in Martín Alonso they respected a pilot without equal, a son of Palos and a humane leader. It was Martín Alonso who made Columbus possible.

The admiral would certainly have laughed if anyone had told him any such thing. The Pinzón brothers? Useful partners, good technicians, excellent boatswains, nothing more. The genius, the strong mind, was himself. And in a way he was right. As the day of October 10 ended, so deeply was he moved by messianism that he thought again of Moses leading the Jews out of Egypt. Did not that crowd, too, though delivered from slavery almost in spite of itself, murmur against him who saved them? "Ungrateful people!" the admiral sighed on the evening of the revolt.

Martín Alonso's firm attitude and his show of solidarity with Columbus had their effect. The crew of the *Santa María* no longer faltered, and the intrigues around the galley stove came to an end. Moreover, the weather did not favor anger. During the day the sailors bathed in water that was almost warm; around them salmon and dolphins gamboled. At night they gathered on the forecastle; the perfumed humidity of the tropics made them languid; so did the twanging of their guitars. They saw themselves drifting on the Guadalquivir on an August night: the sky of Seville was not less starry than this unknown heaven. The crystal-clear sob of the strings and the harsh call of the *cante jondo*—the wild, raucous chants of Andalusia—were pleasing to the admiral. A great hope vibrated in that song. In fact, evidences of land close by were multiplying: a floating reed, real sea gulls settling momentarily at the top of the mainmast, a stick covered with snails, a branch with red berries. This time Cipango could not be far away.

On the evening of October 11 Columbus climbed up to his castillo. He was waiting for the men to finish the vesperal office. Then, after the *Salve Regina*, he harangued them in his fine melodious voice. For, when he wished to do so or when it was necessary, he could persuade and charm. He told his men that they were 750 leagues west of Ferro and that in a few hours land would be in sight. He knew how to find poetic and moving words to describe in advance their arrival in the land of the Great Khan and to thank his men for their patience. To the first who sighted land he promised, besides a life annuity of 10,000 gold maravedis from the Queen, a silk doublet as a personal present. Such was Columbus's histrionic gift that all the men acclaimed him, forgetting that two days earlier they had wanted to throw him overboard.

It was night of October 11 to 12. Since sunset the admiral had not ceased to scan the darkness, and at ten o'clock he made out a feeble gleam "like that of a small candle, which alternately rose and fell." It was so pale and so far off! Was it not the reflection of a star? Columbus summoned his intimates: Pedro de Terrenos, his chief steward, and Sánchez de Segovia, the royal comptroller. Both observed the phenomenon. It must be some native's torch. The admiral ordered the sails to be spread. The speed of the caravels reached at least four leagues an hour. For the moment no one, besides Columbus and his confidants, had yet been told the news.

At midnight the slightly cloudy sky cleared. Almost everyone was asleep. It was two in the morning. With all sail spread, the vessels had never moved so fast. Suddenly came a cry, twice repeated: "Land! Land!" Then a cannon shot. A sailor stood up in the bow of the *Pinta*. In the now clear night his frantic gestures could be distinguished. The *Pinta,* leading the flotilla as always, stopped. The flagship joined her. Columbus, leaning over the rail of his castillo, cried to Martín Alonso: "Have you found land?" "No, not I," replied the elder Pinzón, "but one of my sailors, Juan Rodríguez Bermejo, native of Triana."

In fact, in the moonlight the dark outline of a coast appeared. This was land indeed. The captains took in sail and hove to, putting the ships across wind. With a great creaking of rigging and seaweed the caravels came to a standstill. They must wait for daylight.

Bermejo hoped for the promised reward: Isabella's 10,000 gold maravedis and the admiral's silk doublet. Martín Alonso, his master, surprised at Columbus's silence in this respect, thought he must refresh the admiral's memory. But the admiral feigned astonishment. Who but himself had been the first to see that tiny light, wavering on the beach, at ten in the evening of October 11—he, Christopher Columbus, Admiral of the Ocean? Bermejo's cry, four hours later, was only confirmation. Give him the 10,000 maravedis! As to the doublet, he might think about it later.

The brothers Pinzón were appalled. In this unparalleled moment— there had been nothing like it in the history of the world—how could Columbus think of depriving poor Bermejo of the royal gift (for him a fortune) when he, Columbus, was about to collect a tenth of the fabulous riches now within reach! What probability or truth was there in the admiral's claim to have seen a light on the horizon so long before the coast appeared? At the moment when Columbus became the equal of the earth's greatest monarchs, he did not hesitate to engage in a sordid argument with a simple sailor, and dimmed the purity of an instant one could have wished were free of all paltry feelings. For a few golden coins Columbus impaired his prestige. He sullied his own character. While he gave the greatest care to arranging his own postures, this consummate actor could not resist the lure of lucre.

Unaware, perhaps, of his injustice to Bermejo, not knowing that he had just lost the affection of Pinzón, alone on the *Santa María's* castillo, the great man waited for daybreak. Soon the first rays of the sun would blaze upon the famous golden roofs; they would redden the marble quays, setting fire to the Great Khan's lacquered ships with hippogriffs at their bows. And long processions of elephants, draped in red silk and bearing turrets of carved silver on their backs, would pass by endlessly.

Did Columbus really think that such a scene would emerge from the darkness? In truth, he was divided—as he always was—between his measureless appetite for the marvelous and his cold realism. He did not yet know if he was about to touch an island or a continent, but he was persuaded that at sunrise he would set foot on a land subservient to the authority of the Great Khan, whether that might be an island of Cathay (China) or an advanced point of Cipango (Japan).

Facing the darkness that was already troubled by the first pale glimmer of dawn, Columbus prepared his part. He had run his hand under his doublet, less to quiet the beating of his heart than to feel the letter addressed to the Great Khan by the Catholic monarchs. He repeated the first words: "To the Most Serene Prince, our very dear friend . . ." This imaginative man, always ahead of events, pondered his discourse. For he would not only hand the Asiatic emperor his rulers' missive; he would comment on it. He would establish an influence over him. He would tell him . . .

Cipango? The Great Khan? Columbus was twice mistaken.

It was neither Japan nor China but the Bahamas, in the West Indies, about 2000 miles from the future New York. A few degrees farther north and he would have reached Florida—that luxuriant, lake-studded garden in an eternal summer. Had this happened, Spain might perhaps have supplanted England, and its imperial destiny might have been established at Miami. There would not then have been two Americas, one Anglo-Saxon and the other Hispano-Portuguese, but only one: Latin America. A chimera? In any case, if Columbus had rigorously followed the 28th parallel as he had resolved to do, the bridgehead of the conquest would have been somewhere in Florida. But Martín Alonso had made him turn south.

Columbus was not in Asia. But what did that matter? It was a long time since the Chinese dynasty of the Mings had seized power, held until then by the Mongol dynasty of the Yüans, founded by Kublai. The empire of the Great Khan had ceased to exist one hundred and twenty-four years before.

Cipango? The Great Khan? Neither one nor the other.

CHAPTER 3

The Undiscoverable Cipango

D AY came suddenly, as it always does in tropical skies, like a
curtain rising in a theater. But where were the marble pavements and the lacquered junks? The sun's first rays revealed a simple
and verdant island. Beyond the clumps of trees a lake glittered. Not
a building, not a roof, not a single ship betrayed the presence of
man. A deserted island, without a doubt. Was this Cipango?

But the morning of October 12 was so luminous, the scent of
cinnamon and frangipanes so intoxicating, that the Spaniards were
not in the least disappointed. For thirty-three days they had seen
only sea and sky, and at last they were going to touch earth. Was
this not the crown of all their desires? Columbus had kept his
promise. The officers embraced the one who was now indeed the
Admiral of the Ocean. The sailors cast themselves at his feet and
implored pardon. It was a fine moment.

Without suspecting his ill luck, for he had just missed the
American continent, the commander prepared to land. He dressed
in the garnet-red of an admiral, put out the long boat, and took his
place in it, accompanied by an escort that was armed to the teeth.
The boat was low in the water with the weight of sailors turned
into soldiers with helmets and roundels. Some were enclosed in a
cuirass with blunderbuss and bandolier, for they had to be prepared
for anything. Columbus clutched the banner of Castile. The emblem
of Christ nailed to the Cross floated for the first time in the blue
tropical sky. The boats of the Pinzón brothers followed close behind
the admiral's. The two captains held aloft the standard of the expedition: the green cross entwined with the royal initials.

As the boats were about to touch the shore, some men broke out
of the thickets. They were naked. Some of them dragged hollowed
tree trunks over the sand, which they launched on the sea and
paddled toward the Spaniards. So the island was inhabited. For the

moment Columbus scarcely cared; the most urgent matter was to take possession of the land he had discovered. The admiral ran his boat ashore and took a few slow steps across the strand. Behind him walked Rodrigo de Escobedo and Sánchez de Segovia, notary and royal comptroller, witnesses and licensed scribes. Columbus drew his sword, cut a few weeds, and whipped off the bark of neighboring trees: symbolical gestures to mark his right of owner-ship. The officials then drew up the deed by which Columbus took possession, in the name of the Catholic monarchs, of this island which he named San Salvador. The natives called it Guanahani. Later this was to be Watlings Island, part of the Bahama or Lucayas archipelago in the British West Indies.

Thus was America discovered on a bright morning of October 12, 1492—a relative discovery, since Columbus thought he was in Asia, though he was only in the approaches to the real America.

Columbus never lost his head. At the height of triumph, as in the darkest of his reverses, he preserved an astonishing realism. Never did the intoxication of pride affect his practical sense. First of all and in every circumstance he had to have a document, duly signed and initialed. From his father, the Genoese merchant, or perhaps from some Jewish ancestor he had inherited this fear of the one who pays and the necessity of a written contract, without which no valid agreement was possible. Thus as soon as he set foot on new land, his first act was to draw up a legal deed. Only afterward did he kiss the earth, thank God, and order the *Te Deum* to be sung. Business before sentiment.

On the Threshold of the New World

The natives kept at a respectful distance from the Spaniards. But curiosity possessed them. Step by step they drew near to these godlike creatures. Then the boldest of them touched the extraor-dinary objects that were the strangers' beards, for the Spaniards had not shaved since their halt in the Canaries, and Columbus's own beard was almost white; they touched the stuffs that shone brighter than the plumage of parrots, and the hard surfaces of the armor. One native seized the blade of a sword in his hand, and cried aloud at seeing the blood flow. None had ever seen this shining substance that could inflict such wounds.

These natives, on the whole, were good-looking and well built. Their short, stiff hair was bunched together on top of the head and then left to hang down at the back like a mane. The color of their skins, neither light nor dark, was that of Canary Islanders. They were friendly, almost affable. They seemed peaceable.

Columbus did not tarry at San Salvador. There was nothing to be gained from this island of parrots any more than from its simple natives. To the admiral's questions—signs taking the place of words—the natives of Guanahani could reply only with childish laughter. How could Columbus know if there was gold to be found or where Cipango lay? By taking to sea once more.

On October 14 the caravels raised anchor. Columbus had taken seven natives aboard, either willingly or by force. The next evening the flotilla came upon an island which the admiral named Santa María de la Concepción. The day afterward he discovered another island: Fernandina. To the fourth island, more exuberant than the rest—"the parrots' array puts the sun itself in the shade," Columbus noted in his logbook—he gave the name Isabella. Even more perfumes and even more flowers: nature was virgin and the creatures as inno-cent as in the earliest ages. This resurrection of the Earthly Paradise enchanted Columbus but without making him forget his object, which was to make contact with the Great Khan and to find gold. He was convinced that he was nearing his objective, and the information given him by the natives strengthened this conviction. They spoke to him of a rich and powerful king whose empire was not far away. Sometimes his soldiers came as far as the islands in great canoes; they captured the best of the population and carried them into slavery. They were called Caribs. In which direction did they go? The natives stretched out their arms westward. This could only be Cipango or even Quinsay, the Chinese metropolis. Such signs confirmed Columbus's certainty that he was indeed in the eastern part of the Indies, a few days from the residence of the emperor of Tartary. And, smiling, the admiral murmured to himself the strange name that the savages gave to Cipango: Cuba.

On October 28 the fleet reached Cuba. "I have never seen a more beautiful land," Columbus wrote. The palm leaves were so large that they served to roof the houses. On the beach there were millions of pearl shells. The water was limpid, the symphony of bird song was deafening and continuous. On the other hand, the human beings were no different from those of the islands previously visited. The Indians—what else could one call them, since they inhabited the extreme east of the Asiatic continent?—were of a gentle disposition; they could be trained like young animals. Recalling his apostolic mission, Columbus made them repeat the *Salve* and *Ave Maria.* "It will be easy to make good Christians of them," he noted in his logbook.

Until November 2 the caravels ran along the eastern end of the Cuban coast but saw nothing unusual. A delicious air, "neither warm nor cool"; a superabundant flora; a curious fauna; but men were few. Such as there were lived penuriously, in huts of palm leaves, on the products of their fishing. They were poor, or rather, they had no idea of riches. They were timid, for they often spoke of a formidable sovereign with whom their king was at war. Obscure though they were, Columbus grasped at these allusions eagerly. He decided to anchor at the mouth of a river—the Río Máximo— and to send two ambassadors overland to the local ruler, in the hope that they would get information from him about the Great Khan. For this embassy he chose the Jew, Luis de Torres, his principal interpreter, and a sailor from Huelva, reputed as being very resourceful. The mission set out on November 2. It returned four days later, empty-handed. No one knew where the Great Khan lived. Meanwhile, Columbus had taken his bearings. He had calculated that since leaving Ferro the expedition had covered more than 1100 leagues. Furthermore, he had assured himself that Cuba was not an island but a continental province of the Great Khan's empire. As for Cipango, they had left it behind them. The natives gave it the name of Babeque or Bohío. He would have to turn back and postpone the exploration of the continent.

On November 12 Columbus gave the order to leave Cuba, which he called Juana, after the Infante of Spain. The admiral had taken six Cubans aboard with their women and children. On to Babeque! On November 21 a serious incident occurred. The *Pinta*, which since the beginning of the voyage had constantly led the fleet, disappeared over the horizon. Had Martín Alonso lost sight of the *Santa María*'s lanterns, or had he deliberately separated from the expedition? Columbus himself regarded this disappearance as premeditated flight; Martín Alonso wanted to reach Cipango before him, which was a possible hypothesis since, as a result of the admiral's attitude toward Bermejo, relations had been strained. Vicente Yáñez, however, remained faithful.

On December 6 the *Niña* and the flagship reached the island of Bohío, and it was as if the ships had returned to Spain. Before they had even reached the shore, the sailors could descry fields of grain like those in the country around Córdoba. There were wide valleys and high mountains, like the scenery of Old Castile. A nightingale—a *ruiseñor*—sang, awakening a nostalgia in the hearts of the sailors. To this island that was so like Spain Columbus gave the name Hispaniola; later it was called Haiti. While the crews stared about them, moved at finding that Hispaniola looked so much like Spain, Columbus spoke with the natives. They were peaceful but they lived in terror of the Caribs, the cruel cannibals already mentioned by the inhabitants of Isabella. Columbus started. Cannibals! Yet they were supposed to be subjects of the Great Khan. Actually these were the formidable tribes of the West Indian and Central American coasts. But the least sign, however small, gave Columbus hope, so he went from island to island like a lost traveler, asking for Cipango. He staved off his appetite for conquest by naming islands and ports: Tortuga, Puerto de la Paz, Val do Paraiso, and so on. If a stream pleased him, he called it the Guadalquivir. But these were mere hors d'oeuvres to one who was starving for glory. He was seeking an empire and gold. Until now he had found neither.

Christmas was drawing near. On the strength of a vague indication, Columbus headed eastward. He would find the land of gold: Cibao, of which the natives had spoken. Here was a word that greatly resembled Cipango! It was December 24 and would soon be midnight. On the *Santa María* everyone was asleep save the man at the wheel. But, having doubtless celebrated the *navidad* too generously, he too felt slumber stealing over him, so he handed over the wheel to a deck boy and went to sleep. A slight shock suddenly awakened the admiral. He could no longer hear the sound of the open sea, but that of breakers on the reefs.

The caravel was stranded on a sandbank. Columbus aroused the crew. A mast was cut to lighten ship, but Juan de la Cosa shook his head: there was nothing to do but abandon ship, for the bows, which were inadequately protected, were leaking at every seam. So the boats were lowered and in a few minutes the crew of the *Santa María* was transferred to the *Niña*. The flagship was no more than a wooden corpse which a shroud of sand would slowly cover. A sad Christmas night!

The First Return

Once again ill luck had befallen Columbus. He had found nothing of what he had been seeking—neither gold nor empire; his surest companion and best commander had abandoned him; and now he had lost his ship! Of the three caravels only one remained, but she no longer had the freshness and *élan* of the departure. As was his wont when things did not go his way, the admiral was consumed with violent anger. He attacked the elements and his men; he accused Juan de la Cosa of not knowing his job, and the crew of having been asleep. Then, having exhausted his temper, he thought of what steps he should take. For this indomitable man knew nothing of fruitless despair. In this dramatic situation he found precious support in the person of a cacique, Guacanagari, with whom he had struck up a friendship. The Indian and his people cooperated in salvaging what remained of the *Santa María*. The caravel was taken to pieces. From the framework, the two decks, and the fore and aft castles a fort was constructed, called La Navidad—Christmas! In it Columbus installed those he could not take back to Spain: forty-one men in all, among them Diego de Harana (who was appointed governor) and Escobedo, with provisions for a year and the *Santa María*'s artillery for defense. This was the first European colony in the New World, but when, ten months later, Columbus, faithful to his promise, came to seek his companions, he found not one. A head, a few corpses, and the sorrowful silence of the cacique. But that is another story that will be told later.

The Indian chief was not content with giving aid to the admiral. He gave him gold. Very little—a few humble pieces of jewelry—

but just what Columbus needed to avoid facing the Catholic monarchs with empty hands. A little gold proved that gold existed.

At dawn on January 4, 1493, the *Niña*, heavily laden, drew away from La Navidad. Perched on top of a rock, a man followed the fleeing caravel with his eyes, plucking the strings of a harp. He was the Irishman; his English friend was aboard the *Niña*, and it was for him that he played the dirge of La Navidad.

Two days later there was a surprise. The watch signaled a sail. It was the *Pinta*. The *Niña* rejoined her, and the two caravels dropped anchor in a safe harbor. Martín Alonso presented himself to the admiral. Why had he separated from the fleet? The reason was simple: the *Pinta* had a long lead on the other two vessels and had insensibly drawn away from them until they were lost to sight. Columbus accepted Martín Alonso's explanation, at least to all appearances. Actually he did not believe it at all. But that account would be squared later. For the moment Columbus needed the Pinzóns, so he was prodigal with endearments. Nevertheless, he had difficulty concealing his resentment when he learned that Martín Alonso had disembarked at Haiti before him, somewhere in the eastern part of the island. He had brought off some gold. Thus the elder Pinzón was the true discoverer of Hispaniola.

Once more together, the *Pinta* and the *Niña* reached the eastern end of Haiti. There they remained until January 15. On January 16, three hours before dawn, they set out for Spain in a northeasterly direction.

For twenty-eight days the sea was as calm as on the outward voyage. But on February 12 the wind rose and a gale started. It reached its climax on the night of February 14 to 15. For the second time the *Pinta* disappeared. Columbus regarded her as lost, but would the *Niña* survive her? The admiral retained his composure. He took the time to put down on parchment the story of his voyage, to wrap it up in oiled cloth, and to throw it into the sea. It was addressed to the Catholic monarchs. A thousand ducats to the person who should send it to them!

Columbus was not to perish at sea. On the morning of February 15 the gale died down. An island became visible through the mist. "Madeira!" cried the lookout. It was Santa María, one of the Azores.

On February 18 the *Niña* put in to the Azores. She sailed again six days later. Once again a violent gale assailed the unlucky caravel, but this was her last trial. On March 4 the remains of the fleet came within sight of the Cintra rock at the mouth of the Tagus. Portugal! Almost home! On March 8 the admiral was received by John II. The "man in the threadbare cloak" was revenged. Finally, at noon on March 15, the caravel crossed the bar of the Saltés and dropped anchor in the Palos roads. Columbus's first voyage had lasted seven months and a day. A few hours later the *Pinta* reached the port of Palos. Contrary to what Columbus had thought, she had survived the gale; but she arrived too late. Those who watched Martín Alonso disembark from the *Pinta*, carried by his sailors, were few. The sorrow of seeing himself deprived of his part of the triumph, as well as the physical trials he had experienced, got the better of the old sailor. Before he died in the monastery of La Rábida, he had heard the roar of acclamation that accompanied Columbus on the road to Seville, mingled with the surge of the sea.

The court was not at Seville but at Barcelona. Columbus went to Barcelona. About the middle of April a strange procession passed through the Catalan capital. Boys carried long poles on which parrots perched. Others held cushions on their upturned palms, bearing golden masks and jewels. Others displayed fishes, plants—aloes and rhubarb—balls of cotton, all of them rarer in appearance than in value. They might, in fact, be called samples; for had not Columbus once been a commercial traveler? The whole display might have been quite poor, except that at the head of the column there were human specimens: the six Indians captured at Cuba, shivering with the cold in their wretched clothing. It was not so much their copper-colored skin that surprised the Spanish court as their simplicity. What an admirable field for evangelical seed! Millions of men for the cause of Christ! This vision compensated largely for the thinness of the gold plate and the crude jewelry—*guañines*—that Columbus brought back from his voyage. In fact, the King, the Queen, and the Infanta, seated on a brocade dais, had eyes only for the six Indians prostrate at their feet, and the admiral skillfully emphasized the spiritual conquest. As for the material conquest, he remained vague, confining himself to evoking—with more talent than ever before—the riches of Cipango and Cathay that he had

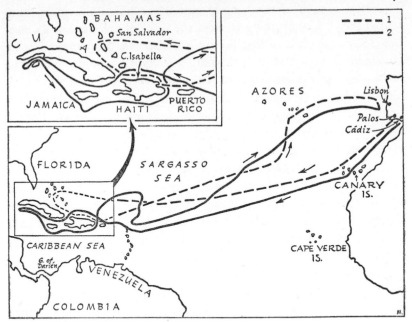

Christopher Columbus's First and Second Voyages

only glimpsed. The heaps of gold were for tomorrow, that was certain, but the harvest of souls had already begun. Columbus was taken in by his own eloquence and burst into sobs. Isabella was not long in following suit. Like a well-orchestrated opera, the singers of the royal chapel entoned the *Te Deum laudamus*, and the whole assembly fell on its knees. Once again, Columbus had humbugged his public.

The Second Voyage

Columbus saw himself confirmed in his privileges. He was Viceroy and Admiral of the Ocean Sea. He acquired the title of "Don" for himself and his descendants. He lacked a coat of arms, but one was given him: a shield with the arms of Castile and León—a castle and a lion—in two of its quarters, in the third quarter a group of golden islands, and in the fourth five golden anchors on an azure field. He could ride beside the King. He supped familiarly at the table of the Catholic monarchs and at that of the Grand Cardinal.

The most exalted of the lords disputed the honor of entertaining him. There was everything to turn the head of anyone but Columbus. He remained cool, for he guessed that the most difficult part remained to be accomplished. This new glory would have to be maintained. His destiny was in the west and it called him.

The admiral savored his triumph for a few weeks. He knew honey and flattery and—already!—the bitterness of jealousy. Hatred raised its head. He saw it in the twitching of a smile, in the shrugging of a shoulder, in a silence. During a banquet some courtiers, half seriously, half jokingly, pretended to regard Columbus's exploit as an easy matter. The admiral then invited these gentlemen to stand an egg upright on the table. Only he succeeded, simply by lightly crushing the egg at its end. The guests then cried out, "That's very simple!" "Very simple, indeed," the admiral replied. "It was only necessary to think of it. Like my voyage to the Indies!"

While Columbus tasted the joys of the victorious return, thinking all the time of his coming departure, the Catholic monarchs worked to get the discovery confirmed, and especially to regularize future discoveries. For Isabella and Ferdinand certainly reckoned there would be others. Until then, Portugal had had the effective monopoly of discovery, but Columbus's voyage had turned Spain into her dangerous rival. From rivalry to hostility is but a step, but the Spanish Pope, Alexander VI, was wise enough to prevent its being taken.

Exactly two months after Columbus had cast anchor at Palos, Alexander VI signed a bull granting to Spain all the lands situated 100 leagues west of the last of the Azores. Portugal should have the right to the territories discovered to the east of that imaginary boundary. How did the Pope define the respective boundaries of the Spanish and Portuguese empires, present and to come? Simply by drawing a line on the globe from one pole to the other. But it was understood that in return the Catholic monarchs would be required to instruct the conquered peoples in the Christian faith. John II of Portugal having protested against this arbitrary boundary, a Spanish-Portuguese treaty was concluded at Tordesillas, carrying the boundary line from 100 to 370 leagues west of the Azores and Cape Verde. That is why Alvarez Cabral, pushed westward by the currents when within sight of the Cape of Good Hope, was able to take possession, in the name of Portugal, of a land situated less than 370 leagues from Cape Verde and thus within the limits of the Portuguese concession. A lucky drift and the courteous bargaining at Tordesillas was to turn Brazil into a Portuguese possession. A contrary wind and a flourish at the foot of a parchment was to put the largest South American state outside the Spanish orbit. Thus are empires born—by chance.

Convinced now of the reality of the West Indies,* the Catholic monarchs decided to pursue their exploration methodically. They set up a political and commercial commission with the function of regulating affairs within the new Spanish territories. Bishop Juan Rodríguez de Fonseca, a member of the Council of Castile and soon the "patriarch of the Indies," presided over this commission. Its powers were wide, including the absolute right to requisition men and materials. In short, it had complete command over colonial affairs.

Fonseca's career was a brilliant one. Originally Archdeacon of Seville, he became successively Bishop of Badajoz, Palencia, and Burgos. Las Casas was to write of him later that he was "*muy capaz para mundanos negocios.*" Very gifted, in fact, in temporal affairs, this farseeing ecclesiastic secured the confidence of the Catholic monarchs. He was less fortunate with Charles V. This young emperor, enlightened by Cortés, deprived Fonseca of the presidency of the Council of the Indies. The Bishop of Burgos detested Columbus, even as he execrated Cortés and, in a general way, all the conquistadors. It was the hatred of a bureaucrat for men of action, the jealousy of a high official, shut up in his office, for the adventurers. Though Minister for the Conquest, he never found conquerors to obey him. However, this skillful maneuverer remained in office for twenty-five years. By exploiting discontents, by setting contrary interests in opposition, and by installing his own men in the principal administrative posts, he succeeded in maintaining a semblance of power and deceiving the Crown. Grand master of intrigue, Fonseca never ceased to persecute the conquistadors in an underhand way; he hunted them down one after the other. Columbus was his most illustrious victim, but no one, during a

* They were, of course, still thought to be the Indies proper, but henceforth, for the purpose of this book, they will be referred to by their present name.

quarter of a century, dared to make a frontal attack upon the Bishop-President—no one, that is, except Cortés.

Columbus was impatient to depart. On September 25 he set out, this time at the head of a real colonial expedition: fourteen caravels and three carracks, fifteen hundred men, and a complete general staff. The admiral had called his younger brother Diego to his side. He had surrounded himself with "technicians": a cartographer, Juan de la Cosa; an astronomer, Father Antonio de Marchena—two old acquaintances; and a doctor, Chanca. He had not forgotten the chaplain, Fray Bernardo Buil, to whom the Pope had given the title "Vicar Apostolic of the Indies." Around the great man revolved the future Conquistadors—his enemies of the morrow—Alonso de Ojeda and Ponce de León, full of courage but as greedy as carnivorous beasts. Assembled in the port of Cádiz, the fleet raised anchor amid salvos of cannon and acclamations. Columbus remembered the sad departure from Palos a year before. Times had changed!

Columbus's destination was Hispaniola. He followed the same route as the first time: Ferro and then a westerly direction, but he steered a little farther south. Twenty days after leaving the Canaries an archipelago was sighted: the Lesser Antilles. One by one the gilded islands ran past: Deseada, Dominica, Marigalante, Santa María la Redonda, Santa María la Antigua, Guadalupe, Once Mil Vírgines, and Puerto Rico. Turning northward, Columbus came to Hispaniola once more and within sight of La Navidad. Not a single light shone from the shore. The admiral ordered the cannons fired, but only the mountains replied. A group of sailors went ashore. At the site of the fort there was nothing but human remains. Columbus made a search for Guacanagari and demanded explanations, which the cacique gave. Left to themselves, the admiral's companions had not been able to resist the pleasures of the climate any more than the primitive beauty of the women. Was this not the place to revive the delights of the Earthly Paradise, here on the Haitian shores? But in this paradise, Mussulman more than Christian, houris were needed. Where could they be found except among the natives? The Spaniards then decided to raid the Indian population. They began by capturing the women, then by making off with the poor possessions of their hosts, claiming the rights of victors. This could last only for a short time, for, rightly angered by their oppressors, the

Indians of La Navidad attacked the Spaniards and effected a terrible massacre. Those who escaped their vengeance fled into the interior but were never found again. Guacanagari's protection was useless. The first European foundation in the New World had been a failure. Passions had to be controlled before men could be governed.

The story of La Navidad depressed the admiral. He began to realize that conquest and colonization are two different things, but he had no time to go deeply into the problem. The continuance of the conquest was his first care. He had promised the Catholic monarchs immense territories, gold in profusion, and the road to Asia. Until now the lands were disappointing, gold was lacking, and Cipango remained undiscovered. Cipango! The name burned him like a fire. Each time that he spoke of it to the natives, they led him to understand that it was quite close. Was it not Cibao that he was trying to say? He explored Cibao—a mountain in Haiti—gave the name Vega Real ("royal plain") to a valley, succeeded in discovering a little gold, took to sea again and steered for Cuba. On the way he dropped anchor at a new island: Jamaica. He ran along the southern coast of Cuba in a westerly direction in search of Cipango or Cathay. He encountered a group of islands—the Jardines de la Reina—which he took for the spice archipelago said by Marco Polo to be off the eastern coast of Asia. He was now certain that he was approaching the Golden Peninsula—Malacca—and was surprised that he did not find any of the great towns described by the travelers. He was convinced that Cuba was an advanced point of the Asiatic continent, but in another two days of sailing he reached its western end. He made his way around it in the direction of his starting point, but decided to turn back at the moment when the coast began to bend. In a fit of puerile anger, he ordered his men to swear before a notary that it was possible to return on foot from Cuba to Spain by the land route across Asia.

While Columbus persisted in his chimerical course, his officers tried their hands at governing. Some, like Alonso de Ojeda, Diego Columbus, and Bartholomew, who had joined his brother at Hispaniola, distinguished themselves by their talents and humanity. The others, among whom were Pedro de Margarit, thought only of enriching themselves by every possible means. Cliques took shape, for or against the admiral. Parties became organized, for or against the Indians. The exactions of certain Spaniards were such that a cacique named Caonabo, having assured himself of the support of all the Haitian chiefs, raised an army against the occupiers. Better equipped and better trained in fighting, the Spaniards defeated the Indian troops and captured Caonabo. The Spanish victory was inevitable, but the effect on the population was unfortunate. In fact, the time had passed when the new arrivals could try to win the good will of the natives. The Spaniards were now no longer ceremonious in requisitioning the labor they needed. It was still too soon to speak of colonization, but soon enough to use the word exploitation. Later, the conditions of work were to be regulated, at least in principle, but for the moment the only law was that of compulsion. The Haitians had to provide a certain quantity of pure gold every three months, and the washing of the metal was very arduous. The Spaniards who had been able to set up farms or agricultural workings were obsessed with the idea of yield. Their domestic animals and cereals, imported from Spain, had to produce a maximum yield. This was a new idea for the Indians, who lived merely from day to day; but whether or not they liked it, they contributed by their forced labor to an increase of production which was not for their own benefit.

Columbus's second stay in the West Indies lasted for three and a half years, but contact was maintained with Spain. The first time, a dozen ships commanded by Antonio de Torres took back the useless or undesirable colonists to their homeland. Torres was the bearer of interesting news: the foundation of Isabella, the first Spanish town, on the Haitian coast; the discovery of gold mines on Cibao; and the submission of the Indians. Columbus made known his great needs in manpower. His special need was for miners for extracting and working the gold. Would it not be possible to consider using slaves? He even suggested trading in them with the homeland. To this question the Catholic monarchs gave a dilatory reply. In Castile it was usual to regard only non-Christian prisoners of war as slaves. Torres reported this message to the admiral. Yet several months later, Torres embarked for Spain a cargo of five hundred Indians. They had revolted against the admiral and he had made them prisoners; and since they were heathens, they had both of the required qualifications. Legal appearances were saved. Five hundred slaves for the Catholic monarchs! Five hundred souls for the Church, too, since they would be converted.

But it was not only good news that Columbus's messengers carried. There were some who complained about the difficult character of the admiral and the mistakes he made in command. It was far from Isabella to Cádiz, but nothing stopped the cry of anger nor the whispered calumny. In any case, these rumors did not fail to influence the Catholic monarchs, for they promulgated an edict granting every Spanish subject the right to trade freely with the newly discovered lands and to settle there.

One morning in October 1495 a caravel anchored in the port of Isabella. It brought Juan de Aguado, royal commissioner, to Hispaniola, charged with inquiring into Columbus's administration. Columbus was not there, for he was waging war against the Indians in the neighborhood. He was told of the arrival of the *visitador*. He returned to Isabella, received Juan de Aguado coldly, put off reading his credentials until the next day, but left him a clear field for his inquiry. For five months the commissioner was free to prepare his dossier. The principal grievance of the colonists was insufficiency of food. But is this not always the complaint of soldiers in the field? Moreover, they were homesick for Spain. "God take me to Castile!" was their common oath.

While the visitor sought his information, Columbus, cruelly mortified, showed nothing of his feelings. As usual when his prestige was at stake, he struck an attitude. He chose humility and dressed himself like a Franciscan. For the five months he remained at Isabella and during the return voyage, he did not abandon the homespun. This was no simple gesture. True, he reckoned on the favorable impression the Franciscan habit would inevitably make on the pious Isabella, and it would be the surest way to obtain pardon. But this selfish calculation was accompanied by sincere repentance. If he had made mistakes, he meant to expiate them from now on. He thought of the five hundred slaves who were rotting in the Andalusian lands of Bishop Fonseca. He thought of the mastiffs he had set at the heels of the Indians in the plain of Vega Real. He beat his breast. But in such penitence there was also arrogance.

An unforeseen event put Aguado under obligation to Columbus. A terrible hurricane struck the port of Isabella, shattering the visitor's ship. Courteously—but with a touch of malice—the admiral had a caravel built for Aguado, and eventually they set sail together like two good friends, for Columbus did not wish to delay his return to Spain any longer. Before leaving he delegated his powers to his brother Bartholomew, and he assigned his other brother, Diego, as an aide to Bartholomew. He established small forts equipped with garrisons. Everything was done to avoid a repetition of the tragedy of La Navidad.

On March 10, 1496, the venerable *Niña* got ready to raise anchor. Columbus was aboard. Thirty Indians—among them Caonabo, who died on the way—accompanied him, as well as two hundred and twenty sad-looking colonists, the disillusioned Conquistadors. The sails were unfurled. The *Niña* drew away from the moorings, flanked by Aguado's caravel.

The voyage was long and difficult. The visitor and the visited did not reach Cádiz until June 11, after a perilous crossing of fifty-two days. It was not an admiral in his garnet-red cloak who landed from the *Niña*, but a penitent in brown wool, with the cord of Saint Francis around his waist. And what had become of his brilliant escort? In truth, they might have been described as survivors of a shipwreck. The crowd on the quay contemplated these almost moribund mariners without a word, and found difficulty in recognizing their own folk among them. Happily, the troop of Indians in their strange apparel mitigated the bad impression of this return.

This time the interview between Columbus and the Catholic monarchs took place at Burgos. More than ever before, the admiral had need of all his powers to disperse the clouds that his enemies had heaped upon his glory. He was ready to justify himself. But of what was he accused? It is easy to imagine him before the royal throne, with raised head—already almost pure white—and the wide movements of the two homespun sleeves. He took up the grievances of his detractors one by one. He refuted them. Five hundred slaves? Had not Pope Innocent VIII once accepted the present of a hundred Moors? The Queen herself had made her cousin, the Queen of Naples, a gift of thirty fine female slaves. Moreover, these Indians were prisoners of war; it was therefore lawful to have made them slaves. Had he been lacking in respect for the gentlemen of the expedition? Had he refused to provide food for the colonists of Hispaniola? Absurdities and falsehoods! His first care had always been to accord the nobility the consideration that it merited. As to provisions, that was not his affair, but he had never heard it said that men had died of hunger. In any case, it was necessary to take to Hispaniola the provisions that were needed there; this was one of the main objects of his third voyage.

His third voyage? Isabella and Ferdinand glanced at each other inquiringly. The moment was scarcely favorable for initiating an affair of such dimensions. Vaster plans absorbed the Catholic monarchs. Spain was at war with France. It was necessary to wind up this adventure and turn to serious things: to establish the young Spanish power in Europe. The marriage of Juana, daughter of Ferdinand and Isabella, to the Archduke of Austria, Philip the Fair, son of Emperor Maximilian, was settled. It was to be celebrated in the autumn. Was this not the germ of a colossal empire that might one day unite, under a Spanish head, besides the heritage of the Catholic monarchs, Germany, Austria, the Low Countries, and the provinces of France and Italy? Columbus welcomed the promise implied by the alliance with the Hapsburgs. It meant, in fact, the possession of the western world. But who would be master of that other part of the world that stretched toward the Orient, as far as the antipodes? It was already quite enough that Portugal had pushed her caravels even farther than was provided for by Alexander VI's bull, to the point of extending the rule of the Aviz dynasty as far as the Cape of Storms (later the Cape of Good Hope). The grandiose plan of the Catholic monarchs—the profitable annexation of the Holy Roman Empire—fell in with the no less grandiose plan that Columbus was in process of carrying out. The admiral displayed the balance sheet of his second voyage: he had reconnoitered 333 leagues of the continent—the southern coast of Cuba—discovered almost seven hundred islands, and completed the conquest of Hispaniola. The riches of these territories were immense. Their Majesties had only to glance at the massive gold collar that had been worn by Caonabo, brother of the cacique of Cibao! They had only to consider for a moment the robust Indians, representatives of innumerable peoples who asked only to be subordinated to the Spanish crown and to pay it tribute! Gold and men: these were what the admiral brought to the Catholic monarchs while they awaited the advantageous alliance with the

Great Khan! Cipango was worth as much as the House of Austria! Once again Ferdinand and Isabella were convinced. They published an edict, in continuation of the Pragmatic Sanction of April 1495, by which they reserved Columbus's rights to the discovered territories. They confirmed the appointment of Bartholomew as the admiral's *adelantado*. Finally, they undertook to assist Columbus in his third voyage. The Franciscan had won.

The Third Voyage

Two years passed before Columbus embarked for the third time.

It was from Sanlúcar de Barrameda, at the mouth of the Guadalquivir, that the admiral's six caravels set out. Having arrived at his usual port of call—Ferro, in the Canaries—he split up his fleet: half of it made straight for Hispaniola, while the other half, under his own command, steered for the equator. What was he seeking there? Cipango, of course.

Columbus took exactly three months to reach Hispaniola. In the course of a difficult crossing—it was so hot that melted pitch ran down the hulls of the ships—he discovered the island of Trinidad and dropped anchor in the Gulf of Paria. There a surprise awaited him. The gulf water was fresh. But Columbus did not let himself be caught by the sailors' questions! Let them drink this water without fear! God had sent it to them. The world, in fact, was not altogether round. Rather, it was shaped like a pear, the top of which was the Earthly Paradise and the stalk the Tree of Life. Four rivers had their sources in that Paradise: the Nile, the Tigris, the Euphrates, and the Ganges. The water at Paria came down from Paradise and the river was the Ganges—certain proof of the proximity of Asia. They were only a couple of steps from the Malacca Straits and the mouth of the Ganges. Paradise was within their grasp. The neighboring landscape gave proof of it: gardens, multicolored birds, and on the beach, the variegated heaps of shells. Columbus did not delay a minute before cutting a quill and reporting the event to the Catholic monarchs.

Once again the admiral was wrong. The river that washed the bows of his caravels was not the Ganges but the Orinoco. It did not descend from Paradise but from the Andes. The luxuriant soil through which it flowed was not Asia, but it was a continent. In fact, without knowing it, and for the first time, Columbus had set foot on the continent. He had passed the archipelagoes. This wonderful land, "one of the most beautiful in the world," was later named Venezuela. The continent was America.

The admiral had no time to pursue his observations further. A sense of urgency—a presentiment?—pushed him on to Hispaniola. What had happened to his two brothers? He drew away from the continent, discovered an island, Margarita, in passing, and steered for his colony.

He reached Hispaniola only to find rebellion. There were two opposing parties, each dependent upon an Indian clan: that of Roldán —the admiral had had such confidence in him that he exercised the office of judge!—and that of the brothers Columbus. Roldán had revolted against the authority of Bartholomew and his brother, and they intended to bring him back to obedience. The conflict had reached the acute stage where the decision could be carried only by force of arms. By alternate promises and threats, the admiral succeeded in avoiding the worst, and the fratricidal war did not take place. After a fashion, he re-established peace among the Spaniards.

During the absence of Christopher, Bartholomew had discovered some gold mines. He had also founded a town, Santo Domingo, on the south of Hispaniola, and he had fortified the island. But he had been less happy in the role of administrator. The need to maintain order and to secure respect for his authority had led him to ill-advised violence. In the name of the King, hundreds of Indians had been reduced to slavery, while in the name of God, natives accused of sacrilege had been burned at the stake. What was Columbus to do?

Actually, the admiral was scarcely better inspired than his brother. After re-establishing Roldán, the originator of the revolt, in office, he tightened his hold on the Indians. Interpreting royal instructions, he introduced into Hispaniola the *repartimento* (apportionment) system: the distribution of the natives among the Spanish colonists who were holders of concessions—the first step toward the *encomienda* system which ten years later was to become general in the territories under the jurisdiction of the Spanish crown. For the moment there was scarcely any difference between these workers subject to requisition and simple slaves, although they were regarded legally as "vassals," at the express wish of Isabella. In fact, the Queen insisted on recording her wish to see the Indians treated humanely: a touching but platonic wish. As in every colonial enterprise at its beginning, he who controls the central authority is one thing and he who acts as local delegate is another. The road to Isabella was a long one. Is it surprising that on the way the royal pragmatic sanctions should have weakened?

In the ensuing two years Columbus showed himself to be as bad an administrator as he had been a persistent navigator. The *Descubridor* (Discoverer) had not been fashioned for public business nor for ruling men. The charmer who had won princes to his cause was not successful with colonists. The gentlemen of Hispaniola gave him anything but a welcoming look: he was a parvenu and a stranger. The rest of the Spaniards—they were both good and bad, from the fine Andalusian merchant who had come to make himself rich, to the common criminal who desired to redeem himself—gave him poor support: he treated them like dogs. A more serious matter was that both sides suspected him of being a Jew, an unpardonable blemish at a time when everyone carefully measured his drops of *limpia sangre*. Columbus was not unaware of these rumors that circulated about him, and he unburdened himself to the Catholic monarchs. How could they accuse him of being a *converso*, he who worked for Christian Spain and never missed Mass!

Cares overwhelmed the admiral. His responsibilities began to weigh upon him. In a letter to the sovereigns, he asked them to send someone to help him—the first sign of weariness in a man who was regarded as tireless. After long reflection, Isabella and Ferdinand complied with his request. Someone would be sent. Did Columbus ask himself if this someone would be his aide or his judge and executioner?

One morning two caravels—the *Gorda* and the *Antigua*—arrived at Santo Domingo. One of them brought the visitor Francisco de Bobadilla, Commander of the Order of Calatrava, *gran caballero y amado de todos* (a great gentleman and beloved by all), according to his friends. His powers, restricted at first to a simple inquiry into the rebellion against the admiral, had been greatly extended by the Catholic monarchs, following new reports that had reached the court. Actually, Bobadilla was about to take over the functions of governor of Hispaniola. Between Bobadilla and Columbus conflict was inevitable. The latter had no trouble proving his rights or those of his brother Bartholomew—rights recognized and patented by royal orders. Bobadilla stated his own claims. Who was right? It is difficult to know, the visitor having received verbal instructions from the Catholic monarchs. In any case, Bobadilla's arrival at Hispaniola caused great commotion among the island's population, for they interpreted it as a mark of disgrace for Columbus. Animated by very evident opposition to the admiral, the visitor ordered the rebels to be freed, proclaimed the freedom of trade, and very cleverly exempted the natives from tribute. These demagogic measures were enthusiastically received and had the effect of ranging all Columbus's enemies, Spanish and Indian, on Bobadilla's side. Finally, determined to complete his activities with a spectacular gesture, the visitor had the three brothers Columbus apprehended, clapped into irons—the admiral was chained by his own cook—and cast into prison.

Bobadilla had arrived in Hispaniola in August. Two months later, Christopher Columbus and his brothers, being regarded as rebels, were embarked for Spain in order to be tried there.

Moved by such ill fortune, the captain of the ship, Alonso de Vallejo, wished to free the admiral from his chains. He refused: he had been chained under orders from the Catholic monarchs, and only the Catholic monarchs could free him from them. Moreover, he had the firm intention of keeping these heavy iron chains all his life, even to the grave, as a reminder of the services he had rendered to Spain and of the reward he had received.

The caravel left Hispaniola eight years to the day after Columbus had discovered Guanahani. The dismal voyage home lasted six weeks —forty days and forty nights. The admiral filled them with his bitter thoughts, but they were not so bitter that a glint of irony could not intrude. Thanks to Bobadilla, he was about to make a striking entry into the Spanish court. Already he was calculating its favorable results. After the Franciscan habit, the criminal's robe! What a blow for the Queen!

On a melancholy November morning the caravel entered the Bay of Cádiz. An innumerable crowd was gathered on the quay. Had the whole of Spain come to the port? An enormous uproar greeted the chained man.

CHAPTER 4

His Greatest Discovery: Himself

THE great sun of the Golden Age rose upon Spain, and its symbol was the birth at Ghent, in February 1500, of the future Charles V, that ambitious prince who was to try to build a powerful Iberian world after the image of the Holy Roman Empire, while, on parallel lines, the great clerics and masters were to construct a still vital mystical universe.

The miserable creature who, in December 1500, fell at the feet of Isabella the Catholic in her palace at Granada also identified himself with the Golden Age. "Look upon my chains, my white hair and my tears!" Through the windows of the Alhambra, wide open to the Sierra Nevada, came the murmur of the mob, as at Cádiz three weeks earlier, indignant and angry to see the one who had discovered the road to Cipango chained like a common malefactor. The people were with him. So was the Queen, who had never abandoned him.

The sovereigns made Columbus rise. He was invited to explain himself, and he did so with his usual eloquence. Although wearied by the bad treatment he had suffered, his eyes inflamed with ophthalmia, his wrists and ankles ravaged by the irons, the admiral still had a fine presence. His voice, broken at first with sobs, grew firmer and became like thunder as he spoke of his enemies. He accused his accusers and twisted the neck of slander. He ended by convincing everyone. He was freed of his irons, and Bobadilla was recalled. Christopher Columbus was reinstated in his dignities and prerogatives. The admiral had won, but it was his last triumph.

His triumph was more apparent than real. Certainly Bobadilla had manifestly overstepped his mandate, and he was relieved of his duties in Hispaniola. But it was Nicolás de Ovando who was appointed in his place. Columbus was no longer governor of Hispaniola. He was forbidden even to return there, in the name of public order. Thus he had become a sort of honorary viceroy, but he continued to draw revenues from the discovered lands. In fact, Columbus had been discharged, without hope of being able to resume an active role.

The decision of the Catholic monarchs—firm in principle, restrained in its nuances—throws light on their feelings with regard to the admiral. They were grateful to him for his first success. They had friendship for him—especially Isabella—and never ceased to furnish proof of it. But they were farseeing. Columbus's ineptitude in command of men and his total absence of administrative capacity were dangerous to the future of the territories he had discovered. He had to be separated from them. At the moment when a tough and victorious Spain was in process of giving birth to her empire, her two rulers, *Yo el Rey, Yo la Reina* (I the King, I the Queen)—could not afford the luxury of favoritism. Moreover, they had done everything for Christopher Columbus except establish him on a throne.

Christopher Columbus Takes to Prophecy

Well informed as they were on the psychology of Columbus, the Catholic monarchs were mistaken in believing that he would be content with this anticipated retreat. He began harassing tactics for the fourth time. He met the same coldness and the same reticence as when he had been preparing for his first voyage. The honors at Barcelona seemed to have been forgotten. Astonishment was feigned that he could dream of further discoveries. He had had his share of triumph: let him make way for younger men! Now that Bishop Fonseca had decreed the freedom of the route to the Indies, the ocean was to become as frequented as the Guadalquivir. The time of the pioneers was ended, and they should know how to retire. But was he not still an admiral and viceroy? Without a fleet and without a kingdom, it is true; but he still had his hands on a tenth of the proceeds. Thus the gentlemen of Castile and Aragon whispered under the porticoes of the Alhambra, with honeyed smiles and much kowtowing, though at heart they were immensely satisfied to see the idol tottering.

Columbus, for his part, did not see things thus. Though he might be very near his fiftieth year, he felt young. Everything had not been discovered; far from it. There was still Cipango to be reconnoitered —the road to Jerusalem. At this point in his life a period of religious exaltation began. He abandoned the court, elected to go into retreat at Granada, where he would be at peace, and passionately threw himself into study. It was no longer the geographers that he preferred, as at Porto Santo; he doubtless thought he had covered all human knowledge in that field. Instead, his meditations and readings were directed toward biblical themes, and the Holy Scriptures became his vital sustenance. After having absorbed the Prophets for nearly a year—especially Isaiah, Jeremiah, and Ezekiel—he produced a synthesis of them in a work called *The Book of Prophecies*. This strange work—heavy reading, but sometimes of superhuman beauty—reveals a new Columbus and makes it possible for us to decipher certain notes hastily scribbled in his logbook. Throughout this torrential book, which is heavy with reminiscences and quotations (clear evidence of a self-taught person at work), one sees the unexpected although suspected figure of a Christopher Columbus who was simultaneously a mystic and a prophet. He regarded himself as a prophet and a father of the Church, and in a sense he was both.

In *The Book of Prophecies* he first stated and defined his own religious doctrine. For the period it was daring and bordered on heresy. "It is my opinion that the Holy Spirit works through Christians, Jews, and Mussulmans, and in men of every sect. And not only among scholars, but also among the ignorant"—a proposition that heralded the Reformation. More daring still, having regard to the edict of proscription which was only eight years old, was his allusion to a universal church that would unite both Jews and Christians. Relying on the Psalms of David, Columbus even went so far as to claim that a convert could remain an infidel. What, in fact, did he want to prove? That conversion to the Christian faith did not perforce imply renunciation of Judaism? Did he intend thus to justify his Hebrew origin? However that may be, the stand he took in defending the Jews and explaining them was striking. What brotherly accents he used in espousing their cause!

This passionate absorption in the prophets raised Columbus to a pitch of exaltation. He was no longer satisfied to comment; he became original and even took to prophecy. Calling upon Saint Augustine and Alfonso the Wise, astronomer and king of Castile, he foretold the end of the world. Everyone knew that the world must end in the seventh millennium of its existence; it was then 6845 years old and had only 155 years to live, just the time needed for all the prophecies to come about. In a sort of mystical trance, the new prophet recalled the historical creation of the people of Israel. They were indeed the chosen people. God had chosen them to rule over men and to bring great things to pass. In skillful disorder, Columbus mingled the brilliant imagery of the Old Testament with the solemn themes of the Spanish crusade. He called upon the Catholic monarchs to complete the reconquest by capturing the Holy Sepulcher from the Mussulmans. Time was short. It was for them to close the history of the world with a gesture at once political and religious. But they must act quickly.

The gold of Cipango, the earthly paradise of the Gulf of Paria, the conversion of the Indians, the conquest of Jerusalem, spices and pearls, the teachings of the Bible, and the calculations of the astrologers—was this the discourse of a visionary or a doctor's thesis? An appearance of logic, however, tied these separate ideas together. The man who made prophecies in his retreat at Granada was not so different from the one who had explained his ideas to the Spanish sovereigns fifteen years earlier. The discovery of the road to the Indies and the alliance with the Great Khan were not an end but a means. It was a matter of harvesting legions of converts in oriental lands. And as for gold—there could never be enough of it—it could serve to finance the colossal expedition that would give Zion back its early grandeur. Even the return of the "Holy Dwelling" to God—it was all there, even though the admiral took care to make clear that both Christians and Jews would have a place in the *Casa Santa*. Columbus was obsessed with the idea of the union of the churches. How far ahead he was of his orthodox century!

The admiral addressed his book to the Catholic monarchs. They never received it. Did Columbus fear at the last moment that he had made his thoughts too obvious? Did he think of Isabella the fanatic and of the fires that flamed at Seville? It is true that in his book he borrowed more often the irritated growling of Jehovah than the tender voice of Christ. The Old Testament inspired him more than did the Gospels. It is also true that his personal religion had all the features of Judaism: an ardent restlessness, a messianic sense, a certain taste for catastrophe and, more than all these, that somber view of the world that the persecuted have. Had not his own life been one long complaint? And as for his Christianity, filled with his own cries and bathed in his own tears, carried along on the apocalyptic waves of a lucid despair, is it that of a *cristiano viejo**?

The color of the hair and of the skin, the beauty of the eyes, the shape of the lips and nose, the gift for trade, and the love of gain—these features are not enough to distinguish a Jew. But to believe oneself chosen, to know how to wait and suffer, to seek martyrdom, to be hard in power and stoical in servitude: these are scarcely mistakable. These were the essential virtues of Christopher Columbus, the Genoese.

Farewell to Cipango

The flotilla which in May 1502 raised anchor in the port of Cádiz was a very meager one. Four caravels of medium tonnage and a crew of not more than one hundred and fifty was all that Columbus was allowed. A royal official was aboard, charged with noting the incidents of the voyage, and especially with watching the admiral's behavior. The latter was forbidden to touch Hispaniola or to use natives as slaves. That he was mistrusted is clear; it was more a study mission that he had been authorized to carry out than a colonial inspection. Once again, only an event of serious consequence for Spain forced the Catholic monarchs to a decision: Vasco da Gama had rounded the Cape of Good Hope. A Portuguese had discovered the sea road to the Indies. As the route followed by Vasco da Gama was east of the line of demarcation fixed by Alexander VI, the Spaniards were excluded from it. Was fortune to turn to the profit of Portugal? Certainly, unless the western route proved shorter. It was necessary to return to Columbus's plan, to give him carte blanche for a last time—the more so, since he said he knew the strait, west of the Gulf of Paria, that gave access to the Indian Ocean.

The road to the Indies, Cipango . . . could it be imagined that the *Almirante Mayor* had abandoned his fabulous plan? The old lion—he was fifty years old—could not live without the odor of salt and tar. And he wanted revenge.

From Cádiz to Martinique—Martinino—by way of the Canaries, the crossing was calm, almost monotonous. Ten years had sufficed for

_____
*A Christian of long standing, i.e., not a recent convert.

this daring exploit to have become an undertaking, if not common-place, at least without mystery. For the five weeks of the voyage the crews were peaceful. Columbus was less so. Since his retreat at Gra-nada, he was no longer the same man. A great peace was in process of descending upon him. Was he about to acquire at last that philos-ophy of events which he had always lacked? Not yet! And the anxiety that possessed him was terribly human. While he drew near to the West Indian archipelago, he thought of all his collaborators who, since his third voyage, had followed and passed beyond his own tracks. He knew their names by heart, their itineraries and adven-tures. Vicente Yáñez Pinzón had crossed the equator, reached the coast of Brazil, and dropped anchor in the Gulf of Paria. Alonso de Ojeda had made the same circuit, accompanied by Juan de la Cosa. All three—his partner, his second-in-command, his pilot—had be-trayed him. The latter two had joined ship with a certain Florentine named Amerigo Vespucci. There was also the Portuguese, Cabral, who had discovered the land of Santa Cruz (Brazil), and the Span-iard, Rodrigo de Bastidas, who had pushed as far as the Gulf of Da-rién. All this in scarcely three years, and at the very time when Co-lumbus—their master—was crossing the ocean chained like a criminal, or meditating upon the fate of Spain while devouring the Bible. In short, all these adventurers had done nothing but repeat his gesture. But this gesture was without meaning if it was not directed toward some grandiose end. He, Christopher Columbus, had fixed that end a long time before: the West Indies, their emperor, their gold, and their people more numerous than the fish of the sea. And Cipango, always Cipango. This prize, simultaneously political and mystical, no one had yet captured. It remained to be taken, and Columbus would take it. This resolute man who challenged the new conquistadors was nevertheless double their age. He was half blind, crippled with gout, exhausted by nameless experiences. But his spirit was young and his will would be broken only by death. He was almost peaceful but not resigned; he would never be that. Such was Columbus during his ultimate struggle with the Dark Sea.

His plan was as follows: to make for Jamaica and from there push on directly to Central America, following the northern coasts until the discovery of the famous strait opening on to China . . . or Japan. Hardly had the fleet lost sight of Martinique than a violent tempest arose, inflicting serious damage to Columbus's caravels. What could he do but seek aid in Hispaniola, whose outlines were visible through the mist? But Hispaniola was the forbidden land. There lay Santo Domingo, the Haitian paradise the admiral had discovered but which was closed to him, though it was his own realm. He sent a boat ashore but his messenger was turned away. Governor Ovando was intractable and referred Columbus to the royal decrees: Columbus was forbidden to land on Hispaniola under any pretext whatsoever. He must continue his voyage.

Columbus received the blow without flinching. While the four wretched caravels cruised off the Haitian coast, a powerful fleet of more than thirty vessels sailed away from it, steering for Spain, laden with riches. The Catholic monarchs were to have their share: four thousand pieces of gold. Bobadilla and Roldán, the hateful conquerors of Columbus, were among the passengers. The two fleets met; they were no more than a few cable lengths from one another when the tempest redoubled its fury. Columbus cried to the captains to turn back to Santo Domingo, but his advice was lost in the uproar of the waves. A few hours later, almost the whole squadron—twenty-seven ships—went to the bottom, and Bobadilla and Roldán were among the victims. Was this the vengeance of heaven? Columbus tended to think so. In any case, his miserable fleet, spared by the tempest, followed its mad course toward a chimerical port.

Columbus's fourth voyage was to last nearly two and a half years. A voyage?—rather a tragic wandering through a liquid labyrinth. The Ariadne's thread that he thought he held was only the insubstantial thread of his own tenacious dream. Let us look at his wayward track on the map. Columbus left the vicinity of Hispaniola, strewn with the wreckage of the sunken fleet. He then ran along the southeast coast of Jamaica; leaving the Jardines de la Reina on his right, he steered for Honduras, which he reached at the level of the present town of Trujillo. He landed and inquired of the natives where gold could be found. They indicated Veragua,* which he believed was Malacca, the Golden Peninsula! He set sail once more. Despite a fiendish tempest, which blew for forty-four days, he succeeded in rounding Cape Gracias a Dios at the present frontier of

* The part of Panama on the northern coast bordering the Mosquito Gulf.

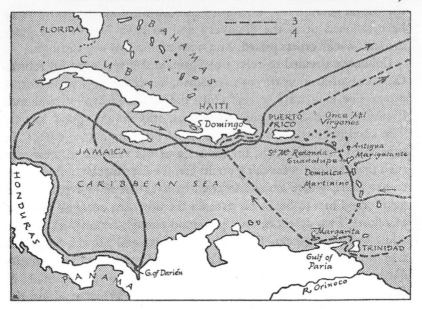

Christopher Columbus's Third and Fourth Voyages

Honduras and Nicaragua. He ran past the coasts of these two lands and continued southward along Costa Rica and Veragua. He reached the Isthmus of Panama, where he expected to find the mouth of the Ganges. Columbus was certain of this; he had recognized the spot on the maritime charts. For several months he prowled around the neighborhood of Panama, but found no break in its abrupt cliff. He then passed on to the Gulf of Darién. But this unlucky man had no idea that he had only to land on the Panamanian coast and to cover 125 miles westward to reach, not the Indian Ocean and the Asiatic empire, but the Pacific Ocean. Who among his companions would have been able to resist the fatal miasmas of those tropical forests? Others, nevertheless, were soon to draw aside the suffocating curtain of the Isthmus of Darién.

Columbus had lost! This daring exploration, from Honduras to the frontiers of Colombia, had taught him nothing. In the north he had missed Yucatán, the point from which Cortés was to start out for the conquest of Mexico; in the south he had missed Colombia, the edge of an immense continent; while in the west he had missed the Pacific, the widest ocean in the world. It had been his misfortune always to have touched upon the discovery and to have half opened gates through which others passed. And what misled him was Cipango.

Columbus decided to return to Spain, and it was a pitiful return. Only two of his four caravels remained. Their bottoms were worm-eaten. The men were weary. Only the admiral's brother and son, Bartholomew and Fernando Columbus, still showed good humor. The admiral himself was calm: he spoke little but wrote much. He supervised the maneuvers, for the state of the vessels and crew was such that the least weakening could involve catastrophe. After a first call at Cuba, where Columbus tried to have the hulls repaired, the gale forced him to beach his fleet on the northern coast of Jamaica. His fleet? Two derelicts, only just good enough to lodge the crews while waiting for help. Two sailors, Méndez and Fieschi, bargained with the natives, procured two pirogues, and carried out the extraordinary feat of covering the distance from Jamaica to Hispaniola in five days: 125 miles with oars on a raging sea. While awaiting the return of these two intrepid oarsmen, Columbus drafted for the Catholic monarchs a missive called *Lettera Rarissima*, which to a certain extent is a sequel to *The Book of Prophecies*. In this letter he was not content to give merely a pathetic account of his last voyage; he demanded justice for himself and his relatives. He demanded that his enemies be punished. With a sort of sad covetousness, he evoked the golden roofs of Cathay, the precious stones of Cipango, and the copper mines, while affirming that he alone knew the road thither. But the great business, *el otro negocio famosíssimo*, was the liberation of Jerusalem, which Columbus had never ceased to din into the royal ears during the seven years he had spent at court. So here he was, again carried away by a storm of prophecy. He harked back to the Psalmist, he cried aloud his despair and his faith, he called upon Jehovah.

Christopher Columbus wrote this letter to the Catholic rulers three years before his death, and in conditions such that one cannot suspect its sincerity. He was sick, incapable of moving, tied to a wreck, surrounded by men he doubted, scarcely seeing them, not knowing if Méndez and Fieschi would ever return, watching the irritated whispering of the Spaniards and the menacing plashing of Indian pirogues. The circumstances scarcely favored delusion, much less so as Columbus had no illusions concerning the fate of his letter. If he died in Jamaica, who would take care of that parchment? It was more a conversation with himself than an appeal to the rulers of Spain—a bewildering conversation, giving strength to the principal features of a personality already known to us, and emphasizing its essential element: contradiction. Weakness and strength, pride and humility, trickery and candor, realism and unconcern; above all, an ardent faith in his own prophetic mission, and for all that, a stoicism and a confidence in God, affirmed by outbursts of genuine emotion. "A hope in that which has created all men sustains me." There is also this exclamation: "Where there is no love, everything ends"—a singular thought, similar to the one that Saint John of the Cross was to formulate three quarters of a century later: "There where there is no love, put love and you will extract love." Columbus already sensed the warning of the Carmelite: "In the evening of your life, you will be asked about love."

Méndez and Fieschi took five days to go from Jamaica to Hispaniola. It took them no less than a year to get back. It was not an easy matter to soften Ovando's hostility; moreover, he was much occupied with suppressing a revolt that had occurred in the colony, and naturally he attached only a secondary importance to his predecessor's worries. As to Columbus, while awaiting the return of his ambassadors he had to face a mutiny among his crew. Both men finally mastered their respective situations. Two ships got under way for Jamaica. Food was already scarce, and the admiral was at the end of his resources.

The two ships steered for Santo Domingo. Columbus was accorded the unexpected privilege of landing there and the surprise of seeing himself cordially welcomed by Ovando. Doubtless the governor of Hispaniola reckoned that the admiral was a "finished" man; he was no longer dangerous, and one could afford to be polite to him. Columbus and his companions stayed at Santo Domingo for three months, then they embarked for Spain. A last look—the Discoverer could distinguish shapes and colors only with difficulty—at the horizon of Cipango. A last tempest off the Canaries, and at the beginning of November the people of Seville saw two dismasted caravels reach the port of Sanlúcar de Barrameda. No one paid any attention to the tall gentleman with white hair and beard who was brought off on a

litter. He turned a blind look westward. Over there were the West
Indies . . . and Cipango.

Swan Song

Columbus landed at Sanlúcar de Barrameda on November 7, 1504.
A short while later, on November 26, Isabella the Catholic died at
Medina del Campo. The admiral had lost his protectress and his only
support. This was all that was lacking in his experience, and God had
sent it him, so he drank his cup to the dregs. The death of Isabella
would make his own death even more bitter.

Columbus had now but one reason to hurry: to get to the court.
But Ferdinand could scarcely bear to receive him, for what would he
have to listen to but the echo of that same aggressive complaint he
had known only too well for twenty years? Under various pretexts,
the King put off from day to day the audience the admiral asked and
even demanded. Meanwhile, Columbus sent letter after letter to his
son Diego, a page at the court, giving him messages for the sovereign.
He must not fail to kiss the King's hands on his behalf. He must find
out if the dead Queen had not, in her will, made known her wish
that he should regain possession of the Indies. He was no longer
obsessed with Cipango, but only that the King should confirm the
Santa Fe agreement: the transmission of his own offices and titles to
his son. He was more interested than ever in what was going on in
the Indies, was surprised that his advice was not asked on the appointment of three bishops in the conquered territories, and demanded
that accounts be rendered to him. He who had shown himself so bad
an administrator now gave the King very wise counsel. Theory was
easier than practice.

Judging that his son Diego's credit at court was insufficient, Columbus sent him reinforcements: his other son, Fernando, and his
brother Bartholomew. The three men of the Columbus family busied
themselves to bring success to the admiral's case, the juridical basis
of which appeared unassailable. The Santa Fe agreement had conceded to Columbus the titles and prerogatives of Admiral of the
Ocean Sea and of the Islands and Continents, transmissible to his heirs.
The titles of Viceroy and Governor General of the discovered territories were personal. But a letter of privilege signed by the Catholic

monarchs some days after the agreement had extended these last titles—even more important because of their material aspects—to the admiral's heirs. It is easy to understand the tenacity of the Columbus family in defending the thesis of "legality." It is easy also to understand the resistance of the Crown. The strict application of the texts would have consecrated, for an unlimited period, the reign of a dynasty of adventurers—foreigners, moreover—over an empire that already seemed to surpass in extent and riches the kingdom of Spain itself.

While the three Columbuses besieged King Ferdinand at Segovia, the admiral seethed with impatience at Seville. There was no possibility that he would regain his health. If he recovered enough energy to get to court, he would consider himself satisfied. He had to find means of transport, for he could not move. The sumptuous litter which, two years earlier, had brought the remains of the Grand Cardinal of Spain from Tendilla to Seville was suggested, but Columbus rejected this macabre offer. He had himself hoisted onto a mule and, six months after his melancholy landing at Sanlúcar de Barrameda, he set out for Segovia. He arrived there, after much difficulty, only to learn that the court had moved to Salamanca. No matter; he would go to Salamanca.

The reception that Ferdinand gave Columbus was correct and no more. The sovereign confined himself to hearing the admiral's requests. He promised to examine them benevolently. These were friendly words but they did not satisfy Columbus. He raised his voice. Ferdinand then suggested naming an official whose special duty at the chancellery would be to look after the admiral's interests. Would he not agree to exchange all his titles—fundamentally questionable—for the governorship of a town in Castile? Columbus was not taken in by such courtly language; he would abandon none of his claims. He demanded, quite simply, that justice be done to him. He withdrew, still very fine and very dignified despite his feeble gait.

The great man was to be seen again in the royal antechambers awaiting his turn among the courtiers. It was now at Valladolid that Ferdinand had taken up residence. Columbus followed him there, pursuing him like a living reproach. How many times was the irritated eye of the monarch to fall upon this motionless phantom standing near a window, wearing over his shoulders the garnet-red cloak of the admirals of Castile, and keeping his hat on his head! To remain covered before the King and to ride at his side were only two of the various privileges the Descubridor intended never to relinquish.

The Princess Juana, daughter of Isabella the Catholic, had succeeded her mother on the throne of Castile and León. Accompanied by her husband, Philip the Fair, son of the Emperor Maximilian of Austria, she arrived at Valladolid, coming from Flanders, to take possession of her kingdom. A last hope rose in the breast of Christopher Columbus. He remembered Isabella—once the small Infanta of Madrigal de las Altas Torres—to whom he had promised Cipango's gold. If only Isabella should live again in her daughter, all would yet be saved. All what? His honor: that is to say, his interests and those of his descendants.

A few hundred yards, no more, separated the modest dwelling of Columbus from the royal residence; after his death, the dukes of Veragua made a palace of it. It was too far for the pilgrim of the Dark Sea. Only the circuit of his room was possible from now on. In a few days it was with difficulty that he could turn in bed. He charged Bartholomew, his brother, with giving Juana a letter written in amazing terms, considering the fact that a man at death's door had penned it. "I can still render you services such as have never been seen. . . ." With his four limbs stricken and his sight extinguished, of what services was Columbus speaking? This last offering to the Crown of Spain—himself, almost a corpse—fits well into the mystical aspect of his personality. He would have given all!

Columbus's message did not hold the new queen's attention for a second. She was naturally taciturn, and in this young woman, anxious and twisting her hands, Juana the Mad could already be seen. Her husband's infidelities tormented her more than the fate of the fallen admiral. As for Philip, the Prince Charming, he led the dance, placed his Flemish friends in the good jobs, and gave his father-in-law a hard time. The last faithful cry of the dying servant was lost among the guttural accents of the favorites of the Austrian archduke.

Christopher Columbus did not understand that he had become an outdated hero, living beyond his time. He was in his own era at the taking of Granada, in the ecstasies of the reconquest, in the chivalrous myths—in short, in the heroic epoch. But while he was wandering upon the ways of the *Ultra Mar*, Spain was growing hard. She was realizing her unity, which the harsh fist of the Flemish emperor was to seal in a few years. For the moment the master of the day was Philip the Fair, merely the Prince Consort, but seeming to be destined for much higher things. He had not come to Valladolid as a visitor; he was the forerunner of the Hapsburgs. He set foot in Spain, and with him in the Trastamare palace was the presence of the House of Austria. Ferdinand was troubled—a little late!—by this nuisance of a son-in-law. With anguish he watched the brief Spanish career of Philip develop. If only he had foreseen it! But the dice had been cast and the game developed very rapidly. On April 15 Philip the Fair arrived in Valladolid. In June he was acknowledged King of Castile jointly with his wife. In July the Cortes at Valladolid took oath to Queen Juana, King Philip, and their son Charles, Prince of Asturias. Ferdinand was no longer anything in Castile, but he kept the sovereignty of Aragon.

In September Philip suddenly died. The trajectory of the new star in the Castilian sky might have been dazzling. But he had only five months: just time to prepare the way for his son (now six years old, grandson of Maximilian, great-grandson of Charles the Bold, and future Charles V) who, ten years later, would arrive at Villaviciosa to inherit all Spain. Ferdinand, whether he wished it or not, and despite fruitless attempts to wrest the heritage of Isabella from the House of Austria, had won the empire. But had he kept Spain?

Thus this month of May 1506 did not belong to any epoch. It was at the crossing of two roads: one that still penetrated the shadows of the Middle Ages, and the other that opened upon imperial prospects. In fact, Columbus could not have died at a worse moment. Periods of transition are not favorable to great men. But Spain's indifference to the admiral was equaled only by her indifference to the events that were developing there.

While Ferdinand clung to the Spanish heritage, Columbus thought of nothing but his own succession. He dictated his will. He wanted to put his affairs in order to protect his children against royal disfavor, which was always possible. But he wrote his testament, too. On May 19, before the notary Pedro de Hinojedo, the Descubridor began his last colloquy with men.

Complex as the personality of Christopher Columbus may have been, it is singularly illuminated by his writings. Freed of their turgidity, swept clear of their contradictions, the admiral's own words explain him better than the testimony of his contemporaries. The notes of his voyages, his *Book of Prophecies*, his correspondence and his letter from Jamaica to the Catholic monarchs find their complement in the last public deed he inscribed. His testament confirms the essential features of his character. He succeeded in portraying his own personality. But he shows us nothing we have not seen already.

Reverting to the terms of a will that he had drafted eight years earlier, Christopher Columbus named his son Diego as his general legatee, reminding him of his rights and duties. His rights? The admiralty of the Ocean Sea, the viceroyalty of the West Indies, and the revenues deriving from them. His duties? To build a chapel where three Masses were to be said every day: one in honor of the Holy Trinity, one to the glory of Our Lady's Conception, and a third for the peace of the souls of Christopher's father, mother, and wife—Felipa Perestrello e Moniz, the gentle and forgotten Portuguese, mother of Diego. Columbus also charged his son with contributing "to the honor and prosperity" of the city of Genoa. Finally, he commended to him Beatriz Enríquez, mother of his other son, Fernando, adding: "And let this be done as a relief to my conscience, for it weighs much on my soul. The reason for it is not licit for me to write here." Thus, before dying, Columbus returned to his old loves: his native land, his wife, and the companion of his evil days. He had been unfaithful to all three: Genoa, Felipa, and Beatriz. Three heavy causes for remorse, but the admiral said no more of them. All comment on this subject seemed to have no place in a testament. But what an admission is contained within this modest phrase! He now knew well that he had sacrificed everything to pride.

There were a few more days. That great peace which, during his retirement to Granada, had brushed him with its wing now enfolded him utterly. Following the example of Queen Isabella, he assumed the habit of the third order of Saint Dominic. His eyes never left the crucifix. The chest that held his relics—the irons with which Bobadilla had laden him on his return from the third voyage—had been drawn close to him. He had never been separated from them. Doubtless they reminded him less of Spanish ingratitude and his own humiliation than of the five hundred Indian slaves shackled by his

orders. The crucifix and the chains! Yes, it was certainly God who
had led his caravels. But gold had wasted all.

The Admiral of the Ocean Sea was watched over by his son Diego
and by the two sailors who had saved him at Jamaica: Méndez and
Fieschi—a Portuguese and a Genoese. Could Columbus have thought
of a more symbolic guard of honor—the presence at his pillow of his
first and second homelands, and the presence, too, of that humble
"troop" who had had faith in his star?

On May 21, Ascension Day, Columbus sighed: "Lord, into thy
hands I surrender my spirit." Then he died. He was fifty-five years
old. His death passed unnoticed. The Valladolid chronicle did not
even mention it.

Columbus died in the midst of his magnificent error, but the error
saved him from despair. For this unlucky man was always unaware
of his own ill fortune. He had *failed*—by a degree farther north—to
reach Florida. He had *failed*—it was necessary only to cross the
Isthmus of Panama—to discover the Pacific. Imagine the destiny of
Spain had she been mistress, before even the fifteenth century was
ended, of the North Atlantic, the South Atlantic, and the Pacific!
Imagine the glory of the man had he discovered the two Americas
and forced the gateway to the Pacific! But Columbus had failed to be
that man. If he had not been obsessed with Cipango; if the sea, the
men, and the period had been constantly in his favor; if the passion
for gold . . . But the conditional tense has nothing to do with the
facts. In any case, it is of little importance that of all the arrows shot
westward of the Dark Sea—north, center, and south—none had really
reached its end. These fiery tracks had lit the Atlantic darkness. The
main point, as regards the man, was that in the last days of his life, in
the dim light of his own sorrows, Columbus had discovered the way
to himself.

Which is the picture we should keep? Master Columbus, the young
mariner; or the outlaw of La Rábida; or Don Cristóbal Colón, Admiral of the Ocean Sea, dressed all in red and wearing about his neck
the collar of Isabella the Catholic; or the Franciscan, full of contrition, returning from the second voyage; or the condemned man,
laden with chains, returning to Spain for the third time; or the tertiary of Saint Dominic, dying, almost alone, a few steps from the mon-

archs whose glory he had made? Each of these pictures is genuine. They illustrate the successive sincerities of Columbus. But the last picture must be held, for it completes the personality. The martyr had ceased to fight. The covetous man had no hunger other than that of penitence. His soul—how light was this caravel that he took to port!—drew near to the Promised Land, which was no longer Cipango but the Kingdom of God.

Columbus Dies and America Is Discovered

Columbus's persistence was rewarded, at least so far as his heritage was concerned. After endless proceedings, Diego, Christopher's general legatee, saw himself confirmed in his father's privileges, including the title "Admiral of the Indies." By an astonishing reversal of fortune, Diego was appointed governor of Hispaniola, replacing Ovando. What a posthumous revenge for the man who was prohibited from landing there!

Fernando Columbus devoted himself to learning, and formed an admirable library at Seville. Both knew the favor of Emperor Charles V. But the two sons of Diego Columbus having died without issue, and Fernando having no heirs, the sumptuous heritage of the admiral was escheated. Nothing remained of Columbus and his two sons but a few bones gathered together beneath a stone in the middle of the central nave of Seville cathedral. It is appropriate here to emphasize a last stroke of ill luck. Transported after his death to the cloister of Santa María de las Cuevas at Seville, Columbus's remains were transferred to Santo Domingo, and from there to Havana, where they were mixed with those of Diego. An earthquake completed the confusion. Nearly four centuries after the death of Christopher Columbus, a coffin from Havana was united with the one holding the remains of Fernando. Four marble heralds in dalmatic, bearing the royal arms of Spain, mount guard around a slab under which a small heap of calcareous dust completes its disintegration: the Discoverer and his sons are mingled together.

More serious even than this physical disappearance was the shadow cast during the first part of the sixteenth century upon the work of Columbus and even upon his name, for which another was substituted: Amerigo Vespucci. Who was this Vespucci? A strange and inquisitive man. Born at Florence of well-to-do parents, he studied mathematics and physics and was entrusted by the Medicis with organizing Columbus's second expedition. It was thus that he established himself at Seville, where he made the acquaintance of the admiral, then at the height of his glory. This scholar-turned-man-of-affairs was soon bitten by the demon of adventure. He participated in numerous reconnoitering voyages, accompanied Vicente Yáñez Pinzón and Coelho on their explorations of the coasts of Central America and Brazil, and was one of those who planted the Portuguese flag on the land of Santa Cruz (original name of Brazil). But he seems, in fact, like a kind of amateur tourist. Though he participated in distant explorations, he took no initiative or responsibility or risks. Aboard the Portuguese and Spanish caravels he was simply a passenger of rank, much respected by the crews because of his knowledge. He advised but did not command. And the certificate of *piloto mayor* (chief pilot) which he was awarded did honor more to his theoretical knowledge than to his capacities as a navigator, of which he had given proof only rarely. It is not that he had not sometimes taken the helm, but just that he had not acquired the knack. Vespucci was not a sailor in the sense that Juan de la Cosa or the Pinzón brothers were sailors. How was it, then, that to him was attributed the paternity of a discovery that seems, in all fairness, to belong wholly to Columbus? A simple sentence explains everything. It was written by Vespucci to Lorenzo de' Medici on his return from his first voyage to Brazil: ". . . I have found, in these southern lands, a continent more peopled with men and animals than our own Europe, than Asia and Africa, with a more temperate climate, softer than any other region known to us. . . . One can, with good reason, name it the New World. . . ." A capital sentence, if it is reconciled to Columbus's statement that "the whole earth is an island" and his conviction that by steering westward he would reach Asia. Thus Vespucci gave the name *Mundus Novus* to the discovered territory, which was clearly distinct from the known world and separated from it by an ocean. Columbus had never even suspected its existence.

To discover is not everything. Discovery must be given a meaning. The incredible hardships, the tears and the blood and sweat of the Admiral of the Ocean Sea would have been to no purpose if a clear mind had not erased the name Cipango and inscribed the words *Mundus Novus* in its place. Columbus had crossed the Dark Sea from one side to the other, forced a reputedly uncrossable barrier, and touched upon marvelous shores without seeing anything but the reflection of his inner dream. This sublime vagabond had given the New World only a blind look. Amerigo Vespucci eyed it clearly and recognized it. Nevertheless, the visionary Genoese and the clear-minded Florentine can take each other by the hand. Columbus remains the Discoverer of America and Vespucci its Explainer.

Master Christopher the Unlucky. Vespucci adds to the tale of bad luck. Without Vespucci we should speak of the Columbias, not of the Americas.

PART TWO

Hernán Cortés;

OR

The Return of the White God

*When the time has come, I will return into your
midst, by the eastern sea, together with white and
bearded men. . . .*

—Proclamation to the Toltec people by Quetzalcoatl, god and king,
in the year 1000 of the Christian era. Aztec legend.

The Conquistadors' March on Tenochtitlán

The Battle on the Great Teocalli

CHAPTER 5

America

Columbus set out on his first voyage in 1492. He died at Valladolid, in 1506. During this same period, other flotillas were sailing the Dark Sea. What was the product of these fifteen years of discovery?

Broadly speaking, Columbus and his companions had reconnoitered the Greater and Lesser Antilles, the Gulf of Mexico, Yucatán, the coasts of Honduras and Nicaragua, the Isthmus of Panama and the Gulf of Darién, as well as the Venezuelan coast and the delta of the Orinoco. If, as many were beginning to think, these countries were not the Indies, a name had to be given to them. It was a German who found that name.

In the year following that of Columbus's death, Martin Waldsee-müller, of German nationality but professor of geography at Saint-Dié, published under the pseudonym "Hylacomylus" a work entitled *Cosmographiae Introductio,* in which, after speaking of three parts of the world, he said: "But these parts of the world are now well known. A fourth part, as we shall soon see, has been discovered by Amerigo Vespucci. Why not therefore call it *Amerige* or *America,* that is to say, the land of Americus—*Americi terram*—from the name of its great and learned discoverer, just as Europe and Asia bear the names of women?" Indeed, why not? Was not Amerigo Vespucci the one who made the discovery intelligible? To him, therefore, the credit and the glory. But it is easier to name an empire than to conquer it; only a little propaganda is required.

Afterward, Waldseemüller felt he had been frivolous. More precise information, perhaps even remorse, caused him to reconsider the suggestion. Vespucci's achievement was undeniable. But should his perspicacity make one forget the labors and tribulations of Columbus, without which there might not have been a New World? The German's honesty found no echo. The idea he had launched made progress; he could no longer stop it. Vespucci's letter to Lorenzo de' Medici brought him to the attention of Europe, while that from Columbus to the Catholic monarchs in the same year passed unnoted.

The term America, which was at first applied to the territories south of the equator, later designated the whole of the New World. In 1541, thirty-five years after the death of Columbus, a Dutch geographer, Gerhardus Mercator, drew a map in which, clearly and for the first time, *Mundus Novus* was separated from Asia: it bore the name America.

The Conquistadors' Ring of Fire

It is time to take a brief look at the world that had just been born, if we wish to judge or to appraise the daring of the first conquerors. The site of the adventure must be located in order to help us estimate the worth of the adventurers. Let us traverse the New World from north to south: the battlefield, empire, and cemetery of the Conquistadors.

Formed of two southward-pointing triangles connected by a narrow strip of land, the American continent stretches in latitude from 72 degrees north to 56 degrees south, that is, through 128 degrees. On the west the Pacific Ocean separates it from Asia.

In reality, the New World consists of two continents connected by a string of islands and isthmuses. That it remained so long unknown to Europe, Africa, and Asia can be understood if the enormous distances from each of them are borne in mind. From Dakar to Natal is 1900 miles, from Lisbon to Buenos Aires is 5300 miles, and from Seville to Lima is 7200 miles. Ninety-four hundred miles separate the coast of Chile from Australian shores, and there are about 12,500 miles—that is, half the circumference of the earth—between Panama and the eastern coast of Indochina. These figures, even in an airborne age, eloquently explain why America remained *terra incognita* until the fifteenth century.

As to the physical aspect of the New World: to the west a moun-

tain ridge curves from the Bering Strait to the Strait of Magellan.
This continuous chain—the Rocky Mountains of North America and
the cordilleras of the Andes in South America—is like a gigantic cliff
overlooking the Pacific Ocean. In the center are the plains: from
Hudson Bay to the Gulf of Mexico in the north, and from the mouth
of the Amazon to Tierra del Fuego in the south. Finally, in the east,
plateaus slope toward, and plunge into, the Atlantic Ocean. In short,
from west to east there are three parallel zones: mountains, plains,
plateaus.

The extreme length of America in terms of latitude (Europe and
Asia are wider than they are long) gives it an astonishing variety of
climate and vegetation. Northern South America has an equatorial
climate: warm and humid; the rains are abundant and constant. A
dense forest of giant trees and a strange and striking flora quiver in
restless vitality. Few men risk themselves there; it is the dark kingdom
of insects, of monkeys with prehensile tails, balancing among the
lianas, and of tapirs. Only the hum of myriads of mosquitoes and the
roar of the jaguar break the silence. On each side of this equatorial
strip are two tropical zones: on the north, Central America and Mexico, and on the south, Brazil and the northern tips of Argentina and
Chile. In the lowlands there is the same steady heat, but it rains only
in summer. The forests, still impressive, are less dense; their leafy
roofs open up and sunlight splashes through in golden droplets. Com-
pact and dense along the rivers, the forests thin out progressively and
disappear. To this succeeds the bush, studded with clumps of trees;
it is peopled by innumerable birds, and the puma is its king. On either
side of the tropical zones begin the zones of temperate continental
climate. The winters are icy and the summers torrid. In North America, the forests and the flora are like those of Europe; then come
immense, scarcely undulating prairies. In South America, there are
the monotonous pampas. Finally, at the two ends of the continents,
in Alaska and northern Canada, and in Tierra del Fuego, are the cold
regions, reaching polar conditions along the icy Arctic coasts.

Very cold, burning hot, or bathed in humidity, the American climate is softened along the western coasts, where it is in contact with
the western winds and the ocean currents. Thus the California and
Chilean coasts, narrowly squeezed between the mountains and the

The Americas in 1550

The Americas in 1950

Pacific Ocean, have an admirable climate: water and sunshine in profusion, a mild wind, orange and lemon trees, and the soft rustling of palms.

The topographic structure of the American continent favors the formation of a powerful hydrographic system. The immense plains, unbroken by any mountains whatsoever, are a vast bed for the waters that run down from the high watersheds in the west. In North America there are two great river systems, the St. Lawrence and the Mississippi-Missouri, while in South America there are three principal rivers: the Orinoco, the Río de la Plata, and the Amazon, whose basin is ten times greater than the area of France.

Although from a physical viewpoint one cannot dissociate the Americas of the north, center, and south, all three of them being included in the same architectural system, only the last two will be dealt with here. What might be called "the America of the Conquistadors" is situated in fact in the central part of the American continent, the frontiers of which are Yucatán on the north, and the Río de la Plata on the south: an area of sunshine, spreading waters, and volcanic regions bounded by the tropics of Cancer and Capricorn and cut in two by the equator.

Thus it is to the south of the United States that the wondrous empire of the conquerors, a hundred times built, destroyed, and rebuilt, begins.

The fantastic loop that the Spanish caravels drew upon the map of the American continent in less than fifty years began at Palos in Andalusia. Let us follow its shining line. It makes its way westward across the Atlantic. First the Canaries and then the Sargasso Sea, and then the Caribbean Sea, the "American Mediterranean." Here lies the tropical archipelago with its dramatic storms, its cyclones, and its giant and brilliantly colored flowers. Cuba, Haiti, Puerto Rico and the Virgin Islands, Jamaica and the Windwards: a necklet of islands abounding in sugar cane and bananas. Then the line leaves the West Indies and winds around Central America, an isthmus 1200 miles in length from Mexico to Colombia—Guatemala, Honduras, Nicaragua, Costa Rica, and Panama. Its shape is such that one might say it had been twisted by the fist of a titan; in its dense dark forests the trees are tied together with lianas, and great blue lakes reflect the cones of volcanoes. And here, as the narrow link between Central and

South America, is Panama, with the Gulf of Darién, the obsession of
the first navigators, on its eastern shore. A landscape like the end of
the world, with nature wild and rebellious against the efforts of man.
Deadly vapors glide over the swamps, and the tropical sun is fierce.
Northward the conquering curve crosses the Caribbean Sea and
passes through the Yucatán peninsula. It is a limestone plateau, arid
in the north and overrun by forests in the south, with little running
water and an alternation of dry savanna and sweet-smelling forest.
Bending westward, the line reaches the main land area of Mexico,
which has three varied aspects. Its northern part is a prolongation of
the United States, with high and sterile plateaus framed by mountain
chains, and the sharp-cut peaks of the western Sierra Madre. In the
center are volcanoes—Popocatepetl, 17,888 feet high—with marvel-
ously fertile soil bearing everything from pines to bananas. All the
earth's climates are found there together: *tierra caliente, tierra tem-
plada*, and *tierra fría*. Lastly comes the Mexican south, with its tropical
beaches and its forests of mahogany and cedar. The Isthmus of
Tehuantepec unites the Atlantic and Pacific shores. The sierra opens
up. The waters foam in the rivers. Innumerable valleys descend into
the plain and die out at the edge of the Gulf of Mexico.

Winding again around Central America, the loop turns southward.
It touches upon the Caribbean Sea, crosses the Isthmus of Panama,
and reaches South America. Now the picture is clear and the junc-
tion of the northern and southern continents is settled. South America presents a gigantic and massive bull's head, a head with two faces:
on the north, looking out upon the Caribbean Sea, the Guianas,
Venezuela, and a part of Colombia; while facing the Pacific are
the rest of Colombia, Ecuador, Peru, Chile. Two faces, each with
its own character.

First, the northern face, north of a line approximating the equator.
The Guiana plateau, bristling with dense forests where rosewood
and rubber flourish side by side. Venezuela, bounded on the north by
the sea, its center watered by the Orinoco, and its *llanos* (plains)
periodically drowned by floods. With plains in the east and mountains in the west, Colombia, like Mexico, includes all types of climate,
from the humidity of Amazonia to the intense cold of the high crests
of the cordillera. On the mountain flanks are mines of precious metals,
and hidden stores of emeralds.

South of Colombia, western South America looks out toward the Pacific. It has a giant backbone in the Andes, which form a formidable barrier stretching from north to south, surmounted by peaks and volcanoes—Chimborazo, 20,702 feet, and Aconcagua, 23,081 feet. The Andean cordillera hugs the Pacific coast closely; the coastal strip is narrow, and the slopes of the high plateaus often descend to the very shore. Enclosed like a wedge between Colombia and Peru, with a coastal plain on the west and mountains in the center, and constantly threatened by earthquakes, is Ecuador. Next, the triple aspect of Peru: a coastal desert, peopled by innumerable birds; then the high lands of the Andes, with snowy summits, massive mountains cut by majestic valleys, and blue lakes as large as seas; and to the northeast, shaped like a crescent, the *oriente*, the Upper Amazon country, covered with forests and traversed by foaming rivers: the Amazon, the Marañón, and the Ucayali. Between the crests of the Andean cordillera and the Pacific, Chile stretches 2500 miles along a narrow coastal strip 220 miles wide at the most, with mountain summits exceeding 19,000 feet. It has an almost tropical climate in the north and a quasi-polar climate in the south at the confines of Tierra del Fuego: a tragic alternation of suffocating deserts, silent heights, and frozen lands. The western part of Bolivia and Paraguay, although not on the coast, complete the South American façade, but the bulk of both these countries lies east of the Andes and is turned toward the Atlantic.

The route of the Conquistadors is nearing its end. Slipping along the Chilean coast, the line of the conquest reaches Patagonia, abandons the Pacific at the Strait of Magellan, and entering the Atlantic once again, ascends northward and settles at the Río de la Plata. Here are the mouths of the Paraná and the Uruguay, the open door to the continent.

Wedged between Brazil and Argentina, Uruguay presents a regular relief: a plain carpeted with tall grasses, widely open to marine influences. A few rare ridges overlook a landscape of woodland and prairie. Argentina, which backs on Chile, occupies the whole Atlantic face of southern South America; it stretches through 30 degrees of latitude from the Tropic of Capricorn to the environs of Cape Horn. The heart of Argentina is the *pampa*, the equivalent of the North American prairie, waving and sighing under the wind like the sea. In the northwest are the high, arid plateaus of the Atacama Desert, with a few scattered oases. To the northeast, the Chaco, a transition between the extreme dryness of the subandean regions and the pampas. In the south is Patagonia, its sky scoured by storms, its shores lined with abrupt cliffs, and its polar seas in constant agitation. Finally, separated from Argentina by the Strait of Magellan, the sinister archipelago of Tierra del Fuego, a chaotic tangle of roaring waters and desolated land. Here the South American continent comes to an end. So severe is nature here and so forsaken by man that one might well believe that the world ends here, too.

From the Río de la Plata, the ring leaps over Brazil without halting (for Brazil fell to Portugal), comes back to the Caribbean Sea, and recrosses the Atlantic in the reverse direction—the Sargasso Sea, the Canaries, and the Andalusian ports.

In broad terms, this is the landscape upon which the first Conquistadors set eyes. For the sake of convenience, modern names have been given here and the land has been divided up geographically, but in fact the places discovered by the Spanish conquerors bore other names and the frontiers were different. But landmarks are needed to follow the stages of the discovery. Later, in the steps of the Conquistadors, we shall penetrate more deeply into the conquered lands.

So here we have, first of all, the back cloth, without people—an over-all view of the New World, of which the prodigious diversity of climate and topography makes clear at once the heroism—the madness—and ecstasy of the Conquistadors.

First, the empty landscape, and now the men.

Men from Other Parts

When the conquerors landed on unknown soil, they first encountered silence and emptiness. They were about to write the first page in the history of the New World; or so they thought. But soon strange men came to meet them, men whose skin was of a color never seen before, neither white nor black, but rather like bronze or sometimes like red sand. The Spaniards named them "Indians," a reasonable appellation, since the new arrivals thought themselves in the Indies. As they advanced farther into the conquered territories, the astonished Spaniards discovered villages, towns, and then great cities bearing the marks of an ancient civilization. The history of America had begun a long time before.

So the New World was inhabited long before Europe had ever imagined the existence of the continent. Aztec, Mayan, and Inca conquerors had preceded the envoys of the King of Spain along the same roads. They, too, had discovered territories, found men and enslaved them. Who were these men, and from where did they come?

To give a date to the appearance of man in America is impossible. Five thousand years before Christ? Perhaps. The interest is much less in the antiquity of what is known as the "pre-Columbian" population than in its origin.

Ought we to believe the Argentine scholar Ameghino Florentino when he tries to prove that American man was born in America, even setting up a genealogical tree of homo sapiens from the Tertiary ape of Patagonia, known as "Homonculus"? It is even claimed that Argentina was the cradle of the world, and the pampa the platform where human migrations took shape and started their journeys.

Another thesis—that of Arius Montana, author of the *Bible Polyglotte*—maintains that the Jews discovered and colonized the New World. The sons of Jactan, great-grandson of Shem, himself son of Noah, may have been the first to people America. Was the Jew the first conquistador of the New World? Why not? Proof and even circumstantial evidence are certainly missing, but who can hope to pierce the mists of the earliest ages? This first American is something we can only guess at.

Should we abandon the idea that he might have been indigenous, and agree that he might have been an immigrant? This is still a controversial question that no one can settle with certainty. But an Asiatic origin is evident throughout the Americas. Are not these faces with prominent cheekbones and narrow, slanting eyes the same that we find in Cambodia and Tibet? Bolivian masks and Chinese masks, Annamese counting strings and Inca quipus, and that musky odor of the women of Ceylon and also of the Indian women, which the Conquistadors found so diverting. Similar analogies, equally striking, are found in customs and architecture. The powerful heads carved in the rocks of Yucatán are replicas of those on the temple façades of Angkor. What is the mysterious kinship that unites the Mayas and the Khmers? Pharoahs and Incas, royal bandeaus and pschents, the pyramid of Memphis and the Mexican teocalli, Thebes "of a hundred gates" and Cuzco—the relationships are evident. Is it not enough to recall that Ra, the Egyptian god, and Inti, the Inca god, carved on the portals of Luxor and in the Peruvian sanctuaries respectively, are one and the same—the Sun?

If the first Americans came from Asia, we must try to imagine how and by what route, which involves another look at the map. The northeastern point of Asia and the northwestern point of North America seem so close that one can easily imagine a time when they were joined. About 60 miles wide and not very deep, the Bering Strait, which today separates Siberia from Alaska, must at one time —in the ice ages—have formed the natural bridge that the Asiatic hordes used in their penetration of the American continent. It would have taken only a few hours' march. South of the strait, the Aleutian archipelago likewise forms a bridge between Asia and America. Having crossed by one of these bridges, the migrants very probably turned their steps eastward, came upon the Great Lakes, followed the great arteries of the Mississippi or the St. Lawrence rivers, and according to whether they followed the western coast or the eastern routes, reached the Isthmus of Panama or the West Indies.

Having arrived in Central America, the nomads from the Bering Strait encountered other columns of migrants who had originated in Australia and crossed by way of the Polynesian islands. This flood of wanderers then spread in successive waves over the immense space of South America, turning back upon itself a hundred times and seeming to move by preference toward the regions of the high plateaus.

A few rare but daring migrants came to America by the sea route. From Australia, Japan, and Melanesia, primitive navigators, borne along by favorable currents and guided by sea birds, were able to beach their rafts on the Pacific coast of South America: an astonishing combination of luck and courage, winds and currents. Between Africa and the South American coast, maritime connections—if there were any—were ephemeral, provided we ignore the myth of Atlantis and the Island of the Gods that made a bridge between North Africa and America and from which the great legendary invasions might have taken off. When Montezuma told the Aztec people of the distant memories of his ancestors, who came from the east, the north, and the northeast, he mentioned their arrival "from cold and icy regions, over a dreary and cloudy sea." On what facts did this tradition rest, and what sea could it have been but the Atlantic Ocean?

To sum up, in the present state of knowledge it is agreed that the American population was formed of four great streams of migration. The first—after the Ice Age—came from Asia by way of the Bering Strait. The second came from Australia by the sea route. The third, composed principally of Polynesian elements, started out from Oceania across the Pacific islands. Finally, the fourth, of more recent origin, was that of the Eskimos, who spread through the polar regions of America and Eurasia.

In any case, whatever may have been the routes by which American territory was entered, imagination falters before the cheerless march—almost a hunger march—of men dressed in the skins of beasts, over enormous stretches of land, much of it icy, from the Bering Strait to the Strait of Magellan—almost from one pole to the other. Or, even more, the journey made by canoe from one island to another, to be destroyed by storms on unknown shores.

So these men who had come from other parts were Asiatics mixed with Malayo-Polynesians. They knew nothing of the plow or of cereals and had no domestic animals; they followed neither an agricultural nor a pastoral life. Hunting and fishing were their only activities: they killed in order to eat—a fact that explains their nomadism. Gold, for these starving creatures, consisted of the great lakes with their miraculous fish, and the North American plains teeming with game. The hour of the glittering metal had not yet sounded, for the conquerors of the Stone Age coveted only raw meat and fresh blood. They were cold. They were hungry. They wanted sunshine and food.

The peopling of America, which probably began about the time of the Ice Age, continued during the Paleolithic period, then the Neolithic, and expanded as the circumstances of the primitive tribes improved. It is possible to conceive this peopling as a very slow but continuous penetration, by sea and by land, along the coasts. It took thousands of years for these human herds, wandering along the rivers and straying in the alternately icy and torrid labyrinths of America, to coordinate their movements. Nevertheless, this thin trickle of humanity already constituted the conquest of the soil. Such was the basis, the substratum, on which the pre-Columbian civilizations were built.

A Spreading Patch of Oil

Christopher Columbus had discovered a world. Amerigo Vespucci had given it a name. Henceforth, Haiti and Cuba, the great West Indian islands, were to be the platforms from which the Conquistadors took off. For it was no longer a question of linking Spain to the Antilles, and the adventure was no longer confined to the Dark Sea. It had its point of departure not in Andalusian ports but at Santo Domingo, the future capital of the Dominican Republic on the island of Hispaniola. The question now arose of pushing the discovery farther forward, from and beyond the West Indies. In this way Santo Domingo became the bridgehead of the conquest. Progress had indeed been great.

Like a spreading patch of oil, the Spanish penetration of America was about to spread toward the center, north, and south. Happy indeed were the young men who, at the dawn of the sixteenth century, were about to open up the greatest field of activity of all time! They were numerous, even legion, those who burned to follow in the tracks of their predecessors. For many the opportunity to quench this thirst for adventure never came. The majority only repeated the exploits that others had carried out. But some, the best, daringly prolonged the furrow cut in the ocean by the *Santa María*. These were the Conquistadors.

The best? Certainly not in the sense of goodness! In that respect they showed themselves the worst. Their excellence was in their toughness: whatever their social origins, whether they were hidalgos, former soldiers from the Italian wars, onetime convicts, or poets in search of strong emotions, they had to adapt themselves to the special conditions imposed by nature and men. Muscles of iron, stomachs that knew nothing of nausea and defied famine, backs that were able to bear armor under the tropical sun, a skin resistant to Caribbean arrows and the bite of giant ants: these were the physical qualities required. Such a hardening of the body necessarily involved a hardening of the heart. The souls of the Conquistadors were tempered like their swords. No weakness; no pity. To be hard or to die, to resist or to succumb: these were the alternatives for those who advanced the conquest.

From Yucatán to Darién

A new period of fifteen years began with 1506, the year of Columbus's death, and extended to 1521, the year in which Hernán Cortés took possession of Mexico. Between these two superb personalities, the Descubridor and the Conquistador, armed figures stole in. During these fifteen years the Conquistadors fumbled, for it was a period of trial and improvisation. But what a bloody apprenticeship it was! Among this pitiless troop certain names stand out: old acquaintances such as Alonso de Ojeda, Juan de la Cosa, Ponce de León, Vicente Yáñez Pinzón; then the younger men: Diego de Nicuesa, Diego Velásquez, and Francisco Pizarro. We shall see them again later, bound up with the destiny of Cortés or, like Pizarro, founding an empire. For the moment they plunged head on toward an objective still obscured by hoary legend.

Here are a few of the stages of the discovery during the first quarter of the sixteenth century.

While Vicente Yáñez Pinzón was making a landing on the Yucatán peninsula, Alonso de Ojeda and Diego de Nicuesa got together to reconnoiter and exploit the Caribbean coasts. Ojeda himself took over the administration of the territory extending from the Cape de la Vela to the Gulf of Urabá, at the inner end of the Gulf of Darién between Colombia and Panama—in other words, the face that Colombia turns to the Caribbean Sea; while Nicuesa took—"on paper"—the coast from Urabá to Cape Gracias a Dios, at the frontier of Nicaragua and Honduras. The eastern arm of this gigantic V was already named New Andalusia, and the western arm was called Golden Castile.

Provided with royal prerogatives, Ojeda and Nicuesa left Santo Domingo for their colony. Juan de la Cosa and Francisco Pizarro accompanied Ojeda. Among his crew, Nicuesa had a young Estremaduran of whom he had great hopes: Núñez de Balboa. Pizarro and Balboa! Soon the pupils would outstrip their masters. The two governors steered, each on his own, toward what they thought to be fortune. They met with misfortune. It was all very fine to have a sovereign's support and to trace on parchment the boundaries of a concession. The mark of a scribe's pen and the *puño y letra* of the King of Spain as yet had no legal value in the Caribbean lands, as Ojeda and Nicuesa learned to their sorrow.

Ojeda's expedition landed near Cartagena in Colombia, which was the home of the Caribs. Renowned for their cruelty, the Caribs terrorized the people of Central America and the West Indies. Ojeda's Spaniards knew no fear. They plunged into the bush in search of these Caribs, whom they wished to enslave. But they had not gone far when a cloud of poisoned arrows fell upon them and annihilated half the group. Ojeda escaped death, but Juan de la Cosa, tied to a tree and shot through with arrows, succumbed to his wounds. The veteran of the Conquistadors, the companion of Christopher Columbus and pilot of the *Santa María* was no more than a bloated corpse —one might even say a porcupine, for his body bristled with so many arrows. Ojeda and his men re-embarked precipitately. On the way back they encountered Nicuesa's expedition, joined up with it, and successfully carried out several raids on coastal villages. Then Ojeda and Nicuesa split up. While Nicuesa made for Veragua, Ojeda settled down for a time on the shore of the Gulf of Urabá, where he founded the colony of San Sebastián. Exhausted by his wounds, Ojeda handed over his command to Pizarro and returned to Santo Domingo, where he died in poverty and oblivion.

When Ojeda failed to return, Pizarro decided to leave San Sebastián. He ran into Fernández de Enciso's expedition and turned back toward Darién. Both Pizarro's and Enciso's troops landed west of the Gulf of Darién and there established themselves. The name Santa María la Antigua was given to this temporary camp, but what would Nicuesa say, since this was in his fief? Never mind! He had doubtless perished over there in the north.

Nicuesa was not dead. At Panama he had founded Nombre de Dios, the future Colón. After innumerable misadventures—hunger had forced his men to devour the half-rotted corpses of Indians— Nicuesa steered for Darién. He reached Santa María la Antigua and landed there and found compatriots at last. But for him they were worse than the Caribs. Although he had legal jurisdiction over the colony, he was driven from it. He and his men were loaded into a

worm-eaten ship that was taking water at all seams, and sent off to
Spain, if they could get there. These unfortunate men did not reach
even Hispaniola; they foundered off the coast. All this had been
maneuvered by one man—Balboa; he had rid himself of Nicuesa, and
some weeks earlier, in the same way, he had ousted Enciso. Now he
was governor.

Ponce de León, another of Columbus's comrades, turned his eyes
toward Borinquen, now Puerto Rico. He obtained the governorship
of the island and there founded the colony of Caparra. His object?
To find gold. There was plenty, but not enough for his taste. Would
there ever be a Conquistador who found enough of this yellow
metal? Would the royal power ever be moved by the excesses of
Ponce de León and his harsh treatment of the natives? He received
the order to leave Borinquen and explore a mysterious country
northwest of the Antilles, which was known as the island of Bimini.
Ponce de León set out. He left Hispaniola to the west, went straight
to the archipelago of the Bahamas, passed them by, and came upon
a flowering coast. This was Florida, and it well deserved its name.
For hundreds of miles it was, one might say, a scented replica
of an Andalusian *huerta*. But in this bright-colored picture there
was a shadow: coral abounded but gold was rare, and the Indians,
as ferocious as the Caribs, handled their bows with accuracy. Ponce
de León prudently withdrew from those enchanted shores, though
he was to return later as governor, at the head of a larger expedition.
Then he was stronger than the Indians, but the latter harassed him
and his men; an arrow in the heart ended the career of Ponce de
León, Conquistador of Borinquen and discoverer of Florida.

Diego Velásquez was governor of Cuba. Some bold gentlemen
assisted him in his task: Hernández de Córdoba, Juan de Grijalva,
Pánfilo de Narváez, Pedro de Alvarado. . . . These names were soon
to shine in the Mexican firmament. Velásquez had chosen a young
student from Salamanca as secretary: Hernán Cortés. He located his
capital at Santiago on the southeast coast of Cuba, 1250 miles from
Yucatán.

Velásquez' first concern was to bring the territorial discovery
of Cuba to an end. He made a circuit of the island and plunged into
the interior. His lieutenant, Pánfilo de Narváez, laid the first stones
of the port of San Cristóbal de la Habana—Havana. Cuba became an

excellent starting base and tended to supplant Haiti. One important event was to increase the importance of Cuba, which was in fact to become the natural relay point between the Old World and the New.

One morning in February an expedition led by Hernández de Córdoba set out westward from the Cuban coast. Nine days later it was within sight of a peninsula: Yucatán. Men were running about the beach: not naked and of barbarous appearance like the Caribs, but of noble bearing and wearing cotton garments with grace. From afar the Spaniards could distinguish monuments, temples, and palaces artistically built in stone—a strange kind of stone of an ocher coloring almost like the skin of these Indians. And above all, there were cultivated fields. The expedition rounded Cape Catoche, tried to land at Champoton, where it was turned back by a rain of arrows, and returned to Cuba. These people were doubtless very civilized but not very sociable—of which fact Córdoba was aware, since he came back with a dozen wounds in his body.

Córdoba reported to the governor. Intoxicated with pride, Velásquez was convinced of the proximity in the west of that famous empire that had escaped the clutches of the Conquistadors for twenty years. What a fine gift for Charles on his accession! In fact, at the same time that Córdoba discovered Yucatán, Charles of Ghent, a young and swaggering prince, landed at Villaviciosa to take possession of his Spanish kingdom. These two roads that opened simultaneously, one to Valladolid, capital of the Catholic kings, and the other to Mexico, seat of the legendary emperor, were a marvelous augury for the Flemish heir. He had not yet assumed the crown when he lost sight of the boundary of that empire on which the sun was never to set.

Some months after Córdoba's return to Cuba, a larger fleet set out for Yucatán. Velásquez had entrusted its command to his nephew, Juan de Grijalva. Pedro de Alvarado and the pilot Alaminos were in the expedition, as well as Bernal Díaz del Castillo, Cortés' future historiographer.

After touching the island of Cozumel—the Island of Swallows—Grijalva's ships sailed to the point of the Yucatán peninsula, rounded it, and ran northwest along the coast of the Gulf of Mexico: Campeche, Tabasco, Tampico. They hazarded a landing. With their first step on the North American continent, the Spaniards' surprise increased. The houses were white, with shutters of bright colors, as in Andalusia. There were colossal statues representing princes or gods, strange signs carved in the stone, and well-marked roads. Was this China? The inhabitants became more friendly and tried to engage the visitors in elementary conversation. In their ears and at their ankles and wrists they wore golden jewelry. So there was gold in these regions! To the Spaniards' questions the natives answered with one word: "Mexico!" and pointed in a westerly direction. Was this the name of the country or that of its ruler? For it seemed that a powerful emperor reigned not far away. Grijalva could scarcely restrain his joy. The abundance of gold, the grave majesty of the stone monuments, the nearby king—so many signs of the proximity of the fabulous lands promised by Christopher Columbus. This Moctezuma or Montezuma, whose name recurred frequently on the lips of the inhabitants, though with trembling voices, could only be the Great Khan. They were on his territory; the goal was near. The Spaniards from Cuba were soon to grasp and then destroy the precious chimera they had coveted so long. But now a shadow passed over this intoxicating prospect. In the outskirts of Tabasco clots of blood were drying upon the monstrous idols, while heads grimaced from the ends of planted pikes. To what barbaric cult did the subjects of the Great Khan make sacrifice? The Spaniards would have to return with priests and convert these heathens: the Cross and the Sword, as at Granada. Long live the new *reconquista!*

Preceded by Alvarado, Grijalva sailed for Cuba. He reported his mission to Velásquez. The news was exciting; it crossed the sea and reached the court. Presents of gold attested the reality of the discovery. So colonial affairs were perhaps going to be profitable! Velásquez was given a mandate to prepare a third expedition, and he got busy again. Who should command this enterprise, from which Velásquez expected glory and profit? Córdoba? Grijalva? Cortés, as Velásquez' secretary, was present at these discussions.

Balboa, Conquistador of the Southern Sea

Vasco Núñez de Balboa was born at Jerez de los Caballeros. It was a curious city, perched upon a rock and overlooked by the somber rampart of the Sierra Morena. Although in Estremadura, it was very close to Andalusia. Midway between Badajoz and Huelva, Balboa's homeland was at the crossroads of two provinces as different from each other as are the dun color of the Sierra de Guadalupe and the flamboyant mother-of-pearl of the *marismas* (swamps) bordering the Guadalquivir. The sea was very close, with Sanlúcar de Barrameda, Huelva, and Palos, and the route to the islands.

This landscape of contrast shaped the man, who was at once Estremaduran and Andalusian. To Estremadura Balboa owed his enduring toughness and his passion for work; while to Andalusia he owed his pride. How very early in his life did the child Vasco learn to know the smell of salt and blood! The wind that passed along the Guadiana and beat against the Saracen walls of Jerez de los Caballeros came from the open sea. Balboa was not more than sixteen when Columbus raised anchor at Palos for his first voyage, and Palos was scarcely a day's journey by mule from Jerez. The young man's ears buzzed with sailors' songs and the irresistible song of the Dark Sea, too. He left for the New World when he was twenty-six.

Balboa embarked for Hispaniola in the entourage of Bastidas and Juan de la Cosa. For the moment, exploration interested him less than business, so he became a planter at Santo Domingo, and soon went bankrupt. Pursued by his creditors, he hid in an empty cask, but the barrel was rolled aboard one of Enciso's ships and the fleet made off southward. Once at sea, Balboa leaped from the cask, presented himself to Enciso, threw himself at his feet and embraced his knees. Would Enciso be good enough to accept him as a common sailor? Enciso was moved; but he had reason to rue it, for the man in the cask later rid himself of Enciso and also of the unfortunate Nicuesa. He then reigned at Santa María la Antigua while he awaited a greater kingdom. What kingdom it would be he did not know, but he believed in his star.

It was a cacique, Panciaca, who gave direction to Balboa's career. Surprised to see the Spaniards fighting for gold, the Indian indicated that he knew the country where it was to be found. They had only to march westward for six days and they would come upon the gold fields. An extraordinarily rich people lived in those lands, where everything was to be found in profusion. Ships faster and bigger than the Spanish caravels plowed the sea. Balboa cocked an ear. The sea? So there was an ocean on the other side of the New World? The tale was worth verifying. They must go and see. Balboa was all the more eager to set out since news from Spain was bad: he was out of favor because of his treatment of Nicuesa and Enciso. The former had perished at sea, but the other had survived. Enciso, the lawyer, was doubtless of tougher stuff, and his hatred for Balboa had loosened his already rather glib tongue when he made his report to Ferdinand. Balboa's departure in 1513 for the unknown sea resembled a flight.

The expedition had only modest means at its disposal. A single ship, nine pirogues, scarcely two hundred Spaniards, a few native porters, and a pack of racing greyhounds—*galgos corredores*. It was a sortie rather than an expedition. Balboa dropped anchor, without knowing it, at the spot where the Isthmus of Panama is narrowest— in the neighborhood of Acla—and landed there with his men. One party remained on the beach to look after the little fleet; the other plunged into the bush after Balboa.

The bush? It was a sort of hell. Imagine these men from Castile and Estremadura, helmeted and armored as on a Spanish battlefield, hacking a passage with saber blows through the dense Panamanian forest! For the first time, men were forcing a way through this jungle of trees so densely packed and lianas so tangled that it was like a fortress that had to be demolished wall by wall. It was dark there, even at full noon. Balboa's companions felt the humid breath of the virgin tropical forest weigh heavily upon them, sticking to their skins, beating against their faces. The damp heat streamed over everything.

To cover a hundred miles took this heroic band twenty days. Snake and insect bites—there were spiders as large as tortoises, and serpents indistinguishable from the roots—Indian ambushes, and the polluted water of the swamps destroyed half the members of the expedition, but those who survived the atrocious journey were well repaid for their pains.

On the morning of the twentieth day the detachment reached the foot of a hill. A cool breath suddenly stirred amid the suffocating odors of the jungle. Balboa inhaled deeply at this smell of seaweed and salt. He seized his sword and, slowly and alone, climbed the

slope of the hill. When he was at the summit, his companions saw
him kneel and raise his arms to heaven. Then they joined him. At
the foot of the further slope, something immensely blue mirrored
the blaze of the tropic sun: it was the sea.

Like Christopher Columbus at San Salvador, Balboa broke into
the *Te Deum* and had the record of the discovery drawn up by a
notary in his company in order to legalize its spiritual and material
conquest. Then he had the deed countersigned by the Spaniards who
were present, amongst them Pizarro. The initials of the King of
Spain were cut into the bark of some trees as a sign of possession;
then there was only one more thing to do before descending toward
the unknown sea—plant a great wooden cross on the mountain.

Three days later the expedition trod the shore of the new ocean.
Alone and the first, as at the summit of the hill, Balboa went to
touch the shining water. At low tide he strode forward toward the
sea. His armor, his helmet, and his naked sword flashed in the sunlight. He held aloft the banner of Castile and Aragon. He entered
the sea until it was halfway up his body and took possession, in the
name of Ferdinand and Isabella, sovereigns of Castile, León, and
Aragon, of this southern ocean with all its ports, islands, and coasts.
And he took care to specify possession "royal, corporeal, present,
and eternal."

As reward for this mad escapade, Balboa received the title of
Adelantado of the Southern Sea. How otherwise could they name
this ocean of water so still that it was later named the Pacific?

Now Balboa could savor the intoxicating taste of triumph. It was
to be of short duration. Like the mouthful of water he drank on the
shore of the Southern Sea, that seemed so fresh at first, he had
to spit out again this draught of glory, for it proved as bitter as death.

While Balboa was bravely cutting a path across the Isthmus of
Panama, tongues were busy at Valladolid. Enciso had sworn to hang
the insolent Balboa. In order to achieve this end, he laid siege to
Bishop Fonseca, whose influence remained great in all things concerning the Indies. Enciso had no trouble in instigating the appointment of a governor to replace Nicuesa in the territories of Golden
Castile or Panama. This was Pedro Arias de Avila, familiarly called
Pedrarias Dávila. Was it not proper to take from Balboa what he
had acquired without permission and by force? So Pedrarias Dávila,

governor of Panama, and Enciso, bearing the title of *Alguazil Mayor*, sailed for the Gulf of Darién, the former to take up his post and the other to do justice and take vengeance on the man who had driven him away.

When Pedrarias and Enciso landed at Acla, Balboa had returned from his expedition to the Southern Sea. He apprised his judges of the astonishing news. Before the King's envoys he laid all arrogance aside and declared himself submissive to His Majesty's orders. The embarrassment of Pedrarias and Enciso was extreme. Balboa's humility and his modest bearing disarmed them; having come to punish him, they were obliged to compliment the rebel. A few weeks later, Balboa's confirmation in the dignities of Adelantado of the Southern Sea and Governor of Panama arrived from Spain. What was there to do but submit to the situation? Pedrarias pretended to applaud Balboa's success. He did better: he gave him his daughter in marriage by proxy, she being in Spain.

The Adelantado was mad with pride. He crossed the Isthmus of Panama once again, with even wider ambitions. Hundreds of Indians accompanied him, carrying on their backs the dismantled parts of four vessels. Having reached the Pacific shore, he had the parts reassembled, launched them upon the sea, and steered south. What was his goal? The lands of gold reported by Panciaca. But he was unable to pass beyond the Bay of San Miguel and the Pearl Islands. He turned back, dropped anchor, recrossed the Isthmus of Panama, and returned to Acla. He had scarcely arrived there when he was called into conference. He hastened to the rendezvous. He went toward his father-in-law Pedrarias with hands outstretched, but Pedrarias remained impassive. A man approached Balboa at the head of an armed troop: this was Pizarro, his comrade of the struggle. Pizarro gave a sign. The Adelantado was seized, laden with chains, and dragged before an improvised tribunal and condemned to death. On what pretext? Treason and seditious intrigue. He had succeeded. He had to die.

At the setting of the sun, the same day, on the square at Acla, the head of Vasco Núñez de Balboa rolled in the ocher dust of Golden Castile. Arrested by his dearest friend, condemned by his father-in-law, executed by his own soldiers, this was almost a normal end for a Conquistador.

These stars that blazed for a moment and then suddenly were extinguished; these kinglets of a day, encamped upon the edge of a gulf, believing themselves masters of the world while waiting for another to throw them into the sea; this comradeship "through life and death" that could be changed into mortal enmity by nothing whatsoever: such was the story of the conquest.

CHAPTER 6

A Young Man of Good Family Tries His Luck

EACH step forward by the Conquistadors—stumbling and hazardous though it might be—brought them nearer to an objective of which they knew nothing. Without awareness, they were closing in on that gigantic reality that was still but a great empty space on the maps of the world: America. Like blind men they moved ahead, always westward. All they knew was that they were moving forward, that the road was rough, but that fortune lay at its end. Would there never be an end to this disconcerting voyage? Was this conquered lagoon the end of a world or only its beginning?

Yet although there was no plan to this exploration, it organized itself naturally. Chance has its methods. Individual effort, even when it seems to end in failure, is not lost. It gives rise to another, which yet another prolongs and completes. The movements of the Conquistadors, though apparently haphazard, were part of a kind of logic that went beyond them. It can be said that this still-shapeless Spanish Empire was the fruit of an anonymous improvisation. Brave leaders and calculating princes fixed its shifting outlines.

Where were the Spaniards when Hernán Cortés, still a simple lieutenant under the orders of Velásquez, was meditating his vast plans?

The West Indies were settled. Haiti and Cuba were occupied and firmly held. All the other islands of the archipelago had been recon-

noitered. Darién and the Colombian and Venezuelan coasts were
becoming peopled. Panama was the point from which tracks were
opening up: southward toward Peru, northward toward Costa Rica,
Nicaragua, and Honduras. The Caribbean Sea had thrown off its
exciting mystery. The Gulf of Mexico was ajar. Indeed, Córdoba's
and Grijalva's men had skirted Yucatán from east to west without
really knowing if it was an island or a continent, while Ponce de
León had reached Florida. No one yet had guessed at the colossal
wall that ran from Hudson Bay to Tierra del Fuego, but it was now
known that the lands discovered by Columbus were not Asia and
that it was necessary to cross them from one side to another—provided no one discovered a strait!—to reach the Southern Sea and,
on the far side of another ocean, China and Japan. The myth of
Cipango faded away. The golden chimera was no more; in its place
was the golden reality.

Nevertheless, although Columbus's successors had diverted it both
northward and southward, the westward direction laid down by
the Genoese was still that of the conquistadors. Obedient to the
westward attraction, the conquest's center of gravity slid from Cuba
and Haiti toward Yucatán and Panama. Later it would be at Lima
and Mexico. Meanwhile, Charles I of Spain had become Emperor
Charles V, and in the homeland the center of gravity moved from
Madrid to Vienna. On both sides of the Dark Sea, in the east and in
the west, the colossal domains of the Fleming were expanding. Every
passing month added a link to the chain that stretched from foggy
Pomerania to the burning shores of the Pacific. The Hapsburg was
not twenty when he could reckon upon a kingdom whose frontiers
surpassed imagination.

In the same year that Cortés freed himself from the tutelage
of Diego Velásquez, Fernando de Magalhães—Magellan—a Portuguese gentleman, embarked at Sanlúcar de Barrameda for the first
voyage around the world. He too was seeking the route to the Indies,
but by the southward route. Charles was his patron. Bishop Fonseca had given him his benediction. It was a lucky voyager who
could presume upon imperial support and the Church's recommenda-
tion. In brief, Magellan simply resumed Columbus's old dream: to
reach eastern Asia by the westward route. At the head of a fleet of five
vessels, he steered for the Canaries, rounded the Cape Verde Islands,

and crossed the Atlantic at the level of Sierra Leone. He touched the Brazilian coast at Pernambuco and dropped anchor at Rio de Janeiro. After a brief halt, Magellan continued his voyage: the Río de la Plata, the *Mar Dulce*, then Patagonia. After several months in the Bay of San Julián (icy lands had succeeded the exuberance of the tropics), the expedition steered toward the extreme south. This wintering almost jeopardized everything. Isolated in a snowy land-scape, where the giant forms of Patagonians could occasionally be seen, Magellan's men attempted a mutiny. Action saved them from despair. At the cost of incalculable suffering, and after passing through fearful tempests, the *Exploradores* reached the Cabo de las Vírgenes. They rounded it, entered an arm of the sea, and came out into the Pacific.* This was the Strait of Magellan. The Portuguese was not content with this victory, however exciting it might be. He crossed the Southern Sea, reached the Philippines, and settled down there for some time. He made an attempt at diplomacy, offered an alliance to the king of the island of Zebu, and found death on its shores while fighting his rival. This was an irremediable catastrophe. However, Magellan's chief lieutenant, Sebastián del Cano, took to sea again with the only two vessels remaining of the original five. Two years after its departure from Sanlúcar, the expedition reached the Moluccas. The Indies at last! The meeting of Spain and Asia by the western route had been realized. Almanzor, Sultan of Tidore, welcomed the survivors of the fleet ceremoniously. Then came the return journey: Timor, the Cape of Good Hope, the Cape Verde Islands. A single vessel came back to the port of Sanlúcar in 1522 after sailing for three years and making the circuit of the world. Sebastián del Cano could well inscribe on his coat of arms, encircling a globe, *Primus circumdedisti me*.

For the time being, Magellan ranked as the one who had closed the circle. His contract with the king was not as advantageous as that of Columbus, for the lesson of Santa Fe had not been forgotten. But the Portuguese knew where he was going. He was certain of the existence of a strait crossing the New World and leading into the Southern Sea. He was certain that the circuit of the world could

---

* Magellan named this sea *El Mar Pacífico* because he first saw it in fair weather and calm conditions, in great contrast to the storms experienced previously.

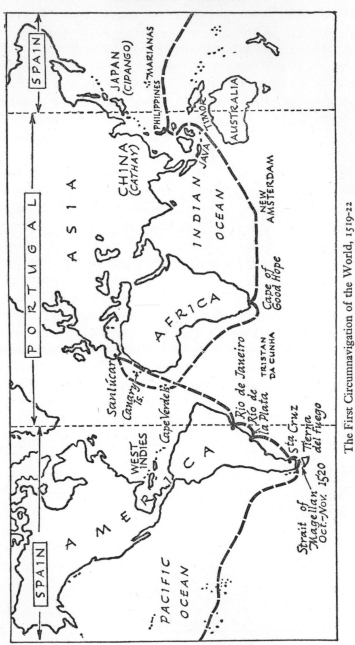

The First Circumnavigation of the World, 1519-22

be carried out. He was certain of returning to Spain with the holds of his vessels filled with gold and spices and with treaties of alliance in his doublet. But he succumbed at the age of fifty years to the assagais of the Philippinos, and another was to bring his plans to realization. One action gives rise to another. The history of the conquest is that of a succession of conquests, each of which was made possible only by its predecessor. Magellan was dependent upon Balboa, as Balboa was upon Columbus. And in the end, was it not Columbus who owed nothing to anyone?

Magellan's departure for his voyage around the world, the election of Charles of Spain to the empire, the flight of Cortés toward Mexico, all took place in the year 1519. It was indeed a year resplendent with promise.

A Lawyer from Salamanca Exchanges the Pen for the Sword

Who at Medellín, a small town in Estremadura between Mérida and Guadalupe, would have imagined the prodigious career of Hernán Cortés when he was born there? No one thought of the New World yet. The year 1485 was marked by the death of Abdul Hassan, Sultan of Granada, which for the Spaniards meant the intensification and perhaps the victorious conclusion of the reconquest. The people of Córdoba spoke of a Genoese who had visited the Catholic monarchs and who had undertaken to reach the Indies by the western route but had been turned away. The thoughts and hopes of the people were all centered on Granada.

Cortés was of good family. His parents belonged to the lesser nobility of Estremadura. They set great store by their coat of arms, but less by their fortune, for these gentlemen were poor. Martín Cortés de Monroy, infantry captain, had acquired more wounds than gold in the service of the Crown. Ought we to add that before becoming a loyal subject of Queen Isabella, Martín Cortés had borne arms against her at the time when the sovereign was bringing the provincial aristocracy to heel? A youthful transgression that Isabella had pardoned long before.

Hernán lived his early years in a sunburned landscape, treeless and almost unpeopled, between the quivering azure of the sky and

the naked earth. He was watched over—for he was the only son—by
a proud mother (she had been born Pizarro Altamirano) and by a
father from the lesser nobility, but *viejo cristiano* and of honorable
lineage. Like Don Quixote, Martín occupied his leisure in reading
the books of chivalry and in hunting. His habits were no better than
those of the hero of La Mancha. He placed great hope in his son,
whom he intended for a soldier's career, although the boy was rather
puny. But could there be any other profession for the son of a
hidalgo?

At fourteen Hernán Cortés was sent to the University of Salamanca. There he showed himself an uneven and temperamental
pupil, gifted in letters, refractory at mathematics: in fact, a dilet-
tante. Did he make the grade as bachelor of law? History does not
say, just as it is silent about how he employed his time between his
return to Medellín and his departure for the New World. Nevertheless, one can guess that the Salamancan student would have found
ways to enjoy himself when he was suddenly freed from the family
circle and its constraints. Courting the *doncellas*, frequenting the
taverns with his comrades, playing the guitar under the lattices of
an emblazoned palace—what rapture for this young man whom his
father could still beat for a *pecadillo!* For the old captain had a
heavy hand with the whip, when Hernán was guilty of some lack of
morale, honor, or faith. But to such discipline the student submitted
like a child. To accept the parental whip was an honor for the son
of a gentleman.

When Cortés reached the age of eighteen, the French and Spanish
were fighting in Apulia for the possession of the Kingdom of Naples.
Two illustrious adversaries faced each other: Gonzalo de Córdoba,
the "Great Captain," and Bayard, "*le Chevalier sans peur et sans
reproche.*" Rather than a war, it was a succession of duels in which
the Frenchmen and the Spaniards alternately covered themselves
with courtly glory. Gonzalo's lancers cavalcaded before the walls
of Barletta as if at a tourney, with a sort of heroic gallantry. Blood
ran, but it did so with elegance. Under the plumed helms, the same
gentlemanly smile lit those noble faces. Was not Hernán's place at
these chivalrous jousts? His father thought so. Nevertheless, despite
earnest requests, he could not persuade his son to set out for Italy.
Not that the young man was reluctant to fight; rather he was ab-

sorbed with more urgent cares—love, certainly, but especially with a frantic desire to cross the sea. In the year that he should have devoted to the profession of arms, he was entirely occupied with roaming the ports from Seville to Cádiz.

The monotonous and harsh horizon of Estremadura, the rigid education of his early years, his sojourn at Salamanca, the smell of powder that came from the Italian battlefields, and his truancy along the Andalusian coast had given young Cortés a taste for freedom, for war, and for letters. Moreover, he was ready for big things. One day, at Medellín, he disclosed his plans to his parents, asked their benediction, and fled. The next day he embarked at Sanlúcar de Barrameda on a merchant ship bound for Santo Domingo. He was nineteen years old. The adventure had begun.

Among the Gerfalcons

The first stage was Santo Domingo, capital of Haiti, capital also of the Spanish Empire in gestation. Since its discovery by Columbus, Santo Domingo had taken on the appearance of a city: stone houses had been built, a church had been erected, and the semblance of a port had been organized. These were rudimentary constructions, but they were enough to dazzle, perhaps to delude, young Cortés, who had thought to find there only jungles and Indians.

Ovando was governor of Haiti. His jurisdiction extended to Cuba, the neighboring island, and even farther still to the vague outlines of a world that had scarcely emerged from legend: the Indies. Little was known about this world: men were ignorant of its dimensions or structure; Cuba passed for the continent, and the Venezuela coast for an island. At the time when Cortés landed at Santo Domingo, Columbus had just left it after his brief visit to Ovando. While the Genoese completed his fourth and last voyage, Cortés began his own. The youth and the old man crossed paths without knowing it. Thus it was throughout the period of discovery: there would always be someone to carry on the torch. But the young were ungrateful to the old or failed to value them.

Cortés began his career of Conquistador as a public scrivener. "Intellectuals" were rare in the Spanish ranks, but they were needed for administrative details. Resigned to anything, once he was on the spot, Cortés was busy with paper work while waiting to polish his sword. But the opportunity soon came to show what he was made of. Diego Columbus, son and heir of the Discoverer, had just succeeded Ovando as governor and Viceroy of the Indies. He decided to pursue the conquest methodically, and especially to complete the exploration of Cuba. It was time to know if it was an island or a prolongation of the continent. Diego entrusted the command of the expedition to Velásquez. Three hundred men in all, among whom Pánfilo de Narváez and Bartolomé de Las Casas, the future "Apostle of the Indies," stand out. Cortés was one of this band.

Diego Velásquez was first and foremost a pleasant gentleman, liking to joke with his men while maintaining his authority over them. He was liked and feared simultaneously. Pánfilo de Narváez little resembled his captain: he was a great, strapping redhaired fellow, combative and always ready to return blow for blow. He had common sense but no political mind. His conversation was lively and his manners courtly; he was not the stuff of which a leader is made, though he loyally carried out the duties of a second-in-command. As for Bartolomé de Las Casas, who had been established in Haiti for several years, where he administered the lands of his father Francisco, a former comrade of Columbus, he participated in the Cuban campaign as an observer. He burned with Christian ardor and dreamed only of the conversion of the Indians. He proclaimed himself their protector at the very conclusion of the Cuban expedition, which Velásquez carried out with implacable cruelty.

Cuba was reconnoitered, explored, and conquered. Velásquez was its governor. He had appointed Cortés his secretary and treasurer. The young man received at the same time an allotment of slaves and a concession of land. So there he was, at twenty-six, a planter, a royal official, and the governor's favorite. Any man other than Cortés would have been satisfied with this enviable situation. But he had not come to the New World to graduate in administration, any more than to take up agriculture. His spirit and mind were with the Conquistadors—Córdoba, Grijalva, Narváez, and Alvarado—who, luckier than himself, had visited Yucatán and the coast of the Gulf of Mexico. But why had Cortés been absent from these expeditions?

It would seem that no thing or person would have prevented him from joining the men who had pushed as far as Campeche and

Tabasco. They were his comrades and the same age as himself. There
could therefore be no question of precedence or seniority. The truth
is that Cortés was holding himself in reserve. Just as at Medellín he
had put off from day to day the date of his departure for Italy, so
at Santiago de Cuba he willingly allowed the time to pass. He was
awaiting his moment. His companions were at the gates of the forbidden kingdom. They were paving the way for him. He would
enter the scene at a moment of his own choosing. What good would
there be in exhausting himself with the preliminaries of an enterprise
that he would take over when the time was ripe?

While keeping an eye on what was happening in the west, Cortés
was busy. His plantations prospered and he put money aside. To
dispel his boredom, he launched out on an amorous intrigue. The
story should be told, for it is not unconnected with the tension that
was already evident between Cortés and Velásquez. The play began
as a comedy in the classic Spanish style. An expatriate from Granada,
named Juárez, was living in Cuba with his four sisters, who were
poor, beautiful, and virtuous. Handsome Cortés declared his passion
to one of them, Catalina, and she gladly allowed herself to be convinced. But once victory had been achieved, Cortés was slow to
consecrate it officially. The brother became indignant and frightened.
He sought out the Governor. Was not a gentleman's promise of
marriage sacred? Velásquez took the victim's part with such energy
that he himself began to pay court to another of the sisters, a situation that made him feel even more deeply the affront to Catalina.
But there was more to come. Besides the outraged brother's story,
another reached him which was even more serious for Cortés. The
Governor's favorite, his own secretary, was conspiring against him:
Cortés aimed at nothing less than overthrowing the Governor and
usurping his place. Rebel and perjurer, he deserved the gallows.
He was punished with a spell in prison; he escaped, was retaken,
escaped again, and—height of audacity— sought refuge in the very
house of the injured brother. The adventure ended as in the theater:
Cortés maried Catalina, and Velásquez pardoned him. But though the
brother's honor was saved, the blow to Velásquez had struck home;
he now knew that Cortés was not reliable and that he would betray
him again at the first opportunity. Thus, beneath the lively appearance of a comedy of manners that might have been penned by Lope

de Rueda, another drama continued: that of an underground war between Velásquez and Cortés, which would be settled only by the death of one of them; a drama of hate and jealousy, the echo of which was to reach the very throne of Charles. The conquest of Mexico would be poisoned by it.

Velásquez and Cortés to all appearances had made their peace. It was then that the Governor, encouraged by the results of Grijalva's and Córdoba's expeditions, decided to arm a large fleet, with strong royal support. This time the objective was not limited to simple exploration. Velásquez' ambition was to found, in the mysterious western lands, settlements that would be responsible to his authority. Who would lead this expedition? Candidates were not lacking: they surrounded the Governor as a pack surrounds a stag. To everyone's surprise, perhaps even to his own surprise, Cortés was appointed. It was indeed a surprising decision, in view of Cortés' indiscretions. Barring an imperceptible afterthought, it seems that, having silenced his justifiable ill feeling, Velásquez thought only of the success of the enterprise. To choose Cortés was proof of intelligence and a fine forgiveness of injury.

Thus the hour had sounded for the son of Captain Cortés de Monroy. He was at the full strength of his years—thirty-four; he had had time to learn to know men, to exercise his physical courage in the struggles in Cuba, and to perfect his natural aptitude for the art of governing. He had taught himself in Velásquez' antechamber. Finally, his popularity among the Spanish sailors and soldiers was great. There was not one among them whose name and secrets Cortés did not know. Almost every man had some sin upon his conscience, sometimes murder. Some had had altercations with the Santa Hermandad, the police of Ferdinand and Isabella, or—more serious still—with the Holy Office, and had had to flee to the islands. They no longer had much to lose, but everything to gain, including honor. Cortés closed his eyes to the past. From his companions he required only their obedience and never-failing bravery.

In order to succeed, what does a captain general require? A disciplined troop and a general staff. His mission was religious and military, since it was a question of conquering and converting. As lieutenants, Cortés chose Pedro de Alvarado, a magnificent fellow with a golden beard, Cristóbal de Olid, Gonzalo de Sandoval, Juan

Velásquez de León, kinsman of the Governor, Alonso Hernández de Puertocarrero, Juan de Escalante, Montejo, Diego de Ordaz, Francisco de Morla—all gentlemen and all veterans of the conquest. Father Bartolomé de Olmedo was entrusted with the spiritual affairs of the expedition. He was simultaneously the military chaplain and the moral adviser. Finally, Bernal Díaz del Castillo was chronicler. In actual fact, they were not all at Santiago de Cuba: a large number were at Trinidad or Havana. But Cortés would assemble his men in good time. Only one of the brilliant Conquistadors had not been sought out: Pánfilo de Narváez, the Governor's favorite.

A Departure That Resembled a Flight

At Santiago de Cuba the excitement was great. Crowded upon the quay, the Indians and Spaniards lost no detail of Cortés' preparations. Cuban women adorned with flowers, monks telling their beads, and rich planters with heavy earrings packed close together in a roar of voices and a blaze of color. Cortés had had no trouble in recruiting the three hundred men he needed, for he enjoyed great prestige among the population. Moreover, he was alcalde of Santiago. The provisions were more difficult to assemble, for he had to provide on a large scale, since only God knew how long the expedition would last. Officially, Cortés had received authority to set up strong points on the Mexican coast, to establish colonies there, and to pick up those companions of Grijalva and Nicuesa—if they were still alive—who had disappeared during earlier voyages. But the Conquistador knew perfectly well that he would go beyond his mission. He meant to penetrate to the heart of the unknown empire, not as Velásquez' vassal but as master.

Cortés' six vessels rode upon the waters of the port. From the mast of the largest a flag of black velvet embroidered in gold floated in the wind. A red cross encircled by blue and white flames stood out upon it. This was the banner of the new Captain General, and it bore this device: "Brothers and comrades, let us follow the Cross, and if we have true faith in this symbol, we will conquer." *In hoc signo vinces!* The same words shone on the imperial standard of Constantine. Thus Cortés thought to emphasize the evangelical character of his enterprise. But he had not failed to have the arms of Castile

Cortés' Approach to the Aztec Empire

embroidered upon his standard, too. Was he not also, by proxy, the representative of the King of Spain? But the idea that Cortés was sent by God and also by the future Charles V was not pleasing to Velásquez, and he began to regret his choice. Cortés' annexation of the Church and the Crown to his own profit, and the ostentation of his preparations, revived unhappy memories in the Governor's mind. Had his secretary not already betrayed him twice? Cortés meanwhile realized his impudence. He hurried his men and quickened the operations of embarcation. The important thing was to depart before Velásquez changed his mind.

Just as Cortés was about to raise anchor one day in November 1518, he received an order from the Governor enjoining him to delay his departure. What should he do? Lie and use trickery. The Captain General pretended to submit to the wishes of Velásquez, assured him of his entire devotion, and protested his loyalty. Thus he gained a few hours; that same night he slipped his moorings and in the deep silence of the tropical sea, fled. For it was indeed a fugitive—soon a rebel—who, at the head of his six ships, looked that evening upon Santiago de Cuba as it was being swallowed rapidly by the darkness.

So Cortés was beyond the reach of Velásquez. But his precipitate departure had not left him time to complete his preparations in per-

sonnel and material. He put into Trinidad. There he found Alvarado,
Velásquez de León, Cristóbal de Olid, and Hernández de Puertocarrero. He enrolled them. Then he took to sea again and sailed for
Havana. It was in this town, situated at the western point of Cuba,
that Cortés put the finishing touches to his enterprise: he completed
his recruitment, gave special attention to his artillery, and stuffed
the holds of his ships with provisions. Meanwhile, Velásquez had
sent letter after letter to the officers of Trinidad and Havana, ordering them to arrest Cortés, but they turned a deaf ear. Better still,
some of them joined the rebel and embarked under his banner. Cortés,
following a wise policy, declined to make an open break with
Velásquez. When Father de Olmedo reported to him the Governor's
doings, the Captain General pretended surprise. The whole affair
rested on a misunderstanding, but what this misunderstanding was he
did not make clear. He wrote Velásquez a moving letter in which he
reiterated his loyalty. Thus he hoped to safeguard his rear. Cortés'
facility with his pen and his skill in the turning of a phrase were of
great service to his career.

Early in the month of February 1519 everything was ready. The
army comprised 11 ships, 580 soldiers and captains, 100 sailors, 16
horses, 10 cannons, 4 falconers, 13 arquebuses, and 32 crossbowmen.
During his brief stay at Havana, Cortés had made new recruits. The
majority of Grijalva's former companions had enrolled under his
standard. Furthermore, Alvarado and Sandoval were with him, as
well as Bernal Díaz del Castillo—still in his twenties—and Alaminos.
The latter, an experienced pilot, had guided Columbus on his fourth
voyage and knew the Gulf of Mexico. He took over the helm of the
flagship. Thus Cortés had carried off the best technicians and fighters
the islands possessed. He had provided for everything, even a musi-
cian, Ortiz, and even women for domestic duties. He had not forgotten the interpreter, Melchor, nor the astrologer, Botello. There
was no more to do but get under way. This time the squadron that
drew away from Havana to the acclamations of a great crowd had all
the appearance of a conquering fleet. The real voyage was beginning.

The first stage was to the island of Cozumel, off the Yucatán coast.
Its scenery was known to some but not to Cortés. The Spaniards
dropped anchor and went ashore. Alvarado, always ready to do
battle, started to plunder among the islanders and hold them for

ransom, but Cortés curbed his lieutenant's enthusiasm: it was not his intention to conquer in this fashion. Through Melchor, he exchanged words with the natives. Conversations ensued and exchanges were effected. Cortés looked closely at the stone temples, the columns of which were sometimes ornamented with crosses. Were these the vestiges of some distant Christian influence? He was tempted to think so until the occasion when he was present at the celebration of the cult. A priest dressed in a black cotton robe, his hair braided and hanging down over his shoulders, gesticulated before a silent assembly of the faithful. He pointed out for their adoration the ponderous idols carved in granite and smeared with blood—human blood, the interpreter made clear. These were rites that little resembled the Catholic religion.

Cortés then broke into his first political discourse; if the people wished to remain his friends, he said, these stone monsters must be cast down at once. The Indians, dumb with dismay, did not know what to think of such a surprising speech. Could there be other gods, better than theirs? They trembled with horror at seeing the white soldiers pull down the sacred statues, wash the blood-smeared walls and altar with water, and chase away the shaggy-haired priests with the flats of their swords. Cortés had a statue of the Virgin and the Infant Jesus set up in place of the idols; the touching symbol of maternity was substituted for the dismal faces of the cruel gods. Father de Olmedo celebrated Mass at the purified altar, and through the interpreter Melchor he preached to the heathens. Because of his eloquence, perhaps, or the passivity of the Indians, the latter seemed easy to convince. Many accepted baptism. It should be mentioned that those who were unwilling were considered by the Spaniards as unruly and paid dearly for their obstinacy.

A surprise awaited Cortés during his stay at Cozumel. An Indian came before him, threw himself at his feet, and bathed them with tears. This Indian was wholly Castilian; eight years previously he had been one of Nicuesa's expedition and, captured by the natives, had become a cacique's slave—a bitter fate for a deacon of the Roman Church, for Jerónimo de Aguilar had taken minor orders. The Captain General rejoiced at this encounter: here was the interpreter he needed to make himself understood by the rulers of this land. Melchor, an Indian prisoner taken to Spain and converted to the

Christian faith, was good enough for jabbering with the people; but Aguilar would be simultaneously an interpreter and a diplomat. Cortés did not suspect that he would be even better: an interpreter and an ambassador.

The second stage took them to Tabasco. Cortés sent Aguilar to the local caciques to give them his message of peace, which was at the same time a declaration of annexation. Cortés' argument was clear: God had given Saint Peter the care of all men, whether princes or beggars; Peter's successor was the Pope, and the Pope had given the islands and continents of the ocean to the king of Spain. Was it not just—indeed, legal—that the Indians should submit without resistance to the laws of Cortés, the delegate of Charles of Spain? The people of Tabasco did not understand a word of this specious language. What had they to do with this distant prince and his exacting grand priest? They understood nothing of the Spaniard's discourse but its implied threat; it was clear that if they rejected Cortés' proposition, the yoke would be placed on them by force. The Indians were brave. They accepted the struggle.

The battle was fierce. In a cloud of reddish dust, Indians and Spaniards confronted one another furiously. On one side were javelins, arrows, and obsidian swords; on the other, steel sabers, lances, and, especially, cannons. For a long while the struggle was equal. On their side, the Indians had numbers and the ferocious combativeness of primitive people. The Spaniards had military science and gunpowder. Nevertheless, it was feared that the Indians might prevail, for Cortés' men weakened and gave ground. Suddenly, furious neighings drowned the uproar of arms: from the swamps of Tabasco surged the plumed heads of the Spanish horses. From what supernatural world had these fantastic beasts emerged, spitting fire from their nostrils and with sparks flying from their feet? The Indians had never seen such monsters. They fled in disorder, pursued by the "great stags," deafened by the artillery, and harassed by the Spanish outriders.

Cortés' cannons and horses had done more than any harangue to demonstrate the power of Spain to the natives. The caciques of Tabasco could do nothing but submit. They assured the Captain General of their loyalty. To seal the alliance they loaded him with presents: cotton garments, provisions, gold dust, four diadems, jewels in the shapes of lizards and dogs, earrings, and a thousand precious things. Further, the caciques offered the victor twenty women, chosen from the most beautiful in the land. One of the latter stood out clearly from the rest by her distinction and grace. Her story was a moving one. She came from the great tribe of Aztecs in the north; her father had been a great lord, but he died while still young, and his widow, who soon remarried, had sold the girl to slave traders, who in their turn had passed her over to a cacique of Tabasco. Her princely bearing, her clear complexion, and her doelike eyes made an impression on Cortés. Was he going to make the beautiful captive his own? Not yet. The hour of love had not yet sounded for this Conquistador. Other cares pressed upon him; another ambition burned him. He dreamed of a fabulous prize, not one of flesh but of metal. Would he yield to impulses of the heart when an irresistible impetus was bearing him toward an unimaginable empire? Eager as he was for glory, even more than for embraces, nothing would turn the captain from his plan. For the time being he was content to distribute the Indian women among his officers, after having them baptized by Father de Olmedo. He allotted the cacique's daughter to Puertocarrero, his friend and confidant, but in his innermost heart he well knew that when the time came he would make her his favorite.

His companions suspected this and already treated her with great respect. Had she not the air of a lady? So, quite naturally, she was given the title of Doña and was known as Doña Marina until the day when the Indians changed her name to Malintzin, a word formed from "Marina" and the suffix *tzin*, signifying nobility. Counselor and interpreter to Cortés, it was to her that the natives addressed themselves in matters great or small. Friend of the humble and spokesman for the red-skinned princes, she protected the unfortunate and was confessor to the war chiefs. People became so used to treating with Cortés through Malintzin that they ended by giving her name to the Spanish captain, too, so that to the Indians Cortés became Malintzin or Malinche. By her tact, by her political intelligence, by her skillful and generous attitude toward natives and Spaniards, and by her beneficent role as mediator, Marina well deserved these honors. To see herself given by Cortés' companions—none of whom, not even himself, had the right to be called "Don"—the title of Doña, which is hereditarily reserved for Spanish nobility; and by a roundabout and unforeseen way to give her own Hispano-Indian name to the son of Captain Martín Cortés de Monroy—this was distinction indeed for the one who, though of noble blood, had been the slave of a cacique not long before.

To the Frontiers of the Aztec Empire

Although bloody, the fight at Tabasco had been only a skirmish. So Cortés thought, now that he had emerged from it with honor. Nevertheless, it had given him the opportunity to try the opposing defenses and to prove his own strength. Thanks be to God, he felt himself strong. The adventure was beginning well.

Setting out from Tabasco, the eleven ships ran along the continent in a northerly direction. They were close enough to the land to distinguish the golden shore backing onto the forest, and above the forest the snowy peaks cutting the intense blue of the sky. The Captain General's enthusiasm had infected the crews. Everyone, sailors and gentlemen, as they breathed the air of the Gulf of Mexico, inhaled also the mysterious odors of the Promised Land. Discipline, inflexible on land, was relaxed at sea. Could it be otherwise in the narrow caravels where officers and men, captive Indians and beasts, were jammed together? Doña Marina was in the flagship. Puertocarrero kept close to her. But the languorous eyes of the beautiful Aztec never left the face of Cortés.

On Maundy Thursday of the year 1519, two months after its departure from Havana, the Spanish fleet dropped anchor at San Juan de Ulúa. Hardly were these operations completed when several boats from the shore approached the flagship, which was recognizable by its pennon. When they had come alongside, their occupants—fine-looking Indians adorned with feathers—sought information from Cortés, through Doña Marina, about his intentions. Reassured by the Captain General's friendly words, the Indians returned to the shore. The next day, Good Friday, the Spaniards landed.

A silent crowd watched the foreigners install themselves. The firing of the cannons astonished the natives, but not so much as did the hobbling of the horses, for none had ever seen these prancing creatures before. Cortés' first concern was to have an altar erected, and Father de Olmedo straightway celebrated Mass. Was this not the anniversary of the death of Christ? The Indians, amazed but respectful, did not miss a gesture of this strange ceremony.

On Easter Saturday, an envoy of the local governor, Cuitlalpitoc, came for news. What did the white men want? Nothing but to pay a visit to a powerful neighbor, said Cortés. The following day, the governor himself, Tendile, presented himself to the Spaniard. He was the bearer of rich presents and was attended by a large party. Cortés begged him to attend Mass. A furtive smile lit Tendile's face at the moment of Communion; obscure as the procedure of Catholic Mass might seem to him, he understood that the white men ate the flesh of their god. Here was a peculiarity he would not fail to report to his emperor.

After Mass, the Indian and Spanish chiefs feasted. Tendile and Cortés spoke of their emperors. One spoke of Charles and the other of Montezuma.

Montezuma! At last the name was spoken which until then had only been whispered. The survivors of Grijalva's expedition and the warriors of Tabasco spoke of him as an almost legendary sovereign. Tendile had just seen him; he was one of the Emperor's familiars. This time it was no longer a matter of allusion but of actuality. A strange dialogue, translated by Doña Marina, took place between the Spaniard and the Indian: of short, clipped phrases, of elementary remarks separated by long silences. Each tried to imagine the features of the unknown emperor and to assess his power. Cortés' white complexion and black beard fascinated Tendile, and several times he ventured to touch his face. Did it remind him of something, of a prophecy about a white and bearded man?

Cortés did nothing to dispel the awe he inspired in the Indian. On the contrary, he decided to give a striking demonstration of his power. The cannons were loaded and the horses saddled, and when evening came the Spanish cavalry raced at full gallop across the beach, brandishing their lances, while the artificers fired the cannons. The neighing of the horses, the roar of the guns echoing in the hills, and the shouts of the horsemen filled the native party with fright. Surely these men from the east were of divine race. They had command over thunder and animals. Meanwhile, skillful scribes were tracing these extraordinary scenes on sheets of maguey, and thanks to their rapid brushes, Montezuma learned about the invaders' bearded faces, their enormous ships surmounted by towers, the sailors in multicolored garments, and the furious charge of the Castilian *jinetes*.

Dazzled by so many wonders, but not allowing his astonishment to be too apparent, Tendile took leave of Cortés. Before his departure, the Captain General gave him for Montezuma a carved chair and a red silk cap, hoping that the former would serve as a throne and the latter as an ornament when he agreed to give Cortés an audience. He added a few glass beads from the King of Spain; paltry gifts which Tendile received with great dignity. Noticing the gilded helmet of a passing soldier, Tendile expressed the desire to take it to his master, for it was the very likeness of a helmet worn by Huitzilopochtli, the god of war. Cortés pricked up his ears at the words. The god of war; this was promising! Meanwhile, under the pretense of comparing Spanish and Mexican gold, the Captain General begged Tendile to return the helmet filled with gold dust. He would then make a gift of it to his emperor. Tendile departed.

In brief, the first interview between Cortés and the Indian ambassador had informed neither party. Each was bluffing and had tried to impose on the other. To probe the secret intentions of the eventual enemy, to touch swords: this was the game, masked by a show of deadly courtesy. But both remained imperturbable. Indian guile and Spanish *sutileza* canceled one another. Nevertheless, Tendile had difficulty in concealing his anxiety, as witness his quasi-religious reverence when he faced Cortés. Without doubt, his hesitant attitude—he seemed alternately to fear Cortés' visit to Montezuma and to desire it—reflected the uncertainty of the monarch himself. Perhaps, too, he lacked precise instructions from his master. In any case, Tendile's reticence encountered Cortés' inflexible resolution: whether the Indian emperor desired it or not, he was going to see him in his palace, armed or disarmed, according to whether he was treated as friend or enemy.

Several weeks passed. Tendile returned, together with a plenipotentiary named Quintalbor. An impressive column of nobles and slaves followed him. The nobles glittered with emblems. The slaves carried bundles and chests on their shoulders, which were striped with the marks of whips. With a smile Tendile returned Cortés' helmet; it was overflowing with pieces of gold. Then, after spreading incense at the Conquistador's feet, he had the chests opened. Under the amazed eyes of the Spaniards, the slaves spread Montezuma's presents on some mats: a golden disk as big as a cartwheel and representing the sun; a silver disk representing the moon; animals—lizards, dogs, tigers, lions—carved in solid gold; pendants, a great alligator's head, shields, arrows, fans, all of gold; and five enormous emeralds. An immense burst of enthusiasm filled the Spanish camp, but while his officers and men gaped in admiration, Cortés mentally reckoned how many gold pesos this miraculous mountain represented. The golden disk alone must surely be worth 20,000 pesos. There was enough there, and more, to cover the cost of the campaign.

While Cortés was absorbed in a dream full of calculations, Tendile drew near. Without relaxing his fixed smile, he begged Cortés to regard these gifts as a pledge of Montezuma's friendship. The Emperor asked only to maintain good relations with him. But Tendile dissuaded Cortés from undertaking the journey to the capital: there were too many difficulties on the road. Calmly, Cortés made clear that these were no obstacles for a Spanish horseman, and furthermore that he must complete the mission given him by his own emperor. He would therefore go and greet Montezuma on behalf of Charles of Spain, even though he had to move mountains. Tendile bowed. He had only passed on his master's message. He bowed lower still when Cortés, in order not to be indebted to the Indian monarch, handed his emissary a cut-crystal cup from Florence and three shirts of Holland cloth—miserable gifts that Tendile received as if they were sumptuous presents. Before this, however, Montezuma's sorcerers gave the Spaniards a performance of magic. Then Tendile departed.

Cortés was now faced with a serious problem, that of his relations with Diego Velásquez. The latter's partisans, led by Escudero and Cermeño, did not hesitate to criticize the Captain General's conduct openly. It was all very fine to promise them an empire, but in actuality they were camping empty-bellied on a torrid beach, devoured by mosquitoes. How much longer were they going to feed on hope? To appease these malcontents, Cortés sent Montejo to reconnoiter the coast in search of a healthier spot. At the same time he gave his attention to regularizing his own position with respect to the governor of Cuba, or more exactly, vis-à-vis the Spanish crown. The fact remained that since he was still subordinate to Velásquez, he should report to him. Having made a rebel of himself by his flight from Cuba, he ought to return to Santiago, humble and repentant. After honorable amends, perhaps he would be authorized by Velásquez to continue the conquest. An unthinkable situation. He intended to account only to one master: Charles. Furthermore, humility and repentance were not in his nature. For him it was therefore a question of breaking his allegiance to Velásquez forever. The difficulty was to find a legal formula. He found it.

On the advice of Montejo, who had returned from his reconnaissance, the Spaniards moved their camp farther north to a place called Quiahuitzlan. The road passed through the town of Cempoala, inhabited by the Totonacs. There the conquerors saw houses for the first time in many weeks. They ate fruits that were new to them, and found them pleasant. They gathered flowers and stretched themselves out on garden lawns. These reminders of Andalusia disturbed them.

The landscape was pleasant and so were the people. The cacique of Cempoala could not do enough to make himself agreeable to the strangers. Why such a reception? Cortés was not long in finding out. As it happened, Aztec officers had arrived at Cempoala at the same time as the Spaniards. They had come to collect ritual taxes, in the name of Montezuma. The Totonac chief seized the opportunity to complain bitterly to Cortés of the exactions made by the Emperor. Never had there been such an insatiable despot! If only he were content with ordinary tribute! But he also required blood to appease his gods. Periodically, Montezuma's tax-gatherers carried out raids on Cempoala's population, choosing the most beautiful young men to be butchered on the sacrificial stone. Horrified, Cortés suggested capturing the Aztec officers by way of reprisal, which the Totonacs did at once, trembling with joy. But the very night after their arrest, Cortés secretly freed the prisoners, assuring them he had nothing to do with the affair. However, they must return to Montezuma at once and tell him of his coming visit. The Aztecs having vanished, Cortés promised the Totonacs that he would take their part against Montezuma and support their just claims with arms. He had one condition: that they abandon human sacrifices and destroy their idols. The Totonacs cried out loudly. Abandon their gods? Never! At a brief order from Cortés, fifty Spaniards sprang up the temple steps, seized the holy images, and broke them. The cries of the Totonac crowd became even more piercing, but they stopped short when Cortés observed that the fall of the idols had not involved any celestial intervention. Were these gods not therefore false? The Totonacs were convinced. They gathered together the debris of their fallen gods and cast it into the fire. This task completed, they made no difficulty about taking an oath of obedience to the King of Spain and recognizing as the only god the one whose crucified image Father de Olmedo hastened to erect in the place of the heathen statues.

While Cortés was releasing the Totonac tribes from Montezuma's authority and imposing the Christian religion upon them, he was perfecting the plan he had conceived for legalizing his position vis-à-vis the sovereign. With the aid of his friends in Cempoala, he had a town rapidly built in the plain stretching in front of Quiahuitzlan. He named it Villa Rica de la Vera Cruz, the "Rich Town of the True Cross," a resounding name that contained the promise of gold and also of the Kingdom of God. Then he appointed Puertocarrero and Montejo alcaldes of the new town. To them he added regidores, alguazils, and a municipal council. He forgot nothing, not even the gallows. He called a solemn meeting of the municipal council, had himself summoned there by the assembly, and presented the council with the powers he held from Diego Velásquez. After gravely examining these powers, the council declared that they were not valid. Consequently, Cortés' functions were brought to an end, and there was nothing for him to do but tender his resignation. But at the same time that Cortés solemnly renounced his responsibility and the municipal council took cognizance of the fact, the council appointed him Captain General and Supreme Judge of the new colony—*Capitán General y Justicia Mayor*—in the name of His Spanish Majesty. The trick had been played. The colonists had founded a town under royal jurisdiction and had freely given themselves a leader by universal suffrage. What could be more regular? Henceforth, Cortés was no longer a rebel captain but a citizen of Villa Rica de la Vera Cruz, "elected" by his comrades to administrative and military command. The most punctilious of lawyers would find nothing there to take exception to. Cortés had had himself appointed by plebiscite. Have not the conquering generals of every epoch acted thus in order to succeed legitimately to civil power?

Freed from his Cuban obligations, Cortés felt relieved. He now had the power to act. His first concern was to draw up a report for the King, signed by all the soldiers and all the captains with the exception of the partisans of Velásquez, relating the most recent events, especially the foundation of Villa Rica de la Vera Cruz and his nomination as Captain General. His Majesty was begged to ratify this nomination. The report accompanied a considerable treasure—material evidence of the conquest—to which everyone had added his own part of the booty. Puertocarrero and Montejo, the most faithful of all, were appointed to take the missive and the treasure to the sovereign. They embarked at San Juan de Ulúa, after Cortés had enjoined them to skirt the Cuban coast as widely as possible.

Cortés was in a hurry to start out for Montezuma's residence. But he wanted to be sure of his rear. His election and his message to the King of Spain conspicuously weakened the danger personified by Velásquez, but they did not eliminate it entirely. The "Velásquists" were still numerous in the colony of Vera Cruz. Some of them even fostered the plan of capturing several vessels and returning in them to Cuba. It was necessary to nip the revolt in the bud, so Cortés did not hesitate. He had all the ships, with one exception, dismantled and sent to the bottom, so that contact with Cuba and Spain was broken. There was no longer the possibility of retreat for anyone. Cortés reserved the sole remaining ship for those who grumbled: the poltroons. The Captain General's biting words had their effect, for no one wanted to be taken for a coward. The Conquistador did not rest at that, for a rebellion is not liquidated without making examples. Cortés had a gallows erected on the main square of the new town: Escudero and Cermeño were hanged there. A pilot named Umbria, regarded as less guilty, was cruelly flogged and had his feet cut off. There was no more opposition.

Cortés readily alternated between violence and affection, and now that he had sunk the fleet and annihilated his adversaries, he could afford the luxury of eloquence. On the eve of the campaign, the hour had come to "inflate" his soldiers. Facing his troop, assembled on the main square of Cempoala, Cortés delivered a passionate harangue. Those who were to remain at Villa Rica—a hundred soldiers and sailors—he enjoined to be patient, to watch the coast, and to complete the construction of the church and fortress. To those who were going with him, he emphasized the difficulties they would have to overcome, but at the end of the road they would find fortune and glory. Montezuma's presents were only crumbs from the feast of gold that awaited them. "To Mexico!" he cried in a vibrant voice. "To Mexico!" the Conquistadors repeated. Cortés gave the order to depart.

Just as the expedition was about to start, Cortés received a messenger from Juan de Escalante advising him that suspicious ships were cruising along the coast and making signals. Entrusting his army to Alvarado and Sandoval, the Captain General went by horseback to Villa Rica. Three ships were in fact riding offshore. Four men had landed from them and were looking for Cortés; they had been sent by Alonso Pinedo, captain of the flotilla, to inform Cortés that possession of the whole of this territory had been taken in the name of Francisco de Garay, governor of Jamaica. Cortés found this embassy amusing, so he made prisoners of Garay's four emissaries, collected three sailors who had escaped from the ships, and departed with them for Cempoala. Pinedo understood that he was up against someone stronger than himself, so he rasied anchor for Jamaica. As for Cortés, he had acquired seven more soldiers; with light heart he rejoined his troop and, leaving Cempoala—this time, for good—set out on the road to Mexico.

Cortés had left Havana on February 15, 1519. He left Cempoala for Mexico on August 16 of the same year—six months exactly. What was the reckoning for this half year? He had freed himself from the tutelage of Velásquez. In taking the part of the Totonacs against the Aztecs, he had acquired allies, unknown to Montezuma. Four hundred warriors from Cempoala, fifty of whom were nobles, swelled his rear guard. At the same time he had assumed the guise of defender of the oppressed. By breaking the idols, he had affirmed his mission as propagator of the Faith. Thus he was beginning to take on the character long meditated at Medellín and Cuba. He had now to complete it.

So here he was, setting out for the unknown. Of the empire he coveted he knew almost nothing, either of its dimensions or men. He knew that numerous peoples inhabited it, forming a vast confederation. But what did he know of the cruel emperor who reigned at Mexico, except that his very name made the bravest soldiers tremble and stammer with terror? Was this at last the fabulous Great Khan of whom the whole world spoke but none had ever seen?

Cortés was uncertain of his route. But he was sure that no Conquistador had preceded him in penetrating so far into the western lands.

On this last point Cortés was mistaken. He was not the first Conquistador at all.

CHAPTER 7

The Red Conquistadors

THE pre-Columbian civilizations came into being and developed in the southwest of North America, in Central America, and in the northwest part of South America on its Pacific side. In the main, they were to be found in Mexico and Peru: the Aztecs in central Mexico; the Mayas in southern Mexico, in the Yucatán peninsula, and as far as Guatemala; and the Incas in Peru and Bolivia. But beyond Peru, the farther south we go, the rarer the traces of civilization become, and it is no longer possible to speak of peoples but only of tribes: primitive peoples roughly gathered into clans, who, when their territory no longer offered them the resources necessary to their existence, moved elsewhere.

Contrary to the general belief concerning the influences of climate on human activity, the great pre-Columbian civilizations—with the exception of that of the Mayas—flourished in the arid lands around the equator, and not in the temperate regions. But this was characteristic, too, of certain other nations, the mothers of humanity—Egypt and Persia, for example—that labored on a sterile soil and carved from the hard rock the works of art and science that we still revere. These were unprofitable lands for the laborer, but they were productive for the genius.

So it was in the heart of the American continent, on a Mexico-Lima axis, that the dawn of this civilization arose, as well as that of the conquest. It was there, in fact, in the same places, that the

Spanish Conquistadors first set foot, though preceded by several centuries by the Indian conquistadors. Men always fight on the same battlefields.

America at the beginning of our era is veiled by a mist, through which straying peoples can be distinguished dimly. Like columns of ants, they come and go, zigzagging. To feed themselves, to defend themselves against enemies, to fish, hunt, make slings and weapons, shields of bark, boats of stretched skin, to weave sisal, fire pottery, and draw some sort of music from the conch or the panpipes—such were the concerns of the earliest Indians. But about the sixth century A.D. the fog dispersed.

The Toltec Master Builders

Led by an astrologer-priest, the Toltec tribe broke into the valley of Mexico in the eighth century. They came from California, and it was like Moses leading the Hebrews into the Promised Land. The Toltecs founded the city of Tollan and elected a king—undoubtedly the first in America. In Mexican annals they are known as the "master builders," and Teotihuacán was their masterpiece, a city consecrated to the gods. It was also the political capital of the Toltec empire, but the rulers counted less than the gods, to whom majestic monuments were dedicated. The Pyramids of the Sun and the Moon, two hundred feet high, dominated a forest of columns and temples, proclaiming the glory of the sun god and the moon goddess. Three hundred years later a mysterious personage appeared, named Quetzalcoatl, "the plumed serpent," at once hero and sage. He preached to the multitudes, was a healer, and taught ethics and science. He was extolled and men prostrated themselves at his passing. Then, in course of time, men wearied of the too austere messiah, so he withdrew into the desert and foretold the end of the world. Some time after his death he became the God of Knowledge, the object of worship, and at Teotihuacán the Toltecs built him a temple decorated with immense plumed serpents with polished obsidian eyes. It would be interesting to know the language this Indian spoke, this sage and worker of miracles, who was finally deified and knew both the adoration and persecution of man, as well as posthumous glory. Yet nothing but images of stone remains of his gospel or teaching.

While the Toltecs were climbing the steps of the sacred pyramids and somewhere in Yucatán a group of scholars was inventing a calendar, Charlemagne was crowned emperor on the other side of the Atlantic.

Almost at the same time a great danger threatened the Toltec empire. Decimated by epidemics, softened by too easy living, and divided by religious and political quarrels, it was ripe for invasion, which came from the north. The powerful army of the Chichimecs poured over the valley of Mexico. The Toltecs were forced to flee, abandoning Tollan and Teotihuacán, the American Byzantium. It was then that the first conquistador intervened.

A Toltec dynasty had reigned at Tollan, but a power more absolute than the king's was exercised by the high priest, the religious leader and earthly representative of Quetzalcoatl, the man-become-god. As was customary in the ritual ceremonial, he himself bore the name of the god. In the midst of the general disorder, Quetzalcoatl alone remained calm. He gathered together the Toltec people and led them to the borders of Yucatán. On his way, he encountered the Tzentals, fought and mastered them, and then, to make certain of victory, married his officers and soldiers to Tzental women. Thus the Tzentals were absorbed by the Toltecs. Quetzalcoatl, having become the master of a great tribe, then decided to found great cities. The Toltecs were builders, and several cities soon rose from the earth. As at Tollan, the temples were even more numerous than the palaces. In fact, Quetzalcoatl did not forget that he was also the religious leader and representative of the only true god, whose name he bore. On the conquered country he imposed the doctrine and liturgy of the god with the feathered head. He created a church and instituted a clergy, for already the military-political conquest and the spiritual conquest were closely allied. The conqueror brought his altars along with his arms, for now he was to gather souls.

Thus, having started out from the valley of Mexico, the Toltecs now occupied the region between the Tehuantepec isthmus and the city of Tabasco at the base of the Yucatán peninsula. But this empire did not satisfy the ambitions of Quetzalcoatl, and the Toltec conquistador turned his eyes northward. He knew that Yucatán was in the hands of the powerful Mayas. There were no better soldiers than the Mayas. However, travelers and merchants had brought Quetzalcoatl some singular and, on the whole, encouraging news. The great Maya families—the Itzas, Quichés, Tzutuhiles—were no longer on good terms with one another. Some were even emigrating toward Guatemala and Honduras. Quetzalcoatl acted quickly: the opportunity was unexpected, and he seized it. He organized his army. He armed a war fleet, which cruised along the coast. Then at the right moment he marched upon Champoton, the first Itza town.

Surprised by the mass arrival of the Toltec army, the Itzas offered only feeble resistance. Quetzalcoatl burned the town and continued on his way. Advancing along the Gulf of Mexico, he captured in turn Campeche, Tihoo, and Chichén Itzá. Running parallel to the Toltec army, the fleet mastered the shores of the Yucatán peninsula, and only the island of Cozumel escaped invasion. While Quetzalcoatl was organizing the conquered territory, the Tzutuhiles regrouped in the center of Yucatán. They even built a town, Uxmal, on the borders of the new Toltec state, which retaliated by founding a holy city, Mayapán, near where Mérida stands today. Quetzalcoatl was about to install his gods in suitable dwellings, for he was the messiah of the new religion, the spiritual descendant and disciple of the Plumed Serpent—*quetzali*, precious plume; *coatl*, serpent. Temples were raised that foreshadowed the Aztec teocallis,* access being by steps cut in the stone. Blood was soon streaming over the altars, sealing the alliance of the Tollan god and the Itza deities. Quetzalcoatl, a politically prudent man, had chosen peace. Henceforth, the new federated empire had three capitals: Mayapán, Uxmal, and Chichén Itzá. Three kings exercised power, each in his own realm, but they consulted one another in the political, administrative, and religious matters that interested the peninsula as a whole. The unity of Yucatán was realized.

Quetzalcoatl looked with satisfaction upon his work. He had given peace to this vast land, which until then had been torn by

---

* Teocallis—the Mexican temples—were solid masses of earth, cased in brick or stone, in general aspect like the Egyptian pyramids. In area they were often more than 100 feet square, and were of even greater height. They were ascended by a series of galleries on the outside, or even directly up one side, to the sanctuaries of the gods and to the sacrificial stone on the flat summit.

hatred. Gathered together under the three-headed scepter of the triarchy, welded by marriages and associated by the same rites, the Toltec, Tzental, Itza, Quiché, and Tzutuhil tribes now formed a single community: the Yucatec people. Then Quetzalcoatl took a last glance at the fine thing he had built up: temples for the gods, palaces for the princes, seminaries for the clerks, barracks for the soldiers, hospitals for the sick, laws for all. The Plumed Serpent had labored well! He could retire, and he did. Followed by a few faithful disciples, he crossed the frontiers of the empire he had created. He reversed the route that had been marked by his victories. He progressed southward and took possession of Guatemala. Here his track is lost, but no one imagined that he could be dead, for had he not promised to return one day by the eastern sea, together with white and bearded men, in the fulfillment of time?

While a Toltec hero was shaping an empire, Europe was giving painful birth to the year 1000. She was besieged by barbarians. The Carolingians collapsed. The cruel Magyars, the Normans, and the Saracens paused for breath before flinging themselves again upon their bleeding prey. Olaf the Viking was devastating the plains of France. Al-Mansur the Moor was pillaging and destroying Santiago de Compostela. Pressed on all sides, morally sick with the virus engendered by despair and hunger, ceaselessly at war, and bleeding from a thousand wounds, Europe showed all the signs of approaching death. Nevertheless, she lived.

The Aztec Dictatorship: From the Plumed Serpent to the Teocallis

What was happening, meanwhile, in the valley of Mexico? Columns of immigrants, still arriving from the north, had submerged the Chichimec people. A new dynasty reigned at Tollan: that of the Culhuas. Later they were to found their own capital: Culhuacán or Coyoacán, south of Mexico. Overlooking the lagoons, the temple of the Hill of the Star remained for several centuries the most important religious institution in the valley. The rite of "the New Fire" was celebrated there until the arrival of the Spanish conquerors.

On the other side of the lagoon of Mexico, on its eastern shore,

facing Culhuacán, a rival town grew up: Texcoco. It became the
seat of a wide empire whose frontiers reached to the coast at Vera
Cruz.

The history of the valley of Mexico from the year 1000 to the
Aztec monarchy was that of a bloody quarrel between tribes. It
was also that of intrepid and unscrupulous chiefs who knew how to
assemble troops, equip them, inspire them, and lead them into battle
—and to victory.

Shut up within the narrow confines of the town of Azcapotzalco,
the Tepanec people were hungry. Tezocomoc, a chief, appeared.
He pointed out the route to be followed, and it led to Culhuacán.
The capital of the Culhuas was sacked by the Tepanecs. They continued their raid, and the power of Texcoco was then broken.
Tezocomoc had conquered the whole northern part of the valley.
His son, Maxtla, succeeded him, but the son was not his father's
equal. Although he tried by alternate intrigue and oppression to
assure his power over the Culhuas and Texcocos, they concluded
a secret alliance to which other oppressed communities were admitted, especially the Tenochcas or Aztecs. Maxtla succumbed to
his adversaries and was put to death. His capital was burned. As to
the Tepanecs who had escaped the massacre, they were forcibly
incorporated into the allied tribes.

Who were these Aztecs whose heroism had turned the scale in
favor of the coalition of the Culhuas and Texcocos? They had once
lived in the distant land of Aztlan, north of Mexico. They were of
the Nahua race. Their god, Huitzilopochtli, the Sorcerer-Hummingbird, ordered them to set out on the conquest of the world.
They did so. As they began their march, Saint Bernard was preaching
the Second Crusade in France. For a long time the Aztecs wandered
in the valley of Mexico. Established on Mount Chapultepec, they
could believe themselves masters of the majestic valley and its five
lakes as wide as the sea and even more blue. They gave it the name
Anáhuac, "neighbor of the water." But they fell to the power of the
Culhuas and their king Coxcox. A brilliant military success at the
side of the Culhuas turned them from vassals into allies.

But the Aztec exodus had not ended. Their god Huitzilopochtli
required them to continue on their way, and, taking the form of a

hummingbird, he showed them the road. One summer morning, a century after their alliance with the Culhuas, they reached the banks of the lake of Texcoco. In the middle of the lake was an island of rocks, between which some prickly pears flourished. Before the wondering eyes of the wandering people, a royal eagle, perched on one of these, was devouring a snake. This was the sign, awaited for five hundred years, by which the Aztec god signified that they could halt, set up their tents, and build a town. They set to work at once, not fearing to undertake the enormous task of building a city in the middle of the water. Before the fourteenth century was ended, the Aztec architects and masons had completed their task. In the center of the Texcoco lagoon, connected with the shore by three causeways, a city had arisen. This was Tenochtitlán or Mexico—Mexitli's place, Mexitli being the second name of Huitzilopochtli. Tenochtitlán was the capital of Mexico, the Venice of the New World, created under the symbol of the Aztec eagle with powerful claws, like the Roman eagles.

While the Aztecs were establishing themselves at Tenochtitlán, the Texcoco kingdom, freed from the Tepanec menace, experienced an era of economic prosperity and political wisdom under the scepter of Netzahualcoyotl. Sovereign-philosopher, friend of the arts and belles-lettres, the king of Texcoco instituted councils and promulgated a civil code. He organized labor and gave a strong impulse to agriculture. Himself a poet, he sang of the beauties of life: "Gather the fairest flowers from your garden to crown your brow. Seize present joys, before they perish." He was also a moralist: "All earthly things have an end. In the course of their vanity and their splendor they lose their strength and sink into the dust." But more surprising and braver still was his act of faith: "Those idols of stone and wood can neither hear nor feel; much less could they have created the heavens, the earth, and man, master of all things. The heavens and the earth must be the work of an unknown and all-powerful god and in him alone I must seek consolation and aid." To this unknown god, whom Netzahualcoyotl called "the Most High," he dedicated a pyramidal temple. No blood sacrifice soiled its altars, before which there was only one offering: the scented smoke of ambered resin burning in the censers.

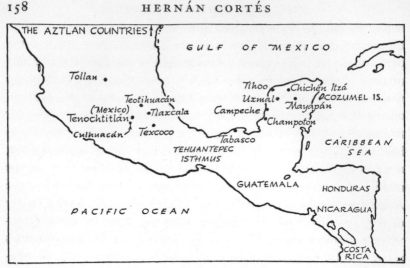

The Aztec Empire

This enlightened king—lawmaker, mystic, builder, and poet—died after a reign of forty years, just as the Hundred Years' War was ending in Europe.

The accession of his son, Netzahualpilli, although he inherited his father's qualities, initiated an era of disorder and difficulty. At first allied to the Aztecs, he became progressively their vassal. His premature death and the bloody quarrels between the candidates to the succession ended in the ruin of Netzahualcoyotl's work. The kingdom of Texcoco fell under Aztec rule. But the philosopher-prince had foreseen this decadence when he said: "When you no longer hold the scepter in your hands, your servants will wander desolated in your palace court, your sons and the sons of your nobles will drink the cup of sadness to its dregs. And all the splendor of your victories will live only in their memory."

The valley of Mexico gradually became a vast confederation. Dynasties were founded by violence or as a result of alliances. But supremacy belonged to the Aztlan people, and became assured during the reign of Itzcoatl. Based upon three principal towns—Tenochtitlán, Texcoco, and Tlacopán—the Aztec Empire had absorbed all the tribes of the valley. It reached from the Pacific to the Atlantic, and southward stretched as far as Nicaragua.

During the hundred years before Cortés landed at San Juan de

Ulúa the Aztecs consolidated their acquisitions and perfected a political system that was communal and dictatorial at the same time. It was a century of organization, but also of fire and blood. In fact, Itzcoatl's successor, Montezuma I Illhuicamina, "the Heavenly Archer," was not content to extend the supremacy of Tenochtitlán north and south, but propagated and glorified the rite of human sacrifice. His son, Axayacatl, accentuated the bloody character of the worship of Huitzilopochtli. It was in his reign and that of his successors that a gigantic temple was raised to the war god. On the day of its inauguration, twenty thousand captives were immolated. Twenty thousand human hearts were burned on the "stone of sacrifice." Then the king of Tenochtitlán had himself proclaimed emperor. All the tribes of Mexico had accepted the Aztec yoke, their laws and their gods. Pacification had been accomplished and unity realized.

Some years after Columbus had set foot in the West Indies, Montezuma II Xocoyotzin ascended the throne of Mexico. He was to be the last native sovereign of an empire that had been brought into being with great difficulty. Now no one dared to dispute Aztec rule. From his palace on the lake, Montezuma contemplated the work of his predecessors. It seemed to him so perfect that he thought less of enlarging than of maintaining it.

How did this enormous machine function? At the head of the state was a triarchy: the kings of Tenochtitlán, Texcoco, and Tlacopán. The first of these bore the title of emperor and took precedence over the other princes. Each king governed a tribe, divided into clans. The land belonged to the caciques. Nevertheless, every member of the clan who cultivated a field had full rights to it. A part of the land reverted by law to the state. This was crown property which was distributed by the government among those who did not possess land, on condition that they improve it; they then enjoyed its possession for life. There were no slaves in Aztec society, apart from prisoners. Nor can one say that there were "classes." Even a man of poor family could make a career insofar as his abilities permitted, either as farmer, artisan, or warrior. An hereditary monarchy by constitution, the Aztec state was socially a democracy, although choice by merit replaced the elective system. In fact, a simple peasant frequently became the chief of a clan. Worth was all that counted. A noble would say to his son: "Devote yourself to agriculture or to making feather mosaics or to some other honorable profession. Your ancestors have done the same. How otherwise could they have provided for their needs? Never has it been said that nobility alone is sufficient to support the noble man." The professions were numerous. Apart from work on the land, the Aztecs devoted themselves to metalwork, commerce, and handicrafts. In the valley of Mexico the people lived happily, provided they blindly accepted the inexorable laws of war and religion.

For the Aztec state could never have achieved its unity had it not equipped itself with a rigid ecclesiastical and military framework. Who would have dared, in the name of freedom of thought, to escape the harsh requirements of a code that was unwritten but all the more imperative? The obligation for the Aztec citizen to participate in the periodic military expeditions, and—more frightful still— the rites of appeasing the wrath of the gods by human sacrifice, was not disputed. For a man's life counted for little. Whether killed in war or immolated on the altar, he served only as a necessary instrument of the community. He knew this in advance. To him nothing seemed more natural.

The Aztec religion was a strange one. It was rich in marvelous symbolism, but practical nevertheless; it allied the highest moral values to repugnant customs. It had tutelary divinities with charming names: Our Lady of the Turquoise Robe, Feather Flower (goddess of flowers), Obsidian Butterfly, God of the House of the Dawn. It had great gods also: the Sorcerer-Hummingbird (Huitzilopochtli) and the Plumed Serpent (Quetzalcoatl), the masters of war and science, and Tlaloc, the rain god and ruler of harvests. There were religious festivals, some rustic and some sacred, but all inspired by the seasons. Ritual was simultaneously simple and barbarous, varying from greased-pole competitions to the flaying of living maidens. Nevertheless, beyond the Aztec pantheon that was peopled with sinister figures was a morality and a doctrine curiously like Christianity. "Clothe the naked and feed the hungry, for you must remember they are flesh of your flesh." So preached the vicars of the high priest. Likewise, they proclaimed the existence of purgatory, heaven, and hell, but love was missing from this implacable religion. The acts of the liturgy followed one another automatically, like the ticking of a clock. Blood never ceased to run upon the teocallis.

The sixteenth century had just begun. Montezuma reigned at Tenochtitlán, the wonderful island that rose out of the waters like a miracle of crystal. The city was still beautiful. But a shadow passed over the steel-blue lagoon. Recent years had been bad. There had been several earthquakes. Whole herds had died mysteriously. Many harvests had been lost. What did all this presage? Nothing good, if it were related to the news that was spreading in the streets of Tenochtitlán. The report was current that white men, coming in ships as big as towns, were cruising along the coast. Montezuma shrugged his shoulders; such distant threats would not prevent him from celebrating the New Fire. An Aztec cycle—fifty-two years —had just come to an end. At that time the fires were extinguished on the altars. Another cycle was about to begin, and a new flame had to replace the dead one. This ceremony of the New Fire, ten years before Córdoba's voyage to Yucatán, was to be the last great religious festival of Aztec theocracy.

Five days earlier, the inhabitants of Tenochtitlán had let their fires go out. They fasted and made lamentation. These were the five days of mourning at the end of the cycle. On the evening of the fifth day an immense crowd—the chiefs of the clans in rich cloaks, musicians beating drums, officials with feathers in their hair—moved toward the Hill of the Star. At its head was a procession of priests dressed in long black robes, their ears still dripping with blood from their mortifications. Throughout the night they stood gathered at the top of the sacred hill, scrutinizing the heavens. How slowly did the constellation that marked the end of the world and its new beginning rise into the skies! But at last the stars completed their course. This was the awaited sign. Then the priests plunged a reddened spear into the open breast of an already immolated captive. Another cycle began. The people of Tenochtitlán raised a wild shout that drowned the fanfare of conchs, the ringing of bells made of shell, and the piercing notes of the bone flutes. Every man lit his torch at the new fire and carried it around the town before going home, and the inky Mexican night was studded with a thousand shining points like dancing fireflies. On the days that followed there was singing and feasting, and the people got drunk on pulque. The Jaguar Knights and the Eagle Knights faced one another in mortal combat. Hearts were torn from other captives. The devotees tore their own flesh with obsidian knives.

Montezuma was satisfied. The festival had been fine. Perhaps all these sacrifices would efface the evil portents: two temples suddenly destroyed, the passage of a comet in full daylight, the appearance of a column of fire, the heartbroken crying of a woman, a tempest on Lake Texcoco. Perhaps, too, this blood, spilled by the bowlful, would drive the white and bearded men—long-announced by the prophets and already on the march—from their shores.

For Montezuma knew that the white men were on the march. The previous year a slave had come to Tenochtitlán from the coast. He had seen three floating towers approach the shore at Chalchiuhuecan —or rather, three mountains moving upon the sea. Neither the blood of slaughtered quails nor the learning of the augurs could give a meaning to this astonishing phenomenon. Montezuma sent his steward to the spot. Having reached the edge of the gulf, the envoy was struck with terror. These enormous monsters, moored to the shore, had vomited beings of an unknown species. With faces white as chalk, with black or red beards descending to their chests, they wore clothes of every color and aimed smoked-filled lances at the heavens. By the time the steward returned to Tenochtitlán, the fantastic visitors had departed. The three towers had vanished in the eastern seas.

Montezuma did not doubt that the mysterious men would return. So he received without surprise, though with a certain mystical terror, the news that the white captain had landed at San Juan de Ulúa. This time his throne and empire were doomed, for Quetzalcoatl had returned to his people. The Aztec had no need to consult the mirror on the head of the magic bird to explain the march of an army toward the palace of his ancestors. Quetzalcoatl must be marching at its head, and Montezuma envisioned him clearly. He was tall, of light coloring and pensive mien. He wore long hair and a patriarchal beard. His tall forehead was crowned by a tiger-skin miter adorned with feathers. At his belt hung plumage studded with golden stars. In his left hand he held a shield on which was painted the rose of the winds. His right hand tightly grasped a scepter like a staff. He marched like a somnambulist, just as, five hundred years before, he had marched toward the sea—that "sad and cloudy" sea which today had cast him back on the gray beach from which his raft, woven of serpents, had set out. The red conquistador was coming back to punish the evildoers and reconquer his throne.

What should Montezuma do? Assure himself, first of all—for he was as artful as he was fearful—that the stranger chief was really Quetzalcoatl. So he planned a stratagem. He decided to send to the Totonac country messengers laden with presents, but he selected presents of the kind that would remind Quetzalcoatl of his divine origin: a tiger-skin miter, a collection of feathers, some serpent-shaped pieces of jewelry, and earrings set with turquoises. The god would be moved at recognizing the jewels with which he was dressed, and his very own emblems! By this astute maneuver, Montezuma thought to make certain that the white man was really the Plumed Serpent, and he hoped at the same time that such gifts would appease the angry god. The messengers were instructed above all to watch the stranger's face carefully when he received the gifts. The least quiver would show that he remembered and that he was indeed the one.

Montezuma's envoys began their march toward the coast. Having reached the edge of the Spanish camp, they joined Tendile and acquired from him exact information about the mysterious arrivals. Then the first interview took place between Cortés and the Indian emissaries. In truth, no sign of emotion, except that of greed, appeared on the face of the Captain General. He was undoubtedly sufficient master of himself not to allow his divine origin to be seen by his people. Faithful to their master's instructions, the Aztec messengers, as well as Tendile, continuously watched Cortés' face. He did not react to the symbols of the Plumed Serpent, but perhaps his words would betray him. Cortés' words were first translated by Aguilar into the language of Tabasco, and Doña Marina then passed them on to Tendile and his companions in the Aztec tongue. Of the original meaning very little remained, but enough nevertheless to catch allusions to a powerful emperor and to a religion of love and kindness. Was this not what Quetzalcoatl had preached?

Many among Montezuma's envoys were convinced that Cortés was the Plumed Serpent and were ready to prostrate themselves at his feet. Tendile stopped them. Nothing proved that the stranger was in fact Quetzalcoatl; he himself remained sceptical. To Cortés' request to meet Montezuma, Tendile replied haughtily: "You have scarcely arrived but you already wish to speak to him!" Would Cortés have received this cutting reply if Tendile had regarded him as a god? In truth, the Indian was divided in his mind: he doubted that the Spanish captain was the incarnation of the expected messiah, but was troubled, nevertheless, by certain signs, such as the golden helmet like Huitzilopochtli's.

Montezuma listened with anguished attention to Tendile's report, the latter having raced at top speed to Tenochtitlán. He studied the drawings of the scribes. He did not share Tendile's scepticism. On the contrary, everything tended to affirm the perfect resemblance of the white chief to Quetzalcoatl. The Emperor gathered together his privy council, summoned his powerful neighbors and allies—the kings of Texcoco and Tlacopán—and acquainted them with the situation. What course should they adopt? Their advice varied: some recommended total submission, while the rest wanted to oppose the marching invader. Montezuma chose a middle course. He decided to send a further embassy to the strangers. At its head, in addition to Tendile, he appointed one of his courtiers named Quintalbor, chosen from the noblest in the land, and also because he resembled Cortés as he was represented in Aztec paintings. The idea was the Emperor's own. Obsessed by the divine origin of Cortés, he ordered the ambassadors to treat him as a god, for it was customary for priests to give themselves the outward appearance and clothes of the idols they served. This is what Quintalbor did: the double of Cortés, and dressed like him, he paid homage to the divinity of Quetzalcoatl. Quintalbor, moreover, was learned in sorcery, and Montezuma thought his talents and demonstrations of magic would persuade Cortés that he, too, possessed supernatural power. In short, the Emperor's instructions to his ambassadors were as follows: to obtain information about the intentions of the white lord, to load him with presents and attentions, to try the effect on him of magic powers, and to strive to persuade him to give up the idea of penetrating farther into the interior.

The second embassy returned, and the results were negative. The white lord had not concealed his intention—more determined than ever—of paying Montezuma a visit. He had accepted the gifts, showed himself enchanted with them, and in return had sent the Indian monarch a worm-eaten armchair and a ridiculous headdress.

He had appreciated the performance of magic, but without seeing in it anything but conjuring tricks. Finally, he had given his troops the order to prepare for departure. Montezuma was utterly crushed by this news: he walked to and fro through the palace rooms like one distracted, wringing his hands and bemoaning the fate of himself and his children. What would become of them when Quetzalcoatl's soldiers killed him? They must be hidden quickly, before the white warriors seized them! He no longer slept; he had ceased to eat. Neither his wives, dancers, nor musicians could distract him from his deep sorrows. With the suffering docility of one condemned to death, he expected that his throne, his empire, and his life were to be torn from him.

Montezuma's attitude when faced with the Spanish threat—his terror and his acceptance of it—filled his entourage with confusion. For he was really a brave man and in numerous battles had given evidence of his physical courage and contempt for death. But here he was in a state of stupefaction on the receipt of only vague information. He was like a bull with the bloodstained *espada* deep in its neck, that stands for a moment immobile before lying down to receive the *coup de grâce* from the *puntillero*.

Certainly the despot of Tenochtitlán had more than one reason for an uneasy conscience. For two centuries he and his predecessors had done nothing but enlarge their empire. The Aztec armies had overflowed the valley of Mexico, invaded the southern lands, and pushed as far as the eastern sea. There was not a tribe that was not tied to the Aztec chariot, like a bleeding body dragged to execution. Not a tribe but had provided Montezuma with gold for his chest, women for his pleasure, men for war, and living hearts for sacrifice. Not a road, from the ruins of Tollan to Cempoala, but had seen the imperial soldiers pass with their obsidian lances held high, and—perhaps even more to be feared—the tax collector, holding a crooked staff in one hand and sniffing a bouquet of roses held in the other.

At the inauguration of the temple built to Huitzilopochtli, twenty thousand prisoners had been immolated. For four consecutive days the blood had flowed in dark streams down the steps to the feet of the allied chiefs, frozen with terror under the fierce eye of the feathered Caesar. Since Montezuma had succeeded Ahuitzotl, the position of the vassal peoples had grown even worse, to say nothing of what had happened to enemies. Hundreds of thousands of slaves had suffered, bled, and died for the king of the lagoon. He was indeed heir to the red conquistadors—red by reason of their daubed faces, and red with the blood they poured upon the stones of the teocallis—who had come from Aztlan, naked and famished, and now strutted arrogantly over stolen lands.

Montezuma had assured the ferocious continuance of the power that his fathers had forged. He had made it even more severe, and at the same time had been overtaken by religious mania. He had built more temples and gorged Huitzilopochtli with the blood of captives, and never lent an ear to the roar of hate that had broken upon the shores of Lake Texcoco. He knew that it was easy to stifle, for he had only to raise the terrifying figure of Huitzilopochtli, whose representative he was. Ally, collaborator, executive, and representative of the war god, Montezuma feared nothing and no one. He was sure of his strength and his right. What, then, was the reason for his bad conscience, if his deeds were justified and sanctioned by his god? Why did he fear Cortés when he had fought enemies just as formidable? Yet there is no doubt that Montezuma was full of fear.

In truth, his attitude is inexplicable if it is separated from the magic and unreal world of the Aztec people. Montezuma's fear was metaphysical. It had its source in the sacred symbols that gave Aztec society its rhythm of life and death. At the dawn of time, the first god and the first goddess were one. Four sons were born of this monstrous marriage: Xipe, Tezcatlipoca, Quetzalcoatl, and Huitzilopochtli. Their lives conditioned those of men. They could die, but blood revived them. Thus the holocaust was the basis of Aztec religion, and blood was needed that the gods might live. But war broke out among the four brothers. Quetzalcoatl had founded a kingdom of peace at Tollan. Jealous of his power, Tezcatlipoca, who was lame and deformed and bore on his forehead a smoking mirror, chased him from Tollan, pushed him toward the sea, and usurped his place, though not for long. Leading the Aztec hordes came Huitzilopochtli, the war god, Son of the Sun, the Sorcerer-Hummingbird, discoverer of Mexico. It was he who led the Aztecs along the roads to victory, who made the greatness of Tenochtitlán and facilitated the promotion of this miserable people to the rank of a tutelary power. But the sun god was vulnerable. He could die. The deaths of men were necessary to maintain his life; blood was the price of his preservation and glory. In exchange for human blood, Huitzilopochtli protected Aztec arms and assured Aztec lives. The blood of sacrifice, constantly replenished and flowing in streams, gave the god eternal youth; it mingled so closely with his own that in truth there was but one blood, simultaneously human and divine.

The solemn step that was drawing near was that of Quetzalcoatl, the avenging messiah. His return signified the defeat and death of his brother-enemy Huitzilopochtli. Two contrary principles cannot co-exist. Before modeling a new human type in his own image, the first concern of the Plumed Serpent would be to break the old idols and cast the war god into darkness. He would restore the ruins of his jade palace at Tollan and of his temple at Tenochtitlán and restore supremacy to the Toltec people. What was to become, then, of Montezuma, the servant of Huitzilopochtli? His temporal power was based only on a spiritual power. He was simultaneously the chief soldier and the chief priest, the *tlacatecutli*, and never did anything without reference to the will of the war god. He was lost. It is not enough to say that Montezuma no longer believed in god. For him god was dead. And the empire was dead, too.

Evening fell—perhaps the last—on Tenochtitlán. The lagoon was like a pool of blood. Montezuma already imagined the solitude, the deserted palace, the servants in flight, and his vassals turning their lances against him. There was nothing to do but fall on his knees and wait until the broken columns of the Aztec pantheon crushed him—unless he ordered his people to give themselves up to death, in accordance with established rites. The idea of a great mass suicide fascinated him. What obsequies for a dead divinity!

CHAPTER 8

Two Worlds Meet

FOUR hundred Spaniards, 400 auxiliaries from Cempoala, 1000 *tamenes* or porters, 15 horses, 10 heavy cannons, 4 pieces of lighter artillery, and a few Indians: this was the small army which, in the month of August 1519, marched across the oppressive jungle of the Totonac lands toward the mountain Cofre de Perote. There were not even a thousand fighters, and half of these were not reliable, for how would the Cempoala recruits react to fire? Yet Cortés had never been so optimistic. He had all the odds on his side, and God would do the rest.

The Battle of Tlaxcala

Cortés had the choice of two routes for reaching the Mexican plateau. The northern route led through Xalapa (now Jalapa), the southern through Orizaba. He chose the northern and shorter route. The Captain General's instructions were to proceed quickly and directly to the goal.

At the head of the army the alferes, bearing aloft the standard of the expedition, galloped upon a dappled horse. Behind him came Cortés, accompanied by Doña Marina—who was now his mistress—Alvarado, Olid, and Father de Olmedo. After them came the Spanish infantry, the artillery, the baggage train, and the group of pikemen and arquebusiers. The Totonac mercenaries and Cempoala nobles brought up the rear. The feathers of the native dignitaries and the Spanish pennons waved in the wind. The beat of drums and the sound of trumpets regulated the pace of the warriors. Crests and breastplates glittered in the sunlight.

As far as Xalapa there was jungle, dense and damp. The Spaniards panted under armor that was stuffed with cotton as a protection against arrows. But soon they were shivering with cold. They had to climb the first cordillera, march along the sinister flank of a volcano—the Cofre de Perote—and cross extensive defiles. This immense land was almost empty; only a few miserable huts gave evidence of the presence of man. Sometimes natives appeared in front of the army and offered fowls, but the majority fled at its approach. The horses, especially, made a great noise with their trappings, terrifying these poor creatures. The echo of military noises broke lugubriously against the hard screen of mountains.

The only pains the troop had to suffer were those of alternating and excessive heat and cold, according to whether they marched in the plain or followed the mountain escarpments. One evening the army arrived within view of a large populated area. The houses were well constructed and were white, as in Andalusia. The inhabitants did not flee but, on the contrary, approached the strangers and fixed them with insistent stares. Thirteen pyramids dominated the town, and bones were piled at the foot of one of them. What with the warlike look of the population, the side glances of the priests who attended the pyramids, and the military style of the houses, the Spaniards realized that they had reached the frontier of the forbidden kingdom and were about to tread upon Montezuma's soil. They would have to act with caution.

The expedition had actually not advanced as far as it thought. The town in which Cortés had chosen to camp was called Xocotlan. It was several days' march from Tlaxcala. The Captain General, relying on information gathered at Cempoala, placed great hopes in Tlaxcala, for it was the agelong enemy of Tenochtitlán and the center of resistance against Montezuma. The Aztec emperor had never been able to subdue completely this focus of rebellion. So Cortés planned to fan the flame and to make further powerful allies of the Tlaxcalans. To use the internal dissensions of a confederacy in order to master it is a classical procedure that almost always assures success.

Cortés was daring but also prudent. Before setting out for Tlaxcala he decided to send there as ambassadors four of the Cempoala nobles who were with him. It was a good idea, for the Totonacs were allies of the Tlaxcalans. After waiting in vain for several days for his plenipotentiaries' return, Cortés ordered the departure from Xocotlan. He had gone only a few leagues from the town when the Spanish army found its road barred by a wall of stone stretching across the

valley from one mountain to the other, with one narrow opening
in the middle. It had been built by the Tlaxcalans to mark the boundaries of their province and protect them from the Totonacs, friends
today but perhaps enemies tomorrow. What a warning it was for the
Spaniards! Once this formidable rampart was passed, who could guarantee that they would come that way again? A wall that closed
behind them, and the dark shape of teocallis outlined against the
hostile sky were enough to freeze the hearts of the most daring
among them. But Cortés knew no fear. He ordered the standard to
be unfurled. "Brothers and comrades, let us follow the Cross. . . ."
And spurring his mount, he was the first to pass the threshold.

A little farther on, the expedition met the four ambassadors returning from Tlaxcala. Cortés realized from their discomfited looks that
the news was bad. Contrary to the Captain General's calculations,
the Tlaxcalans had refused an alliance. Their will for independence
prevailed over their traditional hatred for the Aztecs. They were
preparing for battle under the command of Xicotenga, a great war
leader.

A first engagement took place in the environs of Atalaya. Three
thousand Tlaxcalans tried to halt the Spanish advance, but Cortés
dispersed them with a few cannon shots. The next day's engagement
was more serious. The Tlaxcalans had regrouped and were rein-
forced: six thousand howling Indians rolled down upon the Spanish
vanguard. Their principal weapon was a sort of wooden club tipped
with an obsidian spike, sharp as a razor blade. It was a terrible weapon
in a hand-to-hand struggle, but it lost its efficacy before the two
Spanish arms: artillery and cavalry. This fact did not escape the
Tlaxcalans, who very ingeniously drew Cortés' troops into a ravine
where neither horses nor artillery could be used. Simultaneously
they joined up with Xicotenga's effectives, so that the Spaniards
were now faced with an army of forty thousand Tlaxcalans, led by
Xicotenga. Cortés' companions had to be brave not to flee before this
multicolored flood, the hurricane of noise, the feathers and flags,
the shrill scream of war horns, and the funereal tam-tam of the
teponaztlis. More than one among them remembered the tales of his
childhood: the onrush of the Almoravides in the plain of Zallaka,
their faces veiled in black, lances in their hands, the same frenzy and
the same rolling of drums. Stoic under the rain of javelins and stones,

whirling their swords to turn aside the blows of the Indian clubs, the Spaniards adopted the Tlaxcalan maneuver in reverse by drawing them toward the plain. There in the open country Cortés' soldiers regained the advantage. Driven back by bullets, overthrown by cavalry charges, the enemy ranks broke up. Cortés had won for the second time. His losses were small: one horse and a few men wounded. The legend of his invulnerability spread among the Indians, both friends and enemies. Hence the name *teules*, a synonym for demigods, that they gave the Spaniards from this time on.

During the furious fighting, Cortés had multiplied his peace offers to Xicotenga. But the latter, despite his reverses and his growing conviction that his adversaries belonged to a race of supermen, would not yield. He decided to launch an extended attack upon Cortés' army. Five corps of men were put into line, consisting of the whole able-bodied population of Tlaxcala and neighboring villages. Besides the usual armament—bows and arrows, slings, copper-pointed lances, and obsidian-bladed clubs—the Indians carried bamboo shields and leather helmets. Furthermore, with the object of striking terror into the enemy, Xicotenga ordered his soldiers to paint their faces and to set plumes shaped like serpent and jaguar heads upon their helmets. The Spaniards watched the preparations for this terrible offensive with anxiety, and passed the night in prayer. The battle broke out in the early morning with a thunder of cries and clashing arms. Cortés reckoned the number of Indian warriors at one hundred thousand. A screaming tide swept to assault the Spanish positions, which were then not far from the town of Tzumpantzingo.

This was indeed the battle "*peligrosa y dudosa*"—dangerous and uncertain. The Spanish and Indian arms, although different, balanced one another. On their side the Tlaxcalans had numbers, while the Spaniards had quality. The sky was darkened by the cloud of projectiles. A single cannon shot was enough to sow panic among the Indians; however, it seemed that their reserves were inexhaustible. Scarcely had one enemy rank been mowed down by Cortés' artillery or overthrown by the horses than a second rank took its place. The Spaniards reeled under the weight of a struggle that they began to think was lost. But they were lucky enough to wound fatally several of the most highly reputed Indian chiefs, and this demoralized the enemy. Moreover, rivalries broke out between the Tlaxcalan officers

and those from neighboring towns. The death of the leading chief-
tains and the quarrels in the command destroyed the unity of the
Indian army, and it reeled back in disorder. It was high time, for the
Spaniards could do no more.

Now Cortés was in an excellent position to renew his offers of
peace to Xicotenga. The chief of the Tlaxcalan state still hesitated.
In fact, although the people and civil authorities expected the end of
hostilities with Cortés, the military party intended to continue the
struggle against the invaders—an ambitious plan, but one that seemed
doomed to failure following the events at Tzumpantzingo. The military party had lost its best elements, and the sacred union was broken.
Cortés was encamped at the gates of Tlaxcala. Surrender was necessary. With death in his heart, Xicotenga accepted the alliance which
he was unable to refuse. He decided to send his old blind father and
some high Tlaxcalan dignitaries to meet the Conquistador, including
Maximatzin, who had always favored Cortés. Introduced to their
new ally, the lords of Tlaxcala fell at his feet and burned incense
before him. Then the older Xicotenga, the venerable cacique of
Tlaxcala, spoke in the name of the delegation. For the first time
Cortés was addressed as Malinche—the name of his companion—
which all the people of Anáhuac were soon to use. "Malinche,
Malinche, we have begged you very often to forgive us, now that
we are emerging from war. Although we have joined battle with you,
it was in order to defend ourselves against the wicked Montezuma
and his great power, for we thought that you were on his side. . . ."
After making honorable amends, the elder Xicotenga begged Cortés
not to defer any longer his visit to Tlaxcala, where, he made clear,
"we will serve you with our persons and our possessions." The Captain General responded appropriately and with courtesy. The cacique's noble words and the smoke of the incense had erased the
memory of recent struggles. There was no longer any use for
obsidian weapons except to turn them by common accord against a
mutual enemy, Montezuma. Peace was signed and an alliance concluded, and the sovereign of Tenochtitlán would have to pay the
price.

The next day, at an early hour, Xicotenga the elder and the other
dignitaries returned to Tlaxcala, and behind them came Cortés, followed by his army.

An imposing cohort awaited the Conquistadors at the gates of the capital. First there were the four *tlatoanis*, each of whom governed one of the four cantons constituting the state of Tlaxcala. Then came their officers, superbly arrayed in feathers and cloaks of bright colors. Finally, the priests, dressed in long tunics and black capes, who burned incense at the passing of the victorious army. The priests' hair, which was matted with blood, and their slashed ears aroused disgust in the hearts of the Spaniards. The crowd acclaimed the riders and threw flowers at them. The color of their skins and beards, the steel of their swords, their coats, and the shape of their mounts were so strange that they could belong only to gods.

The Spaniards much admired Tlaxcala, which was a very populous city located 6500 feet above the sea on four hills united by a girdle of thick walls. The low-built houses, the narrow streets and the solidity of the architecture, the tangled lanes, the buildings that clung to the flanks of the mountains, the arrangement of the hills, and the gardens that ringed the town made the Spaniards think of Granada without its Alhambra. There was the same wild nakedness of the plain, the same silver flow of the river (here the Atoyac, there the Genil), the same blinding light on an almost Oriental landscape. And, like the Sierra Nevada, the Mexican cordillera stood out boldly against the turquoise-colored sky. Struck by this resemblance, Cortés wrote to Charles: "This town is so big and so beautiful that all one could say about it would be unbelievable. It is bigger than Granada and better fortified. Its houses, its buildings, and the people that inhabit it are more numerous than at Granada at the time when we conquered it. . . ." The recollection of Granada, symbol of the reconquest, was stimulating to these conquerors on the march!

The richness of the markets and the rigorous order that reigned at Tlaxcala made a strong impression on the Spaniards. An abundance of shops and a good police were to them the signs of good political health. The Tlaxcalan country stretched all around the city within a circumference of 125 miles. The country was fertile and produced cereals, fruits, and forage plants in abundance; especially prolific was the aloe or maguey—a variety of amaryllis—which simultaneously served for the making of cloth and for the preparation of pulque, the drink in common use and a ritual beverage.

A rich city and a fecund soil, yet this peaceful picture had its shadow: the Aztec menace that harassed its frontiers.

A Mad Feat: The Conquest of Popocatepetl

Cortés' great skill was to transform an alliance first imposed by arms into genuine collaboration. While maintaining his prestige, he was able to convince the Tlaxcalans of his good intentions. Was it not to their interest to join with him in overthrowing Montezuma's power, which they could not do alone? United with the teules, the brave Tlaxcalan soldiers could break the Aztec yoke without difficulty. Such frank speech made a great impression on the tlatoanis, and in pronouncing the name of Montezuma, Cortés aggravated an open wound. The elder Xicotenga, his arms trembling and his blind eyes turned heavenward, made this pathetic complaint: "We are poor, Malinche, because these treacherous and evil Mexicans and Montezuma, their lord, have taken all we possessed."

Cortés' first intention on entering Tlaxcala had been to destroy the idols, but Father de Olmedo had dissuaded him. This clumsy gesture would have a most unfortunate effect on the Indian population; it would be better to bring them gently to the Christian religion and not give offense to beliefs that until then had buttressed their morale. But Cortés had a church constructed not far from the teocallis, so that barbarians and Christians performed their rituals side by side and the same copal smoke enveloped both the Catholic altar and the pantheistic stone.

While he was broadening his contacts with the Tlaxcalan chiefs, Cortés gathered information about Aztec strength. But it was difficult for him to obtain precise details about Montezuma's military effectives or his strategic dispositions. Even taking exaggeration and fear into consideration, the Captain General was unable to appraise the war potential and resources of the Aztec kingdom, but he knew enough to figure that he would have to face a formidable adversary.

Meanwhile his companions carried out an adventurous exploit that astonished the Tlaxcalans and did much to establish the Spaniards' reputation of invincibility: this was the ascent of Popocatepetl.

The major part of Mexico is a vast plateau formed by the prolongation of the gigantic Andean cordillera that flanks the western coast of South America. This enormous mountain backbone crosses the narrow regions of Central America, drops toward the Isthmus of Tehuantepec, rises again, and then, having reached Mexico, divides into two branches: the eastern and western Sierra Madre. The two arms of these formidable pincers enclose three plateaus or *mesetas*: the southern, the central or Anáhuac, and the northern plateaus. The central plateau, the heart of the country, is bordered by a volcanic rim with very high peaks: Orizaba (18,700 feet), Iztaccihuatl (or the White Lady, 16,883 feet), and the sinister Popocatepetl (or the Smoking Mountain, 17,887 feet).

From time immemorial the Indians had considered Popocatepetl the god of fire. They had raised temples to it and had consecrated idols to intercede with it. Doubtless the infernal deities were satisfied, for the growling voice of the volcano had been silent for two hundred years. Now, at the very moment when Cortés won the battle of Tlaxcala, the volcano had spoken. A dense column of smoke, laden with cinders, had risen straight into the sky, while incandescent lava slid down the flanks of the mountain. The earth shook. The connection between the volcano's anger and the arrival of the Spaniards was clear. The phenomenon had to be interpreted. What did Popocatepetl require: submission to the teules or rebellion? Was its anger directed toward the Spaniards or the Indians?

Determined to make the most of his psychological weapons, Cortés could only approve Diego de Ordaz' proposal to attempt a reconnaissance of Popocatepetl. The venture was hazardous, and the undertaking required that streak of madness and degree of ignorance that characterized the Conquistadors.

So one morning Ordaz set out from Tlaxcala with nine Spaniards and some Indian porters. The first stage brought them to the limit of the fir forests at about 13,000 feet—Tlaxcala stood at about 6500 feet. They passed the night under the stars on the Tlamanca plateau, a sacred site with temples. The howling of the coyotes, the rumble of explosions, and the roar of the debris composed a plutonian symphony. The Indians refused to go farther. Intrepid, the Spaniards continued on their way. After crossing two barrancas they reached the foot of the volcano where the region of cinders and fire began. Slipping on the pumice or sinking into the burning lava, Diego de Ordaz and his companions reached the snow fields at 15,750 feet.

The summit was not far away. But after 16,400 feet the Spaniards suffered severely: their sandal-shod feet (they had worn their *alpargatas* on this mountain trip) alternately endured the agony of ice and fire. They were overtaken by an overpowering lethargy, and they lacked air. At regular intervals the volcano spat out lava and incandescent coals. Between the monster's fits, the Spaniards, tottering with fatigue and dazed by the sulphurous vapors, went forward a few steps, then let themselves fall upon the shuddering rock. Finally, after superhuman efforts, they hauled themselves to the summit of Popocatepetl, to the very edge of the crater.

Sheltering behind a rock, Cortés' men surveyed the Mexican landscape. Tlaxcala, with fields of corn and aloes, was no bigger than a handful of millet seed, but a gray line could be distinguished that left Tlaxcala, passed through Cholula, then between Popocatepetl and Iztaccihuatl, and ended at Lake Texcoco. It was the road to Tenochtitlán, Montezuma's city, which glittered in the middle of the lake. The causeways that connected the imperial island to the land seemed as tenuous as a spider's thread. To the east lay the mountain of Cofre de Perote—an old acquaintance—and then that king of Mexican peaks, Orizaba. Thus from the top of Popocatepetl Cortés' companions could gauge what they had already conquered and what they had still to conquer.

The earth trembled, and a whirl of vapor and flame enveloped the Spaniards. They had defied and conquered the god of fire. Ordaz and his companions took a last look at Tenochtitlán, and then, after collecting some blocks of ice, descended.

It was a difficult descent but a triumphant return. Now the Indians no longer doubted Spanish strength. The god of the mountain had capitulated to the teules, which meant that the people must obey Malinche, the incarnation of Quetzalcoatl. Cortés again took up his pen and reported the mad escapade to Emperor Charles: "They arrived near the peak. At that moment there was an eruption with a great deal of smoke, which burst forth with such impetuosity and such noise that the whole mountain seemed about to collapse." Charles greatly appreciated Diego de Ordaz' daring and awarded him a title with the device "a burning mountain on a field gules."

Two years later Cortés had to send a second expedition to Popocatepetl, not merely to demonstrate Spanish courage but with a utilitarian purpose: to obtain sulphur for making gunpowder. The expedition was led by Francisco de Montana and its task was facilitated by the volcano's quiescence. The Spaniards followed their predecessors' route and, reaching the cone more easily, were able to set up a hoist at the very edge of the crater and extract a large quantity of sulphur.

But the credit for the idea and the courage to carry it out belongs above all to Diego de Ordaz and his companions. They were the first conquerers of Popocatepetl, and three centuries were to pass before, in 1827, the exploit was carried out for a third time.

The ascent of Popocatepetl in full activity by ten Spaniards in sandals, with their capes rolled around their backs and with nothing for ice axes but the points of their swords, was a heroic interlude in the drama of the conquest.

A Bloody Halt at the Holy City of Cholula

The Spaniards remained at Tlaxcala for seventeen days. The soldiers rested, but Cortés engaged in intense political activity. He strengthened his alliance with the Tlaxcalans, gathered information about Tenochtitlán, and prepared to lunge toward the Aztec capital.

During his stay at Tlaxcala, Cortés twice received an embassy from Montezuma. The Indian Emperor was kept informed by his spies of everything concerning the Spaniards, and he knew all about the furious battles before Tlaxcala and of the peace that followed. Diego de Ordaz' exploit confirmed his belief that the white warriors were of divine origin. Nothing could resist them, neither the forces of men nor those of nature. What else was there to do but appease them with gifts and try to keep them away from Tenochtitlán?

The situation of the Aztec ambassadors was strange. They crossed the Tlaxcalan lines furnished with safe-conducts and were under the protection of the Spanish general. Their diplomatic status and Cortés' caution allowed them to move quite freely in the city and even to participate in the interviews between Cortés and the local chieftains. It was known on both sides that one day war would break out between Tenochtitlán and Tlaxcala; meanwhile both sides presented their points of view courteously.

On their first mission to Cortés, the Aztec ambassadors transmitted

Montezuma's offer to submit to the king of Spain and to pay heavy tribute to him regularly, on condition that Cortés return to his own country. They added that Tenochtitlán did not possess sufficient resources to receive the Spanish captain worthily. Sumptuous presents accompanied the proposal. Cortés accepted the gifts but reiterated his firm intention of paying Montezuma a visit. With their second embassy the tone had changed. Montezuma was astonished that a great lord like Cortés should delay so long among the miserable Tlaxcalans, who were worthless even as slaves. He cordially invited Cortés to his capital. These contradictory messages betrayed Montezuma's confusion. If it was impossible to turn the white leader from the road to Mexico, perhaps he must be lured forward to test his invulnerability.

Cortés reassembled his army and gave the signal to depart. The road to Tenochtitlán passed through Cholula. This was the holy city of the Aztecs. Dominating the three hundred and sixty teocallis was a gigantic pyramid dedicated to Quetzalcoatl. Processions of pilgrims came every year to be present at the ritual ceremonies, when six thousand victims were sacrificed to the gods. The Tlaxcalans were enemies of the Cholulans, who were allies of Montezuma and therefore energetically discouraged Cortés from passing through the city. Seeing that the prospect of danger was more a stimulant than an obstacle to the Captain General, the Tlaxcalans offered him ten thousand soldiers to reinforce his army. Cortés accepted only two thousand. But at the exit from the city the Indian contingent increased by several hundred volunteers. In fact, five thousand Tlaxcalans followed Cortés' banner.

The gray plain was planted with aloes that stood up like raised fists. Then the Spaniards approached Cholula, and from a distance thought they were seeing Toledo, for in the towers and fortified walls there was something reminiscent of Old Castile. While the Tlaxcalans camped outside the town, the Spaniards were received by the Cholulan worthies with dignity. Their words were courteous and their gestures deferential. Incense smoked in the censers. Young girls threw bouquets of flowers to the soldiers. Children obstructed their passage, singing. Crowded on the terraces or pressed against the walls of houses, the Cholulans watched the Spanish horsemen pass, then the infantry, the cannons drawn by the Cempoalans and the wagons loaded with enemy prizes; their attitude was that of any crowd watching a military procession. No hostile cry was raised, not even at the Indian mercenaries. Apparently the welcome was correct, even cordial, and the population seemed friendly—but it seemed too friendly. This organized enthusiasm augured nothing good for Cortés. Cholula reeked of falsehood. He had only to intercept the sly sneer of the Cholulans when they passed a Spanish soldier to know that. A solemn oppressiveness, as on the eve of a catastrophe, hung over the sacred city.

A certain number of suspicious acts had roused the Captain General's distrust: the discovery of sharpened stakes at the bottom of skillfully disguised ditches, the evacuation of Cholulan women and children to the mountains, a sudden lack of foodstuffs. Gradually the Spaniards became isolated: they found themselves cut off in the great temple of Cholula that had been assigned to them as their residence. Finally, the arrival of a third embassy from Montezuma, forbidding Cortés to approach Tenochtitlán, succeeded in perturbing him. What was brewing?

Thanks to her great knowledge of the Indian mind (which was her own), and thanks also to the contacts she had made in the land, Doña Marina had the last word in the story. Something was certainly being prepared. Twenty thousand soldiers from Cholula and Tenochtitlán were hiding in the houses, only awaiting a sign—that of the Spaniards' departure—to fall upon them, capture them, and take them bound to Montezuma's palace, after sacrificing twenty men immediately to the Cholulan gods. Such was Huitzilopochtli's will, interpreted by Montezuma.

So the plot was well organized, and by the very person who had sent suppliant ambassadors to Cortés. Such honeyed words and such rich presents to cloak his treachery! The Spaniard's reaction was terrible. After enjoining silence on his informers and guaranteeing their safety, he officially announced his departure and asked for food and two thousand porters. The muster was to take place in the courtyard of the great temple. Meanwhile he grouped his cannons in well-situated firing positions. What was he plotting? To draw the greatest possible number of Cholulans inside the temple, and as soon as they found it impossible to get out, to cut them to pieces with his artillery. He answered trick with trick and caught his enemies in their own trap.

When day broke, the whole population of Cholula, nobles and plebeians, pressed forward to the doors of the temple. For their part, the Indian warriors held themselves ready to attack the Spaniards as arranged. Then Cortés took a few steps in front of the crowd, crossed his arms, and cried in a resounding voice: "My lords of Cholula, we have come to you as friends, and here you are preparing arms and ropes for our destruction. . . . The laws of our Emperor instruct that such treachery shall be punished. Your punishment shall be death."

Cortés' words, translated by Doña Marina, threw the Cholulans into consternation. They attempted in vain to justify themselves, attributing the responsibility for the affair to Montezuma. The Captain General would listen to none of it. He ordered a musket to be fired—the prearranged signal to his artillery—and at once the cannons began to thunder. Smoke and flame filled the temple courtyard. Despite their courage, the Cholulans were quickly put out of action. Mowed down by bullets, terrified by the bombardment, those who had not perished attempted to flee. But at the city gates they were engaged by the Tlaxcalans, who took their revenge for their abhorred tutelage.

The first part of the battle lasted two hours, during which three thousand Cholulans lost their lives. It was prolonged another three hours in the suburbs. Cortés had great difficulty in getting the Tlaxcalans to stop the fight: they massacred, pillaged, and burned with savage zeal. Houses blazed and teocallis collapsed. The screams of women and children who were burned alive, the regular roar of the cannons, and the war cries of the Tlaxcalans sounded the knell of the sacred city. The fire raged for two days. Cholula had paid. Then Cortés stretched a victor's arm over a now silent city. Henceforth it was under his protection.

The Spaniards long remembered the *matanza* (slaughter) at Cholula. The temple courtyard became a slaughterhouse, with the unbearable stench of decay and burned flesh. It was perhaps the most frightful episode of the campaign. But Cortés' position was now consolidated. Fourteen days passed between the fall of the town and the departure of the Spaniards. During this short delay, Cortés had time to bring off a double political coup: to reconcile the Tlaxcalans and Cholulans, and to secure, if not the alliance, at least the neutrality of the latter. He did not deviate from his inflexible line of conduct: to foster local dissensions when they were profitable to him; to strive to reduce them when he saw it was advantageous to do so; to acquire as many allies as possible; in brief, by arms or by words to conquer the country as he occupied it. His vital objective was to prevent the formation of a front behind him: there must be no enemy at his back!

Cortés was not surprised to see the arrival of a new embassy from Montezuma. He knew this personage now. Of course, the imperial messengers brought the Captain General the monarch's condolences for the tiresome events at Cholula. Montezuma was grieved at the Cholulans' conduct and deplored the fact that Cortés had not punished them more severely. He begged insistently that Cortés visit him at Tenochtitlán. In reality, the Indian emperor had taken the failure of his plan badly. For two days he prayed, imploring advice from Huitzilopochtli. The god, temporarily appeased by the slaughter of a few victims, had pronounced judgment: Malinche must be allowed to enter Tenochtitlán! Once in the city, it would be easy to exterminate him and his people. It was an inflexible verdict, though Montezuma was not sure that he had interpreted it properly.

Cortés pretended to take the fine words of the Aztec envoys seriously. Not for a second did he let them see that he knew of Montezuma's part in the Cholulan plot. It was important, indeed, that the Spanish army should enter the Mexican capital in a friendly fashion, at least officially. Overcoming his disgust at such duplicity, Cortés courteously sent the Indian ambassadors back to their master with the message that he would be at Tenochtitlán in a few days.

Montezuma and Cortés Meet

This was the last stage before the imperial city, which was now no more than sixty miles away. First the road passed through a deep defile between Popocatepetl and Iztaccihuatl and then traversed great forests of mulberries and cedars. The Spaniards advanced cautiously with their arms ready and their eyes watchful. Gradually the plain succeeded the sierra, cultivated fields the bush, and grass the rocks.

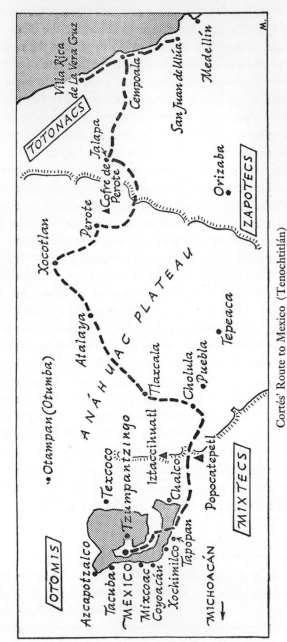

Cortés' Route to Mexico (Tenochtitlán)

Soon the conquerors were in the Anáhuac plateau where the land-scape was soft and voluptuous. In the distance Lake Texcoco could be seen, shining like armor. The colors were gentle, a symphony of greens and blues. Was it possible that so bloody an emperor could reign over a land that seemed made for happiness? From the towns close to the capital—Chalco, Amecameca—delegations came to complain bitterly to the Spaniards of Montezuma's yoke. Did they dare to murmur so close to the imperial palace? This was something that would ease Cortés' task.

Montezuma multiplied his signs of deference. His brother Cuitlahuac, king of Ixtapalapa, came to welcome Cortés as he emerged from the sierra, and soon after passing Chalco, Cacamatzin, king of Texcoco, presented himself to the Spanish general. The two princes apologized that Montezuma was not able to come to meet him, and they put themselves at Cortés' disposal to give him any assistance. At the same time, they discouraged Cortés from continuing his journey to Tenochtitlán: a final but vain attempt to stop the invaders' progress. Cortés simply smiled; the legendary city was now no farther away than a crossbow shot. With his heart leaping for joy, the Conquistador set foot on the Ixtapalapa causeway, followed by his Spaniards, like the Romans on the Via Triumphalis. It was November 8, 1519.

From the opposite direction a magnificent procession advanced slowly toward the Spanish army. Seeing that nothing could stop Malinche, and having exhausted every means in heaven and earth, Montezuma, in order to prevent the catastrophe, decided to meet his adversary.

At the head of the column came the Aztec Emperor in his litter, under a canopy of green feathers. Gold and emeralds shone on his garments. Slaves swept the earth before him. Surrounding the monarch marched the princes of his line and the priests of Huitzilopochtli. Servants carried gilded mats, garlands of flowers, and flasks of perfume. All eyes but the princes' were turned earthward so as not to meet the Emperor's glance. The illustrious chiefs who had come from Tlacopán, Texcoco, and Coyoacán at Montezuma's summons brought up the rear: these were the "Eagles" and "Tigers," and their gem-spangled feathers glittered in the morning sun. Such a gathering of nobles and warriors had never before been seen at

Tenochtitlán, but every face was marked with touching sadness: punishment and war had left their holy stigmata imprinted upon them. Where now were the victory processions? Today the fine flower of Aztec knighthood had a rendezvous with slavery.

Having reached the middle of the Ixtapalapa causeway, the Aztec column stopped. Now the other column approached; at its head was Malinche, mounted on his great "stag." Four captains surrounded him, likewise borne upon "stags." A soldier held aloft a standard. Behind came a crowd of armed men with fair skins and bristling beards. These were indeed the "lords of powder and smoke." They brandished heavy lances that flashed like silver. Finally, with a noise like thunder, the "bronze weapons" rolled along the causeway, followed by thousands of Indians, among whom Montezuma recognized his enemies.

Cortés' chestnut horse and Montezuma's litter stopped face to face. The Aztec descended from his chair. He placed his golden sandals on the cotton tapestry that had just been unrolled and advanced toward the Spaniards, supported by his kinsmen, Cuitlahuac and Cacamatzin, kings respectively of Ixtapalapa and Texcoco. Two other kings accompanied him, those of Tlacopán and Coyoacán. Cortés leaped from his horse and moved toward Montezuma, and the two men bowed deeply. Then they looked at each other.

The two armies were motionless, face to face, and a sudden silence succeeded the tumult of the moment before. The wind stirred the crests of the Spanish helmets and the plumes of the Indian dignitaries; the two war chiefs faced one another, while behind them their motionless general staffs formed a group of statues. It was indeed a historic moment as two worlds met.

Montezuma was tall and well proportioned, and his measured movements were as solemn as those of a priest. His hair was long and he had a sparse beard. His color was pale ocher. Cortés, helmeted and armored, had the manners of a gentleman who has frequented courts as often as military camps. His movements were lively, and his face, dusty and sunburned under his helm, showed resolution. A thick beard hid the strong bones of his jaws. He was covered with steel like a medieval knight. Montezuma was adorned with jewels and feathers. Here, in fact, was the royal eagle.

Two men. Two worlds. Cortés was a hero of the Renaissance. He was imbued with the excellence of the civilization of his day, convinced of the grandeur of Spain, certain of his hold on truth. He knew that he had a role to play: to inform the Indians of Christian morality and to impose on them the laws of his world. His message had the severity of dogma and involved absolute submission. A single god—Christ; a single emperor—Charles of Spain; a single fatherland—Spain. Cortés' mentality was that of a Crusader: *Dieu le veult!* The sidelong glance he cast upon Aztec gold and on the sturdy build of the Indians was not that of a slave trader or a covetous man; his covetousness was political and, in a certain sense, mystical. Gold and slaves, certainly! But for Catholic Spain.

Montezuma was a hero, too. Simultaneously he embodied the fate of a people, the will of their gods, and the symbols of a religion. But the people were passive, the gods were silent, and the religion vacillated. Unlike Cortés, Montezuma could not detach himself from his task. He himself was the people, the god, and the religion, and he succumbed to this triple load. Would he rise again? Not before he received from heaven the sign he awaited. But it was slow in appearing. The silence of the idols—he had not ceased to implore them or to bathe their clay feet with blood—turned Montezuma into this hesitating monarch who for three months had not known what orders to give. He delayed the battle. For if Malinche and Quetzalcoatl were one and the same, was he to take up arms against the god? Montezuma's tragedy was a tragedy of faith. He no longer believed in god; thus he no longer believed in himself. Despair and indecision followed. Cortés believed in God. The cross embroidered on his standard had the shape of a sword. He knew that he would conquer.

Thus the two men meditated, face to face. But the anguish and irresolution of the Emperor were not visible on his stony face.

Around Montezuma's neck Cortés hung a necklet of pearls perfumed with musk. In exchange, the Aztec gave him a golden garland of shellfish and shrimps. With arms outstretched, the Spaniard prepared to embrace Montezuma, but the princes prevented this act of *lèse-majesté.* Who was this Cortés to give himself the right to touch the Emperor? A few courteous words were exchanged and translated by Doña Marina, then the Indian monarch returned to Tenochtitlán. The column re-formed. The nobles, officers, and servants glided slowly over the slabs of the causeway. Their unhappy eyes were turned earthward.

Mexico

"Are these not the delights of which we are told in the legend of Amadis? Is not all we see a dream?" These words of Bernal Díaz del Castillo well express the Spaniards' astonishment at Tenochtitlán. And the chronicler adds: "Before such an admirable spectacle, we no longer knew what to say or whether what was before us was real. . . . And we were not even four hundred soldiers!" Four hundred Conquistadors in a city of three hundred thousand inhabitants!

The Aztec capital was built on an oval island—itself formed of old islets that had gradually come together—situated in the middle of Lake Texcoco. It was connected with the mainland on the north, west, and south by three great dikes or causeways that converged toward the center of the city. The causeways were cut by canals spanned by drawbridges. These had only to be raised to sever all communications. The majority of the houses—there were some sixty thousand in all—were built on piles. There were few streets but many canals, and one went from house to house by pirogue. Gardens abounded, islets of verdure and flowers at the surface of the lagoon. Each garden, born on a bed of mud, was separated from the others by a sort of wickerwork. The history of the city was written on this muddy water.

First there was a lonely lake. Then vegetation began to grow on a patch of mud. A hut was built and then a house, and finally a city, aquatic and plantlike. With its bridges and canals, it was similar to Venice, but bore no resemblance to any city of the Occident in any other respect. The fine dark-red pyramids of the teocallis rose above the green and blue roofs. To the west lay Tacuba, also called Tlacopán; to the north, Tepeyac; to the south, Ixtapalapa; and to the east, Texcoco. Standing out whitely against the dark blue of the sky were the vassal cities and the graceful curve of the Chapultepec aqueduct, which distributed fresh and drinkable water; on the southern periphery of the lagoon, around Lake Chalco, were further towns: Mixcoac, Coyoacán, Tapopan, and Xochimilco.

The three causeways—those of Ixtapalapa to the south, Tacuba to the west, and Tepeyac to the north—led to the center of Tenochtitlán. A smaller causeway started from Coyoacán and joined that of Ixtapalapa at its center, where a fortress stood, named Xoloc.

On the main square of Tenochtitlán rose the city's principal buildings: the temples, palaces, and sanctuaries, including Montezuma's palace and that of his father, Axayacatl, which the Emperor gave the Spaniards as their residence. The square was the political and religious center of the state, where the chiefs assembled. From it, in a northward direction, a road led to Tlatelolco (which at one time was independent and now was a suburb of the capital), to the center of another great square as large as the first. This was the market, where everything was to be found: gold, feathers, honey, and slaves. Tobacco was also sold there, a plant then unknown to the Spaniards, who watched amazed as the Aztecs sucked at long tubes and blew the bluish smoke out through their nostrils.

A double wall separated the market place and its arcades from a closed area where the temples of Tlatelolco stood. The temple of Huitzilopochtli dominated all the rest, for the war god was the real sovereign of the Aztec Empire. His massive figure, carved in stone and incrusted with jade and turquoise, weighed down with necklets of serpents and with golden masks, glittered lugubriously in the darkness of the tabernacle.

The sounds and odors of Tenochtitlán surprised the Spaniards. In the Aztec avenues they found no familiar noises and none of the scents of home: not even the creak of cart wheels or the whinny of a beast of burden. Everything was carried by men or in boats. There were neither shouts nor violent arguments, but only a monotonous and gentle murmur like that of the sea. Sometimes the beat of a wooden drum could be heard, or the shrill complaint of a conch, or the regular strike of a tool. But as for the odors!—the sharp whiff of pimento sauces, the heady aroma of lilies, waves of incense, and suddenly the fearful stench of slaughter from Tlatelolco on the days of sacrifice.

Did this city recall either Venice or Toledo? Neither one nor the other, for there was no point in comparing the Stone Age with the Golden Age. The bright landscape, the delicacy of the architecture, and the quiet grace of the people gave the Aztec city a pleasant

appearance. At first contact its beauty was surprising but not disquieting, and so, while waiting for the sinister secret of such grandeur
to be revealed, the Spaniards could sample the city's voluptuous
peace. From this time forward they knew it only by the name chosen
by Mexitli (Huitzilopochtli) himself, two centuries earlier: Mexico.

Cortés had left Cempoala on August 16 and entered Mexico on
November 8: three months to cover 250 miles, a record time if we
recall the difficulties of the undertaking. Having left the coast with
four hundred Spaniards, not knowing exactly where he was going,
Cortés now found himself in Mexico, in the square at the heart of
the Aztec Empire, in the palace of Montezuma's father. The sovereign had paid him homage, and his army had grown by thousands
of soldiers.

How had he achieved such a tour de force? Above all, how had
he been able to reduce so easily the centers of resistance he encountered on his way? In this connection there is one astonishing fact:
the disproportion of the armies that faced one another. In the fighting
at Tlaxcala there was only one Spaniard to every hundred Indians.
Moved by enthusiasm, the chroniclers have doubtless exaggerated
the number of the Indian effectives, a number about which there is
no agreement. There is the same doubt regarding Cortés' own troops.
Although the figure of four hundred Spaniards really seems near the
truth—all the evidence, including that of Cortés himself, agrees on
this figure, considering the size of the army that had stayed behind
at Vera Cruz—that of the Indian allies varies according to the chronicler. When Cortés left Tlaxcala for Cholula, he took with him several thousands of Tlaxcalans. Bernal Díaz del Castillo gives the figure
of two thousand, while Cortés, in his *Cartas de relación*, speaks of
"five or six thousand." We must therefore consider the figures mentioned by the historiographers—some of whom, like Bernal Díaz,
were actually present at these adventures—as exaggerations, made
greater or smaller according to whether it was a matter of exagger-
ating the enemy peril or exalting Spanish bravery.

Having made this reservation, Cortés' military successes are none
the less astonishing. The Spaniards were courageous, sometimes to
the point of madness; but so were the Indians, who, moreover, had
no fear of death, which for them was the supreme reward of the sol-

dier. On the human level—physical endurance, offensive spirit, and the handling of weapons other than firearms—the Spaniards and the Indians were equal. Cortés' superiority rested on tactics and matériel. This excellent strategist recalled the lessons of his father, old Captain Cortés de Monroy, who had fought on all the battlefields of Europe. When Cortés forced the Tlaxcalans to fight on terrain he had chosen, or when he drew the Cholulans into the great temple under the converging fire of his cannons, he owed his victory to his tactical ability. But we all know that ultimately, in all the world's wars, the decision goes to him who has new weapons at his disposal. The effect of surprise and terror is worth more than the number and bravery of the combatants. Cortés' new weapons were cannons and horses, and although they were in small number (fifteen horses and ten guns), he provoked panic and death in the enemy ranks. Similarly, the muskets and arquebuses—some chroniclers counted them as light artillery—completed the work of the cannons. And the dogs, formidable hounds trained for war, galloped ferociously beside the horses.

So on his side Cortés had military science, cavalry, artillery, dogs, and steel sabers. Against him he had numbers. In acquiring allies, he thought first to equalize and thereafter to reverse the disproportion of manpower. This is what eventually happened.

There is one final point to be made in this attempt to explain Cortés' victories. Sometimes during a fight, without apparent reason, the Indians softened or seemed to want to avoid contact. It was clear that they wanted to spare the Spaniards. This attitude resulted from religious needs: prisoners were wanted so that they could be immolated upon the sacrificial stone. To kill an enemy on the battlefield was an incomplete deed, for thereby a believing Aztec had done nothing, since he had not procured for Huitzilopochtli his quota of warm blood and beating hearts.

How must we think of Cortés, now that he had accomplished his mad march from Cempoala to Mexico? As Caesar or as Parsifal? It is too soon to say. Certainly he had handled his affairs without concern for others. He had fallen upon Mexico like an eagle on its prey. He had massacred the people of Cholula after luring them into a trap—a trick unworthy of a good adversary. His horses and dogs, his muskets and arquebuses, had forced an unrelenting type of war on the people of Anáhuac. One day, during the savage struggles at Tlaxcala, he had sent back fifty of Xicotenga's men with their hands cut off; they were spies, and he needed an example. By doing so, Cortés was defending himself, for the enemy was ferocious and would yield only to force. The enemy? Was it not Cortés who was the aggressor? Although his cause was good, what can be said of the Indians, who were, after all, protecting their own gods and their own houses? Since the juridical and moral problem raised by the conquest is inseparable from historical fact, none can deny that the rights of Cortés were the rights of the strong. But his duty as a Spaniard had its demands, and the first of these was to go forward. *Adelante!*

But legitimate or not, Cortés' actions were prudent. He had recourse to violence only when absolutely necessary and when his troops were in danger. Before making war he offered peace—*his* peace, of course. If he was deceived, he punished. He disliked reprisals but he used them when he had to. He knew how to lull the enemy and how to coax it; he also knew how to subdue it. Divide and rule. Deal with the enemy piecemeal. Cortés had made these formulas his own long before they became famous, but the processes themselves are classic. This Conquistador was more than an excellent general; he had the makings of a statesman on the Renaissance pattern. At Salamanca his reading had not been limited to Plutarch; he had also read Machiavelli.

CHAPTER 9

The Noche Triste

CORTÉS' first concern after entering Axayacatl's palace was to fire a salvo of guns: a necessary demonstration. He intended to confirm at once, in the eyes of the Indians of the capital, the reputation of being a white god that he had had since his landing at San Juan de Ulúa. He was the one who commanded the thunder, and no one must forget it. He thus hoped to avoid fighting, not from fear but from a desire to spare his effectives, for a good captain is economical with his men's blood. Moreover, what would be the result of a trial of strength, with only four hundred Spaniards against Montezuma's whole army? Before this point was reached, he would try diplomacy. He would negotiate, but of course without taking his hand from the hilt of his sword.

From this moment the game was to be played out between Montezuma and himself, man to man.

Montezuma's Vacillations

When Montezuma Xocoyotzin, son of Axayacatl, succeeded his uncle Ahuitzotl on the imperial throne in the same year that Christopher Columbus set out from Cádiz on his last voyage, times were good and the election was no more than a formality. Only the ceremony remained. In fact, for a hundred years the reigning sovereign had designated his successor during his lifetime, and the Aztec monarchy had become hereditary.

The evolution of executive power in the valley of Mexico was linked with that of the regime itself. The passage from an anarchic, nomadic way of life to a municipal regime, then to a governmental and finally to an imperial regime was parallel to the development of Tenochtitlán. These two related phenomena would not have been possible without an elite caste. The severe trials experienced by the Aztecs when they were first established in the lagoon necessitated the emergence of the elite, formed principally of military men. Selection by battle contributed to promoting an aristocracy of the sword. The clergy, too, had a growing influence, and a veritable ecclesiastical and military aristocracy was thus constituted.

The necessities of municipal life and of the defense of the territory led the Aztec aristocracy to choose a leader. His prerogatives, at first limited in space and time like those of the Roman consuls, increased with the spread of the mother city. Little by little the electors lost their power. The leader was elected from the same clan, and later from the same family, until at last the hereditary principle was accepted by all. The foundation of the Aztec dynasty by Acamapichtli consecrated the hegemony of the Aztlan tribe. Itzcoatl, Montezuma's great-uncle, by uniting Mexico, Texcoco, and Tlacopán under his scepter, laid the foundations of the empire. There was scarcely a

century between the arrival of the Aztec horde in the marshes of
Texcoco and the birth of the triple alliance.

Montezuma was the last of this powerful dynasty. His powers
were actually those of an absolute monarch. As supreme leader or
tlacatecutli, he exercised civil and military command, but in his
function as high priest or *teotecuhtli,* he was the leader of the cult—
in fact, he was the god's representative on earth. His spiritual realm
had the majestic dimensions of the universe. As to his temporal kingdom, he reigned in the north as far as the Río Pánuco, in the south
as far as Guatemala, and in the east as far as the Gulf of Mexico. He
had subjugated the Totonacs, the Zapotecs, the Otomis, and the
Tarascos. One state remained resolutely hostile and counterattacked
him vigorously: the republic of Tlaxcala.

A curious man, this Montezuma: a military leader of unquestion-
able worth, a religious leader deeply attached to his faith, a sovereign
by divine right, imbued with the responsibilities of his task. In sacred
matters he thought and acted like a fanatical monk. He missed none
of the rites of his religion: fasting, penitence, and liturgical blood-
letting. At the same time he had a taste for grandeur: his palace had a
hundred rooms, the walls were of porphyry and jade, the ceilings
of carved wood, and the floors of cypress wood. He had two wives
and a number of concubines; five hundred nobles, bright with jewels
and multicolored feathers, watched over the Emperor day and night.
A rigorous ceremony controlled each detail of the etiquette of this
magnificent and barbaric court. Montezuma ate alone and was served
by priests. Gilded screens hid him from the common people while
he dined. His menus were refined: much game, feathered and otherwise, which abounded around the lagoon—quail, partridge, and roe-
buck. His favorite drink was the chocolate extracted from cocoa
beans, which were brought at great expense from the *tierras calientes.*
For dessert, corn tortillas. When he had finished his meal, Montezuma
puffed at his tobacco through long reeds, then he was entertained
by his clowns, dwarfs, and tumblers. Sometimes he gave an audience:
the visitor advanced toward his sovereign with lowered eyes and
naked feet. He bowed three times and began his discourse with these
words: "Lord, my Lord, my very great Lord!"

There was an arsenal near the imperial palace, filled with various
arms: cotton-padded armor, slings, and clubs with obsidian blades.

Adjoining the arsenal was a clothing store where feathered ceremonial garments were carefully piled, then an aviary alive with
birds, from the royal eagle to the dazzling hummingbird. Finally,
Montezuma's menagerie: ocelots, jaguars, wolves, pumas, and bears
made the great square of Mexico echo with their roars day and
night. The Emperor loved wild beasts, and in the great periods of
atonement he gave them live prisoners of war to devour.

Everyone remembered the day when the kings of Texcoco and
Tlacopán, in the name of the empire, installed Montezuma on the
icpalli (throne) of Ahuitzotl. They placed a crown on his head and
hung heavy rings in his ears. Amid clouds of copal and before the
prostrated electors the triarchy slowly ascended the steps of the
temple of Huitzilopochtli. After sticking aloe spines firmly into
his ears, arms, and legs, Montezuma collected live quail in a basket.
He cut their throats and sprinkled the blood on the temple walls and
the sacrificial stone. Then, seizing a golden censer, he cast jets of
blue smoke to the four cardinal points, a grandiose gesture by which
he took possession of the world. Simultaneously he dedicated himself
to the war god and promised happiness for his people. At the height
of his glory he showed himself humble and gentle. One might think
his rule would be that of a father if one were to judge by his open
arms and his smile filled with good will.

Fifteen years and more had passed since Montezuma's enthrone-
ment. The promise of happiness had not been kept. It had not taken
long for the new emperor to cast aside his mask of benevolence.
The arms that had been raised heavenward piously had fallen upon
the confederate tribes. Never had the scepter of the Aztec dynasty
been more harsh.

An ascetic prince, an uncompromising defender of the faith, like
Philip II; an absolute monarch, magnifying the royal person, like
Louis XIV; a fierce conqueror, like Attila. But these were only the
appearances. What did he lack? Character. He doubted his mission,
he doubted his strength, he doubted his god. Caught between the
desire to protect his throne and the desire to respect the divine
will, he still had nobility when he confronted Cortés. But his spirit
was icy. What joy he would have in sacrificing these impudent
strangers to Huitzilopochtli! Yet if Cortés was the incarnation of
Quetzalcoatl, this would be a criminal undertaking. In this conflict

between two divinities, one of whom was silent and the other resolutely human, Montezuma did not know which side to choose.

Such was the person whom the Spanish general contemplated subduing. Followed by his faithful friends Alvarado, Sandoval, Velásquez de León, and Ordaz, and a few soldiers, he went to pay a visit to the Emperor. Friendly words were exchanged. Montezuma offered small presents to each Spaniard. On this occasion he cautioned them against what the Tlaxcalans had told them about his supposed riches. He certainly possessed a little gold, inherited from his ancestors, but much less than was said. His palace was built of stone and lime. He himself was made of flesh and bone like other men. Who could say that he passed himself off as a god? He even went so far as to lift his tunic to show everyone his perishable body. The Aztecs who were present trembled at the sight of their Lord's nakedness laid bare to these strangers, for to the Indian nobles it was an incomprehensible gesture, but it was meant by Montezuma to emphasize his humility before Quetzalcoatl. He was nothing but a poor man and the servant of the gods. "What gods?" Cortés demanded. The Emperor shuddered. He had been expecting that question, and only one reply was possible: to take Malinche to the temple of Huitzilopochtli.

Cortés' visit to the war god could not have turned out worse. After ascending the five stages of the teocallis and the hundred and fourteen steps that gave access to the upper terrace, the Spaniards reached Huitzilopochtli's sanctuary and that of his companion Tezcatlipoca—the god with the pig's snout and glass eyes—just at the moment when the priests had completed their sinister task. Five Indians, their bodies open from breast to pubis, lay at the feet of the idols. Like sections of a severed snake, the hearts still palpitated in the brazier where the copal sizzled. Surprised to see the Emperor and his guests, the priests, with their obsidian knives still in their hands and blood trickling down their black garments, suspended the dismemberment. Mute with horror, the Spaniards gazed upon the funereal chapel. The walls were dark with coagulated blood. It was dim, but not so dim that they could not distinguish trumpets, scalpels, and withered hearts piled together in macabre disorder. In a corner was the enormous teponaztli made of stretched snakeskin, whose melancholy note could be heard leagues away. And the stench of putrefying flesh! Cortés could not overcome his disgust. Were these the gods that Montezuma revered?

Then the Spaniard began his first sermon. These cruel idols must be overthrown and the statue of the Virgin substituted. Montezuma took the proposal very badly. The Aztec people owed everything to Huitzilopochtli. He was as solid in the stone as in their minds. Montezuma begged Malinche to abstain in future from outraging the tutelary gods. Cortés did not insist, for the hour had not yet come, and he simply obtained permission from the Emperor to have a chapel built where Father de Olmedo could celebrate the Catholic rites. Slowly, and filled with nausea, the Spaniards descended the steps of the teocalli.

The Oath to Charles of Spain

It was clear that this state of armed peace could not last long. It was an ambiguous situation which anything could disrupt. For although Cortés was patient and Montezuma indecisive, both felt the need for a solution, which certain events helped to precipitate.

While seeking the best site on which to build their chapel, the Spaniards discovered the entrance to a strongroom that held Axayacatl's treasure. The Emperor's presents and the booty seized by Cortés' soldiers seemed almost paltry beside this incredible accumulation of gold and precious stones. For the time being, it was decided to keep the matter secret, but after a while the Spaniards began to murmur. What reason was there for such inactivity and discipline, unjustifiable by military requirements? They had come to fight and to make their fortunes—or rather, to fight and to go home after sharing the booty, which already totaled 162,000 pesos. Meanwhile, bad news arrived from Villa Rica de la Vera Cruz. During a sortie by the Spanish garrison in the direction of Nautla, Cuauhpopoca, the local chieftain, had taken arms against the expeditionary corps, and although eventually the Spaniards had been victorious, six of them had been killed, including Juan de Escalante, the garrison's commander. To show his zeal, Cuauhpopoca thought fit to send Montezuma the head of one of the Spaniards, Juan de Arguello. The Emperor turned away in disgust.

The Nautla affray strongly impressed Cortés' officers: the death of their comrades, demonstrating the vulnerability of the teules, was a severe blow to Spanish prestige. Moreover, they suspected that Montezuma was no stranger to this act of treachery. If the advantages that had been gained were not to be lost, a heavy blow must be struck at once. What could it be? The capture of Montezuma himself.

After long hesitation, for it would be a risky affair, Cortés yielded to the arguments of those around him. Guards were posted at the crossroads and at the entrances to the streets, and Cortés then marched into the imperial palace together with his general staff.

The interview lasted two hours. Trembling with fear, his hands gripping the arms of his chair, Montezuma lowered his head before the reproaches of Cortés, translated to him by Doña Marina. He begged the Spaniard to spare him such humiliating treatment. What would his ministers say? What would his subjects think? He begged Malinche to take his son and two daughters as hostages instead. But Cortés' biting words and Velásquez de León's resounding voice drowned Montezuma's mumblings. Although he had only to make a sign to his guard and not a Spaniard would leave the palace alive, the monarch submitted to the will of Cortés, and the horror-stricken people of Mexico were faced with the stupefying sight of Montezuma removed as a prisoner to his father's palace, cringing in his litter and with his face bathed in tears. Quetzalcoatl had spoken.

The confinement of the Emperor ended any desire for resistance in the Aztec city. The streets that hitherto had been so frequented were now deserted "as if a jaguar were at large." Although theoretically Montezuma retained his prerogatives, no one was fooled, for who obeys a prisoner? Cortés then felt he was strong enough to destroy the gods, having overthrown their earthly representative. He climbed to the top of the teocalli and, armed with an iron bar, overturned the statues of Huitzilopochtli and Tezcatlipoca. Each blow on the stone echoed in the hearts of the Aztecs. Then the Spaniards whitewashed the bloodstained walls and erected an altar to the Virgin on the sacrificial stone itself. A cross was planted atop the chapel and Father de Olmedo celebrated Mass.

With their sovereign a captive and their gods overthrown, could the Aztecs know humiliation more complete? But they were to experience a final trial. One day they saw Cuauhpopoca, the chieftain of Nautla, his son, and fifteen of his nobles arrive in the main square of Mexico. They were chained, and blood streamed from their wounds. Dragged before Cortés for judgment and put to the torture, they confessed to having acted under orders from Montezuma. Though the Emperor denied it, he was brought down from his throne and put into irons. At the same time a stake was set up facing the temple of Huitzilopochtli, and Cuauhpopoca and his son were burned there, and their screams mingled with the groans of the Emperor and his intimates.

Resolved to stifle any possibility of a revolt, Cortés had Cacamatzin and Cuitlahuac arrested, as well as the ruler of Coyoacán. In a few weeks he had succeeded in removing the Aztec monarchy's heads of state, and, seeking now to put himself on the right side of the law, he thought to sanction by legal text what he had already done by force. He summoned Montezuma to take an oath to Charles V (Charles I of Spain had just become ruler of the empire). Then he was ordered to obtain the same oath from his subjects. The sovereign, submissive to Cortés' orders, called his chiefs and nobles together, and on this occasion the princes were momentarily freed from their irons. Alone with his own people, gathered together in the great hall of Axayacatl's palace, Montezuma exhorted them to do what Malinche required. He reminded them of Quetzalcoatl's prophecy. Henceforth, Huitzilopochtli was effaced before the white and bearded god. The tears ran down the faces of the disarmed warriors; they had to submit. The next day, in front of the troops and the assembled people, the Mexican chiefs solemnly swore fidelity to the unknown emperor. The report was drawn up by Cortés' clerk, so that none could be ignorant of it.

Cortés' soldiers could no longer reproach him for remaining inactive, but they were not the type of men to content themselves with glory. They were tortured by another hunger: the hunger for gold. So they pressed the general to proceed with the sharing of the treasure. To have delayed longer would have gravely affected Spanish morale, so Cortés yielded to their entreaties. With Montezuma's "permission," Axayacatl's treasure chamber was emptied of its contents. Every man received his share; that for the King of Spain—the fifth or quint—was not forgotten. Montezuma added his own personal treasure and charged Cortés with sending it to Charles, remarking ironically: "Pardon the insignificance of these presents, but I have nothing more. You have already taken everything."

In fact, the Spaniards had taken all. Their booty was enormous and almost impossible to calculate, but in modern terms it was some 6,300,000 dollars in gold! The personal loot of each soldier, Montezuma's fortune, Axayacatl's treasure, and the contributions that the Emperor levied on the provinces for Charles's treasury formed an accumulation of riches such as no conqueror had ever amassed. A shining river continued to flow to the feet of Cortés. He watched the stream carefully, setting aside the jewels and precious stones and ordering everything in gold to be melted. Alas for the goldsmith's art! Cortés placed a higher value on gold in bars than on jewelry. Moreover, he reserved to himself a fifth of the booty, like the King of Spain. After the *quinto real*, a *quinto* for the Conquistador. Every Spaniard found himself in possession of a considerable revenue, but they never ceased to plead poverty. They understood nothing of Cortés' arithmetic.

A people dazed with despair, soldiers confined to barracks, chiefs executed or in captivity, the national treasury pillaged, the gods silent: indeed, it seemed that nothing more remained of Aztec grandeur. Cortés still spared Montezuma, keeping him in reserve for the improbable event of a popular uprising, but in reality it was he who governed in the place of the fallen sovereign. He levied taxes, named officials, and above all, had his lieutenants reconnoiter the country that he already considered his own. Small detachments were sent almost everywhere with the task of discovering the gold-bearing regions. Cortés wanted gold. His soldiers whispered that he kept the larger part for himself and gave them only the crumbs. There was some truth in these murmurings. Cortés loved gold.

While the general consolidated his power in Mexico, a double danger hung over his head. Two enemies, an Aztec and a Spaniard, were preparing to attack him. In northern Mexico, at Tlatelolco, resistance against the Spaniards was being organized in the greatest secrecy. Its leader was Cuauhtémoc, son of Ahuitzotl, and Montezuma's first cousin. Elsewhere, a powerful fleet was steering toward Villa Rica de la Vera Cruz, with Pánfilo de Narváez in command. It had been sent by Diego Velásquez to arrest Cortés.

Thus at the very moment when Cortés was receiving the submission of Montezuma's Mexico to Charles's Spain, another Mexico
and another Spain were rising to contest his rights and, if possible,
to break him.

Alvarado Disturbs the Feast

Truth to say, Cortés' thoughts were concerned very little with
Cuba. Although close in terms of time—he had left Havana only
fourteen months before—the island and his own beginnings seemed
to him very far away. So many things had separated him from
them: the cordilleras, the massacre at Cholula, the valley of shining
cities, Doña Marina. . . . How banal Cuba seemed beside all that!
But if Cortés did not think about Cuba, Cuba was thinking about
him. It would not be long before the results of this concern were
felt.

For the moment the Captain General was watching Montezuma,
whose attitude had changed. Since Cortés had overthrown the statue
of Huitzilopochtli and substituted those of the Virgin and the
Infant Jesus, Montezuma had cold-shouldered the Spaniards. Wish-
ing to clear up the matter, Cortés presented himself to the Aztec
monarch. What was going on? In a few words Montezuma acquainted him with the present situation. The gods had spoken at
last. Huitzilopochtli, the war god, Tlaloc, the rain god, Xipe, the
god of spring, and all the rest had given their verdict: that all the
Spaniards should be stretched upon the sacrificial stone! The gods
were hungry for Castilian hearts and thirsty for their blood, and
the hour of oblation could be delayed no longer. Cortés' officers,
present at the interview, put their hands to their swords, but the
general restrained them. He knew his man. Let him finish! In fact,
Montezuma's voice became softer. He would remain deaf to the
voices of the gods. Why? Because Cortés was his friend. But the
Spaniards must leave the country at once.

Cortés had several strings to his bow: patience was one of the
best. He must gain time. He bowed, apparently, to the Emperor's
will. He reminded him simply that he no longer had any ships.
The observation was well founded, and Montezuma made no difficulty about giving the general the time necessary to construct a

small fleet. Cortés planned to use this delay for other purposes. Was he to leave what he already called New Spain because of Indian threats? None of the four hundred Spaniards considered this seriously. In this adventure they had staked not only their lives and their honor, but also their spirits; it was not for them to scamper away like rats at the first growl of the exotic tyrant. Four hundred thousand Indians surrounding them? A thousand to one! But the proportions were right, for was not one Castilian worth a thousand Indians?

A few weeks passed. Cortés' carpenters had set to work. But although the official order was to work fast, the secret order was to drag things out. While pretending to take an interest in the shipyard, the Captain General was busy consolidating his position in the Mexican capital. He multiplied his contacts with the allied chiefs, without ceasing meanwhile to lavish smiles upon Montezuma. He did not hide from himself the delicacy of the situation. They were only a handful of men at grips with a thousand dangers. The numerical inferiority of the Spanish troops would one day end by playing into the hands of the Aztecs if the reinforcements demanded by Cortés did not arrive in Mexico quickly. The silence of Montejo and Puertocarrero was alarming. Had they failed in their mission? Every Spaniard had his eyes turned toward the eastern coast.

One morning in May 1520, Montezuma called for Cortés. Never had his smile been so oblique or his words so honeyed. He had just received surprising news from Cempoala: eighteen ships had dropped anchor at San Juan de Ulúa. Cortés trembled with joy. Here were the Spanish reinforcements. Everything was saved! Without abandoning his irritating politeness, the Emperor then handed Cortés a roll of maguey sheets on which his scribes had recorded the incident. Ships, cannons, horses . . . the drawing was exact. At the head of the disembarking men was one who was distinguished from the rest by his great corpulence, his great height, and the plumes that waved on the crest of his helmet. Cortés frowned. He had recognized Pánfilo de Narváez, Diego Velásquez' lieutenant. The armada had not come from Spain but from Cuba.

Cortés had deluded himself about Velásquez by thinking that the Governor would abandon his thoughts of revenge. But the successes of his former subordinate, who had now become an "elected" Captain General, had only increased Velásquez' resentment. Now, more than ever, he intended to punish Cortés for his disobedience and to recover control of the Mexican expedition.

When the ship that bore Cortés' ambassadors, Montejo and Puertocarrero, passed near Cuba, Velásquez was prepared to stop it. But the crew, properly briefed at the departure, managed to upset Velásquez' maneuver. The main thing was to cross the narrow passage between Florida and the western coast of Cuba without being seen, which was done with great skill.

Cortés' embassy reached Seville without hindrance. From there it went to Barcelona, then La Coruña, and finally Tordesillas, the residence of Queen Juana. Charles of Spain had come there to take leave of his mother before returning to Germany. On the road Cortés' emissaries passed through Medellín in order to take the latest news of his son to old Captain Martín Cortés de Monroy. They persuaded him to accompany them to the court, thinking thereby to give greater weight to their embassy. Young Charles showed interest in the two officers' report, even though he was much preoccupied with Spanish affairs: the Cortes of Castile was showing coolness toward him, and Juan de Padilla was preparing resistance. This was not the first time that Charles had heard of the New World; at the same time he received the missives from Cortés, others reached him from Velásquez. The Governor of Cuba laid persistent siege to the sovereign. There was even a Velásquez party at court, strongly supported by powerful persons, including Rodríguez de Fonseca, Bishop of Burgos and President of the Council for the Indies. After Christopher Columbus, Hernán Cortés. . . . Decidedly, this high-ranking prelate had no liking for the Conquistadors. All the eloquence of the venerable Don Martín was required to force the Emperor's good will. Charles could not remain insensitive to the rough words of the hidalgo, an old soldier stiffened by the wounds of long ago. He admired bravery. But before deciding in favor of either Cortés or Velásquez, he awaited more conclusive results. In the mind of the adolescent monarch—he was only twenty years old—political wisdom already prevailed over enthusiasm.

Then Velásquez, seeing that his influence at court was inadequate, resolved to strengthen it by direct action against Cortés. Having no desire to listen to the counsels of moderation voiced by

Diego Columbus, Viceroy of the Indies, to whom he was answerable, the Governor of Cuba dispatched a large expedition to the Mexican coast, composed of eighteen vessels and nine hundred soldiers, including eighty cavalry, as many arquebuses, one hundred and fifty crossbowmen, two gunners, twenty cannons, and a thousand Cubans. Pánfilo de Narváez commanded these forces, which were much superior to those of Cortés. His mission was precise: to depose Cortés, take him prisoner, and bring him back to Velásquez, alive or dead.

Narváez was established at Cempoala, ready for defense or attack. Meanwhile Montezuma, in his palace, was considering an alliance with the white captain. They were already in secret contact, and together were weaving a web of steel around Cortés. What was the Conquistador going to do? He quickly assembled part of his forces—seventy men—and plunged toward Cempoala. Faithful to his tactic of not engaging in a struggle before exhausting the possibilities of a peaceful settlement, he had previously sent Narváez a conciliatory missive in which he suggested sharing power. However, this had not prevented him from dispatching emissaries to Velásquez de León and Rodríguez de Rangel, who were at that time exploring the country, so that they could join him with their troops. Before leaving the city of Mexico, Cortés entrusted the command of the place to Alvarado.

Alvarado was sensible of the honor Cortés had done him, but his pride was clouded by anxiety. When he heard the clatter of hoofs on the causeway dying away, a great anguish seized him. He was alone—alone in the defense of the treasure, Mexico, and Montezuma. What forces were at his disposal? Eighty Spaniards and four hundred Tlaxcalans, which was sufficient for policing, provided the city remained calm, but not enough to oppose an uprising. Now it was precisely at this moment that the Aztec capital seemed to emerge from its slumber; it stretched itself and growled like a waking giant. In fact, this was the great annual feast of Toxcatl, on the occasion of the beginning of the rainy season in the month of May. It was celebrated in honor of the gods Huitzilopochtli and Tezcatlipoca. Cortés had thought it politic to authorize the celebration, on condition that it not be followed by any human sacrifice. Music and dancing, but no blood except that of quail.

Leaning from one of the windows of Axayacatl's palace, Alvarado watched the crowd growing by the hour. He was a fine-looking fellow, with a red-gold beard and shining armor. The Indians called him *Tonatiuh,* "Sun God." But today the Aztec people had eyes only for the actors in the festival. In the center of the square the statue of Huitzilopochtli that Cortés had cast out of the temple was enthroned, and around the idol crowded warriors covered with emblems, priests with blackened faces, young girls with their arms and thighs decorated with red feathers, and children waving palms. To the sound of drums and flutes the dancers beat the dusty earth rhythmically. One by one the children filed past the priests, who gave them the ritual incisions below the navel and on their arms, consecrating them to the gods. The crowd undulated like a brilliantly colored serpent. The nobles' plumes, the opal jewels, the golden bracelets, and the emerald-incrusted breastplates flashed in the sunlight, as splendid as the spread tail of a peacock. And from the ecstatic people arose a chant in honor of the Lord of Battles. Modulated at first by the priests, it was taken up again by the tribes and grew until it became a raucous incantation accompanied by the booming of conchs and the thunder of drums.

Alvarado was anxious. He felt that the fever of this fanatical crowd was rising. Heedful of the barbaric clamor, he noted the successive nuances: entreaty, love, and then hate. The religious chant had become a war cry. There was no need to understand the Aztec words to guess that it no longer concerned the beneficent rain, but "those whose blood should be drunk and whose flesh should be devoured." Moreover, he had only to watch the grimacing faces that were turned from Huitzilopochtli toward Axayacatl's palace. Alvarado was a rough soldier, but he began to feel something that was perhaps fear. There were close to two thousand people in the square. What should he do? Or rather, what would Cortés do? Never had Alvarado regretted so much his general's absence, for he alone was the genius. While Alvarado was trying to decide, one of his spies whispered in his ear that, contrary to agreement, the priests intended to sacrifice two young people. This put an end to Alvarado's scruples and gave him legitimate cause to intervene. Moreover, he was not displeased to plunge into the mob. He was a man of the people, halfway between the Middle Ages and the Renaissance, and although he had the temperament and violence of an old trooper, he also had the simple mind of a crusader. Such contrasts were not infrequent among the Conquistadors. Alvarado, a son of men who had fought against Israel and Islam, hated heresy even more than paganism. A love of gold he certainly had, but also a desire to defend his Faith. Down with the infidel!

Suddenly, above the clamor of the crowd, a Spanish trumpet sounded and sobered the Indians. The dancers stopped. The savage litany was cut short. Profiting by surprise, Alvarado gave a brief order. The Spaniards ranged themselves in fighting formation. Swords leaped from their sheaths, shields were raised, and while groups of soldiers seized the exits, others mingled with the crowd. The massacre began. Surrounded on all sides, the Aztecs were doomed. Soon the main square of Mexico had become a battlefield. Lances whirled, daggers struck, and blood ran. A murderous madness rose to the heads of the Spaniards. To kill was for them a way of freeing themselves from the anxiety and nervous irritations of the last few days: an atrocious relaxation that turned the soldiers of Christianity into blind beasts for a few hours. After the massacre came the pillage. The dead were trampled underfoot and the wounded were killed, the better to despoil them. Emblems were broken, bracelets were torn off. Jewels, sticky with warm blood, accumulated under Spanish doublets. Alvarado gazed with dismay upon this outburst of rage and wished that he could rescind the order he had given so imprudently.

But the roar of a storm succeeded the groans that rose from the corpse-strewn square. Thousands and thousands of warriors streamed along the two avenues toward Axayacatl's palace. They came from Tlatelolco. Alvarado's men, spattered with blood and laden with their booty, fell back in disorder to the Spanish quarters, and there was no longer any question of saving their honor. What was there to do but flee and barricade themselves against this screaming mass that rolled toward the garrison? Three-pronged javelins and obsidian-pointed arrows darkened the sky like a "yellow cloud" suspended over the heads of the Spaniards, who numbered only eighty.

It was a miracle that Alvarado and his men were able to take refuge in Axayacatl's palace in time. But how long would the walls resist the furious assaults of the Aztec legions? The siege was directed by the most famous warriors: the princes, the Eagles, and the Tigers.

Neither muskets nor cannons could clear a gap in the mass of the assaulting army. The wooden partitions began to give way. Then Alvarado decided to play his last trump card: Montezuma. He was thrust out onto the palace terrace. Alvarado drew his sword and placed the point at the breast of the monarch. The toneless voice of the Emperor could scarcely be heard as he harangued his people, but the uproar died down and then ceased. This frail figure, crowned with a diadem, was no more than the ghost of a king, but his words were still those of a god. The last rays of the setting sun reddened the myriad faces of the barbaric mob as they faced their sad master. He had spoken. The order was given to make peace with Tonatiuh, though no one doubted that it was only temporary. Then the arrows were dropped and the brandished shields lowered. The tribes could return home. Hundreds of canoes glided over Lake Texcoco, and in the violet dusk of evening nothing could be heard but the sound of oars on the surface of the water.

The Noche Triste

Alvarado mopped his brow, but he did not conceal from himself the gravity of the situation. Montezuma had secured only an armistice. The assailants had certainly withdrawn, but this did not mean they had capitulated. They were regrouping in the darkness and continuing the fight in their own fashion. With prodigious speed the canals would be blocked, the streets barred, and the aqueducts cut. The ships that were under construction would be set afire. The intention of the Aztecs was clear: to confine the Spaniards in the city, bar every possible retreat, and besiege them. But before starting operations, the Indian army awaited information about the result of Cortés' conference with Narváez.

Three heavy weeks slipped by. Then one summer morning the Ixtapalapa causeway resounded once more to the clatter of cavalry. Hundreds of steel helmets shone in the sunlight, and a forest of lances quivered in the dust. Gauntlets were raised as a sign of welcome. The Spanish garrison sounded the trumpets from the top of the wall. Cortés had returned.

The Captain General's expedition had succeeded beyond all hopes. Having left Mexico with seventy men, at Cholula he met the reinforcements of Velásquez de León (one hundred and fifty soldiers) and Rodríguez de Rangel (one hundred and ten). Three hundred and thirty men in all, who would later be increased by the hundred Spaniards in quarters at Villa Rica. Cortés reached the gates of Cempoala. Narváez had disposed his troops on the heights overlooking the great teocalli. He himself was peacefully asleep at the summit of the pyramid. Cortés talked with Gonzalo de Sandoval, who, since the death of Juan de Escalante, had commanded the Villa Rica garrison, and they united their forces.

The night was dark and it was raining in torrents. In a short space of time Cortés' and Sandoval's Spaniards crossed a river, took Narváez' sentries by surprise, overwhelmed the outposts, and penetrated Cempoala. The cannons sounded, but it was too late. Cortés was there. Sword in hand and quick as lightning, he climbed the steps of the teocalli and came face to face with Narváez. All night the Spaniards of Mexico and those of Cuba fought one another savagely, and for a long time the victory remained in doubt. Cortés lost three men, but Cristóbal de Olid captured Narváez' artillery. In the early morning Cortés carried the day. His men had set fire to the teocalli and had put out one of Narváez' eyes. Cortés received the submission of Velásquez' lieutenant in the grand manner. To this enemy of yesterday and prisoner of today Cortés opened his arms: a chivalrous gesture immediately followed by taking possession of the fleet and the Cuban army. The eighteen ships were disarmed and Narváez' effectives incorporated under Cortés' banner.

Once again the Captain General had won. Having arrived at Cempoala with a handful of men, he left it at the head of thirteen hundred Spanish fighters and several thousands of Indians whom he had picked up in passing. He had carried through a tour de force by availing himself of those whose task it had been to annihilate him. Meanwhile, he spread propaganda among Narváez' soldiers. He predicted for them a triumphal entry into Mexico. Was he not Quetzalcoatl to the Indians—the White God? But a messenger who had run at top speed from the Aztec capital tempered this optimism, for the news was bad. Cortés showed nothing of his anxiety. He hurried toward Mexico by forced marches.

Where was the enthusiastic welcome? The streets were deserted and the silence of death enveloped the city. Narváez' captains

Mexico, or Tenochtitlán

sneered. Was this, then, the glorious arrival that Cortés had promised?
The general had great difficulty in restraining his anger. He went
straight to Alvarado, whom he rebuked sharply. Then, in the patio
of Axayacatl's palace, he saw Montezuma coming to meet him with
outstretched hand, but he brusquely brushed aside the Emperor's
welcoming arm. For that disastrous day of Toxcatl, Cortés held
Alvarado and Montezuma responsible, the one by reason of his stu-
pidity and the other by his weakness and duplicity. Swallowing his
rage, the general examined the situation and found it tragic. He now
understood why the Ixtapalapa causeway had remained wide open:
his men were to be allowed to enter the city, where they would then
be trapped. The ambush was well laid, but Cortés did not console
himself for having stupidly thrown himself into it. It was a lesson in
strategy for strategy.

In the space of a night and with the nimbleness of primitive people, the Aztec patriots cut the bridges, raised barricades, and obstructed the canals. Reinforcements flowed in from all parts. They occupied the causeways, thus preventing the Spaniards from getting out, and prepared to besiege the town. A new leader was elected: Cuitlahuac, Montezuma's brother. The siege began. Cortés ordered Diego de Ordaz to try a reconnaissance at the head of four hundred soldiers. They left in good order, marching in step like a Roman legion, but they had scarcely passed the gates of Mexico when a holocaust fell upon them. Arrows, stones, and javelins whirled through the fiery sky. Groups of Indians surged from everywhere. Diego de Ordaz and his men withdrew, sweeping their swords wildly. The next day, Cortés himself repeated his lieutenant's attempt, but he was forced to turn back hurriedly under an avalanche of enemy projectiles. The situation was grave: in fact, not only were the attempts at a sortie doomed to failure, but the Spanish camp was not safe. Water was scarce and provisions were shrinking. The attackers fired flaming arrows, which had already set fire to a number of buildings. A veil of smoke and soot covered Axayacatl's palace.

Cortés had returned to the capital on June 24. The month ended. Under the furious pressure of the Aztec warriors, fuddled with pulque and inflamed by their priests, the Spanish camp drew closer and closer together. The Spaniards suffered severe losses. It was no longer a question of leaving the camp, but of holding on with all their strength. How could they withstand the constantly renewed flood of Indian aggressors? Cortés then decided to make use of Montezuma. It is true that he no longer meant anything in the eyes of the Aztec people, for the election of his brother had finally destroyed the little prestige he had retained. But it was possible that the voice of the fallen Emperor might awaken the echo of former terrors in the minds of the tribesmen.

The royal hostage was brought from his apartment. A plumed cloak was thrown over his shoulders; a diadem was placed upon his brow and a scepter in his hand. Dressed again in his insignia, he appeared before his people on the terrace of his father's palace. Protected by Spanish shields, the trembling figure spoke. Was this the one who had ruled as far as Guatemala, who now delivered this embarrassed discourse in a toneless voice? The great Montezuma had become a puppet disguised as a king. Meanwhile the lances were

lowered and the people listened to him. Eight years of reverence are
not easily discarded. In a voice that lacked fire, he exhorted the
Aztecs to lay down their arms. The Spaniards were the stronger; the
Aztecs would have to yield. A long and indignant uproar greeted the
ridiculous prince's declaration; jeers drowned the melancholy thread
of his words. A volley of projectiles fell upon the terrace, and the
Spaniards raised their shields to protect the Emperor. But they were
too late. Montezuma was hit by a stone on the forehead and he fell.
He was carried away. He refused all aid and tore away the dressings.
He cried loudly for death, and some hours afterward, died. Had he
succumbed to his wounds or had the Spaniards finally killed him?
Whether he perished by a Castilian blade or by a blow from an Aztec
sling—Montezuma took the truth of the event with him. Torn between Huitzilopochtli and Quetzalcoatl, his indecision had made a
martyr of him, and his miserable end was that of a desperate man.

Montezuma's death aggravated the Spaniards' situation even further. The tribal council ratified the election of Cuitlahuac. Galvanized by their new king, the Aztecs intensified their siege and gained
ground. Attacks and counterattacks succeeded one another without
respite. The Spaniards were dislodged from Axayacatl's palace and
moved their quarters to neighboring houses in the square. But not
for long, for fires chased them out again. Withdrawal followed withdrawal until they had their backs to the temple of Huitzilopochtli
and there was nothing to do but take refuge on the pyramid. With
shields and swords held high, they climbed the steps of the teocalli,
which was still in the hands of the Indians. Each step conquered was
a victory, but eventually they reached the third terrace and then the
top platform. Below them the battle raged with the roar of a forge.
The whole city was on fire.

Temporarily the Spaniards were safe, but they were condemned
to perish, for there was not a grain of corn or a drop of water; the
dead and wounded baked under the terrible June sun. All around the
teocalli the Indian mob, suddenly silent, awaited the moment when
its prey, worn out, would let itself be devoured. Cortés had tried
everything to pierce the dense human wall of the Aztec tribes. He
had even had four *mantas* built: battle towers mounted on wheels
and protected by the cavalry. From inside them the crossbowmen
fired with all their strength, but a few moments sufficed for the

enemy, perched on the roofs of houses, to smash the Spanish "tanks."
Was the battle lost? Not yet. One last chance remained—to force
the siege, to risk the impossible. How could a few hundred exhausted
Spaniards possibly break through that enormous mass of Indians?
But their nerves were frenzied; rather than surrender or die of
hunger, Cortés' soldiers preferred to make the last desperate effort.
To stay and be slaughtered by the knives of the priests would be an
end too ignoble for caballeros!

It was July 1, and the blockade had lasted a week. Cortés gave the
order to retreat. The moment seemed propitious. Botello, the soldier-
astrologer, had read in the stars that they had to start that very night,
for afterward it would be too late. Rain was falling. The general's
plan was to reach the mainland by the one road not yet completely
severed—the western causeway. Having reached Tacuba, the Spanish
column would move northward, circle Lake Texcoco, and rejoin the
road that led to Tlaxcala by way of Otampan. The plan was a daring
one, but the alternatives were clear: to flee or to die.

In order to cross the breaches in the Tacuba causeway (the Aztecs
had broken it in several places) a portable wooden bridge was built.
The men were assembled, and Father de Olmedo celebrated Mass.
All was ready for departure. Had nothing been forgotten? Yes: the
gold. There were 700,000 pesos, but the general hesitated to burden
himself with them, for the additional weight might slow the soldiers'
progress. The Spaniards needed the gold and had no wish to leave
it to the infidels. By smoky torchlight, the soldiers divided the fabulous treasure: gold in bars, powder, and nuggets, and jewels torn
from Aztec corpses. They filled their pockets and stuffed their saddle-
bows and bags. And now, *adelante!* For what seemed the last time,
for the hope of return was very small, the command rang out in the
Mexican city. The heroes of Tenochtitlán, who had arrived to the
sound of trumpets, scurried away like thieves. The darkness deepened
and the rain poured down upon an army in flight.

The column set out upon the causeway. First went the portable
bridge. Then came Sandoval, leading the advance guard. Cortés commanded the center, while Alvarado and Velásquez de León supervised the rear guard, protected by the artillery. In all, eleven hundred
Spaniards—the rest were dead or captive—several thousand Indian

allies, a few women (including Doña Marina), some thirty cannons, and nearly a hundred horses. The order was to keep silent and to move quickly, for the Aztec warriors were asleep, and the noise of thunder and rain drowned the sounds of the marching army.

Suddenly a woman's shrill cry gave the alarm, and the Indian camp awoke at once. Showers of arrows and stones fell upon the Spaniards. On each side of the causeway an unbroken line of boats harried the advance of Cortés' soldiers. Maddened priests beat the teponaztli, and its continuous rolling—the very voice of the war god—sounded the tocsin for the Spanish retreat. The portable bridge was broken. The horses slipped on the slabs, and the men, weighted down with gold, sank into the water and were drowned. Their bodies choked the breaches. Each man sought to save himself as best he could, and the living trod upon the dead in order to pass from one part of the causeway to another. The vital thing was to reach the mainland. Under blows from Aztec clubs, the Spanish soldiers tumbled into the lake, some of them still clasping chests of jewels in their arms, and in the wan light of early dawn the mud gleamed with Axayacatl's gold.

Breach by breach, the Spaniards eventually reached the Tacuba shore, and the last to come was Alvarado. He had lost his shield, and his horse had been killed beneath him. He was gravely wounded. Responsible for the rear guard and charged with covering the retreat, he turned around. There was no other Spaniard on the causeway, and he could now try to save his own life. Already the Indians were reaching out for him. Without hesitation, covered with mud and blood, the giant plunged his lance into the lagoon and, swinging himself up like a pole vaulter, landed on the bank with a great clatter of armor.

At the moment the Aztecs did not pursue the Spaniards onto the mainland. They were too busy despoiling the dead that floated along the causeway, though they preferred the wounded, whom they loaded with chains and took to Mexico to make a fine harvest of hearts for Huitzilopochtli.

Cortés and his men took refuge on the hill of Los Remedios, above Tacuba, and took count. None had ever known a night more bitter. The general himself retired beneath a cypress and burst into tears, and all the Spaniards wept with him. . . . *El árbol de la Noche Triste!*

This summer solstice had not been a good one for Cortés. In one week he had known the most intoxicating of victories, that of Cempoala, and the most humiliating of defeats. The Spanish lion had allowed himself to be caught like a sparrow in a net, and had escaped only at great peril. This time numbers had vanquished science. In the streets of Mexico Cortés had launched the first armored cars of the New World, but they had been shattered by Indian javelins in a few minutes. Montezuma was dead. Cunning as he was, he had served Cortés' purposes; for to Cortés this puppet had been like the equestrian corpse of the Cid Campeador to Alfonso VI of Castile—a standard and a shield. What was left to him now? Four hundred and forty soldiers, a dozen crossbowmen, seven fusiliers, twenty horses, a few cannons that were beyond use, one hundred Tlaxcalans, and almost no officers, for the best—with the exception of Alvarado—had perished. As for the treasure, it was scattered in the waters of Tacuba. Did this mean that gold had brought misfortune? Cortés almost thought so.

However, the defeat of Cortés bore within it the germ of future victory. None among his prostrate companions suspected that at this precise moment Cortés achieved his real victory—a victory over himself. He had dried his tears. He turned his head toward the lagoon, not to say farewell but to say *au revoir* in a manner that was filled with menace. He no longer heard the sobbing of the Conquistadors in the Mexican night.

CHAPTER 10

The Aztec Agony

FOUR hundred and forty soldiers: no more than when he had entered the city of Mexico. But why despair? Cortés got his people together and ordered them to start for Tlaxcala.

The hate that the people of Tlaxcala bore for the Aztecs was greater than their racial feelings, and it was this that saved the Spaniards. For they could have made short work of this miserable band,

which en route had undergone a terrible attack from the pursuing
Aztecs at Otampan—a band that dragged its useless guns and was
more hungry for sleep than for conquest. However, at the entrance
to the town, Xicotenga, surrounded by the elders, welcomed Cortés
like a great war chief. They embraced him. Tears flowed. Malinche's
prestige was intact, and so was the wild hostility of the Tlaxcalans
against the tribe of Aztlan.

Several weeks passed. For the Spaniards it was a period of relaxation. They nursed their wounds and overhauled their forces. For
Cortés it was a period of intense reflection. Although gravely
wounded in the head and hand, he worked. He made his report to
Charles, searched for the causes of his defeat, discovered and pondered over them. His mistake had been to try to capture Mexico from
within, when the town was surrounded by water and therefore continually exposed to flank attacks from the tribes of the lake shores.
To take and keep Mexico one had to have control of the water. Once
master of the lake, Cortés would merely have to stretch out his hand
to the Aztec city and gather it like a ripe fruit. This beaten general,
who, instead of abandoning himself to despair, analyzed his failure
and at once thought out a plan of victory, certainly showed the
abilities of a leader. He drew a lesson from misfortune, and in the
light of it prepared for the future.

In order to realize his plan, Cortés needed a fleet and an army.
For the moment he had neither, but six months would suffice him to
organize both.

He sent a party of Tlaxcalans to the coast under Spanish command,
charged with recovering all that was still usable of the remains of the
boats that had been sunk the year before: timbers, ropes, ironwork,
and deck material. All these were transported from San Juan de Ulúa
to Tlaxcala in the greatest secrecy. Then, obtaining the necessary
wood on the spot, the carpenters undertook the construction of
thirteen brigantines—light two-masted ships with a single deck. Actually, Cortés' workmen made the ships in sections that would be fitted
together at the site. As soon as the work was finished, the general
ordered the sections of the brigantines to be carried from Tlaxcala
to Texcoco. Thousands of Indian slaves, yoked to rollers like beasts
in harness, carried out this incredible tour de force of dragging a
whole fleet in separate pieces over a distance of fifty miles. As soon

as they had reached the edge of the lagoon, the brigantines were assembled. It remained only to launch them, though this involved digging a canal over a mile long and four yards wide. Forty thousand Indians worked there under the Tlaxcalan lash, and in the spring of 1521 the thirteen brigantines, each armed with a cannon in the bow, were anchored in Lake Texcoco. Sixteen thousand allied canoes formed an escort to Cortés' flotilla.

Paralleling the construction of the ships, the Spanish general reconstituted his army. First he assembled the remnant of his company. Meanwhile Velásquez, knowing nothing of Mexican events and believing Narváez to be master of the situation, sent another expedition to Villa Rica de la Vera Cruz. Cortés easily took over the men and matériel after they had landed on the coast. Thanks to these unexpected reinforcements, he was able to get together five hundred and fifty soldiers, including eighty arquebusiers and forty cavalry. Further, he was amply supplied with munitions and arms: muskets, crossbows, and powder. Twenty-five thousand Indians, forced or voluntary, enrolled under the Spanish banner.

In a few months Cortés had managed a complete re-establishment. Now the vanquished leader had at his disposal a naval base and a wholly fresh army, and awaited only the favorable moment for launching his counterattack.

The Falling Eagle

While the vigil of arms went on in the Spanish camp, what was happening in Mexico?

After the departure of Cortés, the first reaction of the Aztecs was that of a liberated people. For some days a gust of madness swept over the lagoon. The Indian mob insulted the Spanish corpses as they lay naked and despoiled. The unfortunate survivors were stretched upon the sacrificial stone; the priests opened their breasts with swift blows of the obsidian knife and, like barbarous hosts, presented the people with their dripping hearts. Huitzilopochtli—was he not the real victor?—had resumed his place on the profaned sanctuary. The grimacing idols with their quetzal feathers and turquoise masks were seen again at the altars. A savage joy shone upon the faces of the Aztecs, and the whole city was one triumphal song: "The earth trembles. The Mexican native strikes up his song. As soon as they hear it, the Eagles and the Tigers begin to dance." A lugubrious paean whose echoes added to the agony of the Spanish prisoners.

In the midst of all this, Cuitlahuac died of smallpox, brought to Mexico by Narváez' soldiers. The tribal council elected Cuauhtémoc, son of Ahuitzotl, to replace him. It gave formal sanction to a power that Cuauhtémoc had actually held for a long time, for while the weak Montezuma still reigned, Cuauhtémoc had been preparing and directing resistance to the Spaniards in the suburbs of Tlatelolco. The Noche Triste was his work. This time its hero was to confront the enemy openly.

Predestined by birth to rule, Cuauhtémoc had been educated with a view to accession to the throne. While still a child he was entered at the Calmecac—the seminary for the king's sons—and there had been instructed in religion and the art of war while simultaneously hardening his body by fasting and mortification. Penitence and pain had been his first masters. Beside his cousin Montezuma, he had covered himself with glory in the fighting at Tlaxcala. Then, having retired to his domain at Tlatelolco, he awaited his hour. Now it had come.

Preceded by the chieftains and priests, he went on foot from his palace to the temple of Huitzilopochtli. He had donned the royal mantle and in his right hand he swung a censer of smoking copal. He prostrated himself before the sanctuary and prayed to the cruel god. He had himself become the god: "I am now thy mouth and thy face and thine ears and thy teeth and thy nails, wretched and poor as I am." The new emperor turned to his people and gazed beyond the bowed heads toward the invisible frontiers of his empire that had now to be reconquered. Responsible for Aztec grandeur, the son of Ahuitzotl knew the danger that threatened it, and was perhaps the only one to have presentiments of tragedy. The thought came to him that perhaps he would be the last of the Aztlan dynasty. He was the very incarnation of the fatherland, but would he be able to save it, or would he drag the Mexican people with him in his fall? His name, Cuauhtémoc, means "the falling eagle."

No one had any doubt that Malinche was preparing an offensive in the grand manner. The spies were well informed: the attack on Mexico was imminent. Where and when would it take place? Cortés' intentions were inscrutable. This time surprise would work in his favor. But Cuauhtémoc did not remain inactive; he was preparing for the shock. Foreseeing a siege that he considered inevitable, he had the useless people evacuated: women, children, old people, and the sick. Hastily, ditches were enlarged, traps were erected and walls built, and arms and munitions were accumulated in the arsenals. While preparing his defenses, Cuauhtémoc strove to win over the greatest possible number of tribes. He invoked "the sacred union." He exalted the community of race. For all the confederated peoples of the valley of Mexico there could be only one enemy: the white man. These were intelligent politics, but they were to fail. Although for the first time an Aztec king embodied in the same national union all the tribes of the *imperium*, the Aztec fist was unclenched too late, for two centuries of servitude are not forgotten in a few days. The very name "Aztec" gritted the teeth of Tarascos, Tlaxcalans, and Cempoalans, who remembered their own people immolated on Mexican altars or reduced to slavery. Deaf to Cuauhtémoc's supplications, Montezuma's former slaves followed the call of Cortés: "liberation," or rather, "vengeance." Cuauhtémoc and the Aztec people with him were to pay for the mistakes of the Mexican tyrants.

Events took a sudden turn. On December 28, 1520, the Spanish army stood in battle order before Texcoco. War had begun.

Mexico Besieged

Cortés had divided his army into three corps, each at the head of one of the causeways. His plan was to launch the columns toward the Mexican city while protecting their flanks with the brigantines. The Spanish fleet would destroy the Aztec boats as the army progressed, and the assault columns would meet in the center of the town. This type of offensive was classic in European wars but was being tried out in the New World for the first time.

Before launching his great land and water maneuver, Cortés engaged in a series of small attacks. By harassing the adversary with rapid blows he tired him, tried his defenses, and at the same time tested his own resources. Five months passed, and then one morning in May 1521—the Monday of Pentecost—Cortés gave the order to attack. The three columns moved off. They advanced slowly along the causeways while the fleet simultaneously got under way. While the brigantines methodically cleared the lagoon with their cannons, the Spanish infantry freed the causeways. The operation began favorably. Under the fleet's fire, the Aztec boats found it difficult to approach the causeways. Cortés' soldiers, protected on both sides, gained ground. They did so cautiously, for the general's order was definite: to avoid encirclement at all costs. Anxiety to protect the rear and to advance only with certainty slowed the Spaniards' progress. It was a matter of two steps forward and one step back. Moreover, operations were possible only by day, and when night came the attackers retired into their quarters at Texcoco, the bridgehead of the Spanish invasion. Under cover of darkness, the Aztecs demolished the work accomplished by Cortés' men during the day. They cut the bridges and opened new breaches in the causeways, so everything had to begin again the next day.

Tired of weaving this Penelope's cloth, Cortés invented a new system. He sent his Indian allies in advance with the task of preparing the ground, that is, dismantling the obstacles put up by the Aztecs and using the debris to fill the breaches. The allies occupied the causeways during the intervals between military engagements. They fell back and gave place to the Spaniards as soon as a counterattack developed. Thus Cortés' soldiers advanced along the ways prepared for them by the Indian mercenaries.

How long was the road from Texcoco to Cuauhtémoc's city! One day, carried along by their own impetus, the Spaniards reached the suburbs of Mexico. Cortés attempted an assault. It was repulsed, and sixty-two Spaniards were taken prisoner. The soldiers withdrew precipitately but had time to see the bodies of their companions, with gaping breasts, hurled down the steps of the great teocalli. The Spaniards flowed back toward Texcoco in a cloud of ocher dust and under a rain of arrows. The funereal roll of the teponaztli and the braying of the conchs told Cortés that the game was not yet won.

The general regrouped his troops. Reinforcements had reached him from the coast, and he had now more than nine hundred Spaniards, though the Indian contingents varied according to the day and the circumstances, their number being related to the fortunes of the struggle. Desertions were frequent in both camps, but the twenty-five thousand allies Cortés had brought from Tlaxcala had at least quadrupled since the beginning of the campaign. The enormous human masses on both sides, mobilized and similarly armed, tended to balance one another. It seemed that the decision would never be reached.

Cortés had cause to reflect. Numerically his army was too weak to take the city by assault, and to nibble at the defenses, which were tough and full of ambushes, would be like filing at an iron bar. However, an end had to be put to the interminable conflict. Thinking to propose an armistice, his overtures to Cuauhtémoc provoked only an outburst of scornful laughter. One solution remained: blockade. Neither force nor attrition nor diplomacy had succeeded in defeating the Aztecs. Would they resist famine, that pale ally of generals?

With the siege of Mexico the last page of Aztec history was reached. The agony of the Aztlan tribe lasted for seventy-five days. Cortés destroyed the Chapultepec aqueduct that supplied Mexico with drinking water. All exits from the city were blocked, and the fleet completely surrounded the Mexican island. Any attempt at a sortie was broken by cannon fire. The general slackened his attacks and contented himself with advancing very slowly along the causeways, without approaching too close to the invested city. The Aztecs no longer had anything to eat or drink; they slaked their thirst on the blood of Tlaxcalan corpses and fed on lizards or on leather from shields. The besieged died by hundreds, but the survivors, munching the salt grass from the lagoon, continued to fight. While there was still a stone or a javelin within the walls, it was thrown at the Spaniards.

Cortés multiplied his offers of peace, and Cuauhtémoc obstinately rejected them. Mexico was no more than a vast charnel house above which the standards of the Eagles and Tigers still floated. Mingled with the unbearable stench of decay was the odor of copal, which the famished priests burned at the feet of Huitzilopochtli.

Now the Spanish army took over the city. Having crossed all the causeways, it methodically occupied every quarter, one after the other. The soldiers had to step over piles of bodies. Fifty thousand Aztecs had perished, and those who still lived tried to flee. They threw themselves into the water with their women and children. Mad with joy, the Tlaxcalans pursued this miserable prey and killed fifteen thousand of them, and as the Aztec prisoners passed they cried: "Death to this race of savage hearts!" From among this pestilence-ridden troop the Spaniards chose the youngest—the "recoverable" ones—and branded the letter G, for *guerra* (war), on their faces with red-hot irons.

It was August 13, 1521. The city had capitulated; Cuauhtémoc, on an islet with a handful of faithful comrades, abandoned the last struggle. The glow of the setting sun lit the heavy obsidian sword he brandished as the last symbol of Aztec grandeur. Indians and Spaniards fixed their eyes upon the sword reddened with the sunset and with blood. Then it was lowered and fell. The Aztec Empire was dead.

Almost encircled, Cuauhtémoc leaped into a boat and tried to reach land. Darkness had fallen. The pirogue slid into the shadows among the rushes. Muskets and crossbows were leveled at the fugitive, but just when the Spaniards were about to fire, Cuauhtémoc's voice was heard in the darkness, saying: "Take me to Malinche!" He was seized and escorted to the terrace of Axayacatl's reconquered palace. Victor and vanquished gazed at each other, then Cuauhtémoc said: "I have done my duty for the defense of my city and my subjects. I can do no more. Since force brings me to you a prisoner, do with me what you please." Then the slender emperor swiftly snatched the dagger from Cortés' belt and, handing it to the victor by the hilt, cried: "Take this dagger and kill me!"

The Triumph of Cortés

The Aztec Empire had become the empire of the dead. The earth was in disorder as after an earthquake. Of the three hundred thousand inhabitants of Mexico, only a few thousands had survived, and these were in a terrible state. The princes, Eagles, and Tigers were no more. "They were emeralds and they were broken!" Bernal Díaz del Castillo was to say. "Never in the world had a people suffered so much!" Mexico was nothing but a sepulcher.

Cortés' first gesture was to offer a banquet to his soldiers. A ship had just arrived from Cuba, laden with casks and pigs. Spanish wine and hams! The feast took place at Coyoacán. Under the influence of wine the Conquistadors lost their heads; they rolled under the tables, ravished Spanish and Indian women, and invented grotesque dances. After the Noche Triste this was the night of madness.

The soldiers of Cortés were sated with pork, wine, and caresses.

Would they be content with love and feasting? But another appetite gripped them: the hunger for gold. They had already turned over the debris of the city, but the harvest had been small: some fans, shields edged with silver, heron's feathers. Where was the gold? The question was put to Cortés. If only he could manage his own people as easily as he managed his Indian allies! The latter had returned home, very satisfied with paltry presents: priests' copes and chieftains' plumes that the general had distributed among them. And what better trophies than slices of Aztec flesh, salted and dried in the sun! In the villages they made merry with these macabre remains.

Where was the gold? Cortés passed on the question to Cuauhtémoc. The last Aztec sovereign's life had been spared, and the general had taken him under his protection. Superficially, Cuauhtémoc was treated with the honors due to his rank, but he was not fooled by this. He knew well enough that Cortés held him in reserve for some final blackmail. Where was the gold? Cuauhtémoc knew nothing. Cortés persisted. Where was the hiding place? The Indian remained silent. Then, together with two men of his suite, he was tied to a rack. Their feet and hands were rubbed with oil. Brands were brought close and the flesh crackled. When one of the victims began to groan, Cuauhtémoc cast him a withering glance and said: "Am I on a bed of roses?" Seeing that nothing could be learned from the Aztec, Cortés suspended the torture. Fifty years later the sceptical Montaigne remarked: "The king, half roasted, was carried away, not so much from pity—for what pity ever touched hearts so barbarous—but because such constancy rendered their cruelty more and more shameful."

The waters of the lake were plumbed. All the houses were searched. Every Indian was examined minutely. Not a stone remained unturned nor an Indian body unstripped. Grain by grain the metal was recovered, and all these scraps of gold added up to a great deal. Cortés had it melted, took the fifth for the King of Spain and a share for himself, and distributed the rest to his soldiers. The Aztec people—its gods, its suppressed kings, its massacred elite, and its annihilated army—was now as poor as at the dawn of its history.

The war was ended. Spain's hour had sounded. Cortés now had to secure recognition of his conquest from Charles V. Ten months earlier, when he had founded Segura de la Frontera, he had suggested to Charles that the conquered territory be named "New Spain of the Ocean Sea," and the Emperor had agreed to this name. But Cortés had to wait more than a year after the fall of Mexico to receive from Valladolid his appointment as governer and captain general of New Spain.

Cortés' triumph was complete. All he had to do now was to make his conquest secure. First he had to raze the remains of the capital and construct a new city in the middle of the lagoon. Every trace of Aztec presence there was effaced, and on the site of the great teocalli arose the cathedral of San Francisco. A Franciscan monastery took the place of Montezuma's aviary, and in the city center was built a *plaza mayor* that was soon noisy with Spanish gatherings. Cortés' palace surpassed Axayacatl's in its splendor. Thirteen churches witnessed to the True God. It took the Indian slaves four years, under the lash of the conquerors, to destroy the face of the former Tenochtitlán, and it was a bitter paradox that Aztec hands carved the first capital of the Spanish Empire in America from ancestral stones.

Once built, the new city had to be peopled. Two thousand families arrived from Spain to settle there and if possible to make their fortunes in the colony that was in process of creation. The economic system was that of *repartimientos*, already established in the West Indies. Every immigrant Spaniard received a concession of land and native labor, on condition that he secure a maximum product from both. Plants and seed were imported from the homeland, and thanks to the water from the Chapultepec aqueduct, which had been Cortés' first concern to repair, the gardens were restored to life. The first attempts at cultivation produced excellent results: oranges and peaches, as well as sugar cane and cotton, acclimatized themselves very well. Gradually the houses multiplied, and with their patios and colonnades they reminded the exiles of the *solares* of southern Spain. Crenelated towers, orchards very like the *vega* of Granada, monasteries that looked like fortresses, and the odor of jasmine . . . was this not Andalusia, risen again under the Anáhuac sun?

So at last the master of New Spain had found a role to suit him: that of legendary prince. In the magnificent lord of today the warrior of yesterday could no longer be seen, nor the unlucky planter of Cuba, nor the man who fled from the Noche Triste. In the residence that he set up at Coyoacán, which he preferred to his palace at

Mexico, Cortés kept court like a sovereign. He had his counselors, his gentlemen of the chamber, his civil and military households. He ate from vessels of gold. He never moved unless surrounded by armed valets and pages. The Governor's clowns and musicians were ready at any hour of the day or night to distract him. His women—their color was not important to him!—shared his favors. Don Juan? This was the epoch when that type of man, dressed in black velvet, with a rapier at the ready, frequented the palaces of the dukes of Seville, and Cortés was the Don Juan of the New World and was never separated from his "little allies," Indian and Spanish. The earlier ones—María de Estrada the Asturian, Doña Marina the favorite, and all those whom he had drawn to his retinue since Cuba and Tabasco—were honored, which was only just. They, like the men, had been under fire, and had been through the terrible retreat from Mexico. They had bandaged the wounded and buried the dead. Cortés considered them as companions-at-arms. But the faithful cohort had been swollen with new recruits: daughters of caciques who had been handed over to the victor by farseeing fathers, and Spanish ladies who had come from Cuba or Spain. The general had his seraglio.

There was one shadow on this splendid scene: the sudden arrival in Mexico of Catalina Juárez, Cortés' lawful wife. Was it jealousy that drove her to cross the sea, or was it ambition? The general's court was also a salon, and Catalina intended to be the queen of this salon. She was coldly received by her husband, but she persisted in trying her hand at the difficult role of general's wife.

A rigorous etiquette regulated this still barbaric yet Castilian court. Cortés had re-established the high local officials in office, and Cuauhtémoc himself, although a prisoner, had the title of governor of Mexico. By this means, and under the guise of generosity, the general transferred to the Indian administration the delicate responsibilities of recruiting labor, levying taxes, and maintaining order. Quite a composite crowd gathered at the Governor's audiences: alcaldes, captains coming to receive their orders, and native chiefs, silent and grave. And at one table, under the trees of Coyoacán, were gathered together the clerics from Valladolid and the caciques from the lagoon. Catalina presided over the banquets and received visits, but her presence revived in Cortés the bitter regrets of a forced marriage. Had she forgotten that he had married her in order to escape the alguazils? He tried vainly to bring her to reason, but she pursued him with her recriminations and ceaselessly demanded further honors. One morning Catalina was found dead in her bed, apparently strangled. By whom?

Cortés' amusements and his conjugal vexations did not keep him from his main objective—to complete the conquest—and the moment had come to confirm its evangelical character. At his request, religious missions were sent from Spain to begin the struggle against idolatry. Franciscans and Dominicans were the pioneers of the spiritual conquest. Thenceforth and as a preamble to every public catechization, the Indian chiefs and their families were led to baptism. Cortés built great hopes on the value of example at these spectacular conversions. First in importance was Cuauhtémoc. His religious instruction was begun, but what did he retain of all this teaching? Was he truly touched by grace, or did he make his submission to Christ because he planned some last and secret stratagem? However that may be, he docilely let himself be taken to the baptistry, where he knelt with bared shoulders and clasped hands, while behind him stood his sponsors, Hernán Cortés and Pedro de Alvarado. Behind them was Doña Marina, and all around stood Spanish cavaliers and befeathered caciques. While a herald sounded a trumpet, the purifying water ran over the brow of Ahuitzotl's son. He had renounced his Aztec gods, at least in appearance. He was now called Hernando de Alvarado Cuauhtémoc.

The Twilight of a Hero

Cortés had triumphed, but evil omens were already visible in his sky. A success as brilliant and total as his could be followed only by vexations. From the moment of the creation of New Spain, his star began to fall.

Cortés' principal enemy was Spain. Captivated at first by the Conquistador's personality and by his gifts, Charles of Spain lent an increasingly attentive ear to those of his counselors who disapproved of Cortés' colonial policy. They knew how to stress very skillfully the danger Cortés was to the young Emperor's own power. He had more gold and would soon have more soldiers than Charles himself!

His powers must be limited. Such language was not new, for a quarter of a century earlier the enemies of Columbus had spoken to the Catholic monarchs in the same way. It was still Bishop Fonseca who led the game.

Commissioners were sent to Mexico, and then inquisitors. They settled down near Cortés and watched his actions, but as yet there was no question of supplanting him. He alone had the situation in hand, and to overthrow Cortés would mean losing New Spain. The imperial magistrates temporized.

While Fonseca intrigued at Valladolid, treachery worked its way into the very entourage of Cortés. Intoxicated by his victory over the Aztecs, he had the imprudence to call Narváez to his side. It was like introducing the worm into the fruit. Conspiracy started in the Spanish camp. Men plotted even in the antechambers of Cortés' palace. Encouraged by the dissensions of the white leaders, Cuauhtémoc broke his long silence and addressed a pathetic proclamation to the tribes, in which he evoked the grandeur of their past. Even more, he declared Cortés' powers unlawful and recalled that Mexico belonged to the Mexicans. "I have never," he said, "ceased to watch over the waters of the lagoon." The order to resist was clear, but it was not followed, for although the tribes well remembered their past glory, the memory of their recent reverses was even clearer. They bowed their heads and wept. Cuauhtémoc relapsed into silence.

Scorning the dangers that surrounded him, Cortés enlarged his conquest. He dispatched his lieutenants to the shores of the Gulf of Mexico from the Río Pánuco to Yucatán, to the shores of the Pacific as far as present-day San Francisco, and into Michoacán. But his ambition was not simply to reconnoiter and embrace the whole of Mexico; he was seeking a strait that would lead to the Southern Sea and thus open up the spice route. With this end in view, he entrusted Cristóbal de Olid with the command of an expedition toward Honduras. Shortly afterward he learned of the treachery of his old companion-at-arms, for Olid had gone to Cuba, come to terms with Diego Velásquez, and marched in the direction of Honduras on his own behalf. Five years earlier Cortés had freed himself of Velásquez in the same way, but now he became violently angry, organized a column under his own command, and left for Honduras. He took Cuauhtémoc with him.

Preceded by his musicians, surrounded by his court, and followed by the vanquished chiefs, Cortés set out for the unknown, crossing forests, marshes, and rivers. A passage was cut through the jungle, the rivers were crossed and the sierras climbed. On the way, obsessed with the idea of treachery, Cortés decided to put Cuauhtémoc to death. The execution took place in the square of a Mayan village. A rope was passed over the branch of a ceiba, the totem tree of the Mayas. Cuauhtémoc was led to the place of execution and, as he passed Cortés, said: "Oh, Malinche! I have known for a long time that you were reserving this death for me and I have known the falseness of your words. . . . Your god will make you pay for it!" Cuauhtémoc's head was passed through the noose; the eagle fell.

After burning Cuauhtémoc's remains and scattering his ashes, Cortés resumed his journey. With immense difficulty he reached Honduras, but he did not meet Cristóbal de Olid, for he had been assassinated by his companions; what was worse, Cortés found there a Spanish expedition sent from Darién by the governor, Pedrarias Dávila. Contact between the two columns was stormy. A fight started, but Cortés calmed the men, quieted their minds, and laid the foundations of a colony. Then he returned to Mexico.

Cortés' journey had lasted a year and a half. In his absence conspirators and intriguers had rejoiced. Was it not said that the general was dead? Everyone cast covetous eyes at the place he wanted to assume, but Cortés' return cast a great chill over the conspirators and they were obliged to quell their ambitions. Meanwhile, Charles's eyes were fixed upon New Spain, and the visits of inquisitors with steadily increasing powers multiplied. At first Cortés treated the emissaries of the Council of the Indies with disdain, for he intended to have dealings only with the Emperor; in this concealed struggle with the administration, the general won the first round. He had little difficulty in ridding himself of the mediocre Cristóbal de Tapia. He even succeeded in destroying the influence of Bishop Fonseca and in bringing about the disgrace of Diego Velásquez, but intervention from the homeland became increasingly insistent. *Missi dominici* followed one after the other: Luis Ponce de León, Aguilar, and Estrada, who went so far as to threaten to banish the conqueror from New Spain.

This was too much, and Cortés decided to go and justify his position with Charles. He embarked for Spain and presented himself to the Emperor at Toledo. One by one he took up the charges that had been made against him, including the abuse of personal power, the exploitation of the Indians, and the murder of his own wife, and refuted them with somber eloquence. He expounded upon his campaigns. The Emperor listened and asked questions about the Indians and the nature of the country. Cortés seized a sheet of parchment, rumpled it, and threw it upon the table. There was the map of New Spain—bristling with peaks, hollowed out into valleys, blistered with mountains, it was an inhuman land, but men had conquered it for the greater glory of His Catholic Majesty.

Charles was convinced, and Cortés was loaded with honors. He received the titles of Admiral of the Southern Sea and Marquis of the Valley—the valley of Oaxaca, southeast of Mexico, of which he was given inalienable possession for himself and his descendants. Charles placed the collar of the Order of Santiago around his neck. Finally, Cortés married the niece of the Duke of Bejar, one of the most prominent personages at court. One might think that now, six years after the capture of Mexico, he was at the height of his triumph, but it was not so, for, offsetting the honors conferred on him, an *audiencia* was created at Mexico. Thus New Spain became a viceroyalty, and thereafter Antonio de Mendoza ruled at Mexico in the name of Charles V.

Returning to Mexico, Cortés tried his new role as a planter for a while. He took possession of his domain at Oaxaca and busied himself with improving the land. But soon he felt too restricted in his palace at Cuernavaca. Did they think him old? He was not yet fifty and he was rich. He raised an expedition at his own expense and set off northward. For four years Cortés explored the Pacific coast, discovering Lower California. He founded settlements and planted his pennon on empty shores. He pushed his exploration as far as the 30th degree north latitude. A great part of his fortune was swallowed up in this affair, and hundreds of Spaniards died without profit to the Crown. Then Mendoza forbade him to continue an experiment costly in gold and human life, and with death in his heart Cortés looked for a last time at the valley of Mexico and left for Spain.

Did this signify the Conquistador's renunciation? Cortés was not one to accept defeat, and while breath remained in his body he was to use it in demanding justice for himself. New Spain was his, and it must be given back to him. For seven years this continued: a tragedy in two acts, one heroic and the other funereal, completing the portrait of the hero.

The first act took place before Algiers, where Charles was determined to undertake a punitive action against the capital of the Barbary pirates. The imperial galleys had taken to sea, but having reached the African port they were violently assailed and, after a disastrous land battle, the Spanish soldiers re-embarked precipitately, pursued by the Barbary corsairs. The rout was complete. Forty galleys were shattered on the reefs and a hundred boats were sunk, while the rest returned with great difficulty to Cartagena. At Charles's side, deep in the forepart of the flagship, an old man cried out that he would undertake to capture Algiers if they would follow him. This simple white-haired soldier was Hernán Cortés. The expedition to Algiers was his last foray, and to it he had committed all that remained of his strength and money. During the battle he lost three emeralds that had come to him from Montezuma. Rain and darkness shrouded the vanquished fleet, just as at Mexico during the retreat.

The second act took place in an Andalusian village about four miles from Seville: Castilleja de la Cuesta. Cortés was preparing to leave for New Spain, where he wished to die. He was sixty-two years old. But his body, exhausted by superhuman labors, betrayed his heart's intention. Death left him no time to prepare, but struck him down unaware. So he expired, not on the shores of the Aztec lagoon but under the Andalusian sky. Solitude, indifference, and poverty were the companions of his agony.

It was while the Emperor was hanging the Cross of Santiago around the neck of Cortés that his administration was preparing the Conquistador's succession: honors and caresses to hide a dismissal. Cortés' last years were occupied with soliciting an audience that was adjourned indefinitely. The specter of the great man haunted the antechambers, and he importuned everyone. In this last season of his life Cortés resembled Columbus very much. Forty years earlier the same tragedy had been played out at Valladolid in King Ferdinand's palace. Like Columbus, Cortés demanded power that was refused him; like him, he died almost poor, after enriching the royal treasury and giving Charles of Spain, according to Cortés' own words, "more provinces than he had inherited towns from his parents and ancestors." Also like Columbus, Cortés died alone and abandoned by those whose fortunes he had made.

Did Cortés ever have doubts at the end of the Mexican story? Did he remember the blood that was spilled, the Indians devoured by dogs, the gold torn from corpses, the slaves toiling under the lash, and the ashes of Cuauhtémoc scattered in the forest? If we reread his testament, if we consult the testimony of his contemporaries, Cortés at the end of his life seems to have been filled less with contrition than with mystic pride. He was no longer the conqueror consumed by his conquest, but at last he had prevailed over it. He retained of it nothing but its spiritual meaning. All the personages he had been—captain, chief of the army, trafficker in gold, and explorer—reveal the successive faces of a single person, the Defender of the Faith. The victory of which he was proudest was having planted the Cross above the teocallis. His principal enemy? Huitzilopochtli—the Devil. His master? Not Charles of Spain, but Jesus Christ. *"Esta obra que Dios hizo por mi medio . . ."* By this phrase Cortés defined himself: he had been the instrument of God. He had brandished the crucifix at the same time as the sword. But the cause was just. At least, he thought so.

In Mexico today no monument commemorates the prodigious adventure of Cortés. His ashes, preserved for three centuries at the hospital of Jesus of Nazareth, were dispersed by revolutionaries, just as were those of the last Aztec king. Is there no stone, then, to recall the deeds of the Conquistador? Yes, there is one: a statue of Cuauhtémoc.

PART THREE

Francisco Pizarro in Peru;

OR

War in the Land of Inca Communism

VIRACOCHA

The Incas governed their subjects in such a fashion that among them there was neither a thief, nor a depraved man, nor an adulterous woman. . . . The mountains and the mines, the pastures, the game, the wood, and all kinds of resources were controlled and shared so that each knew and possessed his own, without anyone else being able to take it. . . . Matters of war, although numerous, did not hinder those of commerce. . . . Order and harmony reigned in everything. . . . By our bad example we have destroyed this well-governed people. . . .

—*Verdadera confesión y protestación en artículo de muerte* made by one of the first Conquistadors of Peru, Mancio Sierra Lejesema, in his testament of September 15, 1589.

Death of Pizarro

CHAPTER 11

The Empire of the Sun

In the same year that Cortés received the title of Captain General
of New Spain from the King, and Charles himself took possession
of his Spanish kingdom after suppressing the revolt of the *comu-
neros* with some difficulty, Pascual de Andagoya made his voyage
from Panama. After skirting and reconnoitering the western coast
of the mainland, Andagoya brought back some strange news from
his expedition, foremost among which was the certainty of a vast
continent southwest of the Gulf of Darién. Moreover, he had encountered some pirogues that carried Indians who repeatedly used
the name "*Pirú, Pirú . . .*" as they pointed to the coast—probably
indicating a river that led into the interior of the land. The native
tales made allusion to a powerful empire governed by a sovereign of
divine origin and fabulously rich. In this land of dreams, gold was
used instead of stone.

Such was the report that Andagoya made to the governor, Pedrarias
Dávila. In his innermost heart the *adelantado* gave thanks to Balboa,
for in discovering the Southern Sea his unfortunate son-in-law had
struck the true road to gold, which started from Panama.

Andagoya's report was passed from mouth to mouth, discussed and
interpreted. The spark took flame and set fire to Spanish minds. The
simultaneous triumph of Cortés in Mexico and of King Charles at
Valladolid, consecrating the reality of the empire, excited the Conquistadors of Panama less than did the vague promise of that unknown realm: *la Tierra de Pirú.*

Three Resolute Partners

But the Spaniards of the mainland were not the sort of men to be content for long with chimeras. It was not enough simply to imagine this Eldorado: they had to go and see it. Three brave companions were to open up the track across the waters of the Pacific and through the tropical jungle by which the conquest would be extended southward as far as Tierra del Fuego.

Francisco Pizarro: we have seen him already, a simple sailor sailing with Diego Columbus. Afterward, he served successively under Ojeda, Balboa, Pedrarias Dávila, and Cortés. He changed his "patron" according to circumstances—or rather, to better his immediate interests. A faithful collaborator when it was to his benefit, he did not hesitate, at the first contrary wind of fortune, to leave his master of the moment or even to betray him. Núñez de Balboa had been his chief and companion, but he did not falter in arresting and handing him over to the executioner. Among the Conquistadors he was one of the hardest. There was not a soft spot in a heart that beat only for gold.

Natural son of a Spanish colonel and a prostitute, he was born in secret at Trujillo in Estremadura, some thirty miles from Yurta, where Charles V was to die. His mother abandoned him on the steps of a church, and it was said that his first nurse was a sow; without her he would have died. Then when he was old enough to walk he earned his living as a swineherd. As an adolescent he enlisted as a simple soldier in the army of Italy and never passed beyond that rank. Could one entrust a command, however modest, to an illiterate? For Pizarro did not know even how to sign his name. Tired of dragging his arquebus along the roads of Italy, without glory or profit except for paltry pillage, Pizarro returned to Seville. For an adventurer of his kind, what was there to do but embark for the islands? He was enrolled aboard a caravel as one of the crew. He was forty years old. Swineherd, soldier, sailor . . . until middle age he had been engaged only in lowly tasks in lowly company: the *pícaros* of Estremadura, the soldiery of the camps, and the *desperados* without faith or law who were saved from the gallows by sailing for the west. God? Fatherland? King? These were words that were scarcely uttered in Pizarro's entourage. As to honor, the "*punto de honor*" was a refinement for gentlemen only. To make a fortune, that was everything. It was a fortune that Pizarro went to seek in the New World. Ten years after his arrival in the islands he had acquired it. While clearing a way for successive leaders, he had filled his pockets. The pearls of the Gulf of Paria and the gold of Panama had made Francisco Pizarro one of the richest colonists of the mainland. What a sweet irony for the bastard of Trujillo!

Diego de Almagro: Pizarro's best friend and his companion-at-arms. He, too, was a foundling, abandoned, it is said, on the porch of a church at Malagón near Cuidad Real. Like Pizarro, he made his fortune in the islands. He was illiterate, but brave and ambitious, with a sort of rough vulgar charm. He knew how to be debonair when he pleased. Such was not the case with Pizarro, whose mailed fist never unclenched except at the end of his life, when he could afford the luxury of looking pleasant.

Ferdinand de Luque: this priest had come to Panama in order to teach, which had not prevented him from making excellent investments. The schoolmaster was rich. Beside the two veteran Conquistadors, already past their fiftieth year, Father Luque appeared like a neophyte. Andagoya's tales went to his head; he jumped for joy in the streets. They called Luque "*el loco*," the madman, a play on words which his excitement justified. He already saw himself the discoverer of the Tierra de Pirú.

These were the three men—Pizarro, Almagro, and Luque—who were going to confirm the confused tales of Andagoya and give them reality. They formed a sort of shareholding company, and before a notary undertook to divide the profits of the expedition. This involved nothing less than exploring the mysterious southern empire and taking possession of it.

At the Frontiers of the Tierra de Pirú

Each had his part to play in the syndicate. Pizarro was the military leader; Almagro did the recruiting and organizing; Luque did the administrative work: a soldier, a manager, and a financier. Actually it was Pizarro who commanded, and as for Luque, he confined himself to following the voyages of the two Conquistadors from afar. He remained on shore while his two team mates vanished into the golden mists of the Pacific.

There was nothing mystical about the projected cruise. There was no question of civilizing or converting. The object was clear: to make a fortune—and what a fortune it would be if Andagoya's tale was to be believed! Yet when the moment came, crosses and banners waved together in the high wind of the Andes. Was this a contradiction? Not for men who had emerged from the Middle Ages. Even though the aim was not one of evangelization, that would be accomplished nevertheless. Pizarro's companions, like those of Cortés, were imbued with dogmatism. Their faith was as solid as a rock, and the religious reflex was to them as natural as the instinct for conquest. Moreover, the two were complementary: one acquired gold and one saved souls, a matter of right and duty. The Conquistadors showed equal enthusiasm for brutalizing bodies and catechizing souls, and an equal sincerity, too.

For one can reproach them with everything but hypocrisy. Convinced of the racial inferiority of the natives and of their own excellence, not for a moment questioning the legitimacy of pontifical bulls any more than the rightful leadership of Spain, and utterly persuaded of the pre-eminence of the Catholic church, why should these rough adventurers from Castile and Estremadura feel even the shadow of remorse or hesitation? They were sure that God and the king were with them, and this quiet certainty gave them a clear conscience, freeing them from any hindering scruples. Not hypocrisy, then, but candid submission to unquestioned laws. And so, once again, as on the road to Mexico, the clatter of swords and the rustle of rosaries were to be heard on the Conquistadors' march.

When Pizarro embarked at Panama in November 1524, he imagined that he was close to his prey. But he and his companions were not to enter the mysterious capital until November 1532, eight years later to the day: eight years of nameless experiences and such incredible struggles against nature and man that one might doubt that these Spaniards were of flesh, so great was the fortitude they showed. Their physical endurance was indeed exceptional, but they were spurred on by something in addition: their fear of the master. Who could fail to tremble before Pizarro? The former swineherd of Trujillo knew how to enforce obedience. His sunburned face with its black beard was severe; he spoke little and never laughed. His officers secretly detested him; his soldiers feared him. But though they had no love for him, they submitted to him. By his brutal presence alone he imposed respect. He himself slept on the bare earth and was always at the head of his troops; he preached by example, and there was no choice but to follow him. *Adelante!* Woe to them who showed reluctance or betrayed him, for they were crushed without pity. To bring a superhuman task to success, an inhuman hero was doubtless needed.

Duly furnished with the governor's authorization, Pizarro set sail. The expedition was a modest one: two ships and one hundred and forty soldiers and sailors. But this was only the advance guard; Almagro was proceeding with his preparations and planned to join his associate later. For the moment, Pizarro was carrying out only a simple reconnaissance. His first goal was the mouth of the River of Pirú (in reality, the San Juan River), and he reached it only after several weeks of difficult sailing. He anchored one of his two ships on the coast, landed, and decided to rest part of his men while Montenegro, one of his officers, continued the exploration.

Was this the beginning of the magic empire—this sinister bay, wind-swept and infested with caimans, where there was nothing to eat but the bitter fruit of the mangrove? While waiting for Montenegro to return, Pizarro tried to make contact with the natives, but they fled at his approach. Days passed. Famine entered the Spanish camp, and men were reduced to chewing the boiled leather of their sword belts. This desolate haven well deserved the name of Puerto del Hambre (Port of Hunger) that Pizarro gave it. At the end of a month and a half Montenegro returned to base; he had been as far as the Pearl Islands but had brought back no interesting information. It was then decided to explore the interior, but they did not get far. Having reached a promontory—Pueblo Quemado or "the burned village"—they fell into an Indian ambush. Pizarro left five men on the field and just missed being killed himself. The Spanish troops re-embarked under a rain of arrows. The return to Panama was a melancholy one.

During this time Almagro had not been inactive. Following

Pizarro's expedition at a short distance, he had embarked with seventy men in a southerly direction in search of his associate. During his voyage he discovered the San Juan River, and he, too, tried to establish himself at Pueblo Quemado, from which Pizarro had just been chased. The Indians, encouraged by their recent victory, had no difficulty in routing Almagro's troops, and Almagro himself lost an eye in the battle. Despairing of finding Pizarro and sorely tried by his reverses, Almagro turned back to the isthmus.

Pizarro and Almagro met at Chicamá, near their starting point. They compared information, which was still vague, though it agreed. There was no doubt of the existence of a vast kingdom south of Panama or of the inexhaustible gold mines. More than ever did the business seem profitable. This was the moment to ratify the famous tripartite contract. First it was important to keep Pedrarias Dávila out of the partnership, for, scenting the odor of metal, he suddenly became demanding. After all, was he not His Majesty's representative on the mainland? Pizarro recalled that Diego Velásquez' claims had failed to obstruct Cortés' campaign. Learning from this precedent, he persuaded Pedrarias to renounce all rights to the territories they discovered, in return for immediate payment of 1000 pesos. Luque, who was increasingly attracted to the project, provided the partnership with 20,000 pesos on the understanding that a third of the riches acquired would be reserved for him. Pizarro and Almagro swore on the Gospels to respect the terms of the contract, and since neither knew how to write, they attested their good faith by a large sign of the Cross. Next to the contract between Christopher Columbus and the Catholic monarchs, that of the three men of Panama was probably the most daring legal deed that had ever been drawn up. What folly it seemed to divide in advance a treasure that was more than hypothetical!

Two years after their first attempt, Pizarro and Almagro took to sea again. The flotilla was composed of two ships of fairly heavy tonnage and eight auxiliary boats. The force numbered one hundred and sixty Spaniards and black slaves. Horses were taken, too, because of the help they had been to Cortés. The famous pilot Bartolomé Ruiz took the helm. It was full summer and the weather was fine. The auspices were favorable.

The itinerary was the same as on the first voyage: the Bay of San

Miguel, the Pearl Islands, the port of Las Penas, and Cape Corrientes. They disembarked at the mouth of the San Juan River on the coast of present-day Colombia. The spot was a desolate one: a muddy coast planted with motionless mangroves; a disquieting silence. Sometimes an arrow from they knew not where passed right through a Spaniard's throat. The three captains split up. Almagro was able to collect a few pearls and golden jewels during a raid on an Indian village. Here was something to attract those recruits who were still hesitating! He went back to Panama to seek reinforcements, while Pizarro decided to camp at the river's edge to investigate the country.

As for Ruiz, he continued southward. He discovered the island of Gallo, passed the equator, and rounded Cape Pasado, facing the Galápagos Islands. On the way he met a *balsa*, a sort of wide raft with a sail and a rudder. Merchants were aboard this strange vessel, and Ruiz questioned them. Where did they come from? From Tumbes. With gestures the Indians described this marvelous town. They spread out their multicolored stuffs, unpacked pearl necklaces, ran powdered gold through their fingers. All this had been bought at Tumbes, but farther south were cities even richer. When pressed with questions, the Indian merchants became silent and trembled with fear. Woe betide strangers who tried to enter the forbidden kingdom!

Ruiz returned to the San Juan River. Pizarro's camp was in a sad way. The natives had harassed the Spaniards continually, making fun of the hair they grew on their chins, and sniping at them with arrows. Fortunately, Almagro arrived from Panama with a reinforcement of eighty men, and the three captains, uniting their forces, set off again southward. The farther they went the more the landscape changed. Cultivated fields and villages succeeded the sandy beaches. They landed, but the people were hostile everywhere, and the expedition had to be on its guard constantly and sometimes to contend with a combative adversary. They advanced step by step, with their eyes watchful and their weapons ready. They came to Tacamez, where thousands of Indians, with gold studs in their cheeks, prohibited entry to the town. What were the Spaniards to do? Fight? But it was not an equal match, so the expedition retired. Almagro went in search of reinforcements at Panama, while Pizarro and Ruiz established themselves on the island of Gallo.

There was news at Panama. Pedro de los Ríos had succeeded Pedrarias Dávila as governor of the mainland, but this appointment robbed Pizarro of an ally. In fact, Pedro de los Ríos meant to put an end to these unsuccessful voyages that had produced no practical result. Men who could be usefully employed at Panama were dying in vain. And it was said, too, that Pizarro and Almagro were at loggerheads, and that revolt was brewing on Gallo. Scurvy, famine, and Indian arrows had ravaged Pizarro's mercenaries, and they had become like wolves ready to devour one another. One morning Pizarro's troops, gathered on the shore, sighted a sail on the horizon; Almagro and his men to their relief at last! The ship beached and an officer landed—Juan Tafur, Pedro de los Ríos's lieutenant. He handed Pizarro a message from the Governor, with the injunction to allow any man who showed a desire to do so to return to Panama. Pizarro was free to continue his mad enterprise—alone!

Pizarro did not flinch. Could he possibly oppose so formal an order? All eyes were on him. Almost all the men were frantic to flee the accursed island, but he was like a lion tamer facing his growling beasts. It was a grave moment and one that would settle the whole fate of the conquest. Suddenly, unable to contain himself any longer, he sprang to a spot in front of his wavering troops, and drawing a dagger from his belt, traced a line in the sand. Then, pointing south, he roared: "*Compañeros*, on that side are toil, hunger, nakedness, the drenching storm, desertion and death; on this side, ease and pleasure. There lies Peru and its riches; here Panama and its poverty. Choose, Castilians. . . . For my own part, I go to the south." And with a leap Pizarro crossed the symbolical furrow. In the silence that followed the men looked at one another. Then Bartolomé Ruiz crossed the line. Twelve companions followed his example, and the rest made for Tafur's boat. They had the air of deserters, but they did not hide their relief. Soon the government ship was heading for Panama, and on Gallo, where dense warm rain was bending the mangroves, there remained only Pizarro and his twelve men, for Bartolomé Ruiz had gone with the ship to pilot it on its return journey. He would return after he had taken it safely to port.

Who were these twelve fanatics? Among them were some who would become hidalgos; some were hidalgos already. There were Castilians: Alonso Briceño of Benavente, Juan de la Torre, Francisco de Cuellar. Antón de Carrión was a compatriot of Pizarro. Cristóbal de Peralta—his device was *ad summum per alta*—was a native of Baeza, and Alonso de Molina was born in Ubeda. Both were Andalusians, just as were Nícolas de Ribera, born at Olvera, and García de Jérez. Pedro de Candia was a Greek; it was he who later burned ten towns and, to expiate his crime, lit ten lamps before the Virgin's altar. Domingo de Soria Luce, Pedro Alcón, and Martín de Paz completed the dozen. Gathered about the terrible Pizarro, the twelve Conquistadors awaited the order to depart for the empire of Peru. For now the name was spoken.

While awaiting Ruiz's return, Pizarro decided to move his camp to a neighboring island, Gorgone, six leagues away. The place seemed better. There were springs and softwood; they could drink and make a fire. But food was lacking, and there was nothing to eat but pimento, crawfish, adders, and sometimes iguano eggs which the Conquistadors collected in their helmets. They disputed this bitter subsistence with the beasts. And what beasts these were! Ferocious creatures like pumas and jaguars, and foul ones like toads and alligators. How hardy these Spaniards were not to have succumbed to snakebites and to the claws of wild beasts! It is true that they never shed their coats of mail by day or by night, for they slept—if their light doze could really be called sleep—booted, armored, and with sword in hand. They had to defend themselves continuously, but in the sticky darkness they were less attentive to the tread of carnivores than to the stealthy flight of vampires. These monsters were watchful and waited for their victims to sleep in order to take their fill of blood.

For seven months Pizarro's companions floundered in this fetid mud. Their heavy horses, cased in steel as at the Crusades, sank in to their breasts. Devoured by mosquitoes, trembling with fever, soaked by the rain and suffocated by their armor, how did the conquerors manage to live? Finally, one morning, Bartolomé Ruiz returned from Panama with a vessel and just sufficient men to sail her. He gave Pizarro an ultimatum from Pedro de los Ríos: he was given six months to return to Panama. Six months! There was not a moment to lose. The little band embarked, not for the north but southward.

After the equator had been passed, the scene changed and the coast took on its wonderful tropical finery. In the foreground were flowers and variegated insects, sparkling like jewels, while amongst the trees macaws and monkeys kept up a deafening chatter. Behind lay the high line of the cordillera and, already visible, the snowy slopes of Chimborazo. The expedition rounded Cape Santa Elena, its beach studded with purple shells, and passing Santa Clara, came to Puná Island in the Gulf of Guayaquil. How soft the air was! The sky seemed to be carved from an enormous sapphire. A last promontory was passed, and suddenly the lookout raised a cry, pointing with his arm to Tumbes. The town that stretched along the indentations in the gulf was indeed Tumbes, and thousands of cube-shaped houses, palaces, and temples reflected the equatorial sun. A port—a real port such as had not been seen since they left Seville—opened to the conquerors' worm-eaten ship, and a motley crowd gathered on the quay to watch the Spanish caravel. There was amazement on both sides: for one group, the sight of the floating tower and white men covered with hair and clothed in steel, and for the other, this bright city that had succeeded the jungle. "They are gods!" whispered the people of Tumbes. "Is this the end of a nightmare?" the Spaniards asked themselves.

The first to land was Pedro de Candia, soon followed by Molina and the others. Everyone judged that caution was essential. A local official welcomed the strangers and led them around the town, which was guarded by a triple wall and a large garrison. There was no question of trying to capture it, and Pizarro restricted himself to establishing political contact with the authorities. Courtesies were exchanged. Pedro de Candia, an excellent marksman, performed wonders with his crossbow. Pizarro received presents of golden vases, precious stuffs, and jewels. There were salaams and smiles, and all parted on good terms. The Spaniards re-embarked, taking a few natives of Tumbes and some llamas with them, for they had never seen llamas before.

In addition to the treasures, Pizarro took back to Panama a harvest of information. He had learned, this time from a reliable source, that some hundreds of miles south of Tumbes, beyond the high mountains, a very powerful king reigned over an immense empire. He was at war with a neighboring king who was preparing to usurp his throne. This information filled Pizarro with pleasure. Like Cortés in Mexico, he planned to exploit the rivalry of these two princes and to apply Machiavelli's formula of "divide and rule."

The past three years had not been in vain. Pizarro now knew the name of those who governed in Peru: the Incas. Better still, he knew the secret of their weakness. The eyes that looked on Tumbes were already those of a conqueror.

Inca Communism

If a line is drawn from Quito, the capital of modern Ecuador, to Trujillo on the Pacific coast of Peru, and prolonged as far as Lake Titicaca on the Peru-Bolivia frontier, an obtuse angle is formed that embraced the Inca Empire—the Tahuantinsuyu—although at the height of its power the empire included Peru, Ecuador, and Bolivia and almost all of Argentina and Chile. This immense territory has four well-defined aspects: the *costa*, narrow and facing the Pacific Ocean; the Andean cordillera; and between the two faces of the cordillera, a plateau surrounded by the *sierra* and its ash-colored *pouna*, the refuge of llamas and the haunt of eagles, and the homeland of the god-emperors. Finally, on the east is the rain forest that stretches its dark fleece as far as Brazil. A tragic and disconcerting landscape that can be characterized only by the word "solitude." Sometimes a shepherd can be seen driving his herd before him. Does he ever dream of the golden shepherd who once watched over the golden vicuñas with emerald eyes in the metallic garden of Cuzco?

Strangely similar to the Aztec legend, the Inca tradition relates the exploits of a white demigod who came from the sea and demonstrated his power by blasting a mountain. Viracocha, "spirit of the deeps, founder of the heavenly light," possessed, like all his precursors, the attributes of a leader of men, an architect, and a priest. Furthermore, he was a creator. He modeled men, not in mud but in stone, and these statues came to life. One day, having astonished everyone with his prodigies, Viracocha departed northward from the edge of the sea.

A long time afterward, years or centuries, a man appeared on the Andean plateau, coming from Lake Titicaca. This was Manco Capac. He was accompanied by Mama Ocllo, his wife and sister. He was the first Son of the Sun.

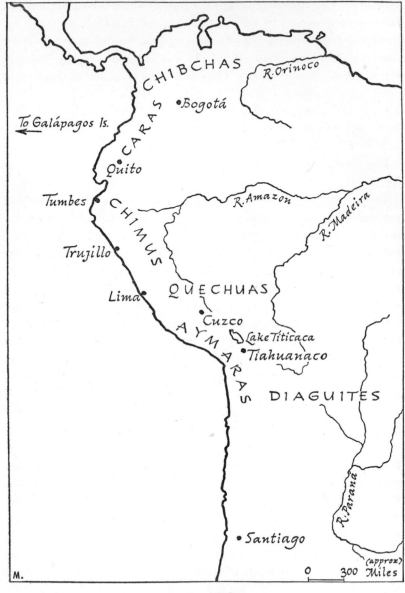

The Inca Empire

Who were the people, then, who inhabited the future Inca Empire, and how long had they been there? From north to south a series of confederations were grouped around the principal centers. The Chibchas at Bogotá; the Caras—a race of giants—at Quito, who were to produce the Schyri dynasty; the Chimus with their capital at Chan-chan near Trujillo (they were descended from the Malay-Polynesian flood that swept against the Pacific coast for thousands of years); the Quechuas, ancestors of the Incas, with their capital at Cuzco on the high Andean plateau, the land of the *soroche* or mountain sickness; and finally, in the south, on the shores of Lake Titicaca at the Peru-Bolivia boundary, the Aymaras, the founders of Tiahuanaco.

These peoples apparently lived on good terms with one another, but their ethics were rudimentary and they were unskilled at the art of governing. They worshiped trees and beasts, and they were past masters in stonework. Pachácamac, Cuzco, Machu Picchu . . . these are so many enigmas. These present-day ruins, sections of walls, terrifying faces carved in the rock, fabrics and ceramics covered with incomprehensible symbols, all bear witness that before the arrival of the Incas a civilization that was wild but in some respects very advanced existed on the Andean plateau. The enigma is insoluble. Perhaps we shall never know what were the men, laws, and gods for the two thousand years—perhaps much longer, for some speak of ten thousand years—before the Inca dynasties took over the empire.

Manco Capac had departed from Tiahuanaco. The first Inca con-quistador started his adventure at the same time that Quetzalcoatl brought about the unity of Yucatán. These deeds were simultaneous but not connected. For, astonishing as it may seem, the Inca Empire and the Aztec Empire were never at war, nor did they ever contract an alliance. They knew nothing of one another, although the road from Mayapán to Cuzco is not very long. They needed only to follow the narrow strip of Central America in order to have met, and what a meeting it would have been! An understanding between Montezuma and Atahualpa, the ruling monarchs at the time of the Spanish conquest, would have given much trouble to both Cortés and Pizarro. But the Inca knew nothing of the Aztec, and the Aztec did not know the Inca.

How was it that neither knew of the other? The great Indian kingdoms of America were highly insular. When Cortés met Montezuma,

the Spaniards had been established at Santo Domingo, about 2200
miles by sea from the Mexican capital, for twenty years, but the
Aztecs knew nothing about them. And the Schyris of Quito did not
suspect that there were white men in Panama, 750 miles away. How
could they have imagined that there were lands and peoples on the
other side of the "eastern" sea?

Wholly occupied with lawgiving, providing for its people, and
reverencing its gods, pre-Columbian America turned its eyes eastward only rarely. We do not know—we will never know—what the
Incas and Aztecs imagined beyond the known lands or beyond the
seas. Moreover, so great was their rulers' pride that they could not
conceive of empires other than their own. Thus it was that the
Aztecs had divided the world into areas corresponding to the four
cardinal points, each inhabited by a god. The power of each god was
confused with the nature of the climate. The sinister lord of death
reigned in the north, and the god of rain and cloud lived in the east,
a climatic concordance with no relation to geography. The first
Americans were very advanced in the realm of astronomy and knew
more about the heavens than about the earth. They could follow the
movements of the sun, moon, and stars, but they did not know about
the frontiers of their own world. The significance of geographical
dimensions escaped them, and the universe appeared to them as a vast
continent surrounded by water, after the fashion of Tenochtitlán
itself. They showed no curiosity on this subject and had no teachings
about it. Moreover, even if the early inhabitants of America had had
a presentiment of the existence of a continent in the east, the feeble
nautical means at their disposal would have prevented their reaching
it. There were voyages by sea between Japan and Australia on the
one hand and America on the other, and probably, also, hardy Negro
navigators had set off from the African coast—Guinea or Congo—
toward South America and reached Brazil. But nothing allows us to
suppose there had been attempts of the same kind in the reverse
direction. In any case, if there had been, they would not have succeeded, for in addition to the mediocre quality of the Indian fleets,
the sea currents and trade winds were against them. We can imagine
Chinese or Japanese junks carried by the currents to the North
American coasts, or Congo boats carried toward South America, but

these ephemeral ties were one-way. The first Americans to set foot on the Old Continent, after having crossed the Atlantic, were those whom Columbus took back with him from his first voyage.

Tiahuanaco was a cyclopean city built upon a gigantic terrace at nearly 13,000 feet above sea level in the very heart of the Andean uplands. On the blue-black surface of the legendary lake bamboo canoes glided along in a splash of gold. All around were summits of over 20,000 feet, forming a violet amphitheater that merged into the soft blue of the sky. It is a poignant landscape, for man has left there the herculean mark of a genius whose meaning and inspiration are obscure but which reached incredible heights.

The originality of Tiahuanaco rests in the superimposition of successive architectures marking the epochs of one of the oldest cities of the world—really the oldest, if tradition is to be believed. Enormous stones, badly squared but bearing human faces in relief, give evidence of the fact that in the most remote periods of prehistory there was a city on the banks of Lake Titicaca. Should we believe those who state that the first Tiahuanaco was the refuge of people driven from their habitat by the great upheavals of the Tertiary period? Some have even suggested that, having survived the drowning of their enchanted island, the Atlanteans reached the Andean plateau; also that it was they who introduced the bronze industry to Peru. The appearance of iron as a raw material was the characteristic of the second epoch: it matches a perfection in the art of stonecutting that has never been equaled.

Tiahuanaco is actually a union of two cities: Acapana, "the belvedere," and Pumapuncu, the "puma gate," scarcely half a mile apart. Of Pumapuncu there remain only some enormous monolithic blocks, pillars of a temple or palace of justice. Some of these blocks lie on the earth in a rough state or only half worked. It is probable that the workers, after moving these colossal stones to the place where they were to be used, were surprised by some cataclysm and abandoned their work precipitately. What epidemic, invasion, or earthquake drove human habitation from the environs of Pumapuncu? Similarly, in the Assuan quarry in upper Egypt one can see the desert strewn with rocks that the stonecutters had scarcely touched. These unfinished Egyptian pylons and the rocks abandoned by Aymara slaves suggest, even more eloquently than the bas-reliefs, the dramatic picture of a terrified people fleeing under a dark sky from some frightful catastrophe.

Acapana includes two circular walls several yards in height and marked by great square pillars. Inside these walls are scattered blocks, overturned platforms, and giant mutilated statues. The remains of canals wind all around. Fortress or temple, Acapana has not surrendered its secret. The substance of the monuments is beautiful: an assembly of red volcanic stone and gray stone. Tiahuanaco is some distance from the quarries, the nearest being about four miles away and the farthest, but best provided, about forty miles. How did the early Peruvians transport these gigantic blocks, some of which weigh more than ten tons? Doubtless they knew something about the lever. It is also probable that they used water transport, or even that they cut canals by which the monstrous monoliths were floated to their workshops, having been torn from the bowels of the earth with tools we know nothing about, neither the shape nor the material.

While men were laboring to build Acapana, others like them were building the pyramids, erecting obelisks, and planting granite columns on the shores of the Nile. One can visualize these millions of slaves, their shoulders striped by whips, streaming with sweat and blood, treading the road from the Assuan quarry to the Valley of Kings, or from the Kayapa quarry to the Acapana temple: parallel events that an ocean separated. But their gods were the same, and the stones would never be heavy enough or beautiful enough, nor would their grain be pure enough, to satisfy the requirements of a pitiless cult—that of the Sun. For the Sun was god both in Egypt and Peru. He was called Inti on the Andean plateau and Amen-Ra in the Nile delta. And the same secondary divinities, hostile or benevolent, peopled the Inca and Egyptian pantheons. Nevertheless, more than six thousand miles separate the portal at Karnak from the Gate of the Sun at Tiahuanaco.

Cut from a single block, 12 feet and 7 inches long by 9 feet wide by 1 foot and 8 inches deep, the Gate of the Sun marks the entrance to a vanished kingdom. Massive, but finely proportioned, it reveals a skillful technique. It reminds one of the Lion Gate at Mycenae. For what Agamemnon was this proud portico erected, and to celebrate what victory? At the center of the monument is a haloed enigmatic figure carrying a scepter in each hand, while all around are human heads surmounted by falcons' beaks. Strange creatures with wings and tails, also bearing scepters, seem to flutter around the principal figure like a burlesque swarm of bees or the principal dancers in a sacred ballet. Among the pillars, from which time has not worn the corners, and the statues with mutilated faces, the indecipherable lintel of the Gate of the Sun is the sole complete vestige of ancient Tiahuanaco. But it sheds no light on what the cyclopean city was like when Manco Capac and his incestuous spouse, in the year 1000 of the Christian era, left the shores of Lake Titicaca to civilize what they thought to be the world.

When the Aymaran Manco Capac reached Cuzco, the Quechua capital, a monarch ruled there, but he was a king of straw, a mere puppet. Actually, the lords gave the orders, for in the Cuzco country the regime was feudal and the intrigues of the nobles undermined what little remained of royal power. Political instability and the excesses and claims of an increasingly demanding feudalism had their effect on morals. The clergy strove in vain to curb the immorality of governing circles, but the zeal that they brought to this task was not very great. In fact, they made common cause with feudalism on the political level. Having plotted in secrecy for a long time, the lords and priests at last drove the sovereign from his palace. He left the capital, fleeing to the mountains. Then Manco Capac assumed power. Endowed with unusual political genius, he invented or appropriated the formula of a state religion and, obtaining support from the clergy, curbed the feudal lords. Once the lords were back in their ranks and the priests cooperating, he had nothing to do but keep his mailed fist firmly on the bent backs of his new people. Henceforth he united the Quechuas and Aymaras under his crown, and to guard his frontiers and maintain internal order, he created a strong and disciplined army. His frequent allusions to his divine origin helped, for how could one resist a man who said: "Viracocha and the Sun, my father, have in their wisdom decided the fate of my race and the path of success that my descendants must follow. . . ."? The Inca dynasty began with Manco Capac.

While these events were taking place in Cuzco, Europe was passing through a curiously similar crisis. In England, Portugal, and Tuscany the feudal lords triumphed. But in France the rise of the

Capetians brought about the decline and then the death of feudal power. Louis le Grand, with the support of the clergy, engaged in a merciless struggle against the lords and forced them to yield. He restored royal authority, made the crown hereditary, and centralized power. That was the end of the great vassals and their arrogance; they were sent back to their domains. The King of France was King, and the Church stood at his right hand. This likeness deserves to be emphasized, for in fact there is nothing new in the government of men.

On his death Manco Capac left a state whose dimensions were still relatively modest, but one endowed with an administrative and political framework that would assure its continuance. Sinchi Roca, his successor, succeeded in breaking the last vestiges of resistance among the lords. Indeed, he did more. He took possession of their lands and annexed them to the Inca crown. By so doing, he affirmed the dual character of the policy that the rulers of Cuzco meant to practice and did practice until the Spanish conquest: to maintain peace and unity within, and to extend the empire to the maximum. These two orders every Inca monarch would pass on to his heir, and none would betray them. The continuity and firmness of such a policy, conducted energetically for five hundred years, was the secret of the empire.

Two hundred years after Manco Capac's seizure of power, a grave danger almost destroyed the empire. It came from the southeast. Some tribes that were moving along the Paraguay had decided to unite, forming a vast confederation. They organized an army and marched upon Bolivia. Emboldened by their early successes—they had overthrown the Chiriguans without difficulty—the Paraguayans then moved toward the plateaus. But before they had time to lay siege to Cuzco, Inti Yupanqui, the fifth Inca, inflicted on them a bloody defeat and then subdued them, thus extending southward the territory he had inherited. At the same time he thrust his armies to the sea not far from Arequipa, near the Bolivian frontier. He had to have exits to the sea, and from this moment the Incas controlled the Pacific along the whole Peruvian coast.

This movement toward the sea was continued by Yahuar Huacac and Yupanqui Pachacutec, who subjugated the Chimu confederation. Tupac, the tenth Inca sovereign, continued and completed this unparalleled expansion. In the north he subdued the tribes of Quito and the Gulf of Guayaquil. In the south he launched a campaign against Chile that succeeded beyond all hope. When Huayna Capac, his son, ascended the throne his power and jurisdiction extended from Quito to Santiago. He transferred his residence from Cuzco to Quito, and from there directed and strove to coordinate the activities of his boundless empire. It was, moreover, an excellent observation point for supervising the Cara and Chimu tribes, who were still unsettled; and it was perhaps also a bridgehead to the mysterious north.

To maintain internal peace and unity and to extend the empire to the maximum—by what means were these policies pursued? The Inca Empire was brought into being by successive leaps. The method was simple and consisted of two stages: first, the military expedition toward a designated point and the subjugation of the adversary, then the occupation of the conquered province. The laws of the conqueror became those of the vanquished, prisoners taken by arms were freed, and the chiefs and officials made their submission to the Inca. A census was taken of the population, the enemies of yesterday became the allies of today, and the defeated soldiers, now enrolled in the Inca ranks, swelled the imperial army. In brief, political conquest closely followed military action. The supreme ruler, like the Roman imperator, aimed less at crushing the adversary than at acquiring new subjects. It was a question of absorption rather than destruction. Sometimes, also, war was avoided, and the expansion of the empire was then effected by diplomatic means; a treaty of alliance took the place of an ultimatum. Political marriages were celebrated with great ceremony; thus Lloque Yupanqui, by marrying the daughter of a powerful neighbor, helped to enlarge the empire.

If the means used by the Incas to carry out their territorial acquisitions were the result of a certain improvisation, taking local situations into account, on the other hand those that controlled internal organization were unalterable. The framework of the Inca state had the rigidity of steel.

The basis of the social system was the ayllu, by origin a simple family but extended to mean a clan or tribe. The chief of the ayllu bore the name *capac*. He was also called the *inca capac*, the term "inca" applying not to the function but to the tribe. Consequently, confusion arose between the name of the tribe and that of the chief.

First elected by the community, the inca capacs emerged gradually from the ranks and formed an aristocracy or college of nobles and then a dynasty. In order that their power might be incontestable, the capacs assumed a divine origin. Descendants of the Sun, Inti, and only awaiting his pleasure to return there, the capacs constituted the inner sanctum of chiefs, the elite, at whose head was the supreme Inca.

The power of the Inca was absolute, even though it was carefully controlled and limited by his council. But his authority over the people was fully exercised: an authority simultaneously good-natured and tyrannical, a paternalism of a good god (for was he not God?) combined with the harshness of a pitiless dictator. He was father and judge; nothing escaped him, not even the most secret thoughts of his subjects. He reigned over their minds. No one had the right to look into the face of this dazzling monarch.

How did this enormous administrative and social mechanism function? All the lands of the empire belonged by right to the Inca, but in practice they were divided into three equal parts: those of the Sun, those of the state, and those of the community. Each family received a fraction of the community part, called the topo. This fraction of land belonged to the family in its own right, with the condition that it could not be given away or left undeveloped. Its size was proportionate to the number of members in the family, and it returned to the state when the family died out. The allotment of a topo did not free men from service on the state's lands from the age of twenty-five to fifty. This kind of obligatory civic service took the place of a tax. The cultivators kept the product of their land, and they were sole proprietors of their houses and livestock. As to the produce from the lands of the Sun and the state, it was usually earmarked for the needs of the clergy and the nation. On reaching the age of fifty, citizens became the charge of the state.

Thus the Inca reigned, inaccessible to the common people, shut up in his golden palace. The elite—the priests, officers, and high officials —organized and directed. Then, in the absence of a middle class and more particularly of a bourgeoisie, there were the people, who never changed, whose vital function was to make war and to till the soil. For the idea of work permeated the social system. Above all, no idlers were permitted. The obligation to work, and its corollary, the control of the product, were never disputed by anyone. Moreover, the Incas took care to make labor bearable and even attractive. When their turn came to cultivate the lands of the Sun, the Peruvians dressed in festal clothes and went forward singing. Feast days were numerous; they were holidays, but not free, for there were ritual exercises, dances, and songs consecrated to the Inca, in praise of the regime. Everything, even leisure, was "directed" in the realm of the Son of the Sun.

The close dependence of the people on the state, the fact that they drew from it, and from it alone, their subsistence, their *raison d'être*, their life, created a special frame of mind. Why should the Peruvian have any anxiety for his children, since the state would take care of them and provide for them? Why should he economize on his harvest when he could count on an equal crop the following year? At the worst, should there be some calamity, the public granaries would disgorge the cereals set aside for the community. Why should he save for his old age when the state would assure his retirement at fifty? And finally, why should he envy the elite, who relieved him of thinking and foresight? What was required of him? To obey—nothing more. What was given him in exchange? Security. Security is not the same as happiness, but this strange word meant nothing to him, for he had never learned it.

At once socialistic and hierarchical, the Inca state was also religious. The Inca pantheon, less peopled than that of the Aztecs, was presided over by the Sun, Inti, the ancestor of the dynasty. His spouse was the moon. Two other gods, Pachacamac and Viracocha, "the spirit of the burning entrails of the earth and of the boiling lava," were represented on the temple façades. Since the Inca nation had been formed by gathering together under one scepter several different peoples—Aymaras, Chimus, Quechuas, Caras—each had contributed his gods. The central power had thought it politic to leave the subjugated tribes or allies the freedom of their cult, but supreme over all these secondary deities there was one official god: Inti.

The splendor of the Coricancha temple, the Temple of the Sun or the "House of Gold," built at Cuzco in honor of Inti, consecrates the glory of the state religion. For Inti was not only the god of the Incas; he was their father. They had striven to emphasize the divine alliance in the minds of the people by the grandest of monuments. They had to dazzle these primitive people so that not even the shadow of a doubt might touch them. A triple rampart made of polished stones placed side by side surrounded the Temple of the Sun. Within, one behind the other, were halls dedicated to Inti, the moon, lightning, the planet Venus, the rainbow, and the stars. The inner walls were entirely covered with sheets of gold. A numerous staff lived in the temple: priests of every class from the capac to those who prepared the *chicha*, vestals appointed to look after the sacred fire, oracles, and servants. Seated on golden chairs or on stone benches incrusted with emeralds, the mummies of the dead Incas mounted a funereal guard.

Thus the heavy Inca machine revolved under the aegis of social security and civic peace. Misdemeanors were rare, not so much because of the rigor of the punishments as because crime had no temptation. What purpose was there in stealing from one's neighbor what one possessed at home or what the state would provide? In order to kill, one must covet, love, or hate, but the ants in the Inca anthill knew little of passion. Moreover, the police would have prevented the gesture even before it was carried out. Secretly or publicly, the police were everywhere, at every crossroad, in every house. They were the most redoubtable auxiliary of power.

Everything was arranged so that the people should never have cause for discontent. In Cuzco there were no poor. Widows were supported, and war casualties received a pension in the form of clothing and food, since money did not exist. The infirm lived at the expense of the community, but they were obliged each year to provide the Inca with a tube filled with insects, a symbolic tribute that justified their right to live.

This impeccable and transparent world was very like one of those old clocks with its mechanism visible under glass: not a speck of dust on the wheels, not a spot on the immaculate marble of the pedestal. An inexorable perfection.

Toward the end of his reign, when he could regard the unity of the empire as accomplished, Huayna Capac was informed by his spies in the Tumbes region that "great floating houses" filled with "bearded monsters" were cruising off the Gulf of Guayaquil. Before he was able to take action he died. By his will he had divided his enormous heritage in two: the southern part of the empire, with its capital at

Cuzco, he had left to Huáscar, his legitimate son, and the northern part, centered on Quito, he had left to Atahualpa, his natural son. The two princes took possession of their kingdoms, but although they were widely separated at Cuzco and Quito, they tolerated each other with difficulty. Soon they would turn against one another. Did they realize, these brother-enemies, that in breaking their alliance they were going to bring to an end the empire of the Sun?

At the moment when Huayna Capac died at Quito in 1525 and his two sons succeeded him, watching each other with bitter hatred, Francis I of France was defeated by the Spaniards at Pavia, and Spaniards, led by Pizarro, set foot on Inca territory in the land of the Chimus.

These "bearded monsters" who haunted the death throes of the old Inca were the Spaniards, the victors over the king of France, and now in search of a prey which would satisfy their hunger. They encountered a static world, mathematical and cold like a constellation of stone.

The Spaniards shattered this minutely organized clock.

So this pre-Columbian America was about to vanish into limbo. We must try to grasp its movements and glimpse its essential architecture, which were as follows.

A continuous mixing of tribes and races, the more robust—or the more crafty—subjugating the weaker: the primacy of the law of the stronger.

Invasions and raids, coming almost always from the north and directed southward, from the desert to the forest, from the glaciers to the burning beaches. To find food and warmth were the urges.

Periods of peace, sometimes of contentment, alternating with seasons of misfortune and famine.

Preceding the armies came the priests, bearing, like monstrances, effigies of their gods. Thus the standard of Constantine, after his victory over Maxentius, bore the words: *In hoc signo vinces*. Raised aloft before the Roman troops, the imperial eagles assured immortality to the soldiers. "You will conquer by this symbol," the eternal symbol of the gods, witnessing that heaven approved the warrior and that the cause was good.

These gods were numerous and varied, although they show a certain family resemblance. Evangelists like Quetzalcoatl, bloodthirsty ones like Huitzilopochtli, and benevolent ones like Inti; thirsty for fresh blood or hungry for tenderness, all agree on one point: man is nothing and can do nothing without them. He must obey.

From the hordes, then from the tribes, and finally from the peoples, there were masters, conquerors, and generals who came to the fore and who were simultaneously military and religious. There were dictators, whose careers were rarely long and whose ends were often tragic. Others took their places, those who, voluntarily leaving the crowd to place themselves at its head, forced the allegiance of the people. This was the mystique of the leader, the mystique of the elected, going back to or even preceding the Mosaic tradition of the people's leader: at once their high priest and army chief, and sometimes their messiah.

Along with the generals and wise men, there were scholars too. The Incas were not only architects, surveyors, astronomers, and cartographers, but probably the fathers of surgery. In making their sick people chew coca they anticipated cocaine, and they invented anesthesia. Moreover, they practiced trepanning. In 1953 two Peruvian surgeons, who were also enthusiastic archeologists, found obsidian scalpels and lancets in the ruins of what was doubtless a sort of Inca hospital, and operated on a gravely injured person, using these instruments. They opened the patient's cranium, removed a blood clot from the left parietal zone, and resorted to the "Inca tourniquet" for ligature. The operation lasted forty minutes and was a complete success. What an extraordinary sight it must have been: these men wearing modern rubber gloves and using the instruments of Inca surgeons!

Empires were made, unmade, and remade. Empires? Rather, they were temporary confederations, torn apart by a puff of wind. The spaces were endless. Yucatán, that small spur pointing toward Havana, is bigger than France, and the Inca Empire covered almost the whole of South America. But only a tenth of these lands was peopled. The net that the red conquistadors had stretched from Mexico to Santiago de Chile had a very wide mesh. There were sumptuous capitals: Tenochtitlán, Cuzco, Tiahuanaco, for instance, and some of them had more than 200,000 inhabitants. But between these powerful cities shadowy zones stretched out—shadowy but inhabited. These human monsters—giants or pygmies—that slipped like insects under leafy vaults denser than cathedral arches—were they citizens of the empire, too? Certainly not, but they could become so.

Firmly marked by the mother cities whose approaches were guarded by fortresses—the Inca *pucaras* were similar to the Saracen watchtowers along the crests of the Pyrenees—the territory where the Indian people lived was surrounded and crossed by endless no man's lands, over which, nevertheless, the nominal sovereignty of Aztec or Inca was exercised.

These empires were fragile and at the mercy of invasion, earthquake, or palace revolution. For they were vulnerable not at the heel, like Achilles, but at the head.

Finally, the codes, the essentials of which varied little, for the laws of politics and economics were as immutable as the laws of physics and as inflexible as the movement of the stars.

CHAPTER I2

The Death of the Inca

PIZARRO'S reappearance at Panama caused some surprise, for he was thought to be dead and there were some, indeed, who hoped he was. Pedro de los Ríos received his subordinate coldly, for he had been a long time in returning to his base. Obviously, the Governor did not like Pizarro, whose turbulence was a nuisance to the administration. Pedro de los Ríos cast a disdainful glance at the booty brought back: in his view they were baubles and no more. Nevertheless, he had a smile for the llamas which, with their languishing eyes, pivoting necks, small upright pointed ears, rolling cruppers, and thick wool, gave him some amusement. As to the natives of Tumbes, he regarded them as savages whose only value was as slaves. Was it necessary to go so far in order to bring back so little? It was the Governor's hope that Pizarro, whose pranks had continued too long, would now rejoin the ranks.

But Pizarro had no intention of joining the ranks. In fact, his only thought was to depart from Panama southward and to free himself from the tutelage of Pedro de los Ríos. Pizarro was never troubled by words, and he coldly informed the Governor of his project of organizing a new expedition to Peru; but he needed matériel, men, and assistance. Pedro de los Ríos burst into laughter. Assistance? He would certainly get none from him. On the contrary, as Pizarro's administrative superior, he ordered him to abandon his costly fantasies and resume his place among the colonists of Panama. An argument developed, with the brutal obstinacy of Pizarro on one side and the intransigent dictatorship of Pedro de los Ríos on the other. Pizarro decided not to obey his superior, but to go to Toledo where there was a higher authority to which he could appeal.

Face to Face with Charles of Spain

Pizarro had scarcely landed at Sanlúcar de Barrameda than he was arrested and taken to Seville under strong escort, where he was jailed in the municipal prison. The charge was an old matter of unpaid debts at the time of the colonization of Darién, and the creditor was none other than Enciso, the ephemeral governor of Santa María la Antigua. It was a poor beginning for his embassy; nevertheless he found unexpected support in the person of Cortés, then on a visit to court. The victor of Mexico interceded with the sovereign and secured Pizarro an audience. It was a chivalrous gesture and much to Cortés' credit. The man who had succeeded—for a few months more he was to remain at the height of his glory—held out his hand to the candidate for glory, showing a disinterest that was rare among the Conquistadors. Perhaps Cortés thought that nothing henceforth could check his rise; Pizarro could not obstruct him. Actually, he had reached the moment in his career when to acquire disciples was a necessity, not so much to set him off as to complete his own personality.

Toledo in the summer of 1528. Prince Philip had been born recently and the Spanish court was merry. A male heir! This was something to compensate for the vexations that Charles was then suffering on the battlefields of Italy. Toledo blazed in the sun under its carapace of ocher-colored stone. A troop of horsemen crossed the Alcántara bridge and trotted toward the imperial palace. These were

Pizarro and his faithful friends. How long the road had been from the island of Gorgone to Toledo!

Charles was in a good humor and welcomed the Conquistadors kindly. The former swineherd from Estremadura knelt before the most powerful emperor in the world. While he listened to Pizarro's recital, Charles passed his fingers absent-mindedly through the thick llama fleeces and weighed the Peruvian jewels in his hand. He leaned over the maps that had been drawn by Bartolomé Ruiz: it was all very interesting, though very vague. Was the affair worth pursuing or worth the sacrifice of the precious blood of Spanish cavaliers? Pizarro drew himself up. In the kingdom of Peru there was not only gold to be gained, but souls for Christ and territories for Spain. Pizarro had touched a sensitive spot. He had discreetly reminded the Emperor of the spiritual mandate he held from the Pope and the hegemonical concept bequeathed by the Hapsburgs. In the end Charles agreed to support Pizarro's cause before the Council of the Indies.

At Toledo some months later, the Queen, in the absence of the Emperor, signed a convention reserving to Pizarro the privilege of conquering Peru, which had been named "New Castile" in anticipation. The bastard from Trujillo became captain general for life and supreme judge of the new province, and furthermore was awarded the collar of the Order of Santiago. His twelve companions of Gallo —thirteen including Ruiz—were not forgotten. These commoners were awarded titles of nobility: *Caballeros de la Espada Dorada*, Knights of the Golden Sword. Luque was appointed Bishop of Tumbes, subject to pontifical authorization, and Universal Protector of the Indians. Bartolomé Ruiz was given the title of Grand Pilot of the Southern Sea. In brief, no one was forgotten, not even Almagro, who was given command of a fortress at Tumbes. Of the three associates, he had the worst deal, although on paper he was awarded an annual payment of 100,000 maravedis, to be taken from the future revenues of the lands to be discovered. More generous with honors than with money, the Crown gave Pizarro a modest grant toward the early expenses of the expedition, but the heaviest financial charge fell to Pizarro; by the terms of the contract, he had to recruit and equip one hundred and fifty men and to embark for Peru within six months.

Pizarro's first concern, now that he was furnished with his new dignities, was to go to his birthplace, Trujillo. It is easy to understand that he was unable to resist the desire to show his Cross of the Order of Santiago to his childhood friends. Captain general and favorite of the Emperor—this was indeed something to inflate his pride! He donned his breastplate; he jingled his spurs; he amiably poked the ribs of the *pícaros*. Doubtless, too, he breathed for the last time the odors of his youth. At the same time he started recruiting, and first of all enrolled his three brothers—Hernando, Gonzalo, and Juan —and his half brother, Martín de Alcántara. There were others too, but enrollments were few, for the people of Trujillo were difficult to convince. Peru? That was a long way off! So the six months expired and Pizarro had been unable to assemble the contingent fixed by the contract. What should he do? Set out nevertheless; this was also the advice that Cortés gave him. To go ahead without long delay had been the tactics of the hero of Mexico. One morning in the month of January 1530 Pizarro hoisted sail on his three ships at Sanlúcar de Barrameda and put to sea.

The Real Start

Twenty-five years earlier, Christopher Columbus had landed at this same port of Sanlúcar on his return from his last voyage. Such was the continuity of the discovery, an invisible chain that connected the Conquistadors and the ports; and on this day, under the great shadow of the Genoese discoverer—the father of the New World—Francisco Pizarro sailed westward, no longer in search of the Great Khan but of the Inca. He too, like Columbus, had in his pocket a contract from the King of Spain. But times had changed. Pizarro knew where he was going, or at least he had a good idea. His contract was precise. Nothing had been forgotten. It was, in fact, a merchant's contract. Columbus had been like a blind man inspired, and for him faith had taken the place of certainty. The Sante Fe convention contained a mystic meaning breathed into it by Isabella: God would lead Columbus's caravels. Pizarro's ships carried hardened men, though among them were a few churchmen, forced on Pizarro by the Crown, with the task of ensuring the evangelical character of the conquest. In this respect they would do everything possible, but they would have much difficulty in keeping the company under control.

Having put in at the Canaries and at Santa María, Pizarro's flotilla anchored at Nombre de Dios. Luque and Almagro were on the quay, and the interview between Pizarro and Almagro was a stormy one. The command of a fortress! Was this all that the new captain general could get from Charles for his earliest associate? Thanks to Luque's diplomacy and Pizarro's promises, a real quarrel between the two shipmates was narrowly avoided. Nevertheless, the poison worked its way in secret and the two Conquistadors were to die of it, though not yet.

A year after leaving Spain, Pizarro embarked from Panama for Peru. He had three ships, one hundred and eighty-three men, and twenty-seven horses, and his expedition had been prepared minutely. He had forgotten nothing, not even an accountant, Antonio Navarra, and a treasurer, Alonso Requelme. The Dominican priest Vicente de Valverde represented the Church. The start was solemn. The Bishop of Panama blessed the fleet and the army. The flags were hauled to the mainmasts and the three caravels sailed away to the singing of *Ave maris stella*. Before separating, Almagro (who was remaining at Panama to gather reinforcements) and Pizarro took Communion. Under the united symbols of the Faith and Spain the true conquest of Peru began.

The first objective was Tumbes, but contrary winds forced the flotilla to drop anchor in the Bay of San Mateo, a hundred leagues from its goal. Pizarro and his troops continued the journey by land. On the way they traversed the province of Coaque, halting in inhabited and well-constructed villages. They were received affably, but the Conquistadors could not resist the urge to pillage their hosts. In the houses were golden objects and emeralds, and a large booty was amassed. A fifth part was put aside for Charles, and Pizarro apportioned the remainder. When the soldiers had received their shares, the Captain General sent a few samples of the booty to the Spanish colonies of Panama and Nicaragua. This was good propaganda and succeeded splendidly. Lured by the gold and the gems, other Conquistadors joined up with Pizarro. Thirty men, including Juan Flores and Sebastián de Belalcázar, rallied to the expedition at

Puerto Viejo, which Pizarro had just founded in the Gulf of Guayaquil. Everything was going fine, although the spines of tropical plants
afflicted the Spaniards cruelly. But of what importance were warts
and ulcers! Pizarro hurried everybody along, for there was no time
to lose.

Now the rainy season approached, and it was a bad time to set off
into the interior. Pizarro set up his camp on Puná Island, facing Tumbes. The Indians attempted an attack, but it was easily repulsed. At
the same time, Hernando de Soto, coming from Nicaragua, joined
Pizarro with two ships and one hundred men. The captain welcomed
these choice reinforcements with open arms, for De Soto was an
experienced man. He was a tough companion and a famous swords-
man. And he, too, was a native of Estremadura, the province of
Conquistadors.

While the men cared for their sores as best they could—they cut
the cactus spines from their flesh with their lances—Pizarro sought
information. Following Cortés' example, he had made interpreters
of captured Indians, and with their help he was kept informed of
events that were taking place in the Peruvian kingdom. The quarrel
between the enemy brothers, Huáscar and Atahualpa, had entered
an acute stage. Under the pretext of paying homage to his brother,
Atahualpa had left his residence at Quito and had moved toward
Cuzco at the head of a powerful army. On the way the Inca raised
other contingents, subdued the caciques, and massacred Huáscar's
partisans. Huáscar, who was not very combative and clung less to
his throne than to his mistress, Golden Star, went to meet his half
brother. The meeting took place in the neighborhood of Cajamarca,
halfway between Cuzco and Quito. The numerical superiority of
Atahualpa's army was crushing: Huáscar's troops were put out of
action, falling back toward the Peruvian capital, and Huáscar, who
was captured, was taken to Cuzco under strong guard. Atahualpa
had triumphed.

Such was the news that spread rapidly and, despite the enormous
distances, reached Pizarro. The sovereign of Peru was being taken to
Cuzco in chains, and Atahualpa, temporarily encamped at Cajamarca, was preparing his victorious entry into the Inca city. One
throne overturned and another still poorly secured: could there be
a more favorable combination of circumstances for Pizarro's plans?

Among the Condors

A legend had preceded Cortés on the road to Mexico: that Quetzalcoatl, the white god, was fulfilling his prophecy and taking possession again of his altars. This myth, more than anything else, made Cortés' victory possible. Remembering his model, Pizarro willingly let the natives believe that he was one of the sons of Viracocha, the god of Tiahuanaco, who was also white-skinned. The same trick served the two conquerors, and it succeeded even better among the Peruvians, for Pizarro had cannons, and Viracocha controlled the thunder. Powder, horses, shining armor . . . The apparatus of terror was ready. How could it be doubted that Viracocha was the organizer of the march that was just starting!

Pizarro's army crossed from Puná Island to Tumbes. It marched southward and reached the river Piura, where Pizarro founded a colony, San Miguel. Then he made for the cordillera, with one hundred and ten foot soldiers and sixty-seven cavalry. Yet they had hardly left San Miguel when five cavaliers and four foot soldiers turned back, so that there were no more than one hundred and sixty-eight in all, only a third the number that Cortés had when he set out from Tlaxcala.

The Cajamarca plateau stretches like a thread between the western and central chains of the cordillera of the Andes. As the crow flies, it is little more than 300 miles from Tumbes to Cajamarca, but it took Pizarro's expedition more than two months to cover this distance—two months to pass from the furnace of the Sechura Desert at sea level to the chill of Cajamarca, at nearly 10,000 feet elevation. While they were on the Peruvian coast the Spaniards found neither trees nor springs; the sun was burning and they were maddened with thirst. Then they reached the foot of the cordillera. Paths were cut in the basalt and the Conquistadors set off along them. The higher they climbed the wider the landscape spread. At a turn in the road the Spaniards came face to face with the glaciers. The sky was translucent blue and a cold sun lit the summits. Sometimes a bunch of cistus, a prickly pear, or the streaming of a cascade reminded the Spaniards of the scenery of Estremadura, enormously enlarged, and even the toughest of them shed a tear. But farther on the horizon

Pizarro's Conquests, 1524-41

changed. Snow succeeded rock, and the soldiers shivered under their armor. The freezing horses refused to advance. The mirage had vanished: it was no longer the valley of the Tajo but a sort of frozen hell. Only a few animals lived on these high Andean lands: the llama with a fine maroon-spotted coat, the alpaca with its heavy black fleece, the fierce vicuña whose wool was used to plait the royal headband of the Incas, and the condor, invisible in the plains, which appeared only on the peaks.

One hundred and six men on foot and sixty-two on horses advanced along the cliffs, skirting the precipices. If Pizarro had not been in command, how many of the Spaniards would have chosen to turn back? But the captain was watching and it was forbidden to complain. Clothed in steel like a medieval knight, he had thrown a gentleman's cloak over his armor. He was at the head of his troops, and such was his power over men that not one of them faltered. There was no need to speak to be obeyed; a glance sufficed, for none could withstand his look.

The Spaniards had reached the summits where the condors soared. Cajamarca was not far off, and Pizarro had already received two embassies from Atahualpa. The first encouraged him to continue his journey; the second, on the other hand, dissuaded him from going farther. Similarly, Montezuma, in an attempt to halt Cortés' progress, had dispatched contradictory messages. Both princes felt the same confusion, though Atahualpa's position was more delicate than that of the Aztec sovereign. Atahualpa had just had difficulty in ascending his throne. His power, although ratified by the Inca council, had been taken by force from Huáscar, an act of usurpation, and the legitimate son of Huayna Capac still had partisans, who had already approached Pizarro. What a fine opportunity for the Conquistador to play the arbitrator! From this moment he was prodigal with friendly words for the envoys of both parties. He wished nothing but good for the inhabitants of this land!

One fine afternoon, having traversed dizzying passes and crossed abysses by bridges of lianas, the Spaniards entered the valley of Cajamarca. On the opposite mountain the slope rose in tiers: from base to summit there was nothing but gardens and terraces. Thousands of tents flapped in the evening breeze. This was Atahualpa's camp.

Pizarro decided to make his quarters in the city of Cajamarca, which had been abandoned by the Inca. It was silent and deserted, for the population had fled to the mountains. Pizarro's soldiers were at large in a depopulated town. They installed themselves shamelessly in Atahualpa's own palace. Then they took counsel.

From all the evidence, the first essential was to contact the Peruvian king without delay. The matter was urgent. Pizarro ordered Hernando de Soto, the most brilliant of his lieutenants, to prepare the way, and on the very evening of the Spaniards' entry into Cajamarca, De Soto, at the head of twenty horsemen, set off at a trot toward Atahualpa's camp some three miles from the city.

Everyone came out of the tents to see the cavalcade pass. The Peruvians were amazed. Who were these fabulous beings, clothed in metal and carried by unknown beasts? The Spanish embassy cut a passage through the crowd and reached Atahualpa's residence. It was an attractive house with a large courtyard in front. The floor was of fine sand, and in the middle a basin of cut stone distributed both cold and warm water. A gathering of lords stood beside the basin, and the importance of their duties could be gauged by the differences in their clothing. But most prominent, by reason of the simplicity of his costume, was Atahualpa, squatting in Turkish fashion on a sort of low seat. He was further distinguished from his nobles by his royal headband, taken from Huáscar. His face was handsome, like the profile of a bird of prey carved in mahogany.

How did the dialogue begin? The Inca maintained silence and did not deign to reply to the courteous words the interpreter passed on to him. Hernando de Soto wondered whether he should substitute actions for words. He was a brilliant cavalier, and he decided to demonstrate the fact. He quickly mounted his horse, and with his legs glued to his mount's flank he became a centaur in silver armor. With a slight pressure of the knees and a touch of the reins the horse galloped, circled, capered, reared, remained upright for a moment, then fell back onto its four feet in a shower of sparks. Throughout this equestrian exhibition, Atahualpa never blinked. At the very most his eyes had flickered a little when De Soto, to prove his skill, had thrust his horse toward a group of Peruvians, who had fled in terror. These were put to death the same evening for showing such shameful cowardice. Meanwhile, Hernando Pizarro and fifteen horsemen rejoined De Soto in the Peruvian camp. A few words were exchanged, and little by little the ice melted. Hernando Pizzaro protested the good intentions of his brother, who was merely an envoy of the king of Spain. Atahualpa stated that he was well disposed toward the foreigners, provided they returned to his subjects the booty collected since leaving Tumbes. The Inca was willing to meet Francisco Pizarro the next day. They separated good friends—at least superficially—after drinking chicha. Each had shown the other what he was capable of: Atahualpa had executed some of his own soldiers under the eyes of the Spaniards, and Hernando de Soto had done his turn by showing his mastery of horsemanship. The Inca exercised absolute power over his subjects: they belonged to him body and soul. The Spaniards tamed monsters. Each side noted points while estimating the strength of the eventual enemy. But they took care not to let this be seen. Their faces were impassive; they feigned indifference; they bluffed.

A Useful Sacrilege

In reality, this reciprocal bluff concealed a great anxiety on both sides. Atahualpa pondered upon the old legends he had heard from his father. The unusual appearance of the strangers, their mysterious origin, and the allusion they had made to a powerful white emperor certainly connected them with the descendants of Viracocha. Having just captured his brother's empire, Atahualpa asked himself if he would have to do battle with the white warriors in order to keep it. Or should he interpret the coming of the strangers as a warning from the gods? Enslavement and death for the usurper!

While the Peruvian was struggling with his conscience, the Spanish embassy returned to Cajamarca. The *caballeros* were anxious about the disproportion of the armies that faced one another. They had been able to estimate the number of the Inca's soldiers: there were one hundred, perhaps two hundred to every Spaniard, and though their armament was primitive—darts, javelins, slings, and lassos—their number was something to be reckoned with. A thousand well-directed arrows could do as much damage as a cannon ball. Night had now fallen over the Cajamarca valley, and on the flanks of the mountain could be seen the great glow of the campfires of the Inca's army.

Hernando Pizarro and De Soto made their report to the Captain General, and though he was not too worried, he did not minimize the gravity of the situation. A bold stroke could make him master of the situation, and once again he turned his thoughts to the Mexican campaign. When Cortés was in difficulties he had drawn inspiration from Plutarch, Caesar, and various others, but Pizarro's classic was Cortés himself. Montezuma's arrest by the Spanish leader had greatly facilitated the Mexican affair, so why not use Atahualpa in the same way? Once the Inca was under lock and key, Pizarro would be in a stronger position to subdue the whole country. He disclosed his plan to his lieutenants. Capture Atahualpa! The undertaking was a daring one. There were only a few dozen Spaniards against thousands of Peruvians. But Pizarro had spoken and there was nothing to do but obey.

There was no question of sleep, and indeed, no one wanted to. Pizarro perfected his battle plan. The rendezvous with Atahualpa must take place on the main square of Cajamarca, which the Spaniards had already named the plaza. It was a large open space flanked on three sides by low rectangular constructions very similar to military buildings. The central building, the most imposing, opened upon a spacious courtyard planted with trees. The disposition of the buildings lent itself perfectly to a tactical operation analogous to the one Cortés had carried out successfully at Cholula. Pizarro divided his cavalry into three bodies, each commanded by one of his brothers, and hid them in the buildings. He did the same with the infantry. The artillery, under the orders of Pedro de Candia, he placed inside a sort of fortress or *pucara*. Pizarro kept for himself only a small number of soldiers, whose purpose was to deceive the Inca about the real number of the Spanish effectives. Everyone was camouflaged and in position, and it was absolutely forbidden to move before the prearranged signal.

But Pizarro made his dispositions for battle only after putting everything right with God. The day that was being prepared was for Spain, certainly, and also for Francisco Pizarro, but above all it was for the Cross. Father de Valverde confessed the soldiers and captains and celebrated Mass by torchlight. All the Conquistadors took Communion, but it was Pizarro and not the Dominican who delivered the sermon. The ruthless warrior promiscuously evoked the Virgin of Guadalupe, the Catholic Faith, and the necessity of converting idolaters. Did they think they had come to Peru only to make their fortunes? God demanded his share, too, and the time had come to give it to Him. The flicker of torches lit the helmet, armor, and brassards of the leader. He held his sword firmly in his steel-gauntleted hand. Was this the archangel Saint Michael preparing to crush the Devil? What was there in common between this somber sermonizer and the plunderer of Peruvian temples? Actually it was one and the same person, for Pizarro had a passion for gold and a hatred of the Devil. This outlaw had respect for divine law. All the Conquistadors, kneeling before improvised altars, knew well that they were children of God. They struck their breasts, proclaimed their guilt, lamented their sins. And all of them entoned the song of Israel: *Ex surge, Domina, et judica causam tuam!* For Pizarro's cause was certainly God's cause too.

Day broke and the Spanish trumpet sounded in the clear morning. The summits of the Andes were rosy, and the valley gently absorbed the mists of night. As in fairyland, the hanging gardens appeared through the dawn vapors. Pizarro and a few companions, grouped in the square, scanned the horizon; the rest of the troops were hidden in the buildings. It was going to be a hard day.

Pizarro was kept informed by his spies about what was happening in the Peruvian camp. Atahualpa had also made his preparations for battle. He had passed the command of his troops—about five thousand Indians—to one of his best officers, Ruminagui. The Inca apparently planned an enveloping maneuver, since he enjoined Ruminagui to occupy all the crossings by which the Spaniards had penetrated the Cajamarca valley. Atahualpa's plan appears to have been to cut off every chance of the enemy's retreat and to encircle and capture them. In any case, the Peruvian army set out by mountain roads unknown to the Spaniards. The Indian camp was deserted. Not a single tent still stood. The valley was silent. Where was the army?

The morning passed. Nerves were strained. Pizarro grew impatient. Any solution was preferable to waiting! At last a messenger asked to see the captain. Atahualpa sent his excuses to the strangers, but he was unable to keep the rendezvous at the time and place arranged. The meeting would have to take place the following day at the city gates. But Pizarro knew that a battle postponed was a battle lost. His men were still inflamed with a mystic and warlike ardor, and he did not know if they could maintain it until the next day. The messenger returned to his master with an invitation to dine with Pizarro. The reply was not long in coming and, contrary to Pizarro's fears, the Inca accepted the invitation: he would come that very evening, accompanied by an unarmed escort. He meant to make a friendly visit to the foreign leader.

A friendly visit! Pizarro trembled with joy. He would receive this friendly overture in his own way. He inspected his troops, checked the horses' harness and the condition of the artillery. The powder was dry and the swords as sharp as razors. The horsemen pinched the noses of their beasts to prevent them from whinnying. The artificers loaded their guns. The arquebuses were in position. Everything was ready for the friendly banquet.

Evening came. A rustle of feathers and fabrics announced the arrival of the Inca. Three hundred Indians dressed in red livery led the procession, sweeping the earth with palm leaves so that no impurity would soil the feet of the royal escort. Next came slaves bearing golden vases and silver hammers. Then officers in blue uniform, their ears stretched by heavy gold charms; these were the *orejones,* who, recruited from the noblest families of Peru and educated in the art and practice of war, formed a *corps d'élite* and constituted the Inca's bodyguard. Finally, borne on the shoulders of his principal dignitaries, came Atahualpa's palanquin, decorated with parrot's feathers and sheets of gold. The throne was also of gold. Behind the royal palanquin came litters bearing the Emperor's familiars. On this day Atahualpa's clothing, which the day before had been modest, was sumptuous. On his head, in addition to the ritual headband, was a crown surmounted by black and white plumes, and around his neck he wore a collar of emeralds. His chest was protected by a golden pectoral set with precious stones. His bearing was dignified, and not a muscle of his face trembled. Sometimes, however, he cast upon the Peruvian crowd the anxious look of one who was not accustomed to command or who doubted his own power, for he had held the scepter a very short time. The procession reached the Cajamarca square: it was empty. He entered the courtyard that lay before the palace: it was deserted. What silence there was in this square, only recently alive with voices! Then the Inca leaned toward his courtiers and asked them: "Where are the strangers?"

How were the pieces placed on the chessboard? Atahualpa was in the palace courtyard with six hundred unarmed Peruvians. Pizarro and his men were posted inside the palace. The Spanish army was hidden in neighboring buildings. Ruminagui and his five thousand soldiers surrounded Cajamarca. The Spanish troops and those of Ruminagui awaited only the signals from their respective masters to go into action. Two war chiefs were about to embrace, but this was the kiss of Judas. Hidden behind the scenes, the soldiers awaited this signal to rush onto the stage and begin the slaughter. Who would give the signal? Alas! it was to be a priest, Vicente de Valverde.

With a crucifix in one hand and the Bible in the other, Father de Valverde left the palace and came face to face with Atahualpa. The silence became even deeper, if that was possible. Valverde began to speak. First a lesson in catechism: the mystery of the Trinity, the creation of heaven and earth, original sin, Christ's redemption. Next a lesson in politics: the Pope, Saint Peter's successor, had divided the world among the Christian princes and had allotted Peru to Emperor Charles V. Finally, an ultimatum: if Atahualpa refused to submit willingly to Pizarro, who was Charles's representative, he would be forced to do so. An interpreter translated the Dominican's discourse as he spoke. The Inca was stupefied. What was this the stranger was saying about dividing the world? All this land and all it contained had been conquered by his father and his ancestors; Huáscar, his brother, had inherited it and he, Atahualpa, victor over Huáscar, was now the lawful possessor. Saint Peter had nothing to do with it. As for this god who was simultaneously single and triple, he had never heard of him. He knew only Pachacamac and, more distant in time, Viracocha—both of them emanations of the Sun, the supreme god.

However, he asked only for information. How did this stranger-priest get his knowledge? "From this book!" the Dominican retorted, holding out the Bible. Atahualpa took it, turning it over and over in his hands. Doubtless he expected the book to speak to him, but the Bible remained silent and he threw it to the ground. Outraged by such sacrilege, Valverde picked up the book and retired in all haste into the palace. He went to Francisco Pizarro, warned him of the perils that threatened him—the fields had filled with swarming Indians while the discussion with this arrogant dog had proceeded—and advised him to take the offensive. In advance he gave absolution to all the Spaniards. *"Salid á el—que yo os absuelvo."*

Then Pizarro waved a white scarf. It was the prearranged signal, and from the top of the fortress a musket shot answered. At once the Spaniards leaped from their hiding places crying: *"Santiago! A ellos!"* The cannons roared. The cavalry dashed into the square like a hurricane. The infantry advanced charging, and in a few minutes the square and the palace courtyard were occupied by Spaniards with arms in their hands. Terrified by the attack, the Peruvians recoiled. Though their numerical superiority was crushing—five thousand of them had just arrived, following the royal procession—they were struck with amazement. Spanish lancers on horseback easily opened a passage through the stunned crowd, and the arquebusiers fired into the solid mass. The Peruvians fell by hundreds under the fire of the cannons. Desperate at being unarmed, Atahualpa's bodyguard made a living rampart around him. The Spanish soldiers struck at the gilded and plumed palanquin with heavy sword blows; it gave way and collapsed, and the bearers, clinging to the handles, were beaten down. The Inca could feel at his throat and breast the points of the Spaniards' swords.

But Pizarro ran up to Atahualpa, brushing aside the blows that were aimed at the Emperor; the hand-to-hand struggle was so fierce and the melee so furious that the captain was wounded by his own soldiers. He seized the Inca's long hair in his bloody hand, dragging him along like a bull on a rope, and placed the fallen monarch in a safe place. From this life that he had saved—though by no means out of generosity—Pizarro planned to draw the substance drop by drop. He would squeeze this heathen until nothing more could be got from him.

While some of the cavalry pursued the fugitives, the rush for the spoils began. The broken litters were ransacked, the corpses (were there two or five thousand of them?) were rifled, and the Peruvian camp was searched to the last nook and cranny. What a booty there was! Fabrics, gold and silver vessels, furniture of precious wood, and finally (a windfall the victors did not expect), several hundreds of women who came to make themselves willing prisoners. Gold and beautiful captives! This time the Conquistadors lived out their dream. Eight years of misery and one day of glory. The victory had been dearly bought, and the Knights of the Golden Sword could now enjoy it with joyful hearts.

Throughout the battle Ruminagui had remained at the post assigned to him by Atahualpa. His troops were placed at the entries to the defiles commanding the valley, and he awaited his master's signal. But the roar of the artillery—the mountains vibrated to its echoes—and the furious gallop of the horses told Ruminagui that the game was up and that the signal would never come. The sound of galloping drew near. The clash of steel and the famous cry of the Spaniards, "Santiago!" could already be heard. The Indian general was not going to be taken by surprise; he gathered together his soldiers and gave the order to retreat. From Cajamarca to Quito is 250 leagues, and Ruminagui accomplished this journey without a break. Darkness favored the flight of the Indian warriors, and in the valley of Cajamarca there was nothing left but silence and shadows.

A Fantastic Wager: Atahualpa's Treasure

The Spaniards celebrated the victory of Cajamarca with an orgy. Pizarro alone kept a cool head. He had shut Atahualpa in one of the most solid buildings in the city, and a carefully selected guard kept watch on him; this seemed a pointless precaution since the royal captive accepted his lot with complete submissiveness. The gods had spoken: their will be done! Pizarro gave his prisoner every consideration. He could receive his ministers and his wives as he pleased, and the appearance of power was left him. But no one, neither Atahualpa nor Pizarro, was deceived, for the Inca knew that he was a hostage in the hands of a pitiless victor and that sooner or later he would have to pay.

The inhabitants of Cajamarca gradually restored their houses and the city came back to life as if nothing had happened. The Peruvian people, trained for several centuries to passive obedience, accepted the new situation without a murmur: for them it was only a change of masters, and those of today were neither more nor less tender than those of yesterday. The invaders' religion was not so very different from the old one, but the Peruvians were surprised by the lack of relationship between the conduct of the Spaniards and the ethics they preached. Under the Inca regime they had been more faithful to moral laws and more respectful of other people's property and women. House visits and searches multiplied, and soon there was not an object of value that had not been taken from the Peruvians and carried to the Spanish camp. Everything was confiscated except working tools. But that was not enough. Pizarro wanted to send Charles the most formidable "fifth" that had ever crossed the sea. He meant to surpass Cortés and to make Peru eclipse Mexico, and it was with this in view that he kept Atahualpa in reserve. The room in which the Inca was imprisoned was 7 yards long by 5 yards wide, and Pizarro proposed that if Atahualpa could fill this room with gold he would be set at liberty. To what height? The Inca raised an arm: 6 feet. A line was traced on the wall, making a block of gold of 70 cubic yards. Such was the fantastic wager that the Peruvian monarch undertook. If there was not enough gold, the cube would be completed with silver.

The Inca's messengers set out at once, for the whole empire had to be prospected from Quito to Cuzco. They hurried, for Pizarro was pressed for time. In order to go quickly they borrowed litters: they covered ten miles an hour, for they were carried at a run by porters in constant relays. In emergency, the porters handed over to the *chasquis*, the Inca's couriers, who were lined along the imperial roads. Atahualpa's envoys carried quipus in their hands, the colored cords of which transmitted the sovereign's orders. The wheels of the Inca system were well oiled, and no one disputed the ruler's will.

The period of two months fixed by Pizarro expired. The heap of gold rose, but the agreed height had not been reached. The Inca smiled. A little patience! Was it not enough that all the roads converging on Cajamarca were dotted with litters that bent beneath the weight of the precious vessels? There was no hurry. But that was not Pizarro's view. Almagro had just arrived with one hundred and fifty men and eighty-four horses, and Almagro was very greedy. He demanded his share and would not be content with promises! Pizarro lost his temper. He had some excellent news to tell the Inca. Hernando de Soto, who had left with the advance guard for Cuzco,

had contacted Huáscar, and although he was a prisoner, the legitimate son of Huayna Capac had not renounced his rights to the
paternal throne. He, too, had promised the Spaniards to repurchase
his crown at the highest price. It was not only to the height of a
man but to the roof and beyond that Huáscar agreed to fill the room
at Cajamarca. The blow struck home and Atahualpa ceased to smile.
A few days later Huáscar was smothered in his prison at Cuzco, on
Atahualpa's orders. Before dying, he voiced these prophetic words:
"I have been king of this land for only a little while. But that traitor
my brother will not be king for longer than I."

July 1533. The agreed amount had been obtained. The Inca's
room was filled with gold and silver treasure. Pizarro was in possession of a fortune such as no European sovereign or banker ever had
in his coffers: 52,000 silver marks and 1,326,000 gold pesos. This heap
of metal in 1950 would have represented about $3,430,000 (£1,225,-
000) on face value! Pizarro proceeded to divide this enormous booty.
First, about $3,080,000 (£1,100,000) for the King of Spain—a fifth
that strangely surpassed the true fraction, but Pizarro wished to make
a great impression. Did Charles V like gold? He would be heaped
with it.

Hernando Pizarro had a right to $78,400 (£28,000), Hernando
de Soto to $39,200 (£14,000), while for the cavalry there remained
$22,400 (£8000) and for the infantry $11,200 (£4000). As for
Francisco Pizarro, he allotted himself Atahualpa's gold plate worth
over $196,000 (£70,000).

Atahualpa had paid, but was he going to recover, if not his throne,
at least his freedom, which seemed only just? But the Conquistadors'
ideas of justice were otherwise. Although a prisoner and ruined, the
Inca was a threat to Spanish authority. In the eyes of the Peruvians
he was the Son of the Sun, the last god of the Inca pantheon, the heir
to Tahuantinsuyu. It was not enough to have conquered his kingdom, emptied his treasury, and subdued his army; the man himself
must be destroyed.

What is easier than to prove the guilt of an innocent man when
it has been decided to condemn him? A tribunal was set up. Witnesses were called. The most aggressive was a Peruvian, Filipillo, who
was employed by the Spaniards as an interpreter. He accused his
master of conspiring with Ruminagui. Atahualpa shrugged his shoul-

ders, for the accusation was absurd. Guarded as he was, how could he communicate with his former general at Quito, hundreds of miles away? He knew only too well the motives that inspired Filipillo, for the traitor was enamored of the Emperor's favorite, and the death of the Inca would favor his amours. But the tribunal took Filipillo's evidence into consideration. Rebel against the King of Spain, Atahualpa was also accused of having usurped the throne of Peru, assassinated his brother, practiced polygamy, and sacrificed to false gods. Father de Valverde was one of the most strenuous in demanding the death of the Inca. He was prepared to sign the sentence, if that was necessary. Doubtless he had not forgotten the public affront he had received from Atahualpa in the Cajamarca square. Did one pardon the insults of a heathen hardened in his crimes? At last the verdict was given: the Indian monarch was to be burned alive. At the last moment he was offered baptism, to which he agreed, and thanks to this he gained the privilege of being strangled.

In that same square at Cajamarca where, nine months earlier, Atahualpa had appeared in his gilded and plumed palanquin, a gibbet was raised. Accompanied by Valverde and Francisco Pizarro, and followed by a large crowd, came the Inca. His name was now Juan de Atahualpa, for his patron saint was John the Baptist. The new Christian was tied to a stake. A running noose was placed around his neck and pulled tight. Fixing his eyes upon Pizarro, the last Inca emperor, the Son of the Sun, died by the garrote.

Francisco Pizarro entered Cajamarca on November 15, 1532; Atahualpa perished by the garrote on August 29, 1533. In nine months Pizarro and his handful of soldiers had mastered a territory that was soon to stretch between the Pacific Ocean and the cordillera of the Andes and from the 2nd parallel north to the 32nd parallel south, an empire inhabited by twelve million people and as large as Spain, France, Germany, and Austria-Hungary put together. It had been a highly developed civilization, with two centuries of Inca rule behind it, with warrior traditions, cadres that seemed fixed for eternity, and wise political leaders. All of this was ground to dust in nine months by a band of Spaniards. A former swineherd had seized the King-God by his hair and put him under arrest. His punishment had been to accumulate the most enormous pile of gold that had ever been seen, and as a reward he had been strangled. The mournful crowd that witnessed the crumbling of its fatherland and its gods made no attempt to stop what seemed to them inevitable. It would have been so easy to toss this pack of conquerors down the slopes of the Andean sierra, but they preferred to let themselves be devoured.

Actually, Pizarro had had everything to bring his *tour de force* to success: first, gunpowder, horses, and well-tempered blades. Steel against stones. The surprise effect of new weapons is not a recent invention, for to terrify an adversary with "modern" machines is a procedure dating from man's earliest battles. Further, Pizarro was preceded by a legend, that of the avenging white god to whom he bore every likeness. Finally, he arrived at the right moment: Huáscar and Atahualpa were disputing the empire, and the fruit for which the two brothers were reaching fell into Pizarro's hands. The two Incas died and the Spaniard was master of the situation.

But Pizarro's principal ally was the Inca regime itself. This empire regarded itself as the world. Tahuantinsuyu—the four quarters of the world! In the Inca universe there was no place for a fifth. Space and time did not exist for the lords of Peru. The word "tomorrow" was unknown to the people, and laws and statistics were for eternity. The machine, constructed for perpetual motion, was well oiled— too well; for to stop it Pizarro had only to capture Atahualpa and thus block the controlling lever. The Peruvian legislator had not foreseen this *coup de force*, which was a surprising omission in a system based upon foresight. Yet when calculating probabilities, would it not have been sacrilege even to consider the assassination of God? The weakness of the regime was that by striking at the head, the entire organization could be crumbled. Separated from the Inca, the officials could no longer administrate and the elite were disoriented. To be sure, the people remained, but they had been taught only one thing, to obey, and they obeyed. Twelve million Peruvians, but ten million robots. While some thousands of upper-class subjects devoted themselves to chosen tasks—surgery, architecture, astronomy—the people, in festival clothing, plowed or harvested singing the praises of the Sun. They had been taught that work was gaiety. This amorphous and sad people worked with joy. For ten generations, ten million Indians had heard it said: "The Inca knows all. The Inca cannot be mistaken. The Inca is immortal." But suddenly the monotonous voice was stilled. The Inca was dead. What could they do when they knew only how to obey? Ten million slaves held out their wrists for Spanish chains.

CHAPTER 13

War between the Conquistadors

THE day following the execution of Atahualpa, a solemn funeral was given him. Father de Valverde celebrated Mass for the dead, and the Spaniards in full uniform surrounded the catafalque. It was a grandiose affair to do honor simultaneously to the last Inca emperor and to the new convert. While the Conquistadors chanted the Requiem, the Dominican priest gave absolution. Pizarro was chief mourner and wore a black sash across his cuirass; a crape veil hung from the hilt of his sword.

When night fell, after Atahualpa's remains had been interred in Christian fashion, a band of the Inca's faithful friends exhumed the body and took it in the greatest secrecy to Quito, his native city. Ruminagui took charge of the royal corpse and summoned the Indian people together. An Inca ceremonial followed the church funeral, and for the second time Atahualpa was laid in the earth. A pit had been dug beside the grave of his father, Huayna Capac, and one by one the dead man's companions stabbed themselves over the tomb of their master.

Cuzco, the Inca Rome

Freed from Atahualpa and Huáscar, Pizarro gave thought to the choice of a successor—a symbolic successor, of course, for he needed an Inca prince at his side when he entered Cuzco. There were two candidates: Tupac Amaru, Atahualpa's brother, and Manco Inca, Huáscar's half brother. The latter lived in Quito, and Tupac Amaru at Cuzco. Pizarro chose Manco. He welcomed Huáscar's half brother to his camp and in exchange for his support, promised to have him crowned at Cuzco. The alliance was concluded and nothing more stood in the way of continuing the adventure.

To go from Cajamarca to Cuzco, the Spaniards took the great road connecting the north and south across the high Andean plateaus. This was the "Inca road." Starting from Pasto, it passed through Quito, Tumipampa, Cajamarca, Huamachuco, Vilcas, and Cuzco, skirted Lake Titicaca, and plunged still farther toward the south. Almost wholly straight and built of hard mortar, it easily bore the weight of armed cavalry and cannons. The Inca road was adapted to the terrain, with steps up the mountainsides, hanging bridges over the rivers, and embankments across the marshes. Nothing was lacking, not even signposts. The surface was smooth and polished; not an ounce of mud spoiled its impeccable cleanliness.

The Spaniards were astonished. How could they avoid comparing these concrete roads with the dusty tracks of Old Castile? Those who had fought in Italy recalled the Roman roads. What were they compared with the royal arteries of Peru? Pizarro was beginning to understand one of the secrets of Inca power. In order to centralize the administration of this enormous empire, a strong network of roads was necessary. The political system depended on communication, and the Incas had solved the problem with good roads, lined with hostelries and relay stations where there were porters always ready to set out. Such meticulously calculated communications enabled the emperor to send and receive messages, the administration to distribute merchandise, and the police to make its contacts in a minimum of time. An order from the Inca took ten days to go from Cuzco to Quito, a distance of about 1250 miles. The chasquis ran in uninterrupted relays, day and night. The Peruvian roads were the ever taut and vibrating nerves that transmitted to the imperial brain the least quiver of this great docile body, the communistic Inca state.

It was November 15, 1533, and two hours before sundown. The Spaniards were within sight of Cuzco, and it was exactly a year to the day since they had entered Cajamarca. Yesterday they had crossed the frontiers of the empire; today they were at the heart of that empire. Everything, in fact, converged on Cuzco: defiles, roads, and canals, as well as thoughts and prayers. Cuzco was for the Peruvians what Rome was for the Latins: the economic, political, and religious

capital. The horizon is bleak, vegetation is sparse, and the sky ice-
blue, for here we are at a height of nearly 11,000 feet—the same as
Etna! The terrain is mineral: quartz, schist, slate. Why did the early
Incas choose this stony spot for their capital? It was as if they had
needed a combination of space and dryness.

The ramparts of Avila could be completely contained within the
shadow of the cyclopean walls that surrounded Cuzco. Nevertheless,
they opened to Pizarro, and the Spaniards entered. They filed by
with arquebuses on their shoulders and swords in their hands. Here
were the districts of Cuzco: that of "the puma's tail" and that of
"the silver snake." Here was the fortress of Saxahuaman and its three
squat towers. Here was the Temple of the Sun: four edifices in gold
and silver encircled by a triple granite wall. Inside was the image of
the Sun in gold, and around it the mummies of dead Incas seated in
golden chairs. Is it surprising that the Temple of the Sun, or Coricancha, was also known as "the place of gold"? Here was the "square
of rejoicing" or parade ground; at the moment when Jesus died in
Jerusalem, the high priest of the Sun, on this very square, held out
to the sun a bowl filled with fermented corn. Flagellants and castrated
monks circled there slowly, for the rites had not changed for fifteen
hundred years.

The day the Spaniards entered Cuzco was also that of a great religious festival, and Pizarro's soldiers ran into sacred processions in
the streets of the Peruvian city. Groups of priests bore massive
golden idols on shields, accompanied by dancers in black robes. The
flagellants flogged themselves until the blood ran. *Oro y sangre!*—
just as at Seville, and, what with the young boys rhythmically stamp-
ing the soil, the penitents, and the *pasas*, the Spaniards felt that they
were once again at the *Fiesta del Corpus*. But the illusion did not
last long. This heathen masquerade was an insult to the True Faith,
and the Andalusians remembered the Virgin of the Sorrows and her
shining mantle. With swords raised, they plunged into the crowd.
The Peruvians replied with stones and javelins, but though superior
in numbers, they were soon crushed by the fury of the Spaniards.
The canticle to the Sun died away, and nothing could be heard but
the clash of armor, the crack of arquebuses, and the cry of the
wounded. But Pizarro's men were seeking gold rather than blood,
and their hands reached out for the idols. The sack of Cuzco began.

Palaces, temples, and houses were pillaged. A mad covetousness possessed the Spaniards, and although it was not long since they had received their share of Atahualpa's treasure and they were rich, it was not enough. They proceeded hurriedly to the distribution of the booty, and no soldier on campaign had ever received such fantastic pay. The Conquistadors were overwhelmed by their fortune. The misers stowed it away in hiding places, but the wastrels staked it on games of chance. On a throw of the dice they chanced what would have given them an income for life. A cavalier named Leguizano received as his share a massive golden disk representing the Sun God. He staked it, during a night of orgy, on a game of *dobladilla* and lost it. He was ruined. But his ill luck became proverbial: *Juega el Sol antes que amanezca,* which means "gamble the sun before sunrise."

Cuzco, the imperial city, "every street, every fortress, and every stone of which was regarded as a sacred mystery," was no more. Without further delay Pizarro meant to make a Spanish city of what had been the Inca capital, for the conqueror was also an architect; he himself drew up the plan of the new city. Wide arteries replaced the squarely laid-out streets; monasteries and convents arose out of the ruins of four hundred Inca temples; the Cathedral of Santo Domingo was built upon the sanctuary of Viracocha, and statues of saints were set up in the niches reserved for the golden tears shed by the Sun. Oriel windows and balconies adorned the cube-shaped dwellings of Peruvian nobles. But this work of reconstruction was not done in a day, though manual labor was abundant. Those who had been able to haul the gigantic blocks of the Saxahuaman fortress to the top of the hill could easily cut the stone for Christian churches, and it mattered little to these passive people whether they worked for the Inca or for the king of Spain.

The Pact of Riobamba

While Pizarro was taking stock of his victory, surprising news reached the Spanish camp. Pedro de Alvarado had landed at Puerto Viejo on the coast of Ecuador at the head of five hundred soldiers, two hundred horses, and a large detachment of Indian mercenaries. Alvarado, Cortés' second-in-command and hero of Tacuba! Pizarro learned through his informers that Alvarado was moving upon Quito

by forced marches, and he learned at the same time—for bad news
never comes singly—that Ruminagui had gathered together a large
force and was preparing for revenge. Quito had become the center
of Peruvian resistance. This double threat had to be countered, so
Almagro and Belalcázar were ordered to go to meet Ruminagui's
Indians and Alvarado's Spaniards. The two detachments set out
northward.

Pedro de Alvarado was not in Ecuador by accident. He was continuing a triumphant march. Sent southward on reconnaissance by
Cortés, he had left Mexico with a few intrepid men. The little troop
had cut a path through the fearful Chiapas bush with their swords
and had reached and discovered Guatemala. Alvarado had always
loved honors, so he proclaimed himself governor of Guatemala. However, Charles V, informed of Alvarado's prowess, confirmed the title
the Conquistador had given himself. Encouraged by the monarch's
favor, Alvarado asked for permission to push still farther southward,
and it was given him. He was conceded a zone of activity outside
that given to Pizarro, but these boundaries were vague, for how
could the administration record on parchment the frontiers of an
almost unknown country? To permit Alvarado to set foot in Peru
was to give him carte blanche. Alvarado, moreover, regarded it as
such.

Belalcázar first had to face Ruminagui, an engagement that took
place at the gates of Quito. The Indian chief was not made of the
same stuff as Cuauhtémoc; nevertheless, he was the incarnation of the
resistance. The ranks had been broken, the Incas killed or imprisoned,
and the corps of elite had become powerless. The figure of Ruminagui
stood out against this melancholy background like a warrior upright
among the dead. It was no longer the dynasty but he himself who
was the incarnation of the fatherland. There was no need for him to
wear the royal headband in order to be king.

Ruminagui was a simple soldier and not particularly concerned
with niceties. His job was fighting, but this did not prevent him
from giving expression to a certain savage humor. As the Spaniards
were approaching Quito, the Indian whispered to his wives: "The
Christians are coming. You will be able to amuse yourselves." It was
a good joke and the women broke into laughter. But this access of

unseasonable gaiety cost them their lives. Ruminagui beheaded them all.

Faced with twelve thousand Indians, Belalcázar lined up his two hundred infantry and eighty cavaliers. Military science was once more to conquer numbers. Belalcázar divided his troops into small mobile groups able to move very quickly from one place to another, and Ruminagui's army was tormented as if by swarms of wasps. Unnerved by these attacks, it lost its cohesion. The Indian warriors were attacked from all sides at once and, not knowing from what direction the blows would come, they were unable to parry them in time and became demoralized. Confused, they turned about, trying to face in every direction, and exhausted themselves in useless counterattacks. Soon they were overtaken by panic, and profiting by their disorder, Belalcázar gently thrust them toward the plain. This tactic, invented by Cortés, had stood the test of experience. In the plain the cavalry could be deployed and the adversary surrounded.

When the Spanish captain judged that the Peruvians were sufficiently exhausted, he launched his horses against them, and a few cannon shots served to terrify them. Ruminagui's furious exhortations were lost among the groans of his soldiers, and it was in vain that he shouted to them that the Spaniards were men like the rest, because no one believed him: these creatures that shone in the sunlight and ran on four feet could not be other than gods. They controlled the thunder; as though to prove this was true, an unexpected ally lent Belalcázar a hand: Cotopaxi. By a coincidence that the Spaniards regarded as providential, the volcano, which had been quiescent a long time, suddenly began to erupt. How could the Indians doubt now that the strangers were of divine origin? They dropped their arms and fled under a rain of lava and ash. Ruminagui, followed by his officers, abandoned Quito and in a final outburst of anger, set fire to Huayna Capac's palace. Then he disappeared toward the northern mountains.

While Belalcázar was fighting before Quito, Almagro was searching the coast for Pedro de Alvarado. Cortés' companion was elusive. He had certainly been seen to land at Puerto Viejo and take the direction toward the mountains. But how could a handful of men be found in the dense *arcabucos* of the virgin equatorial forests?

Almagro turned around and made for Quito, arriving there in time
to help Belalcázar reduce Ruminagui's resistance. While he was col-
laborating in the common victory and cleaning up the suburbs of
the city, Almagro helped himself to his share of the booty. Then,
leaving Belalcázar master and governor of Quito, he turned back
toward Cuzco.

Ecuador is a staircase rising from the Pacific Ocean toward the
summits of the Andes, which project like peninsulas into the sky.
On the last step of this gigantic staircase stands a city, Quito, the
capital of the clouds, the future "Light of America." Now that
Ruminagui and his men had evacuated it, Quito was as sinister as
the crater of a volcano, but still alive with secret life, like a nest of
condors. The Spaniards advanced step by step through the deserted
streets. Temples, towers, and tombs . . . Belalcázar dreamed of planting crosses on the cupolas. Meanwhile he gave the name San Francisco de Quito to the holy city of the Schyris.

Alvarado was not lost. He was climbing the Ecuadorian staircase
step by step. He was undertaking across the cordillera one of the
hardest journeys man had ever accomplished. His Spaniards stag-
gered along the frozen tracks of the "avenue of volcanoes." They
killed their horses for food and sucked snow to quench their thirst.
Sixty died from the cold, among them a soldier and his wife and
two small daughters; unable to do anything to succor them, he took
them in his arms and died with them. The plutonian fury of Cotopaxi
and Chimborazo did not spare the tottering little troop. Heavy
clouds of smoke, the roar of explosions, and a rain of sulphur completed the *décor*.

At last, after crossing dizzy passes and nearly breaking their necks
a hundred times, the Spaniards came out into the plain of Riobamba.
They were rewarded for their struggle. Only yesterday they had
thought they were in hell, and today they trod the green pastures
of paradise. The province of Riobamba is in the middle of the sierra
in an immense valley enclosed by two branches of the cordillera of
the Andes. It is a land of eternal spring: roses, lilacs, tulips, and the
same carnations as in Andalusia. Waterfalls, birds, fruits, and such a
profusion of waters, colors, and perfumes that the Conquistadors
were intoxicated. Why go farther when they could set themselves
up in this wonderful province? A shower of javelins and stones

brought them back to reality. The inhabitants of Riobamba were not going to let themselves be dispossessed. Sobered by the Indian attack, the Spaniards joined battle. In the front rank of the attackers were women with quivers on their shoulders who were no less skillful than the men at drawing the bow. A battle such as the myths record was fought out in the Ecuadorian plain between Spanish cavalry and female archers. Centaurs versus Amazons.

Almagro had scarcely arrived at Cuzco when he learned of Alvarado's presence sixty miles from Quito. Belalcázar received the same information, and each of them, at the head of a column, made for Riobamba. Alvarado awaited his compatriots resolutely. Would he accept battle? It was a chancy business. He had been able to repulse the offensive by the people of Riobamba, but what could his weary troops do, faced with the completely fresh troops of Almagro and Belalcázar? The two captains themselves were hesitant, for though they certainly wanted to oust Alvarado, it had to be at the smallest cost. Soon the three columns were face to face and the leaders made contact. The conditions of battle were regularized as if in a duel, but as they were about to draw swords, the combatants changed their minds. Spanish blood was too precious to waste. Instead of forcing Alvarado's expulsion by arms, why not buy it? Almagro offered 100,000 pesos on condition that Alvarado undertake to return to the coast and set up his government again in Guatemala. Alvarado agreed to the deal, for he had nothing to lose. In fact, although he did not say so, during his perilous journey from Tumbes to Riobamba he had made a fine collection of gold and emeralds. A fortune was worth more to him than power! It was understood that the 100,000 pesos would be paid him by Francisco Pizarro himself. The agreement having been made, Belalcázar returned to Quito. As for Alvarado and Almagro, they made for Pachácamac, where Pizarro was to be found.

There was no fratricidal battle. At least not yet.

Prelude to Strife

Francisco Pizarro paid his 100,000 pesos to Pedro de Alvarado. A bargain made and a bargain kept. With his wallet stuffed, and oiled with good words, the "Sun God" returned to Guatemala; a serious threat had been eliminated. Pizarro could turn his thoughts to construction, for now his chief preoccupation seemed to be building.

First he founded a port on the Peruvian coast. He gave it the name of his native town: Trujillo. Cortés had founded Medellín in the same way. But, more prudent than his model, Pizarro decided to establish the future capital of Peru at a distance from its predecessor. It was not good to install new gods in old sanctuaries. After a minute search, Pizarro chose a site in the valley of the Rimac about six miles from the sea, between the future port of Callao and the mouth of the Rimac river. Callao would give access to the Pacific, and the Rimac would lead to the interior. Excellent from the commercial and political points of view, the site selected by Pizarro was healthful and the climate reminiscent of Andalusia. The new city, founded on the day of Epiphany, was named *Ciudad de los Reyes:* the City of the Kings. Later it was called Lima.

Was Pizarro so absorbed by his new vocation that he would lose sight of his responsibilities as a leader? He was building on soil still scarcely secured, and he could not have any illusions on that subject. His two brothers, Juan and Gonzalo, were at Cuzco, where they were on bad terms with Almagro. Belalcázar was at Quito, at grips with rebel native elements. His third brother, Hernando, was in Spain, and he himself was on the shores of the Pacific. They were indeed far apart. What confidence, moreover, could they have in Manco Inca, who must be champing at the bit in his Cuzco palace? Was Pizarro's place really in the valley of the Rimac among Indian masons, where his cuirass was clouded, not with the dust of battle, but with the dust of a builder's yard? Did he really think the war was ended?

In the midst of all this, Hernando Pizarro returned from Spain. He had seen the Emperor, and the gold of Peru had had its effect. The conquerors of gold must be recompensed! Hernando drew from his doublet a bundle of parchments that contained Charles's gifts. Francisco Pizarro was named Marquis d'Altabillos, and all northern Peru, under the name of New Castile, was assigned to him. Almagro received southern Peru, or New Toledo. Father de Valverde—in gratitude, doubtless, for his attitude toward Atahualpa!—was named Bishop of Cuzco, and Hernando Pizarro had been made a Knight of Santiago. They congratulated one another and embraced, yet the

Emperor's decisions contained the germ of future discord. Where did southern Peru end and northern Peru begin? The day of the geographers had not yet come, and Almagro and Pizarro were to dig their frontiers with their swords.

First of all, to whom did Cuzco belong? Almagro claimed it, but Juan and Gonzalo Pizarro contested his claim. They were, in any case, already at daggers drawn. Warned by his men, Francisco Pizarro went hastily from Lima to Cuzco, torn from his town-planner's dreams. The two partners fell into each other's arms. They had known one another for more than thirty years. They had fought together on the battlefields of Italy. Were they going to forsake their common heritage and break an old friendship for the sake of a misunderstanding? Pizarro promised never to undertake anything against Almagro, and Almagro promised to leave the field free to Pizarro for a radius of 130 leagues from Cuzco. It was understood that he would look farther south for a province to his liking; if he did not find it, he would share power with Pizarro. In order to give divine sanction to their oath, the two Conquistadors crossed hands over the consecrated Host. Addressing himself to the Holy Sacrament, Almagro exclaimed in a loud voice: "Lord, if I break my oath, may you confound me and punish me in my flesh and in my soul!" After this spectacular ceremony, Almagro and Pizarro separated. The former set off southward, and the latter, after confiding the government of Cuzco and the care of Manco Inca to his brothers Juan and Gonzalo, returned to Lima. A rupture between Almagro and Pizarro had been narrowly avoided.

Several months passed. Hernando Pizarro was on a journey, and Almagro gave no sign of life. The Marquis—for Francisco Pizarro was known by this title from now on—gave all his attention to the building of Lima. He seemed to have lost his taste for fighting. One passion consumed him: a passion for stone. He brooded lovingly over this city that was taking shape and could already show miradores, and churches with over-elaborate façades, and palaces with heavy doors cut from equatorial woods. It was "his" city.

Grave events were about tear the Marquis from his peaceful labors again. Manco Inca had succeeded in evading the surveillance of the brothers Pizarro, had fled from Cuzco and raised the standard of revolt. In a few weeks he had recruited an army of two hundred thousand Indians; then, sweeping back on Cuzco at the head of his troops, the Peruvian prince attacked the city. Hernando Pizarro, who had been able to rejoin the besieged garrison in time, took command of the Spanish forces beside Juan and Gonzalo. As to the Marquis, he was blocked at Lima, for the Indians had cut the communications between the two cities. The honor of Spain was in the hands of his three brothers. Confined to Lima, and aware of the threat that weighed upon Spanish Peru, the Marquis asked for help from the governors of the islands and of Terra Firma.

Hernando Pizarro was determined to do everything to break the Indian encirclement of Cuzco. Cost what it might, he had to maintain himself in the city; if not, he and his men were lost. The siege began with a bombardment of flaming arrows: Cuzco was on fire except for its stone buildings. The crux of the battle was the Saxahuaman fortress, and the colossal blockhouse was occupied turn and turn about by Spaniards and Peruvians. For several months the adversaries strove against these enormous walls that were like the armored ram of an antique ship. The keenness of the Indian soldiers amazed the Spanish fighters, but little by little the fighting turned to the advantage of Pizarro. Hernando eventually succeeded in dislodging the Indians from Saxahuaman, and from there he directed and oriented the operations. He had the sorrow of seeing his brother Juan die beside him, struck on the head by a stone from a sling. Shortly afterward the last Peruvian defender, his face covered with soil, threw himself from the top of the fortress, a theatrical suicide that heralded the defeat of Manco. The Inca raised the siege and retreated southward. Hernando Pizarro had only to open his arms to victory. But another was to seize it. It was one whom no one expected: Almagro.

Informed of what was happening in Cuzco, Almagro had interrupted his expedition and had gone to the aid of Hernando Pizarro. This apparently generous gesture concealed a treacherous intent. The love that the Marquis had for Lima, Almagro gave to Cuzco. He had not rushed to the aid of the Pizarros, but to the conquest of Cuzco. He was not upset to find the city that he had had to abandon in the midst of its rebirth burning and mutilated; like the Marquis, he wanted it to be new. But before becoming its master, he had to eliminate the last efforts of Peruvian resistance; that is, he had to complete what Hernando Pizarro had begun.

To be taken in the rear by Almagro's detachment was something Manco Inca did not expect. At the exit from Cuzco he fell into a Spanish ambush. He was powerless and sought only to escape. His strategic retreat became a disorderly flight, and for a long while Almagro's soldiers gave chase to the unfortunate prince, who found refuge only in the desert mountains at the sources of the Amazon, where he announced to his people that the gods had abandoned him. All was lost. To a chorus of cries and groans, the Inca's companions and his last partisans surrendered to death, and a great silence fell upon the final exploit of Huayna Capac's son.

Almagro entered Cuzco and demanded of the Pizarro brothers that the city be handed over to him. It belonged to him, he claimed. But had he forgotten his oath over the Host? Almagro brought a new fact to bear: patents that he had received from His Majesty assuring him possession of Cuzco. Hernando and Gonzalo did not see things thus; Cuzco, in their view, was the fief of the Pizarros. Beside himself with anger, Almagro had Hernando and Gonzalo arrested and thrown into prison. Then he proclaimed himself governor and gave orders that a *Te Deum* be celebrated in the cathedral in his honor.

Conqueror of the Inca, free of the brothers of Francisco Pizarro, and master of Cuzco, Almagro now had only to defy one last adversary in order to complete his triumph: the Marquis himself. Was his ambition going to lead him to take up arms against the friend of his youth? But youth and friendship counted for little when faced with so exciting a prospect: the possession of Peru and its gold. With clenched teeth, his mind and heart empty of memories, Almagro began his march upon Lima. Gonzalo Pizarro remained behind bars; Hernando, on the other hand, went with the troops. Did Almagro think that he might be of some use to him as a hostage or plenipotentiary?

Once again things were arranged peacefully, thanks to the intervention of a priest, Fray Francisco de Bobadilla, Provincial of the Order of Merced. This ecclesiastic arranged an interview between Almagro and Francisco Pizarro at a place called Chinche. The two Conquistadors met cordially and embraced as in the days of their youth. The basis of an agreement was proposed: Almagro would remain governor of Cuzco until the Emperor made his decision known, and Hernando Pizarro would be freed on condition that he returned to Spain.

Then the Marquis invited his friend to supper, but the war feast was cut short, for in the middle of the meal a cavalier ran up to Almagro and whispered in his ear. Gonzalo had escaped from prison and had organized an ambush to assassinate Almagro. The latter had time only to run to his horse and leap into the saddle. His horse's hoofs made the stones fly from the road. He turned around and waved his hand to the Marquis. This was good-by, for they were never to meet again.

The next day Francisco Pizarro received a dispatch from the Emperor. The two captains were maintained in their possessions, which meant that the Marquis was master of Cuzco. Almagro had to be dislodged. Grimly Pizarro ordered his brother Hernando to march upon Cuzco. Almagro accepted the challenge: he would not surrender the holy city of the Incas to the Marquis, but he did not feel strong enough to fight. He was old—sixty-three years!—and his sword seemed heavy. He gave command of his troops to Orgoñez and took refuge on the heights overlooking Cuzco. From there he would be able to follow the fortunes of the battle, for the die was cast and the fratricidal war, so long delayed, was about to begin.

The Duel of Las Salinas

It was indeed a duel that was fought between Hernando Pizarro's Spaniards and those of Almagro. A quarrel was being settled, and Almagro's six hundred men and the eight hundred recruited by Pizarro fought like dogs. Had they forgotten that they served the same king and that they had been born, almost all of them, in Estremadura?

The battle took place some two miles or so from Cuzco in the plain of Las Salinas, thus named because of the salt marshes there. Hernando had chosen as colonel Pedro de Valdivia, who was later the conqueror of the Araucanians. Orgoñez was surrounded by gentlemen who had been proved by experience, including Francisco de Chaves and Juan Tello. The two armies clashed in fury. Grouped upon the hills, the Peruvians jeered as they tasted the unexpected pleasure of seeing their enemies shoot, charge, and disembowel one another as if they were attacking Indians. It was, indeed, their turn to watch the circus. Soon Almagro's soldiers lost ground. They had more lances than the enemy but fewer firearms, and it was gunpowder that was the deciding factor. Almagro's army fell back to the mountains. Orgoñez, wounded on the head by a shot from an arquebus, was captured by an ambush just when he was preparing to rally his troops. Vanquished by numbers, he surrendered his sword to one of Hernando Pizarro's officers. But Pizarro's order was "No quarter!", not even for a gentleman, and as he was dismounting from his horse, Orgoñez received a point-blank shot and collapsed. The leader's death precipitated a rout. Almagro's side had lost.

Was this the same Almagro who, filled with arrogance, had forced conditions upon the Pizarro brothers not so long before? Tied up like a sack on the back of a mule, he made a pitiful entry into Cuzco. He had lost all pride and implored the victor's pardon, but Hernando Pizarro was not disposed toward lenience. He cast Almagro into prison and straightway ordered his prosecution. Supercilious lawyers scrutinized Almagro's slightest deeds and gestures from the day of his departure from Panama, and they had no difficulty in findings proofs of his guilt. Almagro had opposed the Marquis's will with arms; he had set himself up as master of Cuzco; he had led his army, "flags flying," into territory within the jurisdiction of Francisco Pizarro. Accused of high treason, Almagro was condemned to death. When the sentence was announced, the prisoner lost the little dignity that still remained to him and collapsed at Hernando Pizarro's feet, begging Hernando to spare him so ignominious an end. Had he not given Hernando his freedom when he had been in his power? And going farther back into the past, Almagro recalled the part he had played in the Pizarros' fortunes. But Hernando was inflexible and in an icy voice he advised Almagro to commend his soul to God. "How should I, man and sinner, not fear death when Jesus Christ himself feared it!" Did this infirm and dishonored old man love life so much that he should stoop to this miserable confession?

Almagro, who had been known as "Don Diego," received the last sacraments. Earlier he had dictated his testament, naming as his heirs the Emperor and his son Diego. Then a rope was passed around his neck and Pizarro's companion died, garroted, like Atahualpa. His corpse was then dragged into the square at Cuzco and the executioner cut off its head with an ax and presented it to the people. But the next day solemn obsequies were performed for him in the chapel of the monastery of La Merced, where Hernando Pizarro was the chief mourner. The Peruvians who witnessed the execution and the funeral were stupefied. Yesterday Almagro's head rolled on the block, and today Hernando Pizarro intoned the Requiem with tears streaming down his face.

The End of the Marquis

The Marquis learned of Almagro's execution with profound distress. He had not asked for this. But his distress was modified by a feeling of real relief, for the pact that had been concluded fifteen years before was now broken and he was free. Without fear or reflection he could devote himself to the completion of his work.

It was 1541 and the Marquis was sixty-six years old. He had definitely abandoned military expeditions in order to realize his true passion for construction. Lima had become an important city. Other cities had risen, too: Huamanga, Chuquisaca, Arequipa. . . . In the sumptuous palace that had been built to his plans in the middle of the plaza mayor at Lima, Francisco Pizarro kept up the appearance of a king. Nevertheless, the master of Peru was "democratic," or at least pretended to be so when he wished. He played tennis with his servants in his patio planted with orange trees. He walked the streets without escort, wearing a black cape and a white felt hat, with a simple dagger at his belt. One day, passing along a riverbank, he leaped into the water to save an Indian who was drowning. But he could also act as a sovereign. With age and the exercise of power he had acquired a veritable grandeur. One had only to see him in the great hall of his palace, enveloped in his purple cloak or in the marten furs that Cortés had sent him from Mexico, to realize this.

The Marquis's repugnance for war was now complete. Was he tired of arms, or was it remorse? He built, he administered, he governed, but he no longer wished to conquer or to fight. He left this matter to his lieutenants. Pedro de Candia was at Titicaca, Gonzalo Pizarro was exploring eastern Peru, and Pedro de Valdivia was continuing the conquest of Chile that Almagro had begun. As for Hernando Pizarro, he had gone back to Spain, but misfortune had overtaken him. Almagro's partisans at court had convinced the Emperor of Hernando's treason, and he was to end his days in prison long afterward, a centenarian. Juan Pizarro had perished in the siege of Cuzco. The Marquis was alone.

A final conspiracy was being prepared secretly. Diego Almagro, son of the executed man, was its leader. This half-breed—his mother was an Indian woman from Panama—had gathered under him all the elements hostile to Francisco Pizarro. They were numerous, even if one counted only Almagro's companions who burned to avenge his death. The Marquis's faithful friends had not failed to put him on guard against this threat, but the old leader scorned their warnings. He refused to take any precautions. More and more remote and withdrawn into himself, he pursued his imperial dream. Such disdain for death was indeed a sign that the Marquis was approaching those high solitary regions where the man-become-hero believes in his star and in it alone.

One June Sunday the Marquis had invited to dinner a few of his friends, including the Bishop of Quito, Francisco de Chaves, and his lieutenant, Juan Velásquez. It was between noon and one o'clock, and through the open window an uproar reached the ears of the guests. The shouts became clearer: "Death to the tyrant!" Who was the tyrant? None but Francisco Pizarro. About half a score of armed men stood outside the palace, under the command of an officer: Juan de Herrada, Diego Almagro's lieutenant. Very calmly the Marquis ordered all the exits to be closed and retired to his rooms to change his red cloak for armor. Meanwhile, Francisco de Chaves attempted to come to terms. He half opened the door, and Almagro's partisans burst into the palace. Chaves, who was run through by swords, groaned as he died: "They do this even to friends!" The conspirators raced for the stairs and reached the great hall and came to the Marquis's room. At the approach of the attacking party, Francisco Pizarro's intimates fled, leaping through the windows into the street—even Juan Velásquez, who, in order to keep his hands free, held his commander's baton between his teeth.

The Marquis came out of his room. He had not had time to fasten the straps of his cuirass, but protecting himself with his shield, he fell upon his adversaries with raised sword. Five faithful Spaniards fought at his side, but soon the Marquis was alone. Alone against ten. Twirls, thrusts, parries, and clinches followed one another, and Almagro's men were amazed. This old man of nearly seventy handled his sword like a youngster. Juan de Herrada called through the window for reinforcements; then there were twenty against Pizarro, and blows rained upon him, still standing erect. Was he invulnerable after all? Yet he could do no more. His arm weakened. He was like an exhausted stag. A final thrust, and the Marquis crumpled, his throat cut. He cried out his confession and then, unable to speak more, dipped a hand into his own blood and traced a great cross on the floor. He kissed this bloody cross and died with his lips fixed upon the symbol of Christ.

"In this can be seen a fine example of the variety and the uncertainty of the things of this world and the inconstancy of fortune. In a very short time a simple gentleman, who had no great responsibility, had discovered a very large tract of country and powerful kingdoms of which he made himself master and had been made governor with very great authority. He was possessed of prodigious wealth. To several persons he had distributed goods and revenues so considerable that perhaps in the whole of history not one of the richest and most powerful princes of the world will be found who has distributed so much in so little time. Then, in a moment, everything changed. He died, without time for confession, nor to prepare for death, nor to put his affairs in order, nor to arrange his succession. He was massacred in full daylight by a dozen men in the middle of a city, all the inhabitants of which were his creatures, his servants, his kinsmen, his friends, or his soldiers. To all of them he had given the means to live comfortably and even grandly. However, none came to his help in his most pressing need. His domestics and those who were in his house fled and abandoned him. Afterward he was poorly buried. All his grandeur and all his riches vanished, and the means could not be found to pay for candles at his burial."

This was written by a contemporary of Pizarro, the chronicler Augustín de Zarate. It summarizes well the prodigious curve of this incomparable destiny.

The outstanding characteristic of this destiny was the continuity of its rise, but not the continuity of the man. At each point in the life of Pizarro a new Pizarro arose. The Cortés of Mexico and the Marquis of the Valley were not so very different from the student of Salamanca or even from the Medellín youth who already dreamed of becoming a Conquistador. The dying Columbus treasured the same chimeras as at Porto Santo. But there was nothing like this with Pizarro. There were as many quite new personalities as there were epochs in his life. The swineherd of Trujillo; the professional soldier; the Jack-of-all-trades of the captains of the Southern Sea; the island planter; the stubborn sailor who clung on like a dripping shellfish to the rocks of Puerto del Hambre; the conqueror of the Andes; the jailer of Atahualpa; the builder of cities; the red-cloaked Marquis—all these figures rushed along like those in a pack of cards. But one tries in vain to give them a family likeness. What could there be in common, indeed, between this purple-clothed patriarch like a Roman consul and the tough soldier of the Italian wars or the pillager of Tumbes?

However, two pictures—one from the beginning and one from the end—give a sort of unity to the personality. A newborn babe was abandoned on the steps of a church in Estremadura. He survived only by luck. He was alone at an age when even the most unfortunate are surrounded with care. Sixty-six years later, the Conquistador of Peru succumbed to the swords of conspirators, like Julius Caesar. The assassins, once the blow was struck, were confounded. They had killed Pizarro! They made off like thieves. No one dared to touch the corpse for fear of compromising himself. Finally a man from Trujillo and his wife dragged the corpse to the nearest church, wrapped it in a shroud, and buried it. But despite their anxious haste, they took time to envelop the Marquis in the great white mantle of the Order of Santiago and to fasten his spurs.

Francisco Pizarro died alone. Thus, from the first day to the last he had had no other love and no other companion but himself, and he remained constantly faithful to this austere solitude. Yet it must be emphasized that he desired this solitude. It had become, by the end of his life, the only climate in which his pride could live. When a man believes himself to be the elect of God and the interpreter of History, he can tolerate no one.

PART FOUR

Monks Versus Captains

OR

The Conquistadors on Trial

CHARLES V
—COURTESY HISPANIC INSTITUTE,
COLUMBIA UNIVERSITY

Who authorized you to brand us on the face with a red-hot iron?

—Question put by an Araucanian chief to Don Francisco Núñez Pineda y Bascuñan, a Spanish captain.

—FROM *Pioneer Spaniards in America*
by William H. Johnson. Little, 1903.

CHAPTER 14

The Araucanians

Pizarro was dead, Almagro was dead, and to these two men two parties succeeded, the "Pizarrists" and the "Almagrists." Thus the civil war did not end at Las Salinas nor with the death of the two leaders. On the contrary, it became more bitter. In vain did Almagro's son proclaim himself governor of Peru, for no one recognized his title except the *camarilla* that surrounded him. Disorder reached a climax. Here was a last opportunity for the Peruvians to free themselves from Spanish domination, but they did not take advantage of it, despite the favorable combination of circumstances.

Charles V, apprised of the situation, was roused to action. Was he going to see one of his most valued colonies escape him? He sent a judge to Peru with full powers; his name was Vaca de Castro.

The Liquidation of the Peruvian Adventure

Skillful and prudent, Vaca de Castro was wary of attacking the enemy frontally. The focal points of insurrection were at Cuzco and Lima. Vaca de Castro avoided them, and it was at Quito that the imperial delegate set up his residence. Well received by Belalcázar, he began his inquiry, gathered information, and prepared his dossier. He quickly realized that only military action supported by the elements faithful to the dead Marquis could achieve order and peace.

The decisive encounter took place in the Chupas mountains a few miles from Guamanga. The bravest captains of the conquest marched at the head of the Pizarrists: Alvarez Holguín, Pedro de Vergara, and especially the terrible Francisco de Carvajal, known as "the demon of the Andes." Veteran of the Italian wars and formerly

Gonzalo Pizarro's colonel, Carvajal was a colossus dreaded by both his soldiers and his equals. Although he had long since passed his seventieth year, his brutality and physical energy were still proverbial, as were his bouts of drunkenness. Cristobal de Barientos carried the royal standard. The Almagrists were commanded by Diego Almagro himself, surrounded by officers of whom some, like Pedro de Candia, had been among Francisco Pizarro's earliest companions. As for Vaca de Castro, he stayed at the rear with a few cavaliers and did not intend personally to participate in the battle. The licentiate was not a man of war.

Better equipped, more numerous, and encouraged by the Emperor's backing, the Pizarrist troops had no difficulty in vanquishing the small Almagrist army. But the fight was a hard one, and the adversaries were so closely intermingled that they would not have recognized their own men if it were not for the color of their sashes: red for Vaca de Castro's and white for Diego Almagro's soldiers.

When he saw that the battle was turning against him, the half-breed Diego Almagro fled to Cuzco and his troops dispersed, and when night fell not a single Almagrist remained at the scene of the battle. A few days later, after burying the dead and beheading those of the prisoners who had taken part in the assassination of the Marquis, Vaca de Castro made a triumphant entry into Cuzco. His first act was to proclaim himself governor of Peru. This time the appointment was legal, for Vaca de Castro already had it in his pocket when set out from Spain. His second act was to behead Almagro's son in the square at Cuzco, at the same spot where, four years earlier, his father had also lost his head.

The execution signified the end of the Almagrists. What was to happen to the Pizarrists? The majority lined up quite naturally under the king's banner, but not all. There was one who held back: Gonzalo Pizarro. When Vaca de Castro arrived in Quito, the last survivor of the four Pizarro brothers—for one could scarcely count Hernando, imprisoned in Spain, among the living—had made his submission perforce. He had even offered his services, though with no enthusiasm. But though Vaca de Castro had accepted Gonzalo's submission, he coldly declined the offer; for the moment he preferred Gonzalo's neutrality to his alliance. By a sort of tacit understanding, Gonzalo had voluntarily kept apart from the conflict between the Pizarrists and Almagrists, and while the struggle proceeded and throughout the government of Vaca de Castro he remained on his lands at Chuquisaca, not far from Lake Titicaca. He led the peaceful life of a great landed proprietor: a brief entr'acte before the final scene.

Vaca de Castro had re-established order in Peru, not without difficulty, and considering his task completed, he asked the Emperor for his recall. His request was accepted and a successor was appointed: Blasco Núñez Vela, who landed at Tumbes with the title of viceroy. A vast staff came with him: corregidores in crimson cassocks, comptrollers, officers of the Crown. Never had so imposing a delegation come from the homeland. The new viceroy, interpreting the will of Charles, thought to make clear in this way that the reign of the adventurers was ended. Henceforth there would be but one master, the King of Spain. But Núñez Vela was not content simply to bring with him the rods of justice and the royal seal, which lay in a casket set upon a palfrey caparisoned in gold. He was charged with applying to Peru the *Leyes Nuevas* (new laws) which had just been promulgated at Valladolid. Slavery and the encomienda were suppressed, and the Indians were recognized as the free and trusty vassals of His Majesty. The order was given to all the Conquistadors —especially to officials, ecclesiastics, and the partisans of Almagro and Pizarro—to free their slaves at once. In brief, Núñez Vela's mission aimed at nothing less than depriving the conquerors of Peru of all power and dispossessing them of the benefits they had acquired. It was a dangerous mission, doomed to failure because of Núñez Vela's own character: choleric, dogmatic, and brutal.

The reaction was not long delayed. Gathered around Gonzalo Pizarro, the Conquistadors formed an army in the south and marched upon Lima, but the Viceroy did not wait for the arrival of the rebels. He fled toward Quito, and Gonzalo entered the deserted palace, where the Marquis had been assassinated, as victor. Núñez Vela's brief stay had left few traces. Gonzalo was a fine-looking man, and in him the Spaniards and Peruvians saw again the dashing cavalier who, so long before, had cavorted under the amazed eyes of Atahualpa. No one made any difficulty about recognizing Gonzalo as governor of Peru. Beside him old Carvajal, drunk with pride and liquor, shone in his golden cuirass.

But Gonzalo would not be satisfied until he had the hide of Núñez

Vela. He raced for Quito, pursued the unhappy Viceroy into the mountains, captured him, and cut off his head on the spot. Then Gonzalo returned to Lima. In his brother's palace he established the court of an Oriental despot, for Gonzalo dreamed of making immortal the great name of Pizarro which was thought to have died with the Marquis. He was to be the Great Pizarro, and he dismissed the King's officials, for he himself was King.

But the one who was about to wring the neck of this condor was a monk, Pedro de la Gasca, counselor to the Holy Office. This time Charles was lucky. Gasca's arrival in Peru passed almost unobserved. What was he going to do? Carry out a simple inquiry on behalf of His Majesty. This skinny little man, dressed in a threadbare cassock, had a singular gift for authority. He spoke little, but at a single word from him everyone became silent. A gesture, and he was obeyed. One by one, near and far, he approached all those who were favorably disposed toward Gonzalo. He convinced them that Gonzalo was disloyal. He enlisted the aid of some of the leading captains, especially Pedro de Valdivia. Finally he succeeded in raising an army of two thousand men, and a great battle took place at the gates of Cuzco on the Xaguixaguana plain. Gonzalo Pizarro was beaten, and on the very day of his defeat he was tried and condemned to death. Execution followed judgment, and the executioner cut off his head. Afterward it was exposed in a cage hung from the great Lima gallows, with this inscription: "Here is the head of Gonzalo Pizarro, traitor and rebel to his King." At the same time, nine captains were hanged and Carvajal was quartered.

Having spent several months in Peru, Pedro de la Gasca returned to Spain. He had left Spain poor and he returned poor. But he had won an empire for the Crown. The cleric in threadbare clothes and of melancholy face had established peace and restored the colony's administration and finances. There were no more Pizarrists or Almagrists, and Peru was now firmly in the hands of Emperor Charles V. This reconquest was the work of Gasca. Virtue sometimes has its triumphs. In the foreground of the bloody Peruvian fresco with its severed heads and old Carvajal torn apart by four horses, spilling his intestines, rises the cold face of the monk who made "New Castile" out of the Tierra de Pirú, and on the shores of Lake Titicaca founded the future capital of Bolivia, Nuestra Señora de la Paz, Our Lady of Peace, which we now call La Paz.

First Battle in Chile

The geographical shape of Chile is rather absurd: a ribbon twenty-five hundred miles long and two hundred miles wide at its broadest point. Lying between the Andean cordillera and the Pacific Ocean, it embraces the whole gamut of climates. In the north is the great desert of Atacama, its immense salt plains the color of melted lead; in the center is the Great Valley with its eternal summer; and in the south the wastes begin again—a land of fiords and glaciers. Above this narrow ledge hangs the cordillera with its summits that reach to nearly 20,000 feet. Chile, on the slope of the southern Andes that plunges into the waters of the Pacific, is squeezed between the mountains and the sea.

To reach Chile by sea was already possible by the middle of the sixteenth century. In fact, the navigators had only to push their caravels a little farther in order to reach the banks of the "Valley of Paradise"—Valparaíso, the future great port of the southern Pacific. But to reach Chile from the north by land called for madmen and heroes—in short, the Conquistadors.

The first pioneer of Chile was Diego de Almagro, the father. After the Cuzco compromise and the Emperor's decision to award him southern Peru, Pizarro's companion had but one thing to do: to conquer his kingdom. He got busy at once and pushed southward. The expedition was a large one: five hundred and seventy Spaniards and fifteen thousand Indians. Besides his two lieutenants, Gómez de Alvarado and Ruy Díaz, Almagro took with him the Inca Paulus, brother of Manco Inca—a useful precaution in case of conflict with the natives. Ignoring the counsel of the Peruvian chiefs, who advised him to follow the coast, Almagro plunged straight into the cordillera. The intense cold and the deep snow surprised the Spaniards, who were badly shod and lightly clothed. Without concern for human losses—one hundred and fifty Spaniards and ten thousand Indians were frozen to death—Almagro continued the terrible ascent. On his return six months later he found standing in the snow fields groups

The Conquest of Chile

of soldiers petrified by the ice, still holding the bridles of their horses in their hands, like equestrian statues. Having reached the summit of the Andes, Almagro descended upon Copiapó and reached Coquimbo, and from there he went on to the mouth of the Río Aconcagua. Until then he had met with no resistance from Indian tribes; for them the presence of the Son of the Sun at his side validated the expedition. But the situation changed when the Spaniards came to the Río Rapel where, nearly a century earlier, the Promaucas had defeated the army of Prince Sinquiruca, Yupanqui's general, who had come to subdue them. Since then the Rapel had been the frontier of the Inca Empire. On the other side of the river the Promaucas lived free of any allegiance and exempt from tribute; for, powerful as they were, the Incas had never crossed the Rapel frontier with arms since that one unfortunate attempt.

Almagro's pride rose in protest at the very idea of turning back. There, where the Peruvians had been unable to pass, he, a Castilian, would succeed! He gave the order to cross the river. But the Promaucas awaited him on the far side of the water with spears in their hands, and a fight was inevitable. Disconcerted at first by the Spaniards' military array, the native soldiers soon counterattacked with such vigor that Almagro and his men had to fall back, leaving their dead on the field. Full of rage, they recrossed the Rapel.

The return journey to Cuzco was disastrous. More fearful than the Andean passes, the high lands of Atacama almost became the graveyard of the expedition: a stretch five hundred miles long without a plant or even lichen (for in human memory rain had never been seen), where a sort of dry rot flourished. Only the blood of battles occasionally moistened its soil—the vestiges of trees or prehistoric algae mixed with salts and minerals. Even the vulture had fled the Atacama. But men have fought bitter battles there for the possession of fertilizers and iron. The Spaniards almost lost their reason while crossing the "Saltpeter Desert," a phantasmal landscape where the sun's blinding reflection outlined long moving specters on the nitrate fields. In short, Almagro's campaign, a brilliant feat of adventure, ended in failure. The interminable journey gave him neither gold nor cities, and he returned to Cuzco empty-handed. We already know what followed: a year after his return, Almagro died by the garrote.

Pedro de Valdivia

Francisco Pizarro's moral authority and Hernando's arms would probably not have been enough to defeat Almagro had Pedro de Valdivia not lent a hand. With Almagro eliminated, New Toledo became free. It fell by right to Valdivia, who had shown the extent of his military talents and loyalty.

Valdivia was not a newcomer. Born at Villanueva de la Serena about six miles from Medellín, where Cortés was born—Estremadura once more!—he had fought bravely in Italy before setting out for America. After seeking a career for some time on Terra Firma, he had eventually joined up with the Marquis. As Hernando Pizarro's colonel at the battle of Las Salinas, he had been the chief artisan of the Pizarrist victory. A fine fellow, eloquent of speech and noble of manner, still young—only thirty—Pedro de Valdivia was in every way the right person to open for Spain the road to the south, so painfully initiated by Almagro. The Marquis had appointed Pedro de Valdivia as his lieutenant governor of Chile, ignoring the claims of Francisco Camargo and Sancho de la Hoz, who maintained that the Crown had given them authority to explore the south.

Profiting by the unhappy experiences of Almagro, Valdivia neglected nothing, before setting out, that could facilitate the success of the undertaking. To his one hundred and fifty Spaniards, flanked by a large contingent of Indians, he added artisans, workers, and "technicians" provided with the tools indispensable for building, planting, and producing. He took with him not only horses, but pigs and poultry; not only gunpowder, but seed. For beyond the conquest, Valdivia already visualized the business of colonization.

The expedition took the same route as that of Diego de Almagro, but in reverse: the cordillera, the Atacama Desert, Copiapó, Coquimbo. Slanting off toward the sea, the Spaniards discovered a smiling valley at the foot of which was a harbor. To this lovely valley, with almond trees in flower, Valdivia gave the name Valparaíso, Valley of Paradise. Continuing into the interior, the Conquistadors reached the banks of a watercourse: the Mapocho. This place seemed suitable to Valdivia for laying the foundations of a town, and as the site was at the "end of the world," the future city was called Santiago

del Nuevo Extremo. Faithful to the legalist traditions of his predecessors, Valdivia, before even the first stone of the new city was laid,
set up a municipal council or *cabildo*, and a deed was drawn up
before a notary. Four months later the Marquis was dead, assassinated, and the council, which was called together at once, recognized
as governor and captain general of Chile "the Most Magnificent Señor
Pedro de Valdivia, in the name of God and of His Blessed Mother
and of the Apostle Saint James."

Thus was Pedro de Valdivia promoted to omnipotence by a legal
artifice. But he reigned over a desert. The moment had come to
organize the territory of which he was the sole master. Without waiting for Francisco Pizarro's successor to ratify his powers, Valdivia
set to work; his doctrine, expressed in a few words, was: "the best
sights I know are corn, wine, and cattle." The war horses were
harnessed to primitive plows, and Spanish soldiers dressed the vines
and milked the cows. Was the Conquistadors' war cry to change
into some Virgilian song? The months passed, and Santiago took on
the look of a village, then of a small town. Meanwhile Valdivia's
companions grew weary. Native labor was scarce. The population,
moreover, was not reliable. The frequent incursions of the Promaucas
undid in one day the work of several weeks. Valdivia sent Monroy,
one of his officers, to Peru to seek reinforcements. He returned at the
head of fifty cavaliers, while a ship filled with arms, clothing, and
food anchored at Valparaíso. Nothing more was needed to give
Valdivia new optimism. He extended his conquests. Pedro Bohón
founded the town of La Serena in the valley of Coquimbo. The corn
grew and the vintage looked promising. What a fine country and
what a poetic name! "Chile" or "thili" was the Indian word for a
thrush.

While Valdivia tasted the joys of power and the delights of love
with the beautiful Inés Suárez, there was bloody civil war in Peru.
The last act had begun: Pedro de la Gasca was about to face Gonzalo
Pizarro, and Valdivia decided to play his part in the tragedy. He
arrived at Cuzco while the action was still undecided, and in time to
take part in the battle of Xaguixaguana. By placing his military
knowledge at Gasca's disposal, Valdivia assured his victory. In token
of his gratitude, the Emperor's delegate confirmed Valdivia in his
functions as captain and governor general of Chile or New Estre-

madura, but made two conditions: that he pay his debts and that he break off relations with Inés Suárez. If he had need of a wife, there was nothing to prevent him from calling to his side his lawful wife, who was cooling her heels in Badajoz.

Having returned to Santiago, which was now "his" capital, Valdivia took energetic measures. He organized the finances, the administration, and police. No government was possible without internal order and economy! And the conquest continued. Francisco de Aguirre pacified Coquimbo and rebuilt La Serena, which had been burned by the Indians. Valdivia himself pushed boldly southward at the head of a column. He reached the town of Penco on the Pacific shore, which he captured and named Concepción. Would nothing stop the Estremaduran cavalry? Intoxicated with the sense of space, Valdivia left the conquered city to conquer another. To acquire the villages one by one and to dream of turning them into cities was an intoxicating game. Valdivia had now reached the banks of the river Bío-Bío.

In the Land of the Araucanians

The Bío-Bío is the natural frontier of central Chile. Beyond the river lies southern Chile, and the horizon changes. The Andes fall away and dwindle while the valleys become wider. It is colder and it rains. The large island of Chiloé is not far off; it commands the entrance to the world of islands and ice in which Chile ends. Still farther south is the archipelago of Tierra del Fuego, swept by polar blasts, where the Pacific and Atlantic meet.

But the Bío-Bío not only separates two regions of Chile; it marks the frontier of Araucania. The Incas had never ventured beyond the Bío-Bío, for they knew what it would have cost them. Their military science and their arms could do nothing against this elusive people who hid in the depths of the forests: the Araucanians.

Physically the Araucanian somewhat resembled Asiatics: big heads with prominent cheekbones, thick lips, broad noses, and slanting eyes. On the other hand, they were tall and muscular. Skillful in running, excellent swimmers, clever in handling clubs, and excellent marksmen with bows and arrows, the Araucanians also possessed a high degree of trickery and courage, qualities that made them the best hunters in the whole of South America. They were also its most ferocious warriors. Besides hunting and fishing, the Araucanians engaged in agriculture and stock raising. They made chicha from fermented corn, and ponchos from vicuña wool. Generally they fed on fish, game, and vegetables, but they were cannibals, too. Their industry was rudimentary: with fishbones they sewed the skins of animals to make their clothing, and they made tools of stone. For amusement they played the flute, an instrument they made from a thigh bone. They had little taste for the pleasures of family life. Women counted for nothing and were bought and sold like merchandise. From their earliest years children were brought up for hunting and for war. Properly speaking, there was no political or social organization, for the Araucanian found communal life repugnant. Taciturn and proud, he sought solitude. In his wanderings he might come upon a clearing or a riverbank, and if the spot pleased him he settled there. Then he constructed a hut, or *ruca*, and lit his first fire. Disdainful of others, the Araucanian feared god—the Great Spirit of the Universe—and worshiped the stars. He believed simultaneously in the immortality of the soul and the everlastingness of the body. He surrounded the corpses of his people with precautions and respect. He buried his dead seated upright in square pits, and beside them he placed their arms, tools, and food. Each year a matron opened the tombs and washed and dressed the skeletons. The hierarchy was simple: the military chiefs were called *toquis*, and those responsible for the administration were called *ulmens*. A last feature: these hard people spoke a harmonious language with melodious inflections. What ironic creator had placed a language of eloquence and love on the lips of these primitive people?

While Valdivia kept to his own side of the frontier, the Araucanians did not move, for what happened north of the river did not interest them at all. The whinnying of the Spanish horses on the bank of the Bío-Bío gave them the alarm. Like wolves surprised in their haunts and banded together by the threat of danger, the Araucanians formed an army of four thousand men commanded by the toqui Ayavilu. The first engagement took place not far from the Bío-Bío in the plain of Andalion.

Faced with four thousand Araucanians with spears raised and clubs whirling, Valdivia debated whether it would not be better to avoid contact and flee. He knew enough of war to realize that he would not overthrow the Araucanians as easily as he had the Promaucas. On the other hand, it was futile to suggest a compromise, for the Araucanians did not understand diplomacy. But it must not be said that a Spanish captain had refused to fight, so Valdivia gave the order to fire.

The first discharge of muskets was enough to stop the Araucanians. They feared no one, but they respected the gods. Lightning had struck them, as a sign of reprobation. The second discharge killed their best captains, and the toqui Ayavilu fell. The cavalry, launched at a gallop, completed their terror. The Araucanians collected their dead and withdrew in impressive order. Valdivia was victor and, intoxicated with success, continued his advance. He had a free field, so the cavalcade continued, and as the moment had come for the Conquistador to make his name immortal, he gave it to a town and to a river: Valdivia, on the banks of the Valdivia. Had he not already given La Serena the name of his native village? Cities rose like mushrooms: Nueva Imperial, Villarica. . . .

The Araucanians regrouped in the dark forests. In place of Ayavilu, they had elected another toqui: Lincoyan. The new leader was prudent and preached submission to the invader, but a terrible blunder by Valdivia aroused the anger of the Araucanians, whom he probably could have neutralized with a little skill. In the intoxication of victory, thinking to show his strength, Valdivia had sent the prisoners who had been taken on the Andalion field back to their homes with their hands and noses cut off. This futile and barbarous deed was to cost him dear.

How a Tribe Became a People

The Araucanians' first reaction to the Spaniards was instinctive. Each, like a beast at bay, defended his own life, not that of others. But the cruel outrage upon four hundred of their people inspired the Araucanians with a sense of community. Henceforth they were bound together. They lacked only a leader to coordinate their confused aspirations and to make a fatherland out of the Araucanian community. This leader was not long in coming forward. A territory invaded, armed men gathering together, a champion with irresistible speech: thus are nationalisms born.

The man who took charge of the welfare and honor of the Araucanians was called Colocolo. He was an old man reputed for his knowledge, who had been retired from public life for a long time. The crossing of the Bío-Bío by the Spaniards and Valdivia's insolent deed had torn the old sage from his solitary meditations. He gathered the ulmens together and took counsel with them. This Indian Nestor, whose eloquence was famous, begged his compatriots to shake off the foreign yoke before it was too late. The country was already half occupied. The ulmens were convinced, and it was decided to create an army. A toqui was appointed—Caupolican—and they had only to seize the right moment.

While Araucanian resistance was being organized in the greatest secrecy, Valdivia was extending his conquest, and soon all the southern provinces had submitted to him, at least in appearance. He had three small forts constructed in the neighborhood of Concepción: Tucapel, Arauco, and Purén. Thanks to these well-armed garrison points, twenty miles apart, he controlled the land and hoped to hold it.

Keeping an eye on his conquest, Valdivia meanwhile tidied up his love affairs. Who was this Inés Suárez whom he had to abandon on Gasca's orders? When she had arrived in Santiago a few months after the founding of the city, she was the first Spanish woman to have hazarded that fearful journey. It was love that had brought her, for she had come to join her husband Rodrigo, Valdivia's companion. She led the life of the soldiers, and shared all their perils. She was an excellent marksman, and could shoot like a man at a range of one hundred yards. Moreover, she was beautiful, and Valdivia could not fail to be interested in the Spanish Amazon. Having come to Chile for love, Inés stayed there for love, but the object of her love had changed. Now Valdivia, faithful to his promise but in great despair, resigned himself to sending this companion of the evil days back to Spain. Simultaneously he asked his lawful wife to join him at Santiago. Doña Mariana de Gaete, also very beautiful, loved her husband passionately, and Valdivia's invitation was an answer to her prayers. The reunion of these two filled the Spanish colony with pleasure, for the conquerors, imbued with chivalry, needed a lady to ennoble their thoughts and a princess to lead them to victory.

This gallant interlude did not divert Valdivia from his task: the final crushing of the Araucanians. He worked methodically to that end and imagined he was near his goal. But the intrepid general was badly informed. One day when he was at Concepción, grave news reached him: the fort of Tucapel was besieged by an Araucanian detachment. Valdivia at once gathered together some men and set out for Tucapel. He expected only a skirmish and that he would quickly punish the barbarians for their insolence. However, when he came in sight of the fort he found only a heap of ruins, and of the Spanish garrison nothing remained but a severed arm. He had scarcely time to overcome his stupor when he found himself surrounded by an army of some size—Caupolican's. The trap was well laid. There were only fifty Spanish cavaliers and three thousand Indian mercenaries against ten thousand Araucanians in battle order, and behind this mass of fighters other troops could be seen, ready to intervene.

Surrender or die? For Valdivia there was no other alternative, and he chose to die. The fight took place in the marshy plain of Tucapel, which proved disastrous for the cavalry. For many hours the battle remained indecisive, but suddenly an Indian auxiliary detached himself from the Spanish ranks. This was Lautaro, an Araucanian of sixteen years whom Valdivia had carried off and made his page. Having suddenly recovered his patriotic feelings, Lautaro deserted and passed over to his compatriots, whom he upbraided vigorously. Why should they fear these foreigners? They were men like others, for he knew them well.

He placed himself at the head of the Araucanian army, turned about, and rushed upon his former allies with lowered lance. Electrified by this heroic gesture, the Araucanians intensified their action and launched a last assault upon the Spanish soldiers. Not a single soldier came out of the melee alive. Pedro de Valdivia was captured and dragged to the feet of Caupolican and Lautaro, and it was the child who pronounced sentence: death. But Valdivia did not die for three days, during which time, dismembered alive, piece by piece, he served as food for his executioners.

In despair at the fearful death of her husband, Mariana de Gaete retired into a hermitage and founded the order of the Virgin of Solitude.

A Difficult Succession

Valdivia's will named as his successor one of the three following captains: Alderete, Aguirre, or Villagra. Alderete was in Spain, so power was shared by Aguirre and Villagra; while Aguirre held northern Chile, Villagra tried to keep the south.

The victory at Tucapel had aroused the Araucanians, but they did not mean to limit their action to this encounter. They would not rest while a single Spaniard trod on Araucanian soil. Old Colocolo intensified his harangues to the ulmens: "Illustrious defenders of our homeland, oh, caciques! . . ." As everyone was eager to secure a command in the army of liberation, Colocolo had invented a test in order to decide among them: the chieftain's spear would be given to him who held a great wooden beam at arm's length for the longest time. Caupolican still remained the generalissimo, but at his side Lautaro played the role of vice-toqui. The young hero took on the appearance of a demigod.

After an interval, hostilities were resumed and Caupolican laid siege to Nueva Imperial. Lautaro attacked Valdivia and Concepción at the same time. Valdivia held out, but Concepción capitulated. Harassed on all sides, the Spaniards entrenched themselves at Santiago. Lautaro still advanced, while behind him trod six hundred Araucanians in good order, chosen from among the best, and three thousand auxiliaries. Thus they came to the Bío-Bío and had only to cross the river in order to set foot in the suburbs of Santiago. Once Santiago was captured, why not go farther, even perhaps as far as Peru? Nothing seemed impossible to that fierce youth Lautaro. But Villagra awaited him on the banks of the fatal river and opened fire. The Indian archers let fly their missiles. An arrow passed through Lautaro's breast, and the first Chilean *caudillo* was dead.

With Lautaro gone, Caupolican was left alone to bear the brunt of Spanish arms. His experience and his age inclined him to caution. He raised the siege of Nueva Imperial and Valdivia and restricted himself to laying a defensive cordon along the frontiers of Araucania. He felt that the time for offensives was over. Meanwhile the Viceroy of Peru, Andrés Hurtado de Mendoza, decided to put an end to Araucanian resistance. Affairs in Chile irritated him. He ordered his son García to the spot to take the situation in hand. The new governor landed at La Serena with three hundred and fifty men, provisions, and munitions. His first concern was to imprison Villagra and Aguirre. Then he studied the terrain and tested the enemy defenses by a series of small local operations. Despite his youth—he was only twenty-one—García, probably under instructions from his father, maneuvered with patience and without haste.

García had established his headquarters on the island of Quiriquina, facing Coquimbo. Caupolican was established on the shore at the approach to Concepción. The river frontier was still the stake of the battle. Araucanians and Spaniards crossed and recrossed it in turn, and it was fully realized by both sides that final possession of the Bío-Bío would decide the fate of the conquest.

The adversaries watched one another for several months, and the skirmishes they launched did not alter their respective positions. García then decided on an encircling action to take the Araucanians in the rear. He assembled a small squadron and embarked at Coquimbo, taking the direction of Concepción. Off Valparaíso a violent gale caught García's ships, and the Indian auxiliaries saw in this an evil omen. The gods had declared themselves against the Spaniards, that was certain. To complete their terror, the Chilean mercenaries discovered in the stormy sky the face of Lautaro, monstrously enlarged. The chronicler Pedro d'Oña said of this apparition later: "I saw his head emerge like a naked cranium covered with long hair . . . his mouth, surrounded by a black cloud, breathed thick smoke, and along his lifeless body and cadaverous face ran bloodstained sweat. Through the cruel wound that tore his side the hero's heart could be seen, where blood no longer ran, but pus instead." A romantic piece of imagery that clearly illustrates the mark left in the memory of the Araucanians by the brief epic of young Lautaro.

García's fleet escaped shipwreck by a miracle and anchored at Talcahuano, quite near Concepción. The Spaniards had scarcely landed before they were engaged by Caupolican's advance guard, but this time they were in force and powerfully armed. The Araucanians had to give ground. García's detachment of six hundred men crossed the Bío-Bío, gave chase to the enemy, and forced him to fight near a muddy lake. This was the battle of Lagunilla. The Indian column, led by the toqui Galvarino, suffered total defeat, and it might have been a fatal blow to Araucanian resistance if García had not imprudently repeated Valdivia's gesture of sending the vanquished cacique back to his village with his hands cut off. Thinking to make an example, he revived the spirit of revolt.

The return of Galvarino, raising his mutilated wrists to heaven, was greeted with a roar of hatred. The death of Lautaro had brought consternation to the Araucanians, but the torture of the toqui reignited their patriotism. The whole people responded to Caupolican's appeal. Children took arms from their fathers. Women tore away the cutlasses or spears that their lifeless husbands still held. The old men exhorted the youths. All Araucania had risen against the invader, and García and Caupolican faced each other again in the Melipuru plain. The toqui's strength was impressive, but García aligned his best troops, who were now used to the special technique involved in this sort of fighting. A number of valorous captains were in command in the Spanish army, including Ercilla y Zúñiga, who in his leisure hours wrote *La Araucana*. The fight was equal, and for a long time there was doubt who would prevail. But finally García's artillery and horses got the better of Indian fury, and Caupolican abandoned the struggle and retreated southward. García de Mendoza laid the foundations of a town at the place where he carried the day: Cañete.

The buildings that rose on the field of Melipuru were not houses to live in but military constructions. Cañete was to be a strong point, and García had chosen a pitiless man, Alonso de Reinoso, to command it. The new governor instituted a reign of terror. He put all the Araucanian prisoners to the sword, but the ulmens had the privilege of a worse punishment: tied to the mouths of cannons, they were shot into the air and their shapeless remains fell into the Indian camp. Caupolican, followed by his old guard, prowled around Cañete like an enraged beast, seeking the weakest point to strike. Failing victory, Caupolican wanted vengeance, but he was not to know this bitter pleasure, for a last trial was reserved for the old chieftain: treason. Betrayed by one of his own men, he was taken in ambush and brought before Alonso de Reinoso's tribunal. Elated at having the generalissimo of the Araucanian army at his mercy, the governor decided to make the greatest use of his prize. Caupolican was solemnly led into the square at Cañete, impaled upon a pointed stake, and a company of archers riddled the martyr with arrows.

Colocolo had died of grief, Lautaro had been shot down, and Caupolican tortured; what would the Araucanians do now? They had lost their wise man, their hero, and their warrior, the mystical trio indispensable to the people's advancement. But the fanaticism of the Araucanians owed less to the virtues of their chiefs than to the mysterious call of their native forests. Those who embodied the fatherland were dead, yet the fatherland lived on. Without weakening for a moment, the Araucanians continued their struggle. They kept it up until 1850, three centuries after the foundation of Concepción by Pedro de Valdivia. Only then was it possible to speak of a sort of assimilation, which would never be submission. A succession of heroes assured the constant revival of heroism. Thirty years after the death of Lautaro, an adolescent named Nangoniel captured the fort of Arauco and perished with an arrow full in the heart, like his predecessor. About the same time, Jarrequeo took command of the Araucanian army and defeated the troops of Sotomayor, Captain General of Chile. A little later the same Sotomayor had to face a young prince, Quintunguenu. The epic of youth never ceased to inspire Araucanian bravery.

Meanwhile the reconnaissance of Chile progressed. In the north the Spaniards had reached Tucumán; in the south Ercilla had sailed around the Chiloé island in a little ship that was not even ballasted, while Juan Ladrillero explored the Strait of Magellan. The banner of Castile floated at Punta Arenas, for in the same year that Philip II succeeded Charles on the Spanish throne, the Conquistadors had founded the most southerly city in the world at 53 degrees south latitude.

Hernán Cortés landed on the Mexican coast in 1519. He took possession of Mexico in 1521. Thus the conquest had lasted two years.

Francisco Pizarro landed at Tumbes in 1531. Atahualpa was executed in 1533. Thus Peru was also conquered in two years.

Pedro de Valdivia founded Santiago in 1541. He reached the river Bío-Bío in 1550. Villagra built the town of Osorno in 1558. The conquest of Chile had taken seventeen years.

Thus a few months had sufficed the Spaniards to subjugate two old empires and to dislocate a political system that was safe—it seemed— from the worst trials. On the other hand, it took them long years to assure their domination over a simple people without traditions, a domination that remained precarious for a long time. It was the Araucanians, the "savages," who resisted the invaders, while the Incas and Aztecs, believing they were fighting a battle of wits, came to terms with them. Between the barbarians and the nobles, on which side is true nobility to be found? If, in fact, one excepts the brief episodes of Cuauhtémoc and Ruminagui, the two great dynasties of pre-Columbian America allowed themselves to slip quietly into servitude, and their peoples followed. But with the Araucanians there was nothing of the kind: from the first encounter these misanthropes formed a sacred union, and the unsubmissive disciplined themselves. Compared with the superb nonchalance of the Sons of the Sun and the Lords of Aztlan, the stubborn courage of a handful of cannibals leaves one wondering. But there was a precedent. When Christopher Columbus on a certain Sunday in November 1493 landed at Martinique, the Caribs received him with a shower of poisoned arrows and he had to re-embark precipitately. He had the same reception at the Leeward Islands. At Guadalupe the Carib women joined the defenders. For several centuries the soldiers or monks who tried to set foot in the Lesser Antilles were massacred. Ponce de León nearly lost his life there. For the sake of peace, the signatories to the Treaty of Aix-la-Chapelle in 1748 agreed that the Caribs should remain their own masters.

With the Caribs the conquest opened, and with the Araucanians it ended. At the dawn and twilight of their battle for the possession of the New World the Spaniards encountered the same obstacle: the anger of primitive people. What does this mean, if not that attachment to the native soil—a quasi-animal reflex—has no connection with political genius? That the Conquistadors suffered more from the Araucanian and Carib warriors than from Montezuma's legions is nothing new. For it was thus that the Parthians had held the Roman Empire at bay.

CHAPTER 15

From the Río de la Plata
to the Meschacébé

CHRISTOPHER COLUMBUS set foot in the West Indies in October 1492. Pedro de Valdivia founded Santiago de Nuevo Extremo (now Santiago de Chile) in February 1541. The era of the great conquests, which had opened at the moment when the Spanish sailors, exhausted and inebriated by the sea air, sang the *Te Deum* on the beach at San Salvador, ended when Valdivia laid the first stone of the future Chilean capital beside the Mapocho. These dividing lines are, of course, theoretical, but they correspond to reality. The conquest—that is to say, the heroic period of the war and of the improvisation—had lasted fifty years: a half century to take possession of the New World!

But the Spaniards had not restricted their ambitions to the conquest of the great American empires, Aztec and Inca, and to the occupation of operational bases on the coasts and at the mouths of rivers. From the second quarter of the sixteenth century and even before that, the Conquistadors bravely drew away from their bases into the interior of the continent. It was then a matter less of conquering than of exploring and reconnoitering. But the means at the disposal of the Spaniards was not in proportion to the immense territories they discovered. The essential thing was not to die there. The conquering columns became scientific expeditions and prepared the ways for the men who were to follow.

The bridgeheads of these Spanish explorations were the regions already conquered and solidly held, and the three principal ones were, from north to south, Mexico, Central America, and Peru; Mexico City, Panama, and Cuzco were the three bases from which the Spaniards set off in search of a *ne plus ultra* of which the distances had the color of the sea.

The Northern Regions

Let us take for a last time the royal road of the conquerors. From year to year it stretched farther afield, overrunning the jungle, striding across rivers, and coming to a halt upon the ocean shores. Soon it was to complete the circuit—or almost—of this world in creation: the Spanish-American Empire.

The Conquerors of the Meschacébé

The first Conquistador to reach the northern regions—and also the first to obey the call of the north while others bore southward—was Cortés. Still captain general by title, but actually deprived of his command, the conqueror of Mexico organized some unlucky expeditions in a northerly direction, at his own expense. Setting out from Acapulco with three ships, he followed the Pacific coast until he reached the head of the Gulf of California: *el Golfo de Cortés*. But the settlements founded by the tireless conqueror, Santa Cruz and Guaymas, had only an ephemeral life. Of three hundred and twenty colonists, twenty-three died of fever and the rest demanded to return to Mexico. On the practical level, the affair ended in failure.

By an irony of fate it was Pánfilo de Narváez, Cortés' indomitable enemy, who took up and extended the northward move of the Marquis of the Valley—not to the west of Mexico this time, but to the east. After California, it was the turn of Florida. So here he was, once more on the trail, the vanquished soldier of Cempoala, the humiliated captain! He was, moreover, regarded as finished. But the eclipse of the principal star, Cortés, had made it possible for this secondary star to cast its last rays. Narváez had fitted out four ships and behind his pennon had gathered four hundred soldiers and eighty horses—the latter for draft purposes as well as for war. Originally an instrument of conquest, the horse was now the vital tool of colonization: it was scarcely freed from its steel harness before it was tied to a cart. Narváez' flotilla anchored in Tampa Bay on the western coast of Florida and a landing was made. The Conquistador took three hundred men with him and plunged northward into the jungle.

Florida, with its mild winters, its long sandy beaches, the oranges and grapefruit of Tampa, the lovely islands, and the scented sweetness of endless summer. . . . For a time Narváez' expedition advanced with difficulty along a low and marshy peninsula, bristling with dense forests. Occasionally there was a lake. After a harassing march, the Spaniards arrived at a village called Apalache, where Narváez set up his camp. The colonists whom he sent off east and west in search of gold mines came back having found nothing. They returned with empty hands and reached the coast just in time to see the vessels sailing away. The hundred men appointed to guard the fleet had lost patience. So much the worse for those who remained! Narváez ordered rafts to be made of pieces of wood tied together with horsehair, and doublets were hung from the masts to serve as sails. These primitive vessels were launched upon the sea. By one means or another they steered westward hoping to reach Panuco (Tampico), and on the way a gust of wind cast four of the rafts upon the coast at the mouth of the Mississippi, known to the Indians as the Meschacébé, not far from the site of the future New Orleans. The fifth raft, carrying Narváez himself, was borne out to sea, and thus Diego Velásquez' former lieutenant perished.

Luckier than his captain, one man reached an island near Galveston. This was Alvar Núñez Cabeza de Vaca. Captured by the Indians, he won them over by acting as a healer. A few signs of the cross made at the right moment, and he was regarded as a great sorcerer; then, once the Indians' distrust was calmed, this improvised miracle man hastened to desert them. Accompanied by a Moorish slave named Esteban and two other companions, Cabeza de Vaca fled due north.

It took them eight years to make contact with the Spanish command in Mexico, but what a journey it was! On foot they crossed the following states from one side to the other: Mississippi, Arkansas, Colorado, New Mexico, and Arizona. It was at Culiacán, in the Sinaloa country near the Gulf of California, that Cabeza de Vaca, after following the valley of the Sonora and straying in the Chihuahua desert, encountered Melchior Díaz, the commander of the territory. The two Spaniards' embrace can be imagined. Nevertheless, this incredible exploit, like that of Cortés, concealed a failure.

On his return to Mexico, Cabeza de Vaca was inexhaustible in making bombastic speeches about what he had seen during his journey. But this intrepid adventurer was, like the rest, also a boaster, which prevented anyone from paying much attention to him. That there was a "mysterious north" no one doubted; that the lands visited by Cabeza de Vaca might be those of the famous "Seven Cities" many began to believe; but there was no means of knowing more until a large expedition had verified Cabeza de Vaca's tales. A famous Conquistador organized this expedition: Hernando de Soto.

The hero of Darién, Pizarro's lieutenant, had retired to Spain when hostilities broke out between his leader and Almagro. But how could he resist such flattering entreaties as "You alone can succeed . . ." and remain deaf to the call of pride? Hernando de Soto bade adieu to his magnificent retreat in Estremadura and embarked at Sanlúcar de Barrameda. Ten ships, one thousand men, and three hundred and fifty horses: it was a veritable armada. After a brief halt at Havana, the expedition landed in Florida. De Soto left a hundred men to guard the ships and immediately took the northward route. The first stage took him to Apalache and the second to Mobile, near the present boundary of Alabama and Mississippi. Here, eight years after his embassy to Atahualpa, Hernando de Soto gave battle to the Indian warriors. He had not lost his skill, and he defeated the enemy. Then, having accomplished an immense circuit across Alabama and Tennessee, he crossed the Mississippi and passed through Arkansas and into the rich plains of Oklahoma. On the way the Spaniards encountered the fierce resistance of the native tribes, who were lightly equipped but fired by the somber courage of primitive peoples. The only weapon they had was a sort of ax, but they used it effectively. Furthermore, they practiced the peculiar custom of cutting off the scalp and hair of their enemies. Tomahawking and scalping were new to the Spaniards.

Hernando de Soto tried diplomacy, or rather, trickery. But, unlike the conditions he had met in Peru, he was not dealing with an organized power. So, abandoning negotiations, De Soto resorted to strong methods: steel and fire, but especially fire. The Indians of the Mississippi lived in thatched wooden houses, and with the touch of a torch a whole village blazed. Heaps of cinders, Indian women sacrificing their hair on the graves of their husbands, war cries, screams of pain . . . De Soto, sword in hand and armored like a knight, advanced through a tragic landscape. But this march through blood and fire resembled a flight. The Spaniards lost their way, became mired in swamps, circled in their own tracks, and then came back again to the Mississippi. Slowly and with difficulty they approached their goal—but what goal? De Soto claimed to know what it was, but he did not reach the end of his dream, for, succumbing to fever, he died in his tracks at the age of forty-two. To prevent his remains falling into the hands of the Indians, his companions sank him in the deepest part of the Mississippi. Hernando de Soto was to rest in the waters of the old Meschacébé, "the Father of Waters," his own conquest.

The Spaniards had lost their captain, but they continued their mad journey. They had abandoned their rags and gaping shoes long before. They marched barefoot and covered themselves with the skins of animals, like a prehistoric nomad horde. They headed westward, and then one morning they distinguished a bluish line on the horizon: the Rocky Mountains. Among them were some who had crossed the cordillera of the Andes in Francisco Pizarro's train and had not forgotten what it had cost them. They were seized with vertigo as they faced this barrier which seemed to rise to the very zenith. Only the impossible could make these brave men recoil, but with despair in their hearts they turned their backs on the Rocky Mountains—without suspecting that they were a prolongation of the cordilleras—and returned to the Mississippi.

Since the start of the expedition, De Soto's troops had gradually diminished; now there were only about three hundred men and a few horses. Almost all the officers had died, and food was scarce. But they still had courage, and they needed it to realize their plan of descending the Mississippi to the sea and from there returning to Mexico. It was no longer a question of trying to find the anchored fleet again on the coast of Florida. None of the Conquistadors felt strong enough to recross Alabama and Florida, and the precedent of Narváez weakened the best wills. No one believed seriously that De Soto's ten vessels had waited for the expedition's return, and there was no other alternative—except to perish where they stood—but to reach the sea by following the course of the Mississippi. Seven ships were built and launched on the river, but just as the Spaniards were about to start, a thousand canoes barred their passage. Nevertheless they made off southward, rowing hard, under a storm of missiles.

The Indians did not let them escape that easily; they took up the chase, and it was only after several days that the Spaniards succeeded in drawing away and losing sight of their pursuers. They were to remember for a long time those sinister canoes, painted blue and black, that harassed them like savage birds. They descended the river in three weeks and came to the mouth of the Mississippi at the Gulf of Mexico. Bearing westward, they followed the shore in the direction of Mexico, but a storm arose that handled their wretched boats so roughly that they had to abandon them and reach shore by swimming. It was on foot that they completed the last stage. The Spanish sentry on duty at the first post of Panuco presented arms to a troop of half-dead soldiers, almost naked, with bushy beards and hair and eyes that burned with fever in blackened and wrinkled faces. An almost moribund lieutenant still found strength enough to wave De Soto's torn pennon. Not many of the valiant band remained, and those who had escaped were surrounded and plied with questions. Had they found the Seven Cities?

While Hernando de Soto's expedition was ascending the Mississippi halfway to its source and glimpsing the Rocky Mountains, the Viceroy of Mexico, Antonio de Mendoza, having been interested by Cabeza de Vaca's story, entrusted Francisco Vásquez Coronado, the commander of Culiacán, with a reconnaissance. Esteban the Moor, accompanied by a priest, Fray Marcos, left as an advance party. The two Spaniards, escorted by a few Indians, followed the valley of the Sonora and penetrated to the heart of Arizona. The farther they advanced the more certain they felt of the existence of a vast northern city, and they were not long in coming within sight of a large inhabited area known to the natives as Cibola. Without going farther, Fray Marcos planted a cross on a hillock of stones as a mark of annexation and set out on the return, convinced that he had looked from afar upon one of the Seven Cities.

Fray Marcos had no difficulty in winning Coronado over to this opinion. No one cast doubt on the priest's marvelous tale. Moreover, the less credible a tale was, the more the Conquistadors believed it. The road to the Seven Cities had been found at last, and nothing remained but to take possession of them in the name of the King of Spain. So an expedition led by Coronado himself set out for the new Promised Land, comprising about a thousand men, Spaniards and Indians, numerous cattle and some matériel. The itinerary followed that of Fray Marcos: the valley of the Sonora, the Río Gila. . . . After crossing mountains and immense fir forests, the column found itself before Zuñi, near the border of present-day Arizona and New Mexico: this was Cibola.

Cibola! A few hovels of clay and stone built upon a rock. Narrow streets, a filthy watercourse, and a hostile land. A high limestone plateau situated at a height of over 6000 feet, without a tree or a blade of grass. The earth was naked and dry, and the climate was unstable, alternating the rigors of cold with a pitiless burning sun. The Spaniards burst into bitter words about the priest's illusions, and no one doubted that he was deranged. Actually they were among the pueblos of New Mexico. These villages, consisting of houses of three or four stories, were surrounded by a wall flanked with watchtowers. From afar, and in the light of the setting sun, they looked like a Saracen city. Don Quixote mistook farms for fortified castles, so was it surprising that some Conquistadors—these straying knights and spiritual fathers of the hero of La Mancha—thought they had seen cities of stone and crenelated towers where there were only poor hamlets? In the last rays of the sun, adobe had the somber color of granite.

Coronado had no great difficulty in conquering the land of Cibola —that is, Zuñi and its neighboring villages. What arms had the natives to match the steel and gunpowder of the Spaniards? A sort of amity was soon established between the invaders and the conquered people, and, unable to give them a name, the Spaniards called their new subjects Pueblos. Having come probably from the north, the Pueblos had made their first dwellings in caves, and at that time their industry was basketmaking. Then, freed from some mysterious peril, these cave dwellers of New Mexico had abandoned their subterranean habitations and built their curious fortified villages. Agricultural and sedentary, the Pueblos wove goat's wool, made pottery, and tanned the skins of deer and antelopes. Their customs were pacific. Profoundly religious, they worshiped the sun. Each morning at dawn a priest—like the Mussulman muezzin—called the people to prayer from the top of the highest terrace. At the summer solstice they celebrated the great festival of the flutes. When the hunting season opened, the dance of the bison formed the prelude to the departure of the hunters, who were armed only with bows and arrows. Dancing, moreover, was an important element in all communal activity. The sacred rites were accompanied by dances, and the singers beat time by clapping their hands, as in Andalusia. Festivals of germination, of the New Fire (did it derive from, or did it inspire, the Atzec rite?) and of the water were celebrated with dances.

In the land of Cibola the women were beautiful, walking to the fountains with upright carriage, holding jugs on their heads with one hand like the women of ancient Greece. They were not only beautiful, but they held a considerable degree of power. They dominated the home and held the highest positions in the city councils, and their very active sisterhoods were busy in religion as well. The women of the Pueblos were not content with bringing up their children; they also ruled their men. They were without doubt the leading municipal advisers.

The Pueblos can thus, by social and religious organization, be regarded as civilized people, placing somewhere between the nomads of the North American plains and the Lords of Mexico and Peru. It was a transitionary civilization, the product of spontaneous generation, and strangely contradictory (its tools were Neolithic, but feminism had gained its first victory), and it was perhaps the precursor of Aztec civilization. How many were they? About 30,000 men, which is few, considering that the Cibola country extended over the present states of Utah, Colorado, Arizona, and New Mexico, and even overflowed a little beyond Sonora and Chihuahua toward the city of Mexico.

But the Pueblos did not inhabit all this vast territory at one time.

Two great rivers drain it: the Colorado and the Rio Grande. Into the Colorado, before it enters the Gulf of California, flow the San Juan River in the north and the Gila River in the south. The Rio Grande, the present frontier between Mexico and the United States over a great part of its course, runs into the Gulf of Mexico. As the two rivers are very close in their upper courses, the Pueblos passed from one to the other, though it is not possible to speak of real migration. The center of gravity of their settlement remained fixed on Zuñi, the capital of Cibola, which was to stay as such always, for it is now one of the Indian Reservations where the descendants of the pre-Columbian tribes are still living today.

For several months Coronado continued an absurd and wearing circuit around Cibola, and such was his madness for gold that he gullibly accepted the most incredible tales. It was enough for an Indian to indicate same vague point in space—often in order to mock him—for Coronado to go there at once. On one occasion it was a fortified town called Cicuya on the Pecos River, where it was said the chief sat under a gigantic tree from which hung little golden bells; when the evening breeze shook them, the prince fell asleep to the sound of golden music. On another occasion it was the empire of Quivira beside the Arkansas River, where they said there were fish like horses—possibly the hippocampus, the sea horse. Each occasion would be a disappointment, and then the Spaniards would chase other chimeras. Actually there was some basic truth in the native directions: gold was not lacking in the neighborhood of Cibola, but it was under the earth.

An end to this pursuit of fantasies had to come. Coronado and his men returned to Mexico, where they were received by the Viceroy as defeated men—in other words, badly. Nevertheless, one of them, López de Cárdenas, during an exploration northward, had accidentally discovered a natural wonder that surpassed all the illusory beauties of the Seven Cities: the Grand Canyon of the Colorado. This was one of the grandest moments of the conquest. Staring at a landscape that seemed to signify the very creation of the world, the Spaniards crossed themselves, for they had recognized the hand of God.

While Coronado was exhausting himself in the deserts of New

Mexico, grave events were taking place in the province of Jalisco, which was within his jurisdiction. Wearied by the presence of the Spaniards, the Indians of Sinaloa, who were allied to the Zacatecos, had raised the standard of revolt. After setting fire to the churches and butchering some of the Jalisco garrison, the rebels had retired into the mountains, or *peñoles*, north of Guadalajara. Oñate, who acted as governor in the absence of Coronado, was practically besieged in Jalisco, expecting the imminent attack of the Indians. Nevertheless, he was able to send a distress call to Antonio de Mendoza. The request greatly embarrassed the Viceroy, since he did not have sufficient effectives at hand to give immediate and effective help to his subordinate; also, the reputation of the Zacatec Indians was well known, for with them there was no quarter, and death was slow and torture refined. It was then that the providential man appeared: Pedro de Alvarado, the "Sun God," the favorite of the great Conquistadors, the hero of Mexico and Guatemala.

We last saw him at the moment when, following the pact of Riobamba, he took courteous leave of Francisco Pizarro with 100,000 pesos in his pocket, the price of renouncing his interest in Peru. That was six years earlier. Meanwhile Alvarado had returned to Spain and had there provoked a duel with Hernando Pizarro, who had been responsible for the execution of his friend Almagro. He had also become reconciled with his wife, had won the support of Charles V for his plans, and had set out once more for the New World. With the Emperor's consent and his own capital—the Hapsburg was more generous with words than with grants—Alvarado had decided to organize an expedition to China and the Spice Islands. The plan was ambitious and involved nothing less than setting out from the Mexican coast to cross the whole Pacific Ocean.

The shipyards of Mexico and Guatemala had worked hard for Cortés' former lieutenant. But he paid to the last farthing. In a few months thirteen ships were armed and assembled in the little port of Acaxatla, not far from the Isthmus of Tehuantepec. Everything was ready. The flags were hoisted, Alvarado's fleet raised anchor and sailed toward the port of La Purificación on the way to Jalisco. During the halt at La Purificación, Alvarado learned of the danger that threatened Oñate. Could he leave a Spanish officer to perish by Indian arrows? He ordered everyone to land, reefed the sails and saddled the horses. The Moluccas were forgotten, for the life of one of His Majesty's captains had to be saved.

A hundred cavaliers with raised swords debouched into the peñoles of Guadalajara, and it was high time, for Oñate was on the verge of succumbing to the assaults of the Zacatecs. Alvarado's arrival reversed the situation. He was known throughout America from Mexico to Chile, and his exploits were like those of the hero of the *Iliad*. Standing up in his stirrups, firmly gripping his blade in his steel-gauntleted hand, the giant with the glowing beard was as terrible as when he had held back the Aztec mob or calmly protected the refugees from Tacuba. He had donned his cuirass, as in the great days. He was indeed the Sun God, and the Indians fell back defeated. Their grip relaxed and Oñate breathed again.

But at the height of the struggle, which took place at the abrupt summit of a peñol, a horse slipped on the stones of a path, lost its balance, and rolled down the cliff at the foot of which Alvarado was fighting. The Conquistador had no time to leap aside and was struck. The weight of the beast, increased by its battle harness, crushed Pedro de Alvarado to the ground.

The Spanish adventure in North America came to an end with the chivalrous gesture of Alvarado, he who had abandoned the road to the Spice Islands to fly to the aid of a companion who was about to drop his sword. A pure light surrounds his broken body. None more than Alvarado, perhaps, had need to atone for his bloody past, that he might end "in beauty." Was there a single Indian in the isthmus who had forgotten the invasion of Guatemala by Alvarado's columns? From Mexico to Tehuantepec it had been a simple military promenade, but the business had grown worse shortly after the Chiapas country was passed. Irritated at seeing his progress hindered by native elements, the Conquistador had launched all his forces against a practically unarmed adversary. The fights had been so murderous that one of the conquered provinces bore the lugubrious name of Xequiqual, "under blood." Although the Guatemalan operation weighs heavily against Alvarado, to his credit must be placed the generous impulse that cost him his life. Of course, simply because he held out a brotherly hand to Oñate, Alvarado is not absolved of his crimes, but by showing that his heart did not beat for gold alone he becomes more likable. He seems to be more human, and his appearance, which previously had only a sort of brutal grandeur, softens.

Never, perhaps, had the Spaniards made greater efforts than those to penetrate "the northern mystery"—efforts superhuman but fruitless. The balance sheet of the northern expeditions was negative. If only Hernando de Soto, setting out from Florida, had joined up with Coronado, coming from California! Their roads had crossed, but each was working for himself. The discovery of the Mississippi, the splendors of the Grand Canyon, the battlements of the Seven Cities: these were fine pictures and fine memories to relate, with embellishments, during the evenings in Estremadura. The *realities* of North America—its natural resources as well as its geographical outlines—had totally escaped the Conquistadors. This gigantic prey, although attacked on both flanks, east and west, slipped from their grasp, seeming even to withdraw as they advanced. The best of them, including Hernando de Soto and Pedro de Alvarado, struggled vainly. Doubtless at the beginning they lacked a sovereign authority that would have coordinated and planned their haphazard inroads. Doubtless also, the first impulse given to the conquest by the caravels of Christopher Columbus had some responsibility for the failure, for tradition and routine brought the Spanish ships almost mechanically into the same waters, to the same bases, and along the known tracks. These reasons, and others more subtle and concerned with continental politics, had the result that North America, discovered in great part by the subjects of Charles V, was excluded from the Spanish *imperium*, to the benefit of the Anglo-Saxon latecomers.

The Mirage of Eldorado

The conquest of Central America, which had been begun seriously by Pedrarias Dávila, Cristóbal de Olid, and Hernán Cortés himself, was completed by a series of small local expeditions, the leaders of which did not have the wide ambitions of Pizarro or Hernando de Soto but were nevertheless very capable of bringing their endeavors to successful conclusions. The conquering colonists set out simultaneously from Mexico and Panama. This double stream, working in opposite directions, provoked encounters that sometimes ended in tragedy—such as that in Honduras between Cortés and Pedrarias Dávila's men. Each claimed it for his own and would not let go. Like strange game preserves, these lands were bitterly disputed and passed from one to the other according to the fortunes of the fight. No one, of course, respected the rights of the first occupant. Only the right of the strongest regularized possession, and that only for a time. A precarious possession, in fact, constantly menaced by concurrent expeditions.

The history of the conquest of Central America is that of a confused quarrel: lightning changes of captains who, turn and turn about, installed themselves as masters and then gave way to newcomers, more numerous and better armed, and it was lucky when these dispossessions were not accompanied by bloody settlements. Did these daredevil Conquistadors ever know where they were or where they were going? For the most part they had no idea. This 1250-mile isthmus that connects Mexico with Colombia had only one name: Guatemala. Honduras, Salvador, Nicaragua, Costa Rica, and Panama were only provinces, and it was not until the nineteenth century that they became republics. But very soon each province had its Conquistador. Espinosa and González Dávila, setting out from Panama, penetrated Costa Rica and, pushing onward, encountered the cacique Nicarao, the ruler of Nicaragua. Following in their tracks, Hernández de Córdoba explored the San Juan River and made the circuit of Lake Managua and Lake Nicaragua. He continued his progress northward and ran into González Dávila in Honduras. He did not get farther, for Dávila gave battle, defeated him, and obliged him to return to Panama. Meanwhile, Cristóbal de Olid landed in Honduras, having come from Mexico at the head of four hundred men. This time the enemy was considerable, and Olid was one of Cortés' best officers. He captured González Dávila but treated him generously. With Dávila eliminated, would Olid stay master of Honduras? In the intoxication of victory, Cristóbal de Olid too quickly forgot the exact purpose of his mission: the search for a passage between the two oceans—a geographical mission! It is easy to understand that Olid aimed at something higher, for he had been one of those who had conquered Mexico for Cortés and he thought the time had come to carve out a kingdom for himself. But Cortés heard of the affair and at once charged Francisco de Las Casas with seizing the rebel—a double rebel, since Olid, as we remember, had had a talk with Diego Velásquez on his way through Cuba. But Las Casas underestimated his enemy, and after a short battle it was he who was conquered and captured. Just as with Dávila, Olid was magnanimous, for he was very sure of himself. He invited his two prisoners to a banquet of comrades-at-arms, but when the Conquistadors raised their goblets to the King of Spain, Dávila and Las Casas, who had been quick to come to an understanding, stabbed Olid to death.

The field was free for new adventures and new adventurers. Prominent at the top is the massive figure of Pedro de Alvarado. Alvarado, as we have already seen, had cut a bloody furrow from Mexico to the frontiers of Nicaragua. He distributed the native women among his soldiers, loaded the men with irons, and without scruple broke all who opposed him. It was even said that once when he did not have anything with which to feed the thousands of native men he had enrolled for labor or war, he authorized them to eat the flesh of their enemies, that is, their compatriots from neighboring villages. His rages were proverbial. If he was misled by local information—at one time he found copper instead of gold—he made the Indian informers responsible for his failures, and took a cruel revenge on them. He was brutal—with a touch of joviality that colored his worst angers with a false indulgence—brave to madness, and worshiped everything that was of great material value. Alvarado was the great prima donna of Central America. Founder of Santiago de los Caballeros and San Salvador, capital of the future Salvador, he extended his dominions as far as Costa Rica. Ostentatious and sensual as a Medici, Alvarado reigned uncontrolled from Guatemala to Panama for close to twenty years, apart from the intervals in Spain and Peru we already know about. Twenty years of military successes, easy and without glory. One prefers to forget this bantering satrap, presiding over the massacres of the Guatemalans or witnessing their horrible feasts, so that we may remember the hero of the Noche Triste and the Guadalajara peñol.

In actual fact, for a long time the Spaniards did nothing but pass through Central America. The physical structure of the country— its contorted relief, its unstable earth, subject to frequent earthquakes, its lower lands buried under a dense forest entwined with

lianas—was badly adapted to permanent settlements. This long cor-
ridor filled with ambushes was for the Conquistadors coming from
Mexico the land route of the Spanish Main as well as the means of
access to the region of Darién. It was also the road to Eldorado.

Eldorado! After Atlantis, the Fountain of Youth, Antilia, and
the land of the Seven Cities, this was another of those Edens in which
the conquerors had faith as hard as iron. Eldorado bore the name
of its sovereign, El Dorado, the Man of Gold. He was a naked king,
covered all over with grease and then coated with gold dust. At the
end of the day he could be seen standing in his boat, shining in the
light of the setting sun. When he bathed, the gold dissolved in the
water and left nothing but a flaming patch on the surface of the
lake. The Indians of Peru did not doubt the existence of the kingdom of the Man of Gold. But who had seen it? Where was it to be
found? In Ecuador? Colombia? Venezuela? Guiana? Time and space
meant nothing to the Conquistadors, and they searched for Eldorado
everywhere.

Gonzalo Pizarro left Quito with three hundred and forty Spaniards and four thousand Indians. It was not only gold that drew
him, but also the cinnamon in which, it seemed, Eldorado abounded.
Would that old dream of spices at last take substance in the land
of the shining king? Gonzalo climbed the cordillera of the Andes,
descended the other side, and encountered a river, the Napo, which
he followed throughout its length. It flowed into another river, the
Marañón. A brigantine was built at once. Francisco Orellana, also
a native of Trujillo, took command of it. The expedition divided in
two parts. Orellana launched his boat upon the river; Gonzalo for
a while followed the bank but was soon forced to stop. Since the
start of the expedition a warm rain had fallen continuously, rotting
the Spaniards' clothing, rusting their swords, and spoiling their food.
Gonzalo Pizarro and his men—more than half his effectives had
perished—returned to Quito without having discovered Eldorado,
though they did bring back cinnamon. But Orellana carried out an
amazing feat, for in his single brigantine he followed the Marañón
and the Amazon to the sea. Once on the waters of the Atlantic, he
passed within sight of the Gulf of Paria and steered straight for
Haiti. But this was not the end of the voyage. He went to Spain to
tell the Emperor of his extraordinary odyssey. He swore that he was

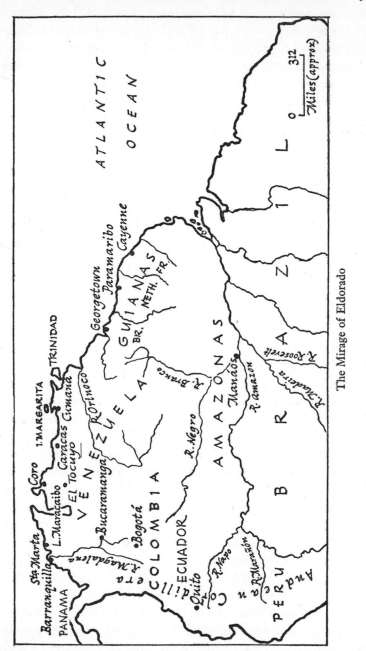

The Mirage of Eldorado

afraid only once: when he found himself face to face with long-haired, pale-faced women who handled their bows as skillfully as men. Orellana had discovered and named the Amazon River.

Next they tried to find Eldorado by starting from the Colombian and Venezuelan coasts. Both were already well known. Thirty years earlier some illustrious Conquistadors—Ojeda and Juan de la Cosa among them—had set foot on the Colombian shores, the part between Cape de la Vela and Darién being known as New Andalusia. Bastidas had founded Santa Marta in 1525. Pedro de Heredia had been busy on the western coast and had pushed his expedition from Cartagena to Antioquia, at the foot of the cordillera. The explorers had violated graves, pillaged, and captured slaves. But the appointment of a responsible governor by Charles V had put an end to such heroic banditry.

One Conquistador in the grand manner then went in search of the Man of Gold: Jiménez de Quesada, who had been appointed as Royal Audience and Chief Justice of the Santa Marta province, situated on the northwest coast of Colombia between Cape de la Vela and Barranquilla. As soon as he landed, Quesada was entrusted by the governor, Hernando de Lugo, with a southward exploration, following the course of the Magdalena River.

Seven hundred Spaniards, with five times as many Indians and one hundred horses, set out. The effective was classic or little short of it, but what was new in an expedition of this kind was the personality of the leader. Austere to asceticism and of scrupulous piety, Jiménez de Quesada was strict in his prayers, but attentive to the affairs of the world. He was one of those great righteous persons who work ardently for the good of their souls, without, however, ceasing to cling to the temporal, and who, although worldly, strictly observe the three monastic vows. Two priests attended upon Jiménez de Quesada, indicating that the inflexible Audience did not intend to take any counsel other than that of the Church. He marched toward Eldorado, not for gold but for Catholic Spain and for God. The intention was pure but his actions were less so.

Setting out from Santa Marta, the expedition followed the course of the Magdalena with difficulty. The country was nothing but a vast swamp covered with dense virgin forest that had to be cut down with axes. The Conquistadors were tortured by famine, which they tried to stave off by the usual means: eating reptiles, dead horses, and the leather of their belts. Then they went further: the corpses of Indian mercenaries and even those of their own comrades helped them to survive. These shameful dismemberments at nightfall can only be imagined. Jiménez de Quesada closed his eyes.

Only a sixth of the conquering column reached the confluence of the Magdalena and the Río Suárez, in the neighborhood of Bucaramanga. The jungle gave place to a wide valley with fields of corn, pastures, and streams of clear water. The Spaniards thought they had awakened from a nightmare. Indians came to meet them, smiling but speaking a language unknown to the interpreters. They were Chibchas.

The history of the Chibchas recalls on a lesser plane that of the Aztecs and Incas. At the beginning one finds the same legend: that of a demigod, a hero and sage called Bochica, father of their civilization, who, having blasted a mountain, disappeared eastward. This messiah, the descendant of the Sun, was the Chibchas' idol. Altars were raised to him, and his cult was celebrated. Bochica joins Quetzalcoatl and Viracocha in the pre-Columbian pantheon.

The Chibchas had been established in Colombia for several centuries. Inhabiting the high plains of the south and the mountains of the north, they concentrated mainly on the Bogotá plateau. It was there that, emerging from the limbo of anarchy, the Chibcha civilization took birth, developed, and flourished. A long quarrel between tribal lords had preceded and paved the way for a sort of Colombian state. As always, it had been possible to establish supreme power only after murderous eliminations; the assassin who escaped assassination became the ruler. When Jiménez de Quesada led his troop of ghosts along the Rió Suárez, Chibcha unity had become a reality, a kind of confederation of tribes, each led by a *zipa* or a *zaque*. They were like dukedoms held in control by a sort of archduke whose name was Bogotá, zipa of the town that bore his name. A curious law of succession transmitted the inheritance from uncle to nephew rather than from father to son. Thus the zipas and zaques were the sons of the defunct monarch's sister. Their initiation, like that of future Aztec rulers, was long and severe. The Chibcha princes held political power and sacerdotal authority, for which double role they were prepared by fasting and maceration. Legislation was sum-mary but just. The administration respected the needs of everyone but did not force anyone beyond his capabilities. These people were skilled cultivators, especially of coca, and were also excellent metallurgists and artistic makers of ceramics. Long before the coming of the Spaniards, they exported their statuettes of gold and copper alloy and vases of cut rock crystal to Peru, where they were admired by the Incas. Their dwellings were primitive: tree trunks cemented by a mixture of earth and straw formed the walls, and the thatched roofs were shaped like pyramids. Such was the Chibcha civilization—still archaic, but sufficiently evolved for the outlines of a political structure to be distinguished, perhaps even the promise of an empire. But in a few days one hundred and fifty Spaniards subjugated the ancient people of Bochica, and the zipa confederation was integrated into the empire of Charles V.

We are, once again, witnesses to an astounding tour de force, that of a company of Spaniards taking possession of a land twice as big as France, and of a capital with twenty thousand inhabitants, almost without striking a blow. All this happened with even greater ease than at Cajamarca. There was not even the semblance of a nominal sovereign, such as gave Pizarro's victory over the Incas the appearance of collaboration, if not of alliance. The success was total. But as in Peru, dissensions among native chiefs favored the conquerors, and Jiménez de Quesada gathered in the Colombian kinglets one after the other. The zaque of Hunza, named Tunja, and those of Sogamoso and Tundama let themselves be taken almost without resistance. As for Bogotá, he fled into the savanna and the Spaniards took possession of the city of the zipas without encountering a living soul. The temple doors were plated with gold and studded with emeralds. Doors were torn off, houses searched, and prisoners tortured in order to learn more. Where was the gold? It was the same eternal question.

Nothing opposed the Conquistadors' advance except natural forces. So funereal was the region traversed by the River Neiva that the Spaniards called it the Valley of Sorrow. Plains, valleys, plateaus. . . . On the return to Bogotá, a few miles from the city Jiménez de installed in the plain at a respectful distance from one another. The Quesada's men saw that they were not alone, for two camps were first was Spanish, certainly, but the second appeared unusual. Who were these soldiers who spoke with so guttural an accent?

The leader of the first camp was known to them: he was Belalcázar, the conqueror of Ecuador. He had grown tired of Quito, and the lure of Eldorado could not fail to interest Pizarro's former captain. Setting out from the Ecuador capital, he had ascended the valley of the Cauca and reached the suburbs of Bogotá by following the left bank of the Magdalena.

The second camp was that of a German officer, Nikolaus Federmann. For the first time a Spanish Conquistador found a foreign conqueror on his path. The Germans were also exploring the continent in search of Eldorado, and this was not to the taste of Jiménez de Quesada. However, their powers had been regularized, for ten years earlier Charles V had given permission to the Alfinger brothers to undertake the conquest of the Maracaibo region in Venezuela. Above all, it was a financial transaction underwritten by the Welsers, bankers of Augsburg, who were creditors of the Spanish crown and hoped by this roundabout means to recover their money. It was thought that the pearl fishing on the coast and the exploitation of gold mines in the interior ought to produce great profits for the concessionaires. Part would serve to repay Spanish debts and part would help to refloat the imperial treasury, which had been exhausted by the wars. The idea was good, but the results did not come up to expectations; far from it. As to mining enterprises, Alfinger was content to establish a *ranchería* on the banks of Lake Maracaibo. After his death in an Indian ambush, the concession was transferred to Hohermuth, commonly known as Espira because of his birthplace, Spire. After vain explorations in the direction of the Andes, Espira joined up with Federmann, who was a protégé of the Welsers, and these two strove to establish a German colony at Coro. It was then that Federmann, braver or more daring than his compatriot, had succeeded in penetrating to the heart of the Chibcha realm.

Thus Belalcázar's column, coming from Quito, Federmann's, which had set out from Coro, and Jiménez de Quesada's, which had started at Santa Marta, had an unforeseen meeting in the plain of Bogotá. Who would have imagined that the three expeditions, originating in the south, east, and west, would have come together at

the gates of the ancient Colombian city? It was a grandiose encounter and one that could have been bloody. But the three captains
remembered in time that they were subjects of the same emperor.
Noblesse oblige! They saluted one another with their swords,
slipped them back in their sheaths, embraced, and celebrated their
meeting with a banquet of venison. Agreement was reached: Belalcázar gave up and returned to Quito, while the practical German
handed his detachment over to Jiménez de Quesada for a payment
of 10,000 gold pesos.

Jiménez de Quesada's mission had come to an end. Instead of
Eldorado, he had discovered the future Colombia, a reservoir of gold
and emeralds. Before embarking for Spain he founded the city of
Santa Fe de Bogotá and named his conquest the New Kingdom of
Granada, in memory of his native land. Still inflexible and austere, he
presented himself to the Emperor and gave an account of his journey.
His voice remained cold when he described the difficult journey, the
tombs of the Magdalena valley filled to the brim with jewels and
animals carved in gold, the surrender of the Chibcha lords, and the
loneliness of the valleys. But he became livelier when he recalled
the courage of his companions, and even more so when he referred
to the thousands of Indians who did not know the True God. A
governor was needed for the territory that he, Jiménez de Quesada,
had conquered. He awaited nothing more than his sovereign's orders
before setting out again, for he did not doubt that the Emperor
would confirm him in his functions. But in this he was mistaken.
He knew nothing of the minds of princes. Charles gave the post of
governor of the New Kingdom of Granada not to Jiménez de
Quesada, its founder, but to a young intriguer, the son of Hernando
de Lugo.

Since Eldorado had not been found in Ecuador or Colombia or
Venezuela, would it be found in Guiana? In that hell? A hot and
humid climate, with violent rains and impenetrable virgin forests—
in short, the most disheartening land the Conquistadors had prospected. Perhaps a few grains of gold were scattered in the alluvial
deposits of the rivers. Perhaps, too, if one searched well in the suffocating heat of the Guiana forests, one might make out the tall and
slender trunks of the tulip-wood trees. But to explore the tiniest
part of this region, which was only slightly smaller than France,

would require an army of woodcutters and tools that were not yet invented. The soldiers were few and had only swords and machetes. Nevertheless they persisted, and Guiana became their grave. Diego de Ordaz, the conqueror of Popocatepetl, wandered along the Río Negro for four years and died there. Pedro de Ursua marched straight ahead toward the legendary Lake Parime and the coveted city of Manáos, the City of Gold. He was not far from it when a volley of Indian arrows killed him. His companions paid him the last honors and stoically continued an enterprise that was lost before it started. It was only in the plain of Manáos, at the edge of the unfathomable forest and of the aquatic kingdom of the Amazon, that the faithful friends of Diego de Ordaz, trembling with fever under the yellow sun of the Guianas, abandoned Eldorado.

In relinquishing the search for Eldorado, the Spaniards simultaneously abandoned Guiana. France was able to settle her convicts there, Holland constructed her polders, and Great Britain annexed a dominion: three Guianas which, three centuries later, were to furnish Europe and the United States with gold, diamonds, strategic bases, and especially bauxite, the raw material of aluminum. For want of perseverance and means, Spain, the discoverer of Guiana, has no place there today. Thus came into being the only fissure in the Spanish-American block—if one excepts Brazil, relinquished voluntarily.

To the failure of Spain in Guiana there is an echo: the failure of Germany in Venezuela. Federmann's capitulation on the high plateaus of Bogotá had not put an end to German expeditions. But the imperial concession had expired without the beneficiaries' having explored a quarter of what had been given them on paper: all the lands between Cape de la Vela and Cumaná, including the islands near the coast and the interior of the land. Meanwhile a handful of German adventurers persisted. One of the Welsers, accompanied by Philipp von Hutten, pushed a reconnaissance from Venezuela to El Tocuyo. They did not go farther; a Spanish detachment commanded by Juan de Carvajal arrested and executed them. For a time the Germans were able to maintain themselves at Coro— with some difficulty, for their rough ways had raised the Spaniards and Indians against them. But had Carvajal a clearer conscience? He ended his career by being well and truly hanged.

While the Welsers made representations at the Spanish court to obtain, if not a renewal of their concessions, at least their continuance in the territories they occupied, a fierce and cunning contest for the possession of Venezuela was being played out around the Maracaibo lagoon by the Conquistadors and the German cavalry. These men cared little for legal arguments. Polished chicanery at Valladolid, but war to the knife—*a cuchillo*—at Coro. The Germans were beaten in the field. After ten years of proceedings, their cause was lost, and it was the Spaniards—Villegas, Villacinde, Fajardo—who laid the first stones of Venezuelan cities. Hutten and Federmann have been forgotten, but Captain Losada, founder of Santiago de León de Caracas, future capital of Venezuela, has been remembered. Ejected from the conquest, the Germans took their revenge three centuries later by colonizing the state of Santa Catarina in Brazil. Another revenge: the same year that Espira was wandering in the cordillera, a German named Cromberger set up the first printing press of America in the Mexican capital.

So was there no such place as Eldorado? There was: a potential Eldorado. Following the Conquistadors who were armed only with swords and arquebuses, modern technicians have forced Eldorado to surrender its gold. Tools and machines have torn open its soil, which had remained impenetrable to Charles's men. What was it that the mirage of the Man of Gold concealed? In Colombia, silver, platinum, and emeralds, the finest in the world. In Guiana, rare essences, diamonds, and the wherewithal to provide all the war industries of the world with aluminum. In Venezuela, petroleum, the black gold of the twentieth century.

The Río de la Plata: The Road to Peru

Around the 35th degree south latitude a vast bay shaped like a funnel drives broadly into the Atlantic coast of South America: the estuary of the Río de la Plata. This is the common mouth of the Paraná and Uruguay rivers and the natural route into the heart of the continent. At the time of the conquest, the country known as the Río de la Plata comprised present-day Argentina, Paraguay, Uruguay, and Bolivia.

The Plata had aroused the curiosity of the Spanish conquerors

The Río de la Plata: The Road to Peru

quite early. Disconcerted by the dimensions of this estuary, which
was nearly 150 miles wide, they examined it long and carefully before
deciding to land there. But they very quickly realized that the Plata
could offer them a shorter route to Peru than those via Panama or
the Strait of Magellan. To cross the continent at the point where it
was beginning to narrow, instead of rounding it on the north or

south, would be a saving of time and money. But there was a double objective. Not only were they seeking to shorten the distance between Spain and Peru, but also to reach the Pacific more rapidly, and thereby China and the Spice Islands as well.

Some heroic pathfinders prepared the way for the advance contingents. Juan Díaz de Solís, the first, set out in search of the famous strait that should permit one to pass from the Atlantic to the Pacific— discovered by Balboa not long before. He touched the coast of Brazil, dropped anchor in a port which he named Nuestra Señora de la Candelaria, and gave the name Mar Dulce to the Río de la Plata. He was killed by an Indian arrow on the bank of the river of which he had taken possession. Eleven years later, Sebastian Cabot (Magellan had meanwhile discovered his strait) followed Solís's route, but continuing northward along the Paraná, extended it as far as Paraguay. The way was therefore well worn when Pedro de Mendoza, one of the noblest gentlemen at the Spanish court, set sail from the port of Bonanza for the Río de la Plata.

It was a large expedition: eleven ships, one thousand men, cattle, and considerable matériel. A brilliant staff surrounded the hidalgo, including the proud figures of Juan de Ayolas, Martínez de Irala, and Felipe de Cáceres, all men of talent and high estate. The fleet reached the Río de la Plata without mishap. Mendoza's first gesture —doubtless inspired by the person of Christopher Columbus—was to found on the river's right bank a city that he named Nuestra Señora Santa María del Buen Aire, the future Buenos Aires. But Mendoza's mission was to be of short duration. Having advanced along the Paraná in search of supplies, he turned back, seized perhaps by some presentiment, and died at sea on the return journey.

While the Spaniards were striving to make the huts of Santa María del Buen Aire habitable, at the very spot where the skyscrapers of Buenos Aires rose later, Juan de Ayolas succeeded Mendoza, but not for long. Two months after the death of his predecessor, Ayolas was caught in an Indian ambush and lost his life, his head crushed by the terrible *boleadora* of the Querandí natives. During his two months, however, Ayolas had ascended the Paraná to the Paraguay and established a post at the confluence of the Paraguay and Pilcomayo rivers. This stopping place between Buenos Aires and Peru bore the name Asunción. Thus it was fated that Mendoza and Ayolas would have time, despite their singularly brief careers, to lay the first stones of the capitals of Argentina and Paraguay: Buenos Aires and Asunción.

In his lifetime Mendoza had designated Ayolas as his successor. Ayolas's successor was elected to power by the Spaniards of the Río de la Plata. The unanimous vote was in favor of Martínez de Irala, a masterful and ambitious captain and a man of great presence. After the king had ratified his election, Irala set about his task. He began by centralizing the administration of the colony at Asunción, leaving at Buen Aire only the personnel necessary for maritime operations. In line with Ayolas's idea, he planned to make Asunción the base for departure for Peru, and he himself was about to set off when disagreeable news reached him: a new adelantado had just landed in the region. This intruder was none other than Núñez Cabeza de Vaca, the healer of the Indians, the hero of the north. The interview between these two captains at Asunción had all appearances of cordiality; each, concealing his ill humor, protested his friendliness. Did they not have need of each other? Moreover, their instructions agreed in all details: it was a matter of establishing communication with Peru, so why fight when they were pursuing a common aim? As token of his trust, Cabeza de Vaca thereupon named Ayolas his second-in-command. The two leaders having agreed, nothing remained but to open the road to Peru, which would bring the Spanish homeland and her empire closer together.

Difficult terrain, hostile natives, and internal dissensions hindered the coming together of the men of La Plata with those of Peru. To reach Cuzco, they had to cross the Chaco and the high plateaus of Bolivia; in other words, conquer changing natural conditions, from the pampas and their howling winds to the high Bolivian ranges at 20,000 feet. They also had to be constantly on guard against wandering native tribes, which were numerous—Querandís, Charruas, Guenoas—although there were some among them that were civilized, such as the Diaguites and Guaranis. The Diaguites occupied the present Argentine provinces of Salta, Catamarca, La Rioja, Tucumán, and Mendoza. The Diaguites, early subjugated by the Incas, did not have their own political organization but were answerable to a *curaca*, a governor delegated by the Peruvian emperor. They were very warlike, however, and handled the sling and lasso with skill. The Guaranis lived on the banks of the Paraná and Paraguay rivers and in the southern part of Brazil. More advanced than the Diaguites, they governed themselves. An elementary hierarchy united the various groups into a sort of society: fifty families constituted a group under the command of a cacique, and in turn the union of these groups formed a tribe, presided over by a superior assembly. Although gentle and melancholy of aspect, the Guaranis were formidable in combat. Brought up from earliest years to the use of the bow and the club—primitive weapons, doubtless, though they rarely missed their mark—Guaranis and Diaguites, like all the tribes of the Río de la Plata, knew how to wage war.

Refractory nature and pugnacious natives: the Spaniards would have mastered these two obstacles with less difficulty and more speed if they had been able to settle their own quarrels. At La Plata, more than elsewhere, everyone worked only for himself. There was no methodical exploration and no over-all plan. There were individual *entradas*, as reconnaissance expeditions were called, as direct as sword blows and, like them, sometimes fatal. Actions were isolated, which did not however prevent the *entradores* from being watchful of the progress of others and from spying on them jealously. Powerless to coordinate the movements of the conquest, Cabeza de Vaca and Irala watched each other, for the sham friendliness of the two men had not lasted long, and their masks had fallen. Each had his coterie: the partisans of Cabeza de Vaca were the *leales*, the loyalists, by contrast with the *tumultuarios*, the turbulent ones who espoused Irala's cause. Cabeza de Vaca, on his return from an expedition westward, was arrested by Irala's guard and cast into prison at Asunción on the pretext of conspiracy, and was then sent back to Spain. This was a coup of great daring—to send the adelantado back to Charles in irons.

Having evicted Cabeza de Vaca, Irala had a free field. He forged ahead, and two years after Cabeza de Vaca's expulsion he reached Lake Titicaca and eventually Cuzco. The distance between the Argentine and Peru had been bridged. Irala presented himself proudly to Pedro de la Gasca, who was then governing in the land of the Incas. He expected compliments as well as his commission as governor, but alas! his reception was icy. Gasca had known for a long time that the Spaniards on the other side of the Bolivian plateaus were trying to make contact with him and had watched their progress with an eagle eye. He awaited these adventurers, not to take them to his heart but to show them harshly that the time for adventure was over. There was but one master, Charles V, under whom he alone, Gasca, possessed and exercised power. Irala and his companions would have to re-enter the ranks and behave obediently. Irala did not even obtain confirmation of his functions as governor of La Plata. This seemed only right to Pedro de la Gasca, for how could he, the austere defender of legality, sanction a rank taken by violence from its lawful possessor? Irala returned to Asunción as a simple captain under orders from the Viceroy. Yet what a victory his actually was! By tracing a line on the map of America from Buenos Aires to Asunción and Cuzco and thus connecting the Atlantic and Pacific sides of the continent, he had completed the grandiose pattern of the Spanish Empire.

Irala's expedition to Peru had taken more than a year. In his absence the colony of Asunción, exposed to the intrigues of the two opposing parties, had changed masters several times. Ambitious claimants tried their hands at ruling turn and turn about, and some, like Diego de Abreu, attempted to hold on to power. It was time Irala returned; with some difficulty, he restored order. Irala governed Paraguay for ten more years, harshly but wisely, and some months before his death he received a parchment from the king officially announcing his appointment as governor.

Irala designated Gonzalo de Mendoza, his son-in-law, as his successor, but after two years in office Mendoza died. The new governor was Ortiz de Vergara, Irala's second son-in-law. While the *gobernación* of La Plata waited to become a viceroyalty and sought administrative balance, courageous Conquistadors were continuing the reconnaissance of the country. Nufrio de Chaves founded Santa Cruz de la Sierra, and Díaz de Melgarejo founded Ciudad Real. Other cities were born: Córdoba, Corrientes, Tucumán, Santiago del Estero, Santa Fe. It seemed easier to build cities than to carry out a good colonial policy.

The conquest of the Río de la Plata was a long and exacting labor. Begun in 1536 at the time when Pedro de Mendoza landed at the mouth of the Paraná, it was scarcely completed by the beginning of the seventeenth century. For a long time the Spaniards who were established on either side of the Cordillera Real knew little of one another, and they received news only through the natives. The Conquistadors of Asunción did know that a white leader ruled at Cuzco, and the Conquistadors of Peru heard of white leaders in the land of the Guaranis. Thus a double movement in opposite directions spread across the Andes: while the Spaniards of Peru and Chile headed for the southeastern regions, those of the Río de la Plata headed north-west. This gigantic game of hide-and-seek ended, as we have seen, with the meeting of Irala and Gasca, but disorder continued in the southern colony. The alternation of elected and designated leaders, which added the faults of the elective system to those of nepotism, the hesitations of a central power that was too far away, and local disputes compromised the pacification of the territory.

The linking up of La Plata to the viceroyalty of Peru did not facili-tate things: too many very difficult men were involved in the affairs of La Plata. The permanent quarrel among these men was that which has existed ever since colonies began: a quarrel of origins. The cap-tains who came direct from Spain to the Río de la Plata had the presumption of new men; they were for the most part young, imbued with a sense of superiority, and they basked in the imperial favor. They heralded a new class of Conquistadors. But those who came from Peru were old campaigners, strong in their acquired rights and determined not to be robbed of them. The old-timers would not allow themselves to be imposed upon by the theoreticians from the homeland, and instead of sharing the prey, young wolves and old wolves fiercely tore it from one another.

Thus the Río de la Plata, discovered by Solís in 1516, reconnoitered by Cabot in 1526, and occupied by Pedro de Mendoza in 1536, was not raised to a viceroyalty independent of Peru until 1776, two hun-dred and sixty years after its conquest. Meanwhile, Juan de Garay had carried out a decisive move in 1580. Setting out from Asunción on orders from Ayolas at the head of sixty-six Spaniards, he pro-ceeded to Nuestra Señora Santa María del Buen Aire, abandoned forty years earlier. On the site of the ruins, Juan de Garay and his party traced a city plan on a chessboard pattern inspired by the Romans. They laid out straight roads intersecting at right angles. Three buildings were built around the main plaza: a church, a town hall, and a school. Later, houses were built. Each of the sixty-six Spaniards received an allotment of land. Before the first stone was laid, the city already had a municipal council, a priest, and judges. This was a decisive move because it thus shifted the center of gravity of the Río de la Plata from the marshy plains of Paraguay toward the Atlantic coast. On the debris of the camp erected by Mendoza, Buenos Aires was born, and over a period of four hundred years the capital of Argentina became the largest city of the Spanish New World and also its masterpiece. Three times greater in extent than Paris, it stretches for nearly twenty miles. Its long, straight arteries, intersecting geometrically, carry out on an enormous scale the primitive design sketched by Juan de Garay. It was Juan de Garay who also devised the city's symbols: as patron of Buenos Aires he chose Saint Martin, the centurion of the divided cloak, and its coat of arms was an armorial crown bearing a black eagle, with the Cross of the Order of Calatrava and four eaglets below.

From the Río de la Plata to the Mississippi, from the pueblos of New Mexico to Tierra del Fuego, the Conquistadors had closed the ring. Our journey is now ended, but a pilgrimage has still to be made to Haiti—not so much to return to our point of departure, to find again the Columbus of the first voyage and once again to watch the *Santa María* approaching Hispaniola, as to pick up the echo of one relentless voice.

CHAPTER 16

The Voice of a Just Man: Bartolomé de Las Casas

SANTO DOMINGO, Haiti, at the dawn of the sixteenth century; Columbus had just founded the first settlement of the New World on the great West Indian island. Spanish colonists, only a few hundreds to begin with, soon numbered several thousands. They had been told that gold was within reach and that the forests were filled with precious woods and spices. Each man dreamed of penetrating to the interior of the country, of discovering new lands and becoming governor of them. But the reality was quite different, for famine, misery, and disease were the constant companions of the colonists. The climate was deceptive; it seemed delightful, but in the long run it was enervating and oppressive. The breeze that gently stirred the great tropical flowers sometimes became furious and blew in hurricanes. The autumn season was accompanied by suffocating rains to which even the heat of summer was preferable, and the rains brought fevers that ravaged the colonists. Work was certainly not easy, and it really was by the sweat of their brows that the Conquistadors made their fortunes. Happily, there were always slaves.

The years passed. One Sunday in the year 1510, in the church of Santo Domingo, Fray Antonio de Montesinos ascended his pulpit with a more assured step than usual. Taking as the theme of his sermon the text of the Evangelist: *vox clamantes in deserto,* a voice crying in the wilderness, he upbraided his parishioners harshly. How long were they going to exploit the Indians? What did the royal edicts have to say about this? That the employment of the natives, the *encomendados,* was conditional upon their being protected and instructed in the Christian faith. The dead queen had been quite clear on this point, but actually the *encomiendas* had become slave markets and the *encomenderos* slave traders. The Spanish colonists were in process of losing their souls.

An ill-concealed tremor passed through the congregation. Such frank speech was obviously not to its taste. Why, when the island of Haiti was beginning to hold out some promise, was it necessary to discourage the well-intentioned? Diego Columbus, son of the Discoverer, had just succeeded Ovando as governor of Haiti. He had arrived at Santo Domingo filled with plans, accompanied by determined men like Diego Velásquez. His intention was clear: to continue the conquest, to reconnoiter the nearby islands and complete the exploration of Haiti and Cuba. It was an ambitious program, and one that did not jibe very well with Montesinos's sermon. The Conquistadors had more need of heroic words than of sermons. Be more gentle with the Indians? As if the honor of a Spanish cavalier was not worth a hundred savage souls! The planters had the same reactions: they had shivered with fever in their huts of leaves long enough, but now they lived in houses of stone and were beginning to grow rich. Were they being asked to till the soil themselves?

But the Dominican did not seek to please. Satisfied, he descended from his pulpit. The significance of his words passed beyond the shores of Haiti. For the first time, in fact, and before colonies were even officially conceived as such, Father de Montesinos had raised the "colonial problem."

While the Conquistadors and colonists returned to their homes in an evil humor, one of them—still young, tall, and slightly stooping—stood motionless at the far end of the chapel, as if amazed. It was not the first sermon he had heard; he attended services regularly and received Communion often. How was it that his mind was filled with tenderness for the natives on that particular morning? Bartolomé de Las Casas had, in fact, been touched by grace.

Bartolomé's father, Don Francisco, was of the old nobility; he was Columbus's loyal companion, having accompanied him on his later voyages. Two centuries earlier, an ancestor of the Las Casas family, a simple soldier named Casaus, from Limousin in France, had fought against the Moors under the banner of Ferdinand III, the Saint. He was distinguished by his bravery at the capture of Seville, and the pious monarch had ennobled him. Thus the blood of a French mercenary ran in Bartolomé's veins.

Las Casas's youth had been divided between study and travel. As soon as he had graduated from Salamanca in letters and law, he embarked with his father. For about ten years the licentiate, fresh from the university, had led the adventurous life of a Conquistador, fighting against the Caribs and carving a road to fortune with his sword. It was a common destiny for all youths of good social position at that time. Without transition, they passed from the classroom to the battlefield and there undertook, sometimes at the peril of their lives, the exploits of which they had heard. Bartolomé's two models were Saint Thomas and Christopher Columbus: Reason and Madness, paradoxically brought together to complete the man. In his first youthful period, Bartolomé forgot Saint Thomas: he was a Conquistador—no more cruel than any other, but as greedy as the rest for power and wealth, and in any event very little concerned with morals and law. Also, he inherited from his father a vast domain in the region of Santo Domingo, and he was now one of the richest planters of the islands. An army of slaves was at his service. His farms prospered. Bartolomé was a happy man, or at least he thought himself happy.

Father de Montesinos's sermon revealed him to himself. He would no longer be a Conquistador and a colonist, but a man of God and soon a priest. He set his slaves free, sold his properties, divested himself of all his goods, and a few months after his conversion was ordained at Santiago de Cuba. The first Mass celebrated by Bartolomé emphasized an important date in the evangelical history of the New World. It was, in fact, the first solemn High Mass to be sung in Cuba. It was a day of tumult and gaiety. Into the Cuban cathedral squeezed thousands of Indians who had come from all parts, not only to be present at the ordination of Las Casas, but also because this was the day ordered by Velásquez for bringing gold to be marked with the seal of the King of Spain.

Bartolomé began as parish priest of Zanguarama, the most wretched parish in Cuba. At the same time he performed the duties of military almoner and accompanied Velásquez and Narváez on their expeditions. He restrained the cruel enthusiasms of the soldiers and intervened between Spaniards and Indians. Then he returned to the Dominicans. His public life had begun.

This monk who was stripped of everything, who fed on cassava flour and slept upon straw, was about to give battle to principles and men. First he attacked the *requerimiento*. This was an institution by which every Conquistador, before taking possession of land, had to call upon the Indians to accept the teaching of the Christian faith; if the Indians bowed to this "request" they kept their lives, their freedom, and their goods, but if they refused, they were reduced to slavery and were dispossessed. Had not Pope Alexander VI's bull given America to Spain? And was not Joshua the first to make use of the requerimiento when he called upon the inhabitants of Jericho to surrender their city to him, in conformity with the divine will? Today the chosen people were the people of Spain. Bartolomé revolted against this pharisaical procedure, for Christ had said that we must go out and teach all the nations—by persuasion, not by threats. The Indian was a free man and must be treated as such.

Bartolomé gave proof of what he expounded. He established a colony in one of the most sinister regions of Guatemala. His only weapons were charity and tenderness, for there were no guns, no forced labor, no chains. To this Spanish-Indian community he gave the name Vera Paz, and indeed, peace and good will reigned there for a long time. But such an enterprise could only be transitory, for this island of peace was beaten down by the fierce influx of neighboring tribes. One day Vera Paz was attacked by the heathens; the houses were burned and a great number of the priests were massacred. Bloody repression followed. All Indians were not "good savages."

But Bartolomé was not in the least discouraged. What he sought so eagerly was the establishment of just laws for the protection of the Indians. He laid siege to the powers at home during his visits and harassed them with letters. At the time of his first journey to Spain, King Ferdinand was near to death, and the Indians interested him less than the problem of the succession. Bishop Fonseca distrusted Bartolomé. What was the good of mixing sentiment and business? Cardinal Jiménez de Cisneros was more understanding. The first results obtained by Las Casas were meager: the dispatch of a Hieronymite mission to the West Indies, his own nomination as "Apostle of the Indies"—a symbolic title that he turned into a reality—and a few minor improvements in the requerimiento system. At the time of his second journey, Cardinal Jiménez had died and Charles V was emperor. What was happening in the New World interested the young ruler, but he had little understanding of colonial matters and had laid the burden of dealing with them on the newly created Council of the Indies. Nevertheless, on the insistence of Las Casas, he promulgated ordinances in the Indians' favor. Bartolomé struggled on step by step. By sheer tenacity he wrested from the administration legal documents restricting the powers of the Conquistadors and giving the Indians legal protection. Thereafter colonial enterprises were controlled by the priests, slavery was suppressed, and the requerimiento lost its absolute character and became a simple exhortation. The encomiendas were abolished.

But it was a long way from Valladolid to Cuba! The official humanity shown by the Spanish court found little echo in the colonies of the New World. In the islands and on the Spanish Main it was a struggle for life. To obtain a maximum return from the conquered territories, a numerous and acclimatized labor force was needed. Were these forced and unpaid laborers slaves? What could one pay them with? It was all a matter of words: they had only to call them peons, and that was the end of it! In any case, without them no colonization was possible. This enlightened Dominican was sabotaging the conquest! The Conquistadors sought to make his task harder. They harried him cunningly, and even went so far as to set up against him a secular priest, Don Carlos de Aragón, who from the pulpit made cruel mock of Las Casas's chimerical struggle. What, exactly, had this former Conquistador contrived? he asked. The laws of Burgos had long before defined the duties of the colonists, prohibiting them from laying burdens on the Indians and from striking or imprisoning them. It was for the royal officials and not for the clergy to supervise the execution of the laws. And what a singular conception of justice it was to suggest to the planters that they replace their Indian slaves with Negroes! Was the nature of the red people of America superior to that of the black people of Africa? This cleric enjoyed himself fully. What a godsend it was to be able, under the protection of the Conquistadors, to insult the Dominicans with complete impunity! But such behavior did not bring the impudent priest much luck. On his return to Spain he tried to disparage the work of Las Casas there, but he went about it the wrong way. One day when he was preaching in the cathedral at Burgos, the Holy Office came to seize him. He had been too talkative.

Indifferent to the stir created by his behavior, Bartolomé continued without letup. In this dangerous game against principles and men, he gained and lost alternately. He thought he had gained when the *Leyes Nuevas* (new laws) were promulgated, decreeing the suppression—this time final—of the encomienda and slavery and prohibiting using the services of Indians without pay, since they had become subjects of the Crown. But to free thousands of slaves suddenly and to assimilate them as vassals was to start new violence. Revolt broke out in the islands and spread to the mainland. Each Conquistador interpreted the Valladolid ordinances in his own fashion. In Peru, Gonzalo Pizarro took up arms against the troops of Charles V and had himself proclaimed governor; the Viceroy, Núñez Vela, was beheaded by the rebels. The royal commissioners were met with arquebuses. Deprived of manpower, the colonists threatened to quit the New World, and some of them actually embarked for Spain.

The Indian question became complicated by the problem of Negro immigration. On the recommendations of Las Casas, a call was sent out for African laborers, who were regarded as healthier than the sickly Indians. What was to be the fate of these increasing numbers of Negroes? By an unpardonable oversight on the part of the legislators, the Leyes Nuevas did not cover them, and they remained slaves. The Indians sneered, the Negroes rose, and disorder reached a climax. In the face of the grave threat to the empire created by the application of the Leyes Nuevas, amendments were made. The principles remained, but injustice, although mitigated, continued. Had Las Casas lost?

Bartolomé was seventy years old. He was proposed for the bishopric of Cuzco, but he refused it because the charge was too profitable, and this formerly wealthy man hated wealth. On the other hand, he accepted the bishopric of Chiapas. A more unhealthy country was scarcely to be found in all Mexico. The state of Chiapas was in the extreme south between the Pacific coast and Guatemala, bordering upon the Isthmus of Tehuantepec. Bartolomé's new residence was in a region swept alternately by the burning breath of the Pacific and the icy north wind of the Sierra de Chiapas. A difficult climate and a wretched population. Nevertheless, the Spanish colony was large and the plantations were prosperous—cacao, vanilla, sugar cane, and sago derived from the breadfruit tree. However, this prosperity was achieved only by means of exploiting the Indians. Bartolomé, more combative than ever, once again embraced the Indians' cause. His exhortations and his threats having no effect upon the Spaniards, the Bishop of Chiapas ordered his priests to refuse absolution to slave-owners. It was a brave decision to take, but an effective one. Brutal and greedy as they were, the Spanish colonists remained passionately Catholic, and there could be no better deterrent for such intrepid men than the thought of Hell. At last Bartolomé had touched a vulnerable spot.

Had Las Casas gone too far in his eagerness to destroy slavery? Had he the right to use his sacramental powers to advance his principles? In any case, his decision raised such a wave of anger in the Spanish colony that he was forced to flee from Chiapas and take refuge in Mexico City. His personal position had become untenable. Everyone was against him except the Indians. They kissed the hem of his robe and prostrated themselves as he passed by. In their eyes he was the incarnation of the white god foretold by all the pre-Columbian traditions.

Spurned by the majority of colonists, supported by the royal officials with bad grace, unappreciated by the clergy, Bartolomé took

the road to Spain once more. This was his fourteenth and last crossing. We can imagine this fine old man blessing the crowd of Indians
before he embarked. Then the sails of the caravel filled and it moved
away from the shore. Hundreds of canoes escorted Las Casas out into
the open sea. The caravel drew away and vanished from sight.

Bartolomé arrived in Valladolid, but he did not think of retiring.
Twenty years remained to him, which he devoted to carrying on his
work. Henceforth the struggle went on in the Spanish capital, where
it became even more dramatic. He had to face formidable adversaries.
He published the *Brevísima relación de la destruyción de las Indias
occidentales,* the most terrible indictment of colonial expeditions ever
written. Taking the history of the conquest country by country, he
demonstrated with facts and figures that it had only been an enterprise of extermination. What, in fact, was the balance sheet of forty
years of conquest? Fifteen million Indian corpses, dead from ex-
haustion, famine, epidemics, or massacres; razed villages; whole populations put to the sword; deserts and ruins. And the Conquistadors
were responsible. But then a reaction against Las Casas took place.
Protests were raised; his accusations were refuted and his figures contested. Father Montolima, Captain Vargas Machuca, and the historian
Saavedra Fajardo gave a very different picture: the conquest had not
been as Bartolomé stated, but a veritable *conquista* in the mystical
sense of the word. The Conquistadors had harvested thousands of
souls. As to the Indians, how could one defend them? "They eat
human flesh, they go naked, they are liars, improvident, drunkards,
ungrateful, cruel. . . ."

For some time the debate remained purely informative. Reports
were sifted, archives examined, evidence collected. Two parties took
shape: for or against the Indians, for or against the Conquistadors.
Each praised his own side excessively, with the sincere bad faith of
the prejudiced. The "good savage" was contrasted with the unscrupulous conqueror, or the humanitarian colonist with the ferocious
Carib. It was a fruitless business which became even more acrimoni-
ous with the entry of Juan Ginés de Sepúlveda into the lists. This
time the principle was raised whether it was right to make war on
the Indians. Sepúlveda said it was, in his treatise entitled *Democrates
alter, sive de justis belli causis apud Indos.* The work had the entire
approval of the Archbishop of Seville, President of the Council of

THE VOICE OF A JUST MAN

the Indies. Only the authority of the Council of Castile was needed in order to publish the work—a simple formality if Las Casas was not involved in the matter. However, the old bishop, who still had a considerable position in the high assemblies of the realm, had the publication of the *Democrates alter* prohibited. Sepúlveda did not consider himself defeated, and he, too, had powerful connections in Spain and Italy. He regarded the Council's decision as an affront, so he took up his pen and restated his views vigorously. A tribunal was then established at Valladolid, composed of officials and theologians, before which Las Casas and Sepúlveda appeared to explain their views.

Taking his stand on the principles enunciated by Saint Thomas, Sepúlveda claimed that war was ethical when ordered by a legitimate authority, when fought for a just cause and inspired by pure intentions. Thus war against the Indians was right because it was the only means of forcing them to give up their barbarous practices and of imposing on them a political and moral system founded on Christianity. Might one reduce the Indians to slavery? Yes, was Sepúlveda's answer, for they were inferior by nature, which justified their submission to superior natures. Had not Aristotle distinguished those men who could legitimately be regarded as slaves? Las Casas protested violently against Sepúlveda's theory. From the moment that war became an instrument of oppression, it was not lawful. There were no inferior and superior natures, but only men with equal rights. Indians and Negroes, as well as Spaniards, could have access to civilization. Bartolomé seized this opportunity to condemn using Negro labor, which he had imprudently advised.

The Valladolid controversy lasted several months, and Sepúlveda and Las Casas defended their theses tirelessly. In the end, the judges failed to reach a decision. Probably the problem was beyond them. But in the practical sphere Bartolomé triumphed. Supúlveda's writings were prohibited. The Bishop of Chiapas died in peace at the age of ninety-two, and all America went into mourning.

Bartolomé's death did not stop his enemies. Passionate discussions about the man and his work continued. It was easy to argue about it, for it must be admitted that very often his apostolic zeal led him astray. He has been reproached with adding two zeroes to the numbers of victims of the conquest, and his *Brevísima relación* (fed more on enthusiasm than on the critical spirit) has been blamed for the lack of understanding of Spanish colonization among the French, English, and Germans. One might deplore the fact that he compromised the work of his compatriots by his blindly generous attitude, and there has been astonishment that public authority should have permitted such sabotage of a national enterprise. It has even been insinuated that by approving the use of Negro slaves, Las Casas was protecting interests he may have had in Portuguese companies trading in Negroes. This last point excepted, one would have to admit the correctness of his enemies' criticisms had not a very great urgency justified his actions. That he was sectarian, naive, more concerned with justice than with truth, that he prejudiced his country's cause by his evangelical anger, that sometimes he felt a sort of "sporting" pleasure in breaking lances with the powers of the day—all this does not modify the essential aspects of his personality. It is not wrong that a sectarian should stand forth under certain circumstances, when faced with problems that concern humanity. The effectiveness of an antidote rests in its violence, and what surer antidote to the brutality of the Conquistadors than the combative charity of a Bartolomé de Las Casas? The Bishop of Chiapas was not a saint, but "a just and God-fearing man." In the fight against iniquity, it was necessary to have such an enthusiast for justice.

When Columbus landed on Haiti, the island had a million inhabitants; twenty years later there were only a thousand or two. But during the same period all Mexico had been gained for the Catholic faith. In a Panamanian village Balboa had Indian prisoners devoured by his dogs. But Jiménez de Quesada, Conquistador of Colombia, ordered his soldiers to treat the natives well and to respect their property. Humane at one point, at others the conquest was barbaric. These were the contradictions of the conquest, reflections of which never ceased to torment the Spanish kings. They had received from the Pope a mandate to convert the Indians, though they also intended to master the New World and to extract from it the gold for financing their European wars. The double imperative, spiritual and temporal, called for the opposing qualities of gentleness and violence. Souls are ruled by love and bodies by force. Since it was impossible to resolve such a contradiction, the Spanish sovereigns strove to put right on their side; the Valladolid conference was one manifestation of their anxiety. To be sure, the obsession with giving evangelical and legal protection to their colonial enterprises concealed an ulterior political motive—the necessity of proving to the world that the conquest was right; but in making appeal to theologians and jurists, the Spanish kings also affirmed their sincere intent to reconcile their consciences and their mission.

Before leaving Bartolomé de Las Casas, one observation must be made. Though he opposed the abuses of the Conquistadors with indomitable courage, though he was the first to demand the abolition of slavery, on the other hand he never questioned the validity of Pope Alexander VI's bull, giving the New World to Spain and charging her with instructing the conquered people in the Catholic faith. Thus Bartolomé agreed to the colonization so long as it respected the liberty of man. He was concerned with procedure and not with the principle itself. The king was the delegate of Providence. Bartolomé was an "anti-Conquistador" and not an "anti-colonial."

Another Dominican, his contemporary, Francisco de Vitoria, professor at the University of Salamanca, stated that Christian rulers had no rights over infidels. The pontifical gift was a diplomatic act having no connection with the conquest. What a stir must have passed through the cold classroom when Vitoria exclaimed: "Difference of religion does not make war lawful. . . . The Christian princes, though protected by the Pope, cannot prevent the barbarians from sinning against nature, nor punish them for it. . . . The extension of the empire is no just cause for war!" Four centuries before one could speak of "conscientious objection," Vitoria dared to say: "The subject cannot fight, even upon the order of a prince, if he knows clearly that a war is unjust." Thus at the very climax of colonial expansion, a university teacher could lecture Charles V ex cathedra at the very time when the Emperor was taking arms against the Lutheran princes and Francisco Pizarro was conquering the fabulous kingdom of the Incas. Vitoria was, in fact, the first anti-colonialist.

The echo of two voices, those of Francisco de Vitoria and Bartolomé de Las Casas, is not yet dead.

CHAPTER 17

Dirge for the Conquistadors

"THERE will come a time when the ocean will loosen the bonds by which things are encircled, when the immense earth will be revealed, when Tethys will discover the universe anew and Thule will no longer be the end of the world." Seneca's mysterious prophecy was fulfilled fifteen centuries later with Bermejo's cry of "Land!" in the night of October 11-12, 1492. Two Spaniards greeted each other through time and space.

Not only was Thule surpassed, but a whole world emerged from the shadows into the light of dawn. What a world it was! It stretched from California to Chile, from the West Indies to Patagonia, and covered all Central America; it was more than 6000 miles from north to south, through 67 degrees of latitude, and covered nearly 10,000,-000 square miles. This was the Spanish Empire, thirty times larger than Spain itself. Brazil was left for Portugal, thanks to the pen of a Borgia, and humid Guiana and the frozen far north were for those who were to come later. Spain had taken the largest share, which was just, for she had been the first to reach the young land of America.

The first Europeans in the New World were Spaniards, and no one has dreamed of contesting their priority. But from the second quarter of the sixteenth century, other Europeans followed in their wake, the first of whom were the French.

In 1534 Cabeza de Vaca crossed North America on foot from the shores of Texas to the western coast of Mexico. In the same year a Frenchman, Jacques Cartier, having set out from Brittany, reached Newfoundland and the gulf of the St. Lawrence; he had discovered Canada. In the years that followed, the colony of Canada gradually acquired the Great Lakes and the valley of the Mississippi. Hernando de Soto went up the Mississippi at the same time that Frenchmen came down it, and it was only by a narrow margin that the subjects of Charles V and Francis I avoided spreading to the Mississippi region the war which was then in progress between Nice and Perpignan, for the two parties failed to meet. Other Frenchmen, cruising along the American coasts, strove to plant the fleur-de-lis banner of the Capetians. Jean Ribaut founded Charlefort, now Port Royal, South Carolina, and went as far as Florida. René Laudonnière built Fort Caroline in Florida.

South America also received a visit from the French: Jean Duperot, sailing on the *La Pèlerine*, touched land at Pernambuco, which is now Recife. The Sire de Villegaignon, following difficulties with the king, went into exile and founded a Protestant colony on an island in the bay of Rio. Eldorado did not fail to draw the French, and they, too, searched for it in Guiana and Amazonia. It is noteworthy that their passage through these territories left an excellent impression in the minds of the Indians. The courtesy and civility of certain gentlemen surprised natives who were used to Spanish arrogance and German stiffness, and sometimes French officers even took up arms by the side of the local people against the Spanish or Portuguese occupiers. It has always been the privilege of European minorities in a territory dominated by another European power to feel sympathy for the conquered populations, provoked for the most part by dislike for the conqueror. Later, France was also to have its piece of Eldorado: Guiana and its sordid towns: Cayenne, Saint Laurent du Maroni, and Oyapock—a sinister Eldorado which, after having been the poor relation of French colonies, in 1947 became the most backward of French *départements*.

The Germans were even less successful than the French, since the latter, by securing Guiana—desolate though this equatorial land might be—could count that they had their hands on part of the New World; but the bank clerks from Augsburg left Venezuela empty-handed and without hope of returning. As for the Dutch, only a part of Guiana and few names elsewhere on the map of South America— Cape Orange on the northern coast of Brazil, Waterhuys, Roohoeck, at the mouth of the Amazon—record their passing. The future founders of New Amsterdam—New York—touched the southern continent only lightly. The English had to wait for Cromwell before becoming aware of their imperial mission. The incursions of Fenton, Withrington, and Cavendish on the Brazilian littoral, Raleigh's trip along the Orinoco—yet another!—in search of Eldorado, the descent of the

famous corsair Drake on Santo Domingo and Cartagena were nothing
but profitable raids or single engagements. Easily last in the conquest,
the English were the first in the share-out. But, like the French, in
South America they secured only a scrap of Guiana—though the best
piece, to be sure.

But all these were only isolated endeavors, like nets cast haphaz-
ardly into the Dark Sea. They had nothing in common with the
Spaniards' ventures, which were carefully prepared, and part of a vast
hegemonical plan sketched by an emperor under the benevolent eye
of a Pope. Frenchmen, Germans, Dutch, Englishmen—contemporaries
of the Spaniards of the conquest, sailing in similar caravels and having
the same means, steered for the same shores. To what end but to
conquer?

Here we face a problem of definition: were these conquerors of
other races conquistadors too? Farther back in time the question
applies also to Genghis Khan and Kublai, the conquerors of Cathay,
or, nearer the present time, to Galliani, Savorgnan de Brazza, and
Lyautey, the founders of the French Empire, and to Ferdinand de
Lesseps, who thought of the canal that cut the isthmus. Could they,
too, be called conquistadors? When Captain Gouraud captured the
Sudanese chief Samory in the heart of his camp, was he so very different from Francisco Pizarro when he captured Atahualpa? These
are attractive analogies, but in truth the Conquistador resembles no
one but himself. He is a Spaniard, the product of the conquering and
mystical Spain of the sixteenth century, made in its image, and re-
flecting the somber glory of its contradictory passions. He carries in
himself, with a sort of terrible ingenuity, the whole of Spain. He *is*
Spain. And just as we cannot define in one word, or reduce to a single
formula, the historic face of Charles V's Spain, so we must consider
successively the various aspects of the Conquistador, so that a true
portrait may emerge, one removed both from the "black legend"
and from the romantic image.

Neither Saints nor Bandits

Here are a few judgments on the Conquistadors. Heinrich Heine
was categorical: "They were bandits," he said. Angel Canivet claims
that they conquered "by spontaneous necessity, by virtue of a natu-

ral impulse toward independence, without other purpose than to reveal the grandeur which hid itself beneath their apparent smallness." Maurice Legendre says: "Spain, by its Conquistadors, was going to seek outside, by sheer energy, the strength which at home she had only potentially and which it was essential for her to realize in order to maintain her independence." Salvador de Madariaga finds in them "the typically Spanish trait: the coexistence of contrary tendencies."

Each of these opinions, even that of Heine, who detested Spain and understood her little, has its share of the truth. Bandits at certain times—crises of panic and greed—the Conquistadors never lost their sense of grandeur. This was one of their contradictions. But the most striking was to have so closely associated the religion of self and the love of country.

The people of Spain, whatever may be her political regime, are the least possible "community-minded." They do not believe in the "collective soul," that invention of sociologists, useful sometimes as a propaganda theme but as sterile as it is theoretical. How could a collection of individuals form a single individual, at least without denying the personal soul? Deny the soul! An old proverb says that every Spaniard "tiene su alma en su almario": a play on words, meaning that he keeps his soul in his closet; it is his own property, a secret thing. Pride and privation: that was the Spaniard of the sixteenth century.

For his soul he was accountable to God alone. Calderón makes the mayor of Zalamea say: "We owe the king our fortune and our life, but honor is the patrimony of our soul. And the soul belongs to God alone." Honor and soul were, for every well-born Spaniard, the supreme freedom. No law, not even the king's will, might prevail against this privilege of making arrangements direct with God and acting accordingly. Hence the individualism of the Conquistadors. Above their local leader, the *visitadores*, and the royal personage there was God, that is to say, the freedom to be themselves. It was Canivet who suggested: "The juridical ideal of Spain would be that every Spaniard should have in his pocket a charter of rights consisting of a single item framed in these brief, clear, and striking terms: 'This Spaniard is authorized to conduct himself as he chooses.'" A joke? Scarcely; for one does not joke about such things beyond the

Pyrenees. By this extravagant but unwritten charter every Conquistador shaped his behavior; thus, having concluded an intimate pact with God, he often thought himself exempt from the duty of obedience.

Although fiercely individualistic, the Conquistadors were no less ardently patriotic. Every Spaniard carried in his heart a fragment of Spain and very often bathed it in his solitary tears. Andalusia had provided the first sailors, and Castile the majority of the soldiers. Columbus's sailors were almost all from Palos and Moguer, and the captains of the conquest came from Estremadura. Francisco Pizarro had recruited his companions at Trujillo, his native village; Cortés was from Medellín, Balboa from Jerez de los Caballeros, Valdivia from Villanueva de la Serena. They must have dreamed constantly of their *casa solariega* and the herd at the bottom of the field tilled by the elder brother. Manor houses with nail-studded doors, or huts of slate—the thought evokes them both. That sunburned landscape of Estremadura, with its wide and melancholy horizons, haunted the Conquistadors, and to their conquests they gave the names of home: Medellín, Guadalajara, Trujillo, Cáceres, Badajoz, and countless Santiagos. This was the compensation of these voluntary exiles, who were so attached to their homeland that one might have been able, it seems, by scratching the soles of their shoes, to find a scrap of the red clay of the Tierra de Baros.

Under the King's Eye

This Conquistador, brightly daring, taking possession of scraps of empire as he galloped along, and listening to nothing but the promptings of his own heart. . . . His plume could be seen on the narrow roads of the Andes, in the vast grasslands, by the edges of leaden lakes and upon the lava flows, and advancing by night along the rims of craters, white in the moonlight. Could nothing stop him but the fear of God? Yes, the fear of the king, for the Conquistador was not the soldier of God alone. He was the liegeman of the Spanish monarch, and his motto was that of Spain: *un monarca, un imperio, y una espada* (one monarch, one realm, and one sword). There was only one who tried to escape from royal tutelage—Gonzalo Pizarro, and he died under the executioner's ax. He who had no fear of cannibals trembled at the thought of incurring the king's wrath. Six thousand miles from Valladolid, his heart froze at the thought of displeasing Charles V. The receipt of a dispatch bearing the royal seal immediately aroused his anxiety. At a single word from the king, he did not hesitate to cross deserts, mountains, and oceans, to take orders, report, or sometimes to give himself up to justice. All, even the greatest, made this humiliating journey. Columbus (three times), Cortés, the Pizarro brothers. . . . The knee had to be bent before the Caesarian monarch if the sheet of parchment legalizing the enterprise was to be secured.

Not a caravel ever left a Spanish port in a westerly direction without a representative of the king aboard. When Columbus left for his first voyage in 1492—for the unknown, moreover—Rodrigo de Escobedo and Sánchez de Segovia, Royal Notary and Comptroller respectively, had been forced upon him. "Master after God," the Admiral of the Ocean Sea saw the king come between himself and God. Thenceforward, the two faces could make only one. Intoxicated as they were by sudden fortune, the Conquistadors never omitted to put aside a fifth part of their booty for the royal treasury. And if any man swindled the accounts, it was at his own risk and peril: all knew that the garrote awaited the man who took it into his head to defraud the king of his share.

Thus from the beginning of the conquest, even in the opening phase when it was less a matter of conquest than discovery, the Spanish monarchy signified its intention of regarding it as a "royal affair." The first act of the conquest—the *Santa María*'s departure from the port of Palos—was sanctioned by the first administrative act: the charter granted to the Genoese by the Catholic monarchs. The following year, the royal grip on this prey that was scarcely yet imaginable became manifest. A superintendence of Indian affairs was created at Valladolid and immediately established a delegation at Santo Domingo: the first "audience." Then, years later, the *Casa de Contratación* was founded at Seville, with the task of supervising the application of the laws concerning trade with America. It registered the vessels that left or returned to Spain, and legislated at the civil and criminal levels on all disputes concerning traffic with the New World. The Casa de Contratación also decided maritime matters: it maintained the register of crews, fixed the departure dates and destinations of ships, and determined freight and tonnage. Furthermore, the chief pilot performed the duties of controller of navigation, technical adviser, and chief of marine personnel. The Casa was at one and the same time a chamber of commerce, a consular office, a naval school, and a cartographic service.

Eight years after the foundation of the Casa de Contratación, Ferdinand the Catholic created the Royal Council of the Indies—a veritable ministry of the colonies that exercised its jurisdiction over all the affairs of the Indies: civil, military, commercial, and religious. All the officials of the New World, from the highest to the humblest, were subordinate to it. Charles V strengthened the powers of this council and gave it his full confidence, going so far as to delegate to it his signature in all matters of justice, with the exception of nominations to "favors and offices." The seat of the Council of the Indies was at Medina. It was more a directory than an assembly, for there were only seven councilors, including the president and the fiscal attorney. Deliberations and conferences took place behind closed doors, and only the king could be present. Public and secret reports from overseas officials were scrutinized, especially the secret ones; compliments were handed out and penalties fixed. In short, the council administered everything, though from a distance.

One very great long-term concern preoccupied the council: that of giving this still-effervescent America a juridical protection that would insure that one day—God willing—colonization would follow the conquest. The Laws of the Indies answered to this anxiety. In preparing them, the royal advisers created the first colonial law. The majority of these laws were just, though it might be difficult to disentangle the essentials of a legislation whose six thousand articles embraced all the forms of Spanish activity in the New World from the running of schools to bodily hygiene. But respect for the human personality was never lost sight of. Doubtless the men who shaped these laws always kept in mind the spirit of Isabella the Catholic's testament: "That the King, my Lord, the Princess, my daughter, and the Prince, my son, do not permit, or will not be the cause, that the Indians, the inhabitants of the Islands and the mainland, should suffer any injury to their persons or to their property. They will keep watch, on the contrary, that these people shall be treated with justice and kindness."

Humane and just in principle, the Laws of the Indies bore in them the germ of future emancipation. Meanwhile, by extending the system of *fueros* (under the name *cabildos*) to the New World, imperial Spain of the sixteenth century laid the foundations of the South American democracies. What, in fact, were the cabildos? They were local municipalities whose members could be non-Spanish, but who were obliged to secure office by popular vote. No one, therefore, opposed the fact that there were Indians among the municipal councilors. The members of the cabildos administered the affairs of the commune, looking after public hygiene, the maintenance of roads, and general welfare. The institution of these local assemblies, born of the people, underlines the extent to which the intentions of the Council of the Indies were genuine. Similarly, by creating a third body known as the Consulate of the Indies, the central power manifested its will to regulate the profession of privateering and to prevent its abuse. This multiplicity of agencies and the abundance of legal texts bear witness to the seriousness with which the Spanish sovereigns took their role as protectors and civilizers of the Indies. In this respect they never ceased to nourish high hopes and noble illusions.

The administration in Spain—the Casa de Contratación, the Council of the Indies, and the Consulate of the Indies—was duplicated by a local administration. First the viceroy, appointed directly by the king; this all-powerful person enjoyed royal prerogatives in his territories. Captain general on sea and on land, chief of the departments of justice and finance—in effect, he held absolute power. At the same time, he was obliged, on the expiration of his mandate, to give an exact and faithful account of it. This sincere, quasi-confessional report was in accord with the intentions of the legislators, for it was necessary that officials in the Indies—and especially the high officials—should feel the constant presence of the royal rod.

At the time of Charles V, Spanish America was divided into two viceroyalties, those of Mexico and Peru. New Granada and Río de la Plata, long subordinated to Peru, were not raised to viceroyalty status until much later. Guatemala, Venezuela, Chile, and Cuba were under the leadership of captains general. Provinces of lesser importance were called *gobernaciones* and were administered by governors. Finally, each province comprised districts placed under the command of a *corregidor*. At the head of each commune was an *alcalde*.

In addition to viceroys and captains general, the sovereign also appointed governors and corregidors. These had to pay a deposit before taking up their duties, and firm moral guarantees were required of them. Their powers were rather those of a colonial administrator or an officer for native affairs than of a prefect, since they were skilled in judging the civil and military differences that occurred in the *encomiendas*. In the event of an appeal, the matter was taken before the Royal Audiences, which sat in the capitals. The "auditors," also designated by the king, were subject to very strict rules: they were forbidden to contract marriage in their place of residence, to take part in public ceremonies, to make friends with the Indians, to go into business, or to lend or accept money. Answerable directly to the Council of the Indies, they were not subject to the authority of the viceroy and sometimes even held it in check. In short, the audiences constituted an intermediate echelon between the administration at home and the local governments. Moreover, the king sent "visitors" to the spot for inquiries and to seek information. It may be deduced that he made every effort to keep himself informed of affairs overseas.

The meticulous precautions taken by the Spanish monarchy in choosing colonial personnel, its mistrust of its most experienced servants, the hierarchical chain linking the royal cabinet to the alcalde of the smallest Mexican hamlet, were evidences of its understanding of men. One could not be sure of anybody. By seeking to insure the total independence of the officers entrusted with judging Indians, by demanding their perfect integrity, the monarchy showed its solicitude for the conquered people. "No Indian can be reduced to slavery . . . since all are vassals of the Royal Crown of Castile. . . ." Isabella, Ferdinand, Charles, and, later, Philip II spoke in the same terms, which expressed good faith and a conviction natural to Christian princes brought up on the Gospel, for whom the "racial question" did not exist. It must not be forgotten that the first colonial charter of the Spanish kings proclaimed the equality of Indians and Spaniards before the law. Doubtless it was a symbolic proclamation, yet it revealed a humane preoccupation on the part of its authors to an extent that no other European sovereign had dreamed of. The distinction between natives and subjects was not a Spanish invention.

Although the system was well conceived, it failed in operation.

The monarchy, in its naive pride, looked upon the territories of the New World in the same way as upon Milan or Flanders, where it was simply a matter of adapting the administrative scheme of Spain. One reproduced the framework of the royal organization on the map of America, and that was the end of it. That was the first error: dogmatism. The countries were different; the natives spoke unknown languages, and for a long time Spaniards and Indians could converse only by signs. It was only after the second half of the sixteenth century that the conquerors made a sincere effort to understand the mores and mentality of the local people. The monarchy committed a second error—psychological this time—in giving too much credit to the reports of its servants or its favorites—an inevitable weakness if one considers the immense ocean barrier between the colonies and the Ministry of Colonies. Is it surprising, therefore, that certain officials, whose principal function was to aid and protect the Indians, amassed enormous fortunes during their regulation five-year stay, simply by buying back from the natives, at low prices, objects that had been sold to them at high prices and for which they had no use, such as razors, silk stockings, and inkstands? This did not prevent these same officials from ascertaining carefully that mixed marriages were celebrated according to the Roman rites.

One Conquistador sighed maliciously: *"Lo que el Rey manda se obedece, no se cumple"*: "What the king orders is obeyed but not executed." This was Belalcázar, the master of Quito. However, Belalcázar's attitude, and that of a few petty tyrants, toward the authority at home was the exception. The Conquistadors' freedom of action was only apparent, and their omnipotence was ephemeral. Attempts at rebellion, even if they succeeded for a while, always ended by being suppressed. A Spanish captain never persisted for long in illegality. The hand of the king, slow to strike, fell sooner or later on the head of the culprit; and the king's eye, though it was such a long way off, never lost sight of the Conquistadors as they marched on.

The Romantics

"Weary of carrying their lofty miseries," "intoxicated by a heroic and brutal dream," "hoping for epic tomorrows": such was the way

in which José María de Heredia, a Cuban descendant of the Conquistadors (Alonso de Heredia had founded the town of Tolu on
the Cauca river), pictured his ancestors steering for Cipango in
search of the "fabulous metal." This is the Conquistador adorned
with all the romantic accessories; nothing is missing, neither violence
nor insupportable pride nor the mirage of gold nor the confusion of
instinct and imagination. Another feature common to the romantics
was stoicism, sometimes theatrical but most often silent. Arrogant
and dignified while they paced up and down the *plazuela* of their
native towns, draped in their ragged capes, waiting for adventure,
the Conquistadors were even more so when in the very midst of the
adventure.

Romantics, indeed, with all the credulity and artless wonder that
is associated with the word. Into the extravagant pact they had made
with fortune the Conquistadors had brought the passionate quest
for risk and the intense curiosity that always made of them something more than old campaigners. In this respect, however, they
differ from the romantics, the eternally unsatisfied. The Conquistadors were overwhelmed. For once, the imagination had to
admit itself surpassed by reality. No adventurer had ever known
such adventure as this, and no actor had ever performed on such a
stage. This splendid prize, outstretched beneath their gaze and within
their reach, seemed the more beautiful to the conquerers even as the
tropical sun burned into their brains. What matter? Atahualpa's
treasure and the magnificence of Mexican possessions were not
mirages. The enchanted forest emerged from legend to become the
tangible virgin forest of America, bathed in twilight shadows. Amadis
of Gaul had turned into Pedro de Alvarado; Bernal Díaz del Castillo
was about to rewrite a chivalrous novel. With eyes wide open, the
Conquistadors lived in a lucid and endless delirium.

The exploits of the Conquistadors have not lacked chroniclers.
But what bard will sing of their amours? It was not always the olive-
skinned Indian women, their long hair decked out with exotic
flowers, stammering childish words, who took the initiative in
dalliance. But they did not reject the Spaniards' advances either. Who
can say what it was that stirred in the hearts and flesh of these girls
or in the wives of the caciques? Submission to the strongest? Curiosity? Sensual comparisons? In any case, no Conquistador was ever

repulsed. In order to break their strict moral rules so joyfully on behalf of the Spaniards, to serve these men with such devotion that they sometimes went so far as to betray their brothers, the Indian women must have been great lovers or profligates. We recall that on the very evening of the fall of Cajamarca, the Peruvian women came in a crowd to offer themselves to the victors. Neither Princesses of the Sun nor vestals seemed to harbor the least resentment against those who had scarcely completed "cleaning up" the city. Were they, then, without rancor, these heavy-breasted women with copper-colored skins who did not seem to have the least hatred for the conqueror? Were they yielding to an unfamiliar pleasure, to the prestige of the invader? Or were they simply seeking to put themselves under the protection of a Spanish shield, on the advice of their fathers and husbands?

There was not one Conquistador, even among the greatest, who did not succumb to the Indian women. Hernán Cortés might not have conquered Mexico if he had not begun by subjugating Doña Marina. But it did not rest at that. His residence at Coyoacán was as full of favorites as the Grand Turk's seraglio. Indian women with Spanish names—Doña Inés, Doña Elvira, and many others—shared Malinche's favors. Francisco Pizarro, that graybeard, lived in concubinage with the sister of Atahualpa, his victim. Only Columbus appears to have remained chaste, tortured as he was until the day of his death by his double attachment to his wife and his mistress, Felipa Perestrello y Moniz and Beatriz Enríquez de Harana. All these romantics had their romances, and the history of the conquest is full of picturesque love stories, such as the one that follows.

When Pizarro landed at Tumbes, Atahualpa and Huáscar were at daggers drawn, but they had not yet taken off their masks. They were watching each other; it was a period of "diplomatic tension." The arrival of the foreign chief in Peru was going to decide the question of war or peace between the two sons of Huayna Capac, but before that, could some solution not be arrived at? The two Inca princes were fully aware that by prolonging their quarrel they were playing into the invader's hands. Atahualpa took the first step. He sent an ambassador to Huáscar with the task of finding some basis for compromise. This man, Quilacou, was one of Atahualpa's most brilliant captains. He reached Cuzco, entered the royal palace, and stood before the legitimate son of the dead emperor. By Huáscar's side stood a young girl who was his mistress: Golden Star. One look between Quilacou and Golden Star was sufficient: they fell hopelessly in love. Quilacou forgot himself, forgot his embassy, and was so daring as to address himself directly to Golden Star. Did he already dream of running off with her? For the moment he was content to smile at her, a rare impropriety that was punished at once. He was driven from the palace, but not before giving the princess the glance of an accomplice: they would meet again!

Meanwhile, negotiations were broken off. Atahualpa's army moved forward, and war began. During the first engagement, Quilacou was gravely wounded and lost consciousness. Rousing from his faint, whom should he see leaning over him but Golden Star. She had abandoned her lover, renounced her position as the favorite of the Inca, and followed the army. In order not to be recognized, she had cut her long hair. Disguised as an adolescent, she mingled with the slaves that carried the baggage and, like them, carried her load. The idyll that had scarcely started at Cuzco unfolded in the midst of the fighting, but it was brief. Both were taken prisoner by the Spaniards and led before Hernando de Soto. Pizarro's captain could recognize true nobility, and he saw at once that the captives were not like the rest of the Indians. He questioned them. Quilacou told their story; De Soto was moved by it and wiped away a tear. The tale was a pretty one, but the woman was prettier still. He took them under his protection. Quilacou died of his wounds, but De Soto married Golden Star, and it proved a marriage of love as well as of profit. Golden Star was in fact the only daughter of a rich Peruvian lord, and she brought her husband a dowry that the most fortunate heiresses of Castile would have envied: gold and silver mines and a multitude of laborers.

On the day Cuzco was taken, Pedro de Barco, a cavalier, entered the gate of the House of the Virgins, who were consecrated to the Sun. There were ten thousand women there! Pedro de Barco set his heart on the one who seemed to him the most beautiful. Passive and smiling, she followed the *caballero*. Was he not the victor? She surrendered. One evening in the main square of Cuzco she observed a number of Spanish soldiers about to cast dice for a golden disk representing the Sun—the effigy of Inti! The vestal could not be witness to such profanation without trembling with horror. The Sun must be saved. This girl, so fragile and so gentle, who had asked nothing of Pedro de Barco until then, was seen to throw herself into his arms, carried away by religious rage. Was he going to allow this sacrilegious game to continue? Had he forgotten that she was still the wife of the Sun? Pedro de Barco shrugged his shoulders. A feminine whim—but he was in love, and what will a man not do for the woman he loves? The Spaniard approached the players, took part in the game, made his throw and won. Pedro de Barco took the shining image back to his wife, but the next day Francisco Pizarro demanded that Pedro de Barco hand over the golden disk, for it had been decided that this symbol of Inca fetishism should be smashed to pieces with hammer blows in the public square before the eyes of the assembled populace. Pedro did not keep them waiting long for his reaction, which was a surprising one for a Spanish cavalier of the sixteenth century. In defiance of discipline and the Faith, he fled with the Indian woman and the disk of the Sun. Love had been stronger than honor.

Pizarro's men rushed in pursuit of the fugitives. The two young people, escorted by a few old priests, took turns carrying the image of the god, but the galloping troop drew nearer. Pedro and his companions reached the shores of Lake Titicaca, but the horsemen were at their heels. Time was short and they had to move fast. They found two pirogues, tied them together with lianas, and laid the golden disk inside. Then they leaped into the boats and drew away from the shore, straining on their oars. Twilight enveloped the raft of the lovers, which went slowly among the rushes. Then torches lit the bank and a boat moved out from it—then two boats, then three. Their wakes traced long luminous tracks on the sacred lake. The two lovers were surrounded, but just as the Spanish boats were about to overtake them, Pedro and his companion lifted the disk and hurled it into the water. Before being captured and without doubt put to death, they had at least saved the god. But instead of sinking to the bottom, the golden disk toppled, rose up, and for an instant stood upright on the waves, no longer yellow, but purple with all the flame of the setting sun. The Spanish cavaliers set up a loud cry of amazement, then the disk tottered, overturned, and sank into the depths. Inti was dead.

While this great drama was taking place, Pedro and the Indian woman had been able to escape from their pursuers and were now beyond reach. It was dark. The hours passed and dawn drew near. Pedro murmured to his love: "The image of your god has sunk. Will it ever cease to haunt the minds of men?" In response the vestal pointed to the horizon and smiled; the first rays of day were beginning to gild the surface of the lake. Having died the day before in crimson glory, the god was reborn in all the youthful beauty of morning.

Under the Pretense of Religion

"*So color de religión—van á buscar plata y oro—del encubierto tesoro . . .* ": "Under the pretense of religion, they went in search of silver and gold and of hidden treasure." These harsh words of Lope de Vega in his play *El Nuevo Mundo* calls for comment, if not for correction. Certainly the injustices and the crimes committed in the name of religion revolt the heart as well as the conscience. Certainly the Conquistadors used the instruments of the Faith to further their ventures. Thus Ovando, when fighting in Cuba, had given the signal to an ambush by placing his hand on his cross of the Knights of Alcántara, while Valverde warned Pizarro's soldiers that the moment of attack had come by waving the Bible at Atahualpa. The system of *requerimiento* inflicted on the primitive people, the mass baptisms, the conversions *in extremis* that preceded strangulation, the expiatory stake, and the massacres that ended in the *Te Deum* seem to justify the words of one Indian, exhorted by a monk to die in the Christian faith: "Are there Spaniards in your Paradise? Then I prefer to die a heathen!" Who would dream of denying that the ceremonial of the liturgy often took on the appearance of a funeral procession? But Lope de Vega was wrong on one pont: the violent acts of the Conquistadors—abduction, robberies, assassinations—though sometimes performed "in the name of" religion, were never "under the pretense of" religion.

The Conquistadors were sincere. The legality of the enterprise was guaranteed them by pontifical bulls. They had been given to understand that they were leaving for a crusade—the one against Islam having ended but recently—and that after the Jew and the Moham-

medan, it was now a question of converting the Heathen. They had
been born into a hatred and terror of heresy. They had wept with
delight at the capture of Granada, trembled before the Inquisition,
and shuddered at the very name of Luther. While still children, they
had often spat at the passing of a Moor or set fire to the booth of a
Jew. Spain in the sixteenth century was nothing but a vast monastery,
noisy with orisons and bells. They had grown up in the shadow of
cathedrals and breathed the odor of incense from their earliest years,
while the first words they had uttered had been the names of the
saints.

The Conquistadors, although for the most part illiterate, had had
no need of letters to feel the same fanatical spirit as did the horsemen of the Prophet when they invaded the old Greco-Latin world,
or the Crusaders when they spread over the Syrian plains, or their
own fathers at the reconquest of Granada. They had been told—
they had been convinced—that millions of Indians would burn forever in Hell if they, the Conquistadors, did not bring them the
Faith. They believed this quite simply. Religion was for them not
a pretext but a banner. The existence of God in three persons, the
immortality of the soul, sin, the Last Judgment—it never occurred
to any one of them to dispute these facts or even to discuss them.
These men of war and passion had retained the faith of little children.
Their confessions were sincere, they participated in the Mass not
only in the flesh but also in the spirit. The worst of them died in
penitence. Pierced by arrows, or with a sword blade in the throat,
or tied to the stake under torture, they called loudly for the last rites.
So color de religión. . . . What an error! No ulterior motive colored
the faith of the Conquistadors. They remained men of the Middle
Ages. Religious hypocrisy had not yet been invented; it was to turn
up later, covering iniquity with its black cloak. The hypocrite is a
creature of the seventeenth century.

The Conquistadors believed in God fiercely and unreservedly.
But they believed also—above all else!—in the Devil. Now, the New
World was the empire of the Devil, a Devil with multiform face,
always hideous. The somber Mexican divinities, Huitzilopochtli (the
Sorcerer-Hummingbird) and Tezcatlipoca (the Smoking Mirror),
the horrible Kinich Kakmo of the Mayas, the Peruvian Viracocha
who symbolized boiling lava, the sinister totems of the Araucanians

and Diaguites. . . . Why, the medieval demon with short horns, lustful eye, and a tail that was curled like a vine shoot seemed a "good devil" besides such as these! Spaniards who in Estremaduran twilights had taken the flight of a bat for the passing of the Evil One were naturally terrified before these monsters of stone, with bared fangs and gleaming eyes, that seemed to come to fantastic life as night fell. How could they have watched an Aztec ceremony without nausea? The black-robed priests with matted hair, burrowing with their knives in the breasts of their victims, the human skulls piled up at the feet of the teocallis, the cannibal feasts around statues spattered with putrid blood, and the charnel-house stench which all the perfumes of Mexico were never able to hide. . . .

Such things froze the spirits of the Conquistadors, surpassing the nightmares of their childhoods. Satan himself was there, and his worship was celebrated among the dismembered corpses. His maleficent power was honored. He was no longer, as in Spain, the familiar accomplice that could be driven off by a flick of the finger, or the shameful specter slipping furtively through one's conscience but put to flight by a sprinkling of holy water. He was enthroned. Carved in granite, incrusted with precious stones and encircled with golden serpents, he was the superb incarnation of Evil. He glorified sin. Nothing was lacking in this perfect representation of Hell, not even the pots in which certain tribes of the Colombian jungle cooked their enemies alive. This indeed was Satan himself, adorned with all his lugubrious attractions.

Why, therefore, should we be astonished at the reactions of the Spaniards? In the depths of the Indian sanctuaries they could see the Prince of Darkness standing in all his macabre splendor. Looking heavenward, they could distinguish the silvery figure of Saint James galloping across the clouds. The conflict between the true and the false, between good and evil, was manifest in this double apparition. The problem was simple and their duty was clear. The Indians were possessed of the Devil, who had to be exorcised, first by destroying the material evidence of Devil worship. This is why the conquerors, activated by the same blind zeal as early Christians when they shattered the Roman statues, overturned the pre-Columbian idols and burned the ritual articles and the manuscripts that transmitted the sacred tradition—in short, showed a holy ardor to abolish the very memory of the heathen liturgy. This they counted as pious work and a salutary need.

Iconoclasts? Vandals? These epithets would have scandalized the Conquistadors. Who would have applied such words except the agents of Satan who served a vile master? But the Conquistadors did not limit themselves to casting down the idols. In order that the exorcism be fully effective, it was not enough to drive away the demons; it was proper also to set up in their places the symbols of the True Faith. Just as holy medals were laid upon flesh that was eaten away with ulcers, the soldiers of Charles V planted crosses on the tops of the teocallis or at crossroads. On the stones that were still spattered with blood from the sacrificial tables, they raised altars to Our Lady of Guadalupe. Tolerance was not for them. Others would follow who would use gentler methods. No one doubts that these booted and armored Christians often lacked the Christian spirit and that charity was almost always missing from their pitiless fervor; but their Faith and their good faith were whole. More even than the love of God and of one's neighbor, the horror of Beelzebub explains certain of the Conquistadors' attitudes, though of course it is understood that to explain is not to absolve.

Gold and Blood

The Conquistadors never ceased to oscillate between the opposing poles of idealism and realism. Were they dreamers or men of action? Does a passion for dreaming master the taste for action? Where does dreaming end and action begin? There is no end to argument on these themes, but the fact remains that from the day the Conquistadors set foot on American soil, they made clear their intention not to be simple voyagers, but to establish themselves there and to remain there. They did not wait until they had finished the war before beginning the peace—by building. During the period between the conquest and colonization, in the middle of the sixteenth century, the conquerors laid the foundations of the colonial edifice which the colonists, later, had the task of completing. To be builders and architects beyond compare, these pursuers of mirages had to be practical men as well.

The first Spanish constructions in the New World were, of course, churches and palaces for the king's representatives, but houses, hospitals, and barracks very quickly arose from the earth as if by magic. Manpower was plentiful and skilled, for masonry and stonework were the arts in which the natives excelled. However, on the instructions of the king himself, the Spaniards at once imposed a special style upon town planning, one that differed completely from the local type of dwelling. This was the famous "checkerboard" plan, inspired by Greco-Latin traditions. The style was simple: a central quadrangular main plaza with a church, municipal buildings, and school. Parallel roads intersected at right angles and formed a regular pattern of squares. Thus the Spaniards transplanted into America an architectural style bequeathed them by their Roman occupiers, who in turn had reproduced Greek models—a curious survival of a scheme some thousands of years old which, revived by Vitruvius and adapted by Hernán Cortés, turned Mexico into a reproduction of the Piraeus.

Had they done nothing but discover the New World, conquer territories, found cities, and teach millions of natives to revere the name of Christ and that of Charles V, the Conquistadors would have done well by their country. These exploits justified such royal favors as commanderies, the Cross of Santiago, spurs of honor, and marquisates. But the ruler would not have looked on his overseas captains in such a friendly fashion if he had not gained the most precious substance of all: gold. The conquerors were the seekers and purveyors of gold for the kings of Spain.

The Spaniards had always been seekers of gold. Far back into antiquity, in fact, gold mines had been exploited in the Iberian peninsula. Strabo spoke of this in his *Geography*. Pliny was more precise. He explained the technique for the treatment of gold at that time: "It is crushed, washed, burned, ground, and finally treated in a mortar," and that was the method still in use in the sixteenth century. The Spaniards therefore knew that gold could be found either in the form of grains or nuggets, mixed with sand or included in sulphites such as quartz. Grains of gold were extracted from rivers or alluvial deposits. Gold incorporated in sulphites was mined. When the Conquistadors arrived in America, the Indians were also familiar with gold, but they preferred to seek it in the rivers. The process which they commonly used was that of "washing." They ran water over the inclined floor of a sort of trough and into it threw the powdered matter containing the gold. The gold fell to the bottom and was held by a screen. When it was washed clear of particles of soil, the gold was smelted with four times its weight of silver. The resulting alloy was then treated with boiling concentrated sulphuric acid—they used sulphur from volcanoes—which dissolved all metals other than gold. This was the refining process. Both operations were known to the Spaniards, although for refining they also used an older process cited by Pliny, which substituted for sulphuric acid a mixture of copper sulphate, schist, and saltpeter.

Thus the Spaniards knew no more than the Indians about the extraction of gold, but they perfected the system and made it more efficient. To begin with, they discovered a new principle of purification: the "patio amalgamation." The auriferous material was pounded by teams of women and old men. It was then placed on a paved surface called an *arrastra*, surrounded by a rim. Beasts trampled the now muddy mineral. It was sprinkled with water, mercury was added, then a final bath separated the gold from its impurities. The Spaniards were not content merely to improve the technique; they created a gold industry. Under their stimulus, the American earth brought forth its hidden treasure. As the technique of seeking gold in the rivers seemed to them archaic and its results inadequate, the conquerors increased the exploitation of mines. Thousands of natives were allocated to this terrible labor of digging into the mountains, extracting the sulphites with picks, crushing them by hand, and pulverizing them in mills. Then came the washing and the refining: a gentle task compared with that of the slaves of gold beneath the earth.

When the Conquistadors arrived in Mexico, they were surprised to note that the Aztecs extracted only silver. Gold did not seem to be of much interest to them. Doubtless the reserves accumulated by the Aztlan dynasties were sufficient for them, or they thought they had exhausted the resources of the Mexican subsoil. In any case, this did not suit the Spaniards. Would they let the Aztecs rest on the heap of gold piled up by their ancestors? The first concern of the conquerors was to set the Indians to working the gold—without, however, abandoning silver, which was also worth acquiring.

It was Carvajal, an officer under Francisco Pizarro, who discovered the famous Potosí mines in Bolivia, south of La Paz, at nearly 14,000 feet elevation. At the summit of this mountain of silver, the Spaniards built the highest town in the world. Under a colorless sky, houses in the Andalusian style raised their arabesques around the yawning pits. Prison and fortress at the same time, the *Casa de la Moneda* (mint) symbolized—by its heavy door and oppressive silence—the power of the Lion of Castile. Here a whole miserable people, secluded forever, made the king of Spain's silver money. It was better, however— a hundred times better—to live and die between the cyclopean walls of the Casa de la Moneda than to go down into the mines. There men labored as once the slaves of Solomon labored in the Manica mines that were dug for the Queen of Sheba. Some of the Peruvian mines, with their dark figures ceaselessly toiling up and down, recall Michelangelo's "Last Judgment," in which terrorized groups of human beings seem to form a sinister chain.

To smell out gold required enthusiasm and patience. What an event it was when the searcher for gold or silver—the *cateador*— thought he had discovered a mine! All activity in the surrounding country was suspended, shops were shut, the schoolmaster dismissed his pupils, the padre ordered the bells rung, and Indians and Spaniards raced toward the site of the miracle. If the find was confirmed, a feast was held at the very place where the vein had appeared, and if there had been a mistake, everyone returned home, only a little disappointed, so strong had been the emotion. It was a curious fact that Spaniards and natives showed the same joyful excitement, al- though for the latter gold had no more value—even less, being of secondary utility—than copper or lead. Moreover, for them the discovery of a nugget foretold the martyrdom of the mine. It is probable that the Spaniards communicated to the Indians their fever for gold and that they thought it a good thing to spread the mirage of Eldorado.

The gold thus discovered, extracted, washed, refined, molded into ingots, and placed in chests or barrels, had now to be transported to Spain, and the caravels, which once had been the messengers of hope and the vehicles of the discovery, now played a new role as carriers of gold. The fifteenth century was not ended before a double movement of caravels became organized between Spain and the New World. There were those that set out and those that returned, and those that started were more numerous than those that came back.

In August 1492 three caravels—the *Santa María,* the *Pinta,* and the *Niña*—left the port of Palos. The moment was a solemn one. Repulsed successively by the Portuguese, French, and English, to whom he had offered the keys to the New World, a Genoese adventurer started off on the golden road on behalf of the King of Castile. These three caravels were the first. In 1506 there were twenty-two, in 1507 thirty-two, and in 1508 there were forty-five. There were only seventeen in 1510, but then there arrived at Seville the astonishing news that Grijalva, having landed in Yucatán, had encountered natives who, in exchange for shoddy goods, had given gold—mere crumbs, it seemed, of the heaps that could be found farther west. Some months later, Cortés, who had made contact with Montezuma's emissaries, confirmed the rumor. The consequences of this information were soon manifest: in 1520 seventy-one caravels crossed the Atlantic; and Charles V, for his twentieth birthday, received the respectable amount of about 13 hundredweights of gold from the future victor of Mexico. Eighteen years earlier his grandmother, Isabella the Catholic, had failed to receive a half ton of gold from Bobadilla, governor of Haiti, a large part of the load having been lost en route. In short, the number of ships that were fitted out for the West Indies and the frequency of their crossings varied in proportion to the traffic in American gold.

A departure from Seville about the year 1540: what a bustle upon the quay! The families of the sailors rub shoulders with hidalgos who have financed the expedition, merchants who have provided the merchandise, and Jewish moneylenders seeking last-moment business. Embraces, final injunctions, tears, and the rocking of the caravels in the violet waters of the port.

The time is past when such ships sailed alone, for the experience was a cruel one. In the space of twelve years, only 270 vessels had come back to Spain of the 490 that had left. Nearly half had been lost! Storms, contrary currents, and reefs had taken their toll, but men had been the cause quite as much as nature. First, the fleets of rival nations or those at war—hot or cold—with Spain. French ships, for instance, lay in wait for the caravels near the Canaries. Returning from his third voyage, Columbus just missed being stopped off Cape St. Vincent. Yet more formidable than the regular squadrons of Francis I and Henry VIII were the corsairs, who operated either on

their own behalf or on that of the nations who were enemies of
Spain and Portugal. In the latter event, they held a commission in
good and proper form, and of course levied an honest share of the
prize. The danger of piracy was nothing new. Even at the beginning
of the century, Ferdinand the Catholic had defended himself by
having strong carracks built after the fashion of the Portuguese and
by posting armed vessels at the Canaries. But the most serious incident had been that in which Verrazzano the Florentine, sailing in
a French ship, had captured three caravels containing Montezuma's
treasure, sent to the emperor by Cortés. To provide against such dis-
asters, costly to the treasury and detrimental to Spanish prestige,
Charles V had ordered that merchant ships should be convoyed by
men-of-war. The sovereign's decision concealed a malicious ulterior
motive. While protecting the merchant ships against corsairs, the
escorting ships at the same time kept watch over them and brought
them safely to the port to which they were consigned. They also
brought them back quite faithfully to the port of departure, so there
was no longer the opportunity for certain dealers to sell their cargoes
in foreign ports. The ships had to unload at Sanlúcar, Seville, or
Cádiz under the eyes of the clerks of the Casa de Contratación, and it
was not easy to swindle His Majesty's bookkeepers.

The armada of the Indies draws away. It is a proud sight with its
graceful caravels and heavy carracks. A captain of highest rank commands the fleet: Blasco Núñez Vela, the future viceroy. The ships
are so heavily laden—stuffs of many colors, glass trinkets, gaudy laces
—that they sink low into the water. How much will they weigh when
all this rubbish has been exchanged for bars of gold! The fleet passes
south of the Canaries, meets the trade winds, and steers straight for
Cuba. Until now there has been nothing to fear, for the corsairs no
longer risk attacking Spanish ships in the middle of the Atlantic.
It is not that they have given up the pursuit, but simply that they
have moved their hiding place: they now await the ships at the very
gates of the New World. For these are indeed gateways which,
across the Antillean archipelago, open wide their doors upon America. Two doors: one, the Florida channel between Havana and the
Bahamas, gives access to the Gulf of Mexico; and the other, the
Windward channel between Cuba and Haiti, commands the entry

to the Caribbean Sea. It is by this second route that the galleons reach Nombre de Dios, the point of departure for Peru.

Thus, having reached the islands, the fleet divides into two: one part goes to seek gold in Mexico, while the other steers for the Isthmus of Panama to take delivery of gold from Peru and silver from the Potosí mines. As soon as the news of the arrival of Spanish ships in the port of Nombre de Dios reaches Lima, the viceroy of Peru gives orders for the fleet anchored at Callao to sail up the Pacific coast to Panama. The cargoes of gold and silver are unloaded and transported on muleback across the isthmus to Nombre de Dios, and then there is nothing more to do but fill the caravels.

It was therefore in the region of the Caribbean Sea that the corsairs prowled. They were numerous and of all nationalities. There were Frenchmen, the legendary Brethren of the Coast, established on the small island of Tortuga off the coast of Haiti. They harassed the Spaniards and maintained the French in the West Indies. They were the ancestors of the celebrated *seigneurs* of Haiti, the gentlemen of Guadaloupe, and the fine people of Martinique of the eighteenth century. There were Englishmen, above all: Hawkins of Plymouth, Reneger of Southampton, and Francis Drake, that king of pirates, whom Elizabeth made a knight as a reward for his services. At San Juan de Ulúa and Nombre de Dios, and on the Colombian and Venezuelan coasts at Santa Marta and Cartagena, the raids multiplied. It was not until the reign of Philip II that a Spaniard, Pedro de Menéndez, organized a system of coast guards and protection for the convoys which proved effective for a while. Piracy did not end then, but lasted as long as the Spanish Empire itself. The pirates transmitted the tradition of adventure from one century to another. However much they changed their name, they were always the same: buccaneers in the seventeenth century or filibusters in the eighteenth, they ceased scouring the Caribbean Sea only when the Spaniards no longer passed that way. They always had mysterious and elusive accomplices: the sea, the night, and sometimes runaway slaves—like the *cimarrones* of Panama who, one evening in 1570, carried off one of the last treasures from Peru under the very noses of the Spanish sentries of Nombre de Dios.

The return to Seville: emptied of their trinkets, but heavily laden with Mexican gold and with silver from Potosí, the caravels have set course for Spain. They have passed through the narrow Antillean channels without falling into any corsair ambush, and are now steering in a northerly direction, carried along by the warm waters of the Gulf Stream, discovered by the pilot Alaminos. A flotilla coming straight from Colombia has joined them in the Sargasso Sea and they run alongside the Bermudas. When they reach the Azores, Europe is near. The escorting gunboat fires a shot from time to time to put to flight the pirates who, setting out from Dieppe, La Rochelle, or Saint-Malo, circle the galleons like cormorants. The Spanish coast comes into view, and already assembled on the quay are the officials of the Casa de Contratación to weigh and stamp the king's fifth, the merchants who supplied the cargo, the lords and the prelates, concessionaires of the New World, and the good people of Seville. It is such an exciting moment that social barriers are relaxed. The beggars of Triana and Andalusian dukes are elbow to elbow, and all have their eyes turned westward, awaiting the fleet. And here it is, the torrent of gold and silver which from Vera Cruz, Nombre de Dios, and Cartagena has cut its shining track across the sapphire-blue sea to mingle with the muddy waters of the Guadalquivir. The fleet has arrived.

A torrent of gold and silver it certainly was! Two figures will show its extent. From 1503 (the year in which Columbus completed his fourth voyage) until 1560 (that in which Francisco Fajardo laid the first stones of Caracas), the New World sent Spain 101 metric tons of gold, or nearly 225,000 pounds. Subsequently the exploitation of the Potosí mines must have multiplied the production of silver tenfold. In fact, from 1560 to 1600, 6872 metric tons—well over 15,000,000 pounds—of silver crossed the Atlantic. In forty years Spain received double the stock of silver existing in Europe before Columbus. If to the precious metals are added the Aztec jewels, the emeralds of Bogotá, the pearls of Venezuela, the beaver skins of New Mexico, the precious woods of Guiana, the indigo, vanilla, and cacao of the islands, one might think that Midas and Croesus are small figures besides Charles V. In contrast with such a torrent, the Pactolus was merely a trickle.

But the wealth of Spain was only temporary, and she was not long in feeling the drawbacks of such prodigious wealth. The abundance of gold caused a rise in prices, without an equivalent stimulus to production. A large part of the monetary wealth remained sterile. The great landed proprietors, enriched by speculation, preferred to live on their capital rather than invest it in agricultural works. The nobility, resting on its laurels, disdained labor and allowed its domains to lie fallow. Certain hidalgos of high rank were even to become moneylenders at high rates of interest, instead of increasing the revenues of their estates. Furthermore, a numerous clergy had to be maintained, as well as increasingly heavier administration and the crowd of parasites who encumbered the antechambers of the Escorial in search of pensions or benefices.

Nothing is more costly than a *politique* of grandeur. This does not mean that Spain died of hunger on its heap of gold, but in order to live on the level of a Great Power—that is, to keep her rank in Europe, and especially to provide for the needs of her American empire—she had to buy abroad what she could not make at home: flax and hemp from Normandy, canvas from Brittany, sailcloth from Saint-Brieuc, cloth from England, and hardwood for shipbuilding from the Baltic. Thus the gold and silver imported from America were exported, in the form of coins, to France, England, and Holland to pay for the merchandise necessary to the homeland and the empire. The consequences of this state of affairs were paradoxical. While the Spain of Philip II and Philip III was at war with the rebellious Low Countries, Anglican England, and Huguenot France, the merchants of those same countries were actively trading with Seville. But that is nothing new! The Spanish imports of goods were so considerable that they had the effect of stimulating the industry of the three enemy nations and contributing to their prosperity. Simultaneously the foe and the client of France, England, and the Low Countries, Spain was to end by being nothing but a dumping-ground for gold between the Atlantic and the Pyrenees until such time as the power founded on the metal yielded irremediably to the power founded on industry.

But before it experienced these vicissitudes, Spain had half a century in which to extract the best part of America's gold. Charles V's plan in 1540 was not only to enrich his inheritance. He had even more wonderful ambitions. The three crowns he had assumed—those of Charlemagne, of Lombardy, and of the Romans—were not enough. He wanted to dominate the world. While the crowns of the

Capetians and the Tudors still shone in the European sky, Charles had not accomplished the task for which he believed he was destined. He needed gold not for investment or to transform into manufactured products, but to pay as ready money for military supplies, soldiers, and arms. In short, he needed gold to make war. Thanks to the immediately available metal, Charles V kept France in check, though she was twice as populous as Spain, much richer in natural resources, and had a regular army of 2500 men-at-arms concentrated on national territory, in contrast to 1900 Spaniards dispersed throughout the Iberian peninsula, the Kingdom of Naples, and Holland. But France was short of specie, while Charles was glutted with it, and thus it was possible for him, by mobilizing the forces of his empire, to bring a permanent threat to bear upon the French and English monarchies. To the 1900 infantry and 3000 light cavalry of his army in time of peace, Charles added several thousands of mercenaries, whom he had the means to buy. One galleon from America paid for a regiment. Charles had won the battle for gold.

A century later, Colbert, that dark, seedy, genial little man, who had been exasperated by Spanish manners, made the following bitter remark: "We see the reigns of Charles V, Philip II, Philip III, and even Philip IV in such abundance of money through the discovery of the West Indies that all Europe has seen the House of a simple Austrian archduke achieve, in the space of sixty or eighty years, sovereignty over all the States of Burgundy, Aragon, Castile, Portugal, Naples, and Milan; has seen her add to all these States the crown of England and Ireland by the marriage of Philip to Mary Tudor; make the Empire almost hereditary; challenge the pre-eminence of our kings to the crown; by secret practices and by arms, place our kingdom in imminent peril of passing into the hands of foreigners; and finally, aspire to the Empire of all Europe—that is, of the whole world." That Spain was rich irritated this French patriot, but that she should spend without thinking provoked him even more. To this devotee of economy, it was something rather immoral and upsetting, for Colbert had no liking for people who lived beyond their means.

One last look at the Conquistadors. We know now how and why they lived. But how did they die? In opulence and glory? One imagines sumptuous places of retirement, or at least comfortable ones, for the captains of the conquest who had returned home with their fortunes made. They would restore the family *solar*, and those who were literate would write their memoirs. Those who were nostalgic for power would hold some honorary position at court; and as for the soldiers—those without rank—they would return to their villages in La Mancha and Estremadura. They would be rich and would buy land, and in the course of endless social gatherings they would relate their campaigns, telling the stories of the Caribbean, of treasure and princesses. They would willingly show their enormous scars, for such wounds were not to be seen every day. Think of it! Scimitars of sharpened obsidian, and darts poisoned with the juice of the manchineel tree! And they would blow out great clouds of smoke from their pipes of Mexican tobacco. . . .

But the reality was quite different. The majority of the Conquistadors died while still in action, by accident, sickness, or violence. Those who survived ended their days in oblivion and, some of them, in poverty. That so melancholy and wretched a fate should have distinguished these enterprises, which at the beginning had been so full of promise, seems scarcely credible. Yet examples abound, and here are some of them, chosen from the most illustrious.

First the Discoverer himself, Christopher Columbus: he died at Valladolid, cast out by the king whose glory he had made. Juan de la Cosa, the father of Atlantic pilots, died riddled with arrows. Núñez de Balboa was beheaded, on his father-in-law's orders. Díaz de Solís was stoned to death. Nicuesa was lost at sea. Ponce de León died of an arrow in the heart. Hernandez de Córdoba was mortally wounded by Indians. Hernando de Soto was carried off by fever. Pedro de Alvarado was crushed by a horse. Juan de Escalante was killed by the natives of Vera Cruz. Hernán Cortés died poor and alone in an Andalusian village. Pánfilo de Narváez was drowned. Pedro de Valdivia was devoured by cannibals. Bastidas was stabbed by one of his own lieutenants. Diego de Ordaz died of sunstroke. Pedro de Mendoza died at sea.

And what happened to the Conquistadors of Peru? Hernando Pizarro ordered Almagro garroted; the latter's son assassinated Francisco Pizarro; Vaca de Castro had the younger Almagro beheaded; and Gonzalo Pizarro, before being condemned to death by Gasca, killed Núñez de Vela. Fifty captains were hanged. Not one of those who governed Peru during a quarter of a century, except Gasca, died other than by violence.

We know now that the alliance of Spain and the New World was sealed with blood. We know, too, that those who profited greatly by the venture were not legion. Is it true, then, that wealth acquired by violence never brings happiness and that there is a curse on gold acquired unjustly? A shadow passes over the flamboyant façade of the temple of Mammon: is it the disheveled figure of the goddess Nemesis?

The drama is ended. The curtain falls slowly on a pyramid of corpses, as in the last act of a Shakespearean tragedy. It is finished, but another play is about to begin. What is its prologue?

The difficult day of the conquest has just ended in a blaze of gold and blood. *Oro y sangre*—a funereal apotheosis! Night descends upon the battlefield of the Conquistadors, and silence follows. But at dawn, into the shadows that slowly pale, phantoms slip one by one. Then day is here, and the morning light falls gradually upon these new beings, lighting their resolute features with its silver gleam. They wear neither helmet nor breastplate, but robes of monkish homespun or the sober doublets of men of law. They carry no swords, but in their hands is the mason's trowel or the ivory staff of the alcalde or the cavalier's lance. At first there are only a few, but soon a numberless crowd emerges from the shadows. They gather up the dead and bury them. The battlefield has become a cemetery. Then, in serried ranks, elbow to elbow, like the Spartan phalanxes, they move off westward. These are the colonists.

Seville, March 1951
Paris, July 1953

CHRONOLOGY

SPANISH OFFICIALS

PLACE NAMES IN USE AT THE
TIME OF THE CONQUEST

INDEX

B.C.
10,000 The submergence of Atlantis?

A.D.
30 The Crucifixion.

200-300 Middle Civilizations in Mexico.

476 Collapse of the Western Roman Empire.

507 Clovis I defeated the West Goths and endeavored to unite all Frankish people in one kingdom.

500-700 The Toltecs reach the valley of Mexico.

800 Charlemagne crowned Emperor of the West.

900 Invasion of Mexico by the Chichimecs.

900-1000 Quetzalcoatl, at the head of the Toltecs, conquers Yucatán and subdues the Tzentals, Itzals, and Mayas.
Quetzalcoatl moves southward and disappears.

1000 Cuzco founded by Manco Capac and Mama Oclo, coming from Lake Titicaca.

1100 Formation of the Inca Empire.

1168 Beginning of the Aztec migration and the invention of the Mexican calendar.

1227 Death of Genghis Khan, founder of the first Mongol Empire.

1232 Foundation of the Chichimec dynasty at Texcoco.

1236 Capture of Córdoba by Ferdinand III of Castile.

1271 Departure from Venice of Marco, Nicolo, and Matteo Polo for India and China.

1279 Kublai, the Great Khan, grandson of Genghis Khan, subdues all China.

1294 Death of Kublai.

1295 Marco Polo's return to Venice.

1350 Foundation of Tenochtitlán, capital of Mexico.

1368 The Mongol dynasty of the Yüans, founded by Kublai, is supplanted by that of the Mings.

1375 Appearance of the "Catalan World Map."

1418-72 Reign of Netzhualcoyotl at Texcoco.

1422 Charles VII ascends the French throne.

1431 Joan of Arc is burned at the stake at Rouen.

c. 1436 Invention of printing by Gutenberg.

1440 Montezuma I succeeds Itzcoatl.

1450 Tupac Yupanqui begins the Inca wars of conquest in the direction of Chile.

1451 Columbus born at Genoa (?).

1452 Birth of Leonardo da Vinci.

1453 End of the Hundred Years' War.
Capture of Constantinople by Mohammed II.

1460 Death of Prince Henry the Navigator.

1461 Death of Charles VII of France; Louis XI succeeds him.

1469 Axayacatl succeeds Montezuma I. Construction of the great stone calendar.
Ferdinand the Catholic marries Isabella of Castile.

1470 Beginning of Chibcha supremacy over the other tribes occupying the territory of Colombia.

1474 Isabella the Catholic becomes Queen of Castile.
Columbus writes to Toscanelli.

c. 1478 Francisco Pizarro born at Trujillo.

1482 Death of Toscanelli.

1483 Columbus's visit to King John II of Portugal. Louis XI of France dies; Charles VIII succeeds him.

1484 Columbus leaves Portugal for Spain. He takes his son Diego to the monastery of La Rábida.
Diogo Cão discovers the Condo.

1485 Accession of the Tudors (Henry VII) in England.
Birth of Cortés at Medellín.

387

1486   Columbus is received by the Catholic monarchs at Córdoba.
He meets Beatriz Enríquez de Harana.

1487   Bartholomeu Diaz rounds the Cape of Good Hope.

1488   Birth at Córdoba of Hernando Columbus, son of Christopher and of Beatriz de Harana.

1491   Birth of Loyola.
Columbus goes to the Santa Fe camp to find the Catholic monarchs.

1492   Death at Florence of Lorenzo de' Medici, "the Magnificent."
Alexander VI (Rodrigo Borgia) becomes Pope.
Martin Behaim constructs a globe.

Jan.   2   Capture of Granada by the Catholic monarchs.

Mar. 31   Proscription of the Jews.

Apr. 17   Santa Fe convention.

May 12   Columbus goes to Palos.

Aug.   3   Columbus raises anchor.

     9   Columbus halts at the Canaries because of rudder trouble on the *Pinta*.

Sept.   6   Columbus leaves the Canaries.

    17   First illusion of land.

    25   Second illusion of land.

Oct.   7   Third illusion of land.

    12   Columbus discovers America (actually Watlings Island in the Bahamas, B.W.I.).

    15   Columbus discovers Santa María de la Concepción.

    16   Columbus discovers Isabella.

    27   Columbus discovers Cuba.

Nov. 21   Martín Alonso separates from the fleet.

Dec.   6   Columbus discovers Hispaniola (Haiti).

    24   The *Santa María* runs aground. The building of the fort of La Navidad is started.

1493
Jan.   4   The *Niña* leaves La Navidad.

    6   The *Pinta* is found again.

    16   Columbus starts the return to Spain.

1493 (*continued*)
Feb. 14   Terrible storm. The *Pinta* disappears again.

    18   The *Niña* calls at Santa María in the Azores.

Mar. 15   The *Niña* and *Pinta* return to Palos.

Apr. 15(?)   Columbus is received by the Catholic monarchs at Barcelona.

May   2   Bull from Pope Alexander VI fixing the Spanish and Portuguese zones of influence.

Sept. 25   Columbus's second departure, from Cádiz.

Nov. 12-25   Columbus discovers the Lesser Antilles: Dominica, Marigalante, Guadalupe, Once Mil Vírgenes, Montserrat, Santa María la Redonda, Santa María la Antigua, Deseada, Puerto Rico.

Dec.   7   Isabella is founded.

1494
Mar. 12   Columbus sets out for the mountain of Cibao, Haiti.

May 13   Columbus discovers Jamaica.

June   7   Treaty of Tordesillas between Spain and Portugal, fixing the spheres of influence of the two countries.

1495
Apr. 10   Pragmatic Sanction by the Catholic monarchs, giving freedom of trade to all Spaniards.

1496
Mar. 10   Columbus leaves for Spain.

June 11   Columbus lands at Cádiz on his return from his second voyage.

August   Columbus is received by the Catholic monarchs at Burgos.

1497
June   2   Royal edict modifying the Pragmatic Sanction of April 10, 1495, in favor of Columbus.
Vasco da Gama rounds the Cape of Good Hope.

1498
May 30 Columbus leaves Sanlucar de Barrameda on his third voyage.
July 31 Columbus discovers the island of Trinidad.
Aug. 2 Columbus enters the Gulf of Paria, finds himself in the delta of the Orinoco, and sets foot on the American continent.
15 Columbus discovers the island of Margarita.
30 Columbus arrives at Hispaniola.
1499 Venezuela is discovered in the spring by Alonso de Ojeda, Juan de la Gosa, and Amerigo Vespucci.
1500 Huayna Capac, son of Tupac Yupanqui, conquers the kingdom of Quito.
Vicente Yáñez Pinzón discovers the coast of Brazil. Pedro Alvares Cabral also reaches Brazil.
Feb. 24 Birth of Charles I of Spain, later Charles V, Holy Roman Emperor.
Aug. 27 Bobadilla arrives in Hispaniola.
Nov. 25 Columbus and his two brothers, in chains, arrive at Cádiz.
Dec. 17 Columbus and his brothers are received by the Catholic monarchs at Granada.

1502
Feb. Nicolás de Ovando leaves for Hispaniola.
May 11 Columbus leaves Cádiz on his fourth voyage.
June 15 Columbus sights the island of Santa Lucia and Matinino (Martinique).
July 30 Columbus discovers Honduras.
Montezuma II becomes Aztec emperor.

1504
Nov. 7 Columbus returns to Sanlúcar de Barrameda.
Death of Isabella the Catholic.

1506
May 21 Death of Columbus.

1513 Ponce de León discovers Florida.
Sept. 6 Balboa sets out from the Bay of San Miguel (Panama isthmus) to discover the Southern Sea.
1515 Diego Velásquez and Pánfilo de Narváez found Havana.
1516 Death of Ferdinand; Charles I becomes King of Spain but is not formally recognized until 1518.
1517 Diego Velásquez lands at Yucatán.
Balboa is executed at Acla on the orders of Pedro Arias de Avila (Pedrarias Dávila), his father-in-law.
1519 Death of Leonardo da Vinci at Amboise.
Apr. 21 Cortés reaches San Juan de Ulúa.
Good Friday Cortés lands in Mexico.
Sept. 5 Battle of Tlaxcala.
20 Magellan leaves on his voyage around the world.
Nov. 1 Cortés masters Cholula and turns toward the city of Mexico.
8 Meeting of Cortés and Montezuma.

1520
Apr. 25 Pánfilo de Narváez lands at San Juan de Ulúa.
Cuauhtémoc succeeds Montezuma II.
June 25 The Spaniards are besieged in Mexico.
30 The Spaniards abandon Mexico; the Noche Triste.
Oct. 23 Charles is crowned Holy Roman Emperor as Charles V.
Magellan discovers the strait that bears his name.
1521 Magellan dies in the Philippines.
May 20 Cortés undertakes the siege of the city of Mexico.
Aug. 13 Final surrender of Mexico to the Spaniards.
1522 Magellan's expedition returns to Spain.
Oct. 15 Charles V appoints Cortés captain general, governor, and supreme chief of the Mexican expedition.

1522 (*continued*)
First expedition to Peru by Pascual de Andagoya.
1523 Pedro de Alvarado conquers Guatemala.
Sept. 12 Cuauhtémoc publishes the Texcoco "Charter for the dividing of the Great Lagoon."
1524 Accession of Tiquesusha, the last Chibcha *zipa* before the Spanish conquest.
González Dávila lands in Honduras.
Oct. 12 Cortés leaves for Honduras (Hibueras).
Nov. Francisco Pizarro embarks for Peru at Panama.
1525 Foundation of Santa María in Colombia by Rodrigo de Bastidas.
Feb. 28 Death of Cuauhtémoc.
1526 Cortés' expedition returns from Honduras.
Mar. 10 Almagro, Luque, and Pizarro make their contract at Chicame.
Lucas Vásquez de Ayllón attempts to explore Florida.
1527 Death of Machiavelli.
1527-31 Diego de Ordaz explores Guiana.
1528 Cortés goes to Spain to clear himself of the charges of which he has been accused. He receives the title of Marquis of the Valley of Oaxaca.
Creation of a Royal Audience at Mexico.
In the spring, Pizarro returns to Spain, and Charles V names him governor, captain general, and *alguazil mayor* for life, and *adelantado* of Peru.
Pánfilo de Narváez reaches Florida.
1529 Charles V signs a convention with Pizarro.
Alfinger, under mandate for the Welsers, bankers of Augsburg, explores Venezuela.
1530 Exploration and foundation of Culiacán by Guzmán.
Copernicus completes his study of the solar system.
1531 Atahualpa takes his brother Huáscar prisoner.
Death of Alfinger.

1532
Nov. 15 Pizarro reaches the valley of Cajamarca.
16 Pizarro's capture of Atahualpa.
1533
Jan. Pedro de Heredia founds Cartagena in Colombia.
Aug. 29 Death of Atahualpa.
Nov. 15 Pizarro's Spaniards penetrate Cuzco.
1535 New Spain becomes a viceroyalty under Antonio de Mendoza.
Aug. 24 Pedro de Mendoza leads an expedition to colonize the Río de la Plata, embarking at Bonanza.
Almagro founds Trujillo in northern Peru. Pizarro founds La Ciudad de Los Reyes (Lima).
Espira leaves in search of Eldorado.
Almagro undertakes the conquest of Chile.
1536 At the beginning of the year, Pedro de Mendoza founds Puerto de Nuestro Señora del Buen Aire (Buenos Aires).
Cortés discovers Lower California.
Apr. 6 An expedition under Gonzalo Jiménez de Quesada explores the Magdalena River and conquers the Chibcha empire and Bogotá.
1537
Apr. Almagro attacks Cuzco.
June Death of Mendoza.
Aug. Juan de Salazar founds Asunción, later capital of Paraguay.
Lorenzino assassinates Alessandro de' Medici, first Duke of Florence.
1537-57 Domingo Martínez de Irala governs Paraguay.
1538
Apr. 26 Almagro is defeated by Pizarro.
July Almagro is garroted by Pizarro.
Aug. 6 Jiménez de Quesada founds the city of Bogotá.

1539 Pedro de Valdivia is named lieutenant general of Chile by Pizarro.

Hernando de Soto lands in Florida.

1540 Cortés finally returns to Spain.

Valdivia leads an expedition into Chile.

García López de Cárdenas reaches the Grand Canyon of the Colorado.

Nikolaus Federmann sets out in search of Eldorado.

Francisco Vásquez Coronado reaches the frontier of Arizona.

1541 De Soto explores the Mississippi.

Feb. 12 Valdivia founds Santiago de Estremadura (the future Santiago de Chile).

June 16 Pizarro is assassinated by the followers of Diego Almagro (the Younger).

Francisco de Orillana crosses South America from the Pacific to the Atlantic.

Death of Alvarado.

1541-45 The bankers Welser explore the Río de la Plata.

1542 Death of De Soto in Florida.

Sept. 16 Diego Almagro (the Younger) is killed; end of the Almagrists.

1543
Aug.   Charles V appoints Núñez de Vela viceroy of Peru.

Death of Copernicus.

1547
Dec. 2 Cortés dies at Castilleja de la Cuesta in Andalusia.

1548 Gonzalo Pizarro is beheaded.

1550
Mar.   Valdivia founds the city of Concepción and reaches the Bío-Bío River.

1553
Dec.   Caupolican and Lautaro massacre the Spaniards at the fort of Tucapel.

1554
Jan.   Death of Valdivia.

1558 End of the Araucanian war and death of Caupolican.

1560 Francisco Fajardo founds Caracas, capital of Venezuela.

1562 Cortés' remains are transported to Mexico City.

1564 Death of Michelangelo. Birth of Galileo at Pisa.

1566 Death of Bartolomé de Las Casas.

1567 Diego de Losada, officer of Ponce de León, again founds Santiago de Léon de Caracas.

1573 Juan de Garay founds Santa Fe de la Vera Cruz in Argentina.

Jerónimo Luis de Cabrera founds Córdoba.

Adelantado: An untranslatable title, to which only the title of "president" could be compared, although the powers of a Spanish adelantado were not exactly similar to those of a president.

Alcalde: In Spain this name is given to certain judges or municipal magistrates whose functions are both civil and judicial. They are simultaneously mayor, justice of the peace, and commissioner of police. Their badge is a white rod surmounted by an ivory hand.

Alférez: Officer who bears the flag or standard.

Alguazil: By this word is implied a sort of provost marshal of the palace charged with arresting, judging, and punishing those guilty of an offense or those whom it pleased the king of Spain to hand over to this kind of expeditious justice. The name was also given to individuals charged with executing orders given by the Inquisition, the Orders of Chivalry, etc.

Auditor: Magistrate, member of the "royal audience," whose decrees were without appeal. The auditors intervened in the choice and appointment of several judicial officials, thus exercising control over the cabildos, consulates, governors, and administrators. They also intervened in conflicts of jurisdiction that broke out between secular and ecclesiastical tribunals. The viceroy was by right the president of the audience.

Corregidor: The leading judicial official of a Spanish town was thus named. When there was neither governor nor royal audience, this magistrate was simultaneously judge, administrator, and head of the municipal body. He thus enjoyed a real predominance that placed the entire government of a town or province at his mercy. The former corregidor has today become an alcalde.

At the time of the conquest of America, corregidors were appointed in the viceroyalties, and some of them were notable for their bad treatment of the natives. Nevertheless, their principal task was to aid the conquered Indians by providing them with the materials essential to their nourishment and maintenance.

Governor: Official appointed by the king. He filled the task of captain general of the place over which he ruled. He directed war operations, the administration of finance, public works, the founding of cities, and, like the viceroy, had the duty of watching over the propagation of Catholicism and good conduct in his province. The responsibility of appointing the alcalde fell to him.

Mestre de camp: Here translated as "colonel," designating the officer who commanded cavalry and infantry under the orders of the general.

Viceroy: The viceroy was appointed directly by the sovereign and was the only real representative of the Spanish monarch. His powers were the greater in proportion to the distance from the homeland. He had to spread the Catholic religion, administrate, govern, and direct justice; in the event of war he was captain general on sea and land.

PLACE NAMES IN USE
AT THE TIME OF THE CONQUEST

Africa

Fortunate Isles	Canary Islands

Asia

Cambaluc	Peking
Cathay	China
Cipango	Japan
Quinsay	Hankow

North America

Cibola, or the Land of the Seven Cities, or the Land of the Pueblos	Zuñi (modern Indian reservation)
Florida, or the Isle of Bimini	Florida
Meschacébé	Mississippi River
New Spain	Mexico
New Navarre and New Biscay	California coast

Central America and West Indies

Antilia, or the Island of the Seven Cities	West Indies
Baracoa	Santiago de Cuba
Borinquén	Puerto Rico
Hispaniola	Haiti
Juana	Cuba
Southern Sea	Pacific Ocean
Northern Sea	Atlantic Ocean
Nombre de Dios	Colon (Panama)
San Cristóbal de la Habana	Havana
San Salvador (Guanahani)	Watlings Island
Golden Castile	The Central American coast from Honduras to Darién

South America

Ciudad de los Reyes	Lima
New Castile	North Peru
New Toledo	South Peru
The Spanish Main:	The region of the Gulf of Darién, by extension, this term was applied afterward to the continental face, turned toward the Caribbean Sea, of Panama, Colombia, and Venezuela, then later to the entire territory in South America within the jurisdiction of the Spanish Crown. The term indicated the "continent" as distinct from the "islands"
Eldorado	The Guianas
New Andalusia	The Colombian coast from Darién to Cape de la Vela
New Estremadura	Chile
New Granada or the New Kingdom of Granada	Colombia

393

INDEX